Summer

THE GUIDE TO THE BIRDS OF IRELAND

To my parents

THE GUIDE TO THE BIRDS of IRELAND

By Gordon D'Arcy

IRISH WILDLIFE PUBLICATIONS
Published in cooperation with
the Irish Wildlife Federation

THE GUIDE TO THE BIRDS OF IRELAND
is the first in a series of Guides on various aspects of Ireland's Natural History which are being published by the I.W.P. at 8, Westland Row, Dublin 2.

Irish Wildlife Publications Natural History Guides
General Editor: Fergus O'Gorman

Acknowledgements

I am indebted to many people, friends and colleagues who over the years have helped and encouraged me to bring this work to completion. In particular I would like to thank Oscar Merne and John Rochford who read the text critically and Killian Mullarney who freely gave his advice on birds and painting them. In addition from an endless list I must select only a few; Robin Ruttledge, Michael O'Brien, Éamon de Buitléar, Andy Barclay and Fergus O'Gorman. I trust all will accept my deep gratitude. Special thanks to Marian for dedicatedly typing the text.

ISBN 0 9507842 0 6

Published by Irish Wildlife Publications,
8 Westland Row, Dublin 2.
Designed by Andy Barclay
Typesetting by Fingerprint
Colour separation by Scanlith
Printed by Ormond Press Dublin

CONTENTS

LIST OF PLATES

Cover illustration of Irish Jay *Garrulus glandarius hibernicus*

FOREWORD

It is amazing that no detailed book describing all of Ireland's birds, including their status, has been published since 1851 when William Thompson produced the last of his great works on the Natural History of Ireland. However, in view of the cost, it is perhaps not surprising that no recent book on the birds — and there have been only four this century — has provided colour illustrations of any species.

I am sure you will agree that Gordon D'Arcy, in writing and illustrating this first complete guide to Ireland's birds in colour, has succeeded in marrying technical lucidity — both in the text and the plates and drawings — with a real artistic sensitivity to the moods of our wild birds.

Gordon D'Arcy is one of a growing group of young ornithologists who have been encouraged by the great names of the past generation, such as Robin Ruttledge, Fr. P. G. Kennedy, George Humphries, Arnold Bennington and Jimmy Deane, to explore our bird fauna in detail. He is one of an even smaller group of gifted ornithologists cum artists whose expert observations in the field are translated into living birds on the page.

The Irish Wildlife Federation, which is dedicated to increasing public awareness and concern for all our wildlife, from butterflies to buttercups, is pleased and honoured to be associated with this the first complete guide to any part of our wildlife heritage.

Fergus O'Gorman
Chairman,
Irish Wildlife Federation

MIGRATION ROUTES TO AND FROM IRELAND

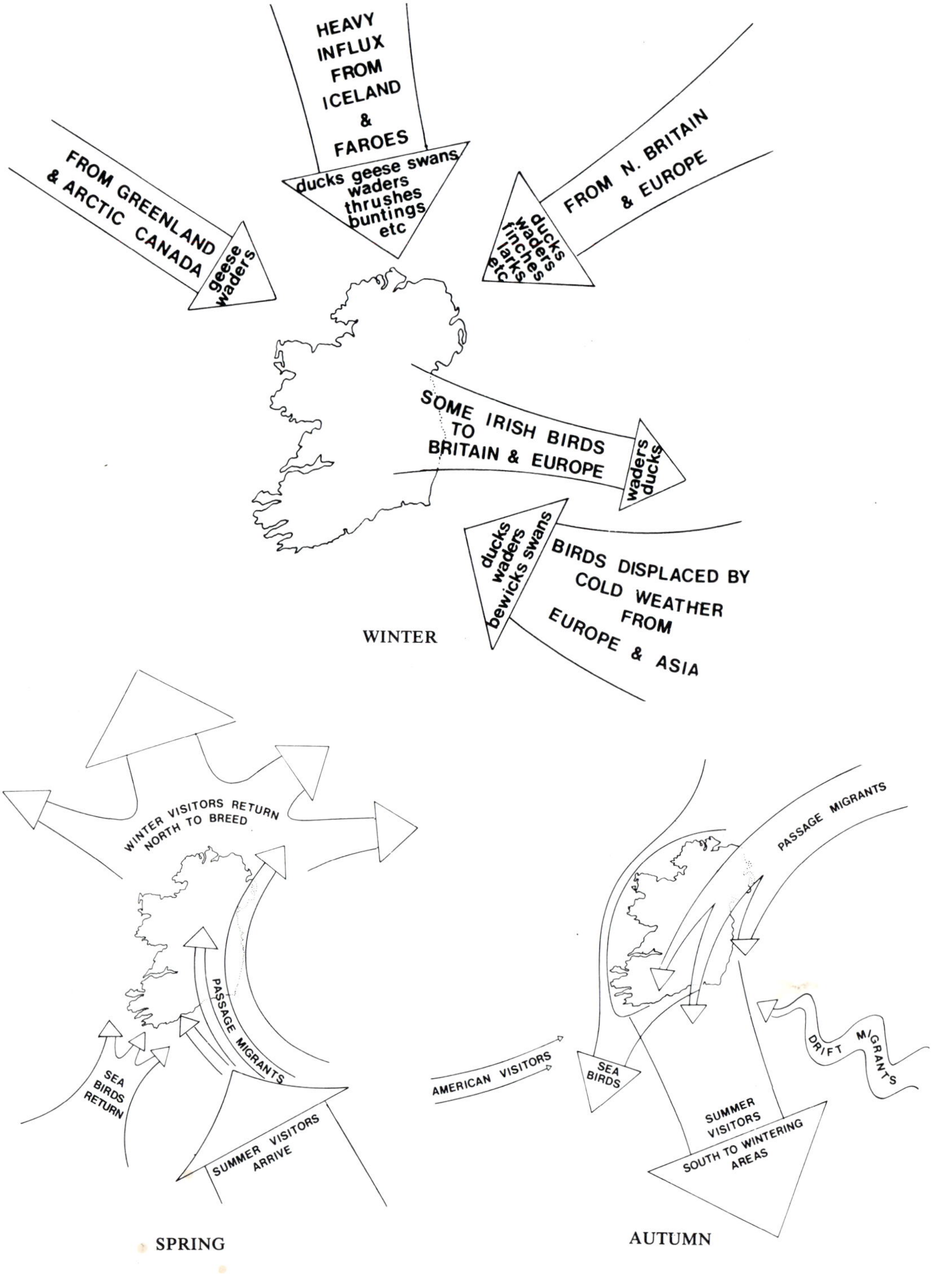

INTRODUCTION
The Past, Present and Future

There have been several books written about the birdlife of Ireland but perhaps the first really comprehensive and reliable work was by William Thompson in the middle of the 19th century. Thompson provides us with a wonderful picture of Ireland's wildlife in the first half of that century. Although the human population was much greater than that of today there was undoubtedly a richer avifauna then. The undrained wetlands still supported large, interesting birds like Bittern and Marsh Harrier, and the Golden and White-tailed Eagles soared around the cliffs and mountains. The unpolluted estuaries harboured masses of wintering waterfowl. The introduction of the mechanical excavator so accelerated the drainage of our marshes, particularly those of the midlands, that the Bittern and the Marsh Harrier had no chance of survival. The poisoning of animal carcasses with strychnine wiped out the last of the eagles which could not be shot in pursuit of the Victorians' craze for introducing and rearing exotic game birds. The use of punt and swivel guns which could shoot dozens of duck at one discharge was surely partly responsible for the decimation of the vast wintering flocks in our estuaries.

It is obvious, that in the past our birdlife has been treated with some insensitivity to say the least. Developers tended to ignore birds, hunters simply regarded them as a boundless food source and farmers regarded all birds of prey as their enemies. The use of the swivel and punt guns has almost been discontinued but, although strychnine has gone, it could be said that poisoning still continues in the form of chemicals used on the land. More sinister still though, is the continued and concerted drainage of the wetlands which has become a real threat to both resident and visiting water birds for which Ireland is renowned.

THE PAST

Most of us have been intrigued by the fantastic story of the Dinosaurs from the dim and distant past. So successful were these creatures that they dominated the earth until their unaccountable disappearance some 70 million years ago. Whatever became of the Dinosaurs, the colossal Tyrannosaurus, the marine Plesiosaur, the flying Pterodactyl, so well known from their fossil remains? They seem to have vanished into oblivion — or did they?

Long before they became extinct a creature existed among the Dinosaurs which had some remarkable characteristics. It has been named Archaeopteryx (ancient feather) and though it possessed many bird features like feathers, wings, beak and so on, it had some features that were decidedly reptilian or dinosaurian. Among these features were, teeth in the beak, and grasping 'hands' at the bends of the wings.

It is now believed, in fact, that the Dinosaurs did not become completely extinct but that they may have evolved into birds! To be more correct, some smaller fleet-footed dinosaurs which seem to have been more successful than the larger ones, gradually adopted bird-like characteristics ultimately taking to the air.

Unfortunately no ancient bird of the vintage of Archaeopteryx has been discovered as a fossil in Irish limestones, as a few have been on the continent of Europe. Nevertheless there are hints in our rocks suggesting that Dinosaurs were at one time found here — a huge footprint in the hill at Scrabo, Co. Down and traces of others elsewhere.

Little is known of these, the earliest fossil birds, of over 100 million years ago, or of those which existed right down to the appearance of man, although evidence of water birds which have representatives today in Ireland, exist from as far back as the Eocene, some 50 million years ago. The main reason for there being so few bird relics is that their flimsy remains are not easily preserved as fossils — they are usually dispersed before mud layers can form over them to be turned, with the passing of time, into stone. However, the famous La Brea Tar Pits in the U.S.A. have revealed birds' remains from many thousands of years ago. These remains are of large vulturine birds, obviously trapped in the tar whilst feeding on the carcasses of large mammals.

The arrival of man in Ireland is comparatively recent. His remains have been carbon-dated to about 8,000 years ago after the ice had retreated and the land was gradually rising from the sea once again. Some of his earliest settlements were in coves on the Antrim coast. Kitchen midden remains from these early dewellings have been shown to contain bones and egg shells of some bird such as auks and include those of the Great Auk — a flightless species once widespread in the North Atlantic but finally extinguished by human persecution in 1844.

Excavations of man's early habitations has taught us much about Ireland's past birdlife, often substantiating evidence from early Irish literature. Cave dwellings and island crannogs have been especially productive. Along with the bones of extinct Irish animals like reindeer, giant Irish deer, bears etc. have been found the remains of many of our present-day birds such as finches, crows, ducks and geese. Among the bones of the commoner species are those of birds which are not now found here, like eagles and cranes.

An inkling of the past birdlife can be gleaned from the wealth of Irish literature. The existence of wild swans, bitterns, cranes and many others is to be found in the ancient annals, the poetry and the mythology of the early authors. The language itself gives a clue to the past birdlife of this country. There are names for Golden and White-tailed Eagles, Marsh Harrier, and so on, birds which have gone from Ireland. It also raises some interesting questions about the range and identity of some birds. The Redstart, now rare here has Irish names which have Scots Gaelic equivalents; 'Snag breac' is one of the several names for the woodpecker in Irish, none of which are now found here (apart from occasional winter visitors). If the Cappercallie was never an indigenous Irish species (as is now suggested), what was the origin of the Irish names cappul coille and caileac coille?

THE PRESENT:

Despite the changes of the past, Ireland has still a diverse and interesting bird fauna — internationally important in many respects. As a fair-sized island on the western extremity of the European Continent, it hosts a good variety of migrant species. Due to its temperate, damp climate it is a haven for thousands of wintering waterfowl. Ireland is, in fact, the age old wintering ground of huge numbers of ducks and waders from northern

Europe, and the Arctic. In addition it is a traditional stopping-off area for thousands of others which continue on to winter further south in Europe. Recent national surveys have shown that a significant percentage of the entire western European population of waterfowl and waders winter here. During periods of extreme cold further to the east in Europe, our normal wintering populations are swollen by large numbers of refugees driven westwards to the ice-free wetlands of Ireland. Our wetlands, though much reduced in recent times, are still some of the finest and least disturbed in western Europe. The indiscriminate drainage of bogs, fens and turloughs, particularly over the past hundred years has been a major factor in the reduction and possible extinction of some of our most interesting birds. This drainage combined with the modern evil of water pollution has seriously limited the feeding habitats available to the masses of migrating and wintering waterfowl in this country.

Though we host large numbers of land birds like thrushes and finches during the winter, Ireland has proved much less inviting to resident dryland birds. This is obviously due in part to our geographic location as well as to general wetness of the country. Ireland, in comparison to Britain, is poor in land birds as it is in mammals and reptiles. Birds like woodpeckers, some warblers, tits and flycatchers, typical of the British countryside are not found here, though this may not always have been the case. The woodlands which mantled much of Ireland until a few hundred years ago have sheltered some of these species but it is probable that the range of some of those now not found here, never extended as far to the west as Ireland. In general therefore, we are proportionately richer in birds associated with water than those of the land.

Yet despite the generally fewer species, some of those we do have are here in greater abundance than elsewhere in Europe. The Corncrake, Chough and Roseate Tern are examples.

In addition there are four species which look sufficiently different from their relatives in Britain or the Continent to have been separated by the Victorians as indigenous Irish birds. These are the Irish Grouse, Dipper, Coal Tit and Jay. Nowadays these are merely regarded as races rather than subspecies or even full species.

Despite having a smaller species list than our neighbouring island, two aspects of our birdlife of major significance have emerged in recent years. The seabird movements which occur annually off the west and south-west coasts in the autumn are a magnificent ornithological spectacle. The islands and headlands of west Cork and Kerry are perhaps the best vantage points to view this spectacle. Most of these birds are British or Irish shearwaters, petrels, Gannets, etc, en route to more southerly Atlantic wintering quarters.

The second of these aspects concerns transatlantic visitors from North America. Ireland provides a first landfall to storm-lost American birds which may be deflected from their normal migration routes by adverse weather. They turn up on Irish soil in an exhausted state, after their involuntary two thousand mile flight. This phenomenon was first noticed over 150 years ago and has proved, with increased observation, to be an annual event. Birds of many types have made the crossing but they are mainly waterfowl and shorebirds, long distance migrants between the Americas. One remarkable feature is that many of those that are blown across are by no means the most abundant of American migrants and it can be difficult to imagine the circumstances that cause their wanderings.

AMERICAN BIRDS IN IRELAND

More than two thousand miles of unbroken sea separate Ireland from Newfoundland, the nearest point on the North American Continent. The eastern seaboard of the United States is considerably further away, and the Florida Panhandle/Gulf of Mexico region five thousand miles from the west coast of Ireland. The vast body of water which lies between, the North Atlantic Ocean, would appear to be an impassible expanse for any airborne animal. This is, however, not the case; winged creatures have managed the crossing on many occasions.

The large Monarch or Milkweed Butterfly is one example of a North American insect which has turned up in Europe on many occasions, to the amazement of many naturalists, and an ever-increasing list of birds are recorded annually as transatlantic wanderers. Since the first was noticed over a hundred and fifty years ago, about fifty species of North American bird have been identified in Ireland. In the normal course of events it should be extremely unlikely that a 'new world' bird should get to the 'old world'. However, a combination of the birds seasonal migration habits and erratic meterological conditions which may coincide with their migration periods, brings this feat into the realms of possibility.

Many of those species which have made the crossing are shorebirds or waders and are strong-flying, long distance migrants. Most nest in the northern part of the continent, often as far north as Arctic Canada, and migrate southwards in autumn. Many spend the winter in the Gulf region of Central America, others cross the Gulf and winter in South America. Some, like the American Golden Plover, fly east from their Canadian breeding grounds and perform a huge cyclic migration which takes them out to sea over the Atlantic for a non-stop flight of over two-thousand miles. They make landfall in northern South America and continue south to their wintering grounds in Patagonia. The northern spring migration takes them the length of both continents, finally completing the cycle at their northern Canadian breeding grounds. The round trip is about fifteen thousand miles every year! Most North American migratory birds are less adventurous but a large proportion either winter around or cross, in the course of their migrations, the Gulf region of Central America.

Hurricanes are a feature of that area in the autumn and it is believed that these dissipating cyclones carry many birds far out into the Atlantic. The majority probably perish but some, converting their body fat into energy to keep them airborne, fly on for days. A few survivors aided by prevailing westerly winds make landfall in Ireland or elsewhere in western Europe. Adverse weather conditions on the eastern seaboard of the U.S.A. may also disorient migrating birds, especially those which fly to South America by the overseas route, like the American Golden Plover.

Not all the American birds which have turned up in Ireland are long-distance migrants. Some are incapable of long flights without regular stops for resting and feeding. It seems that many must have 'hitch-hiked' on ocean-going ships for part or all of the journey. Birds have been noticed alighting on ships in mid-Atlantic and have been seen flying off again when in sight of land. These are usually small perching birds such as finches and warblers. Species as unlikely as woodpeckers and herons have been known to alight on ships and it seems that in an emergency, almost any bird will seek the sanctuary of these floating islands. Nevertheless, much modern ornithological opinion suggests that the majority of those birds which traverse the Atlantic, do so without stopping.

Every year, American birds are spotted in this country and in some years dozens are seen. Indeed, with increased observation the number and variety of species is augmented almost annually. Small numbers of American birds are seen in most West European countries in the autumn. In the Isles of Scilly, however, where observation is highly concentrated there is a remarkable history of transatlantic visitors. It is probable that a similar variety is to be found in this country but due to the small number of observers here, many go unnoticed.

How long do these birds stay on the wrong side of the Atlantic? What do they do when they get here? Do they ever return again to America? The vagrant shorebirds are often in the company of European shorebirds and it seems reasonable that they would follow them on their migrations. It is doubtful if in the course of their lifetime — a few years only, that these birds ever return to America due to the adverse prevailing winds.

Migration routes between the Americas

In 1870 a bird was found in a Dublin poultry market by a keen-eyed naturalist who had it preserved and installed in the National Museum in Dublin. This was a transatlantic vagrant — an Eskimo Curlew which had been shot in Co. Sligo. Remarkably, this little Curlew, one of the most abundant of North American birds in the nineteenth century, was declared extinct to the world in the 1940's, although in recent years one or two Eskimo Curlews have been occasionally seen in Texas on the spring migration northwards and it is now believed that there may be a tiny relict population still surviving. Millions of Eskimo Curlews which nested in Arctic Canada, joined the American Golden Plovers on their huge cyclic migration journey every year. More confiding than the Plover, the Curlews were shot in vast numbers, principally by the Hudson Bay Company which was opening up the Canadian wilderness at that time. Barrel-loads of the birds were salted down for winter food and by the turn of the century nearly all the curlews were gone. Not only is the great spectacle of the migrating myriads of these birds lost forever to new generations but the Eskimo Curlew is one less species for the avid bird-watcher to look for on both sides of the Atlantic.

THE FUTURE

To consider the future of Ireland's birdlife one must first speculate about the future of the country, as we have seen how the variety and abundance of our birds is very much dependent on the habitat available to them.

We would probably find Ireland, after the year 2000, a still-green country but much changed from today. With intensive farming techniques, the field sizes will undoubtedly increase, it being more efficient to work large rather than small fields. This will necessitate the loss of hedgerows, fine wildlife habitat. Fertilisers and chemicals have detrimental effects on watercourses and indirectly on the more extensive wetland habitats. Pig slurry and silage effluent do not help the situation. Already the wildlife has suffered — many older folk comment ruefully about the scarcity of wildflowers and butterflies so common a few decades ago, and a casual conversation with a farmer often raises the questions — where have all the Corncrakes gone? What has happened to the Partridges?

As well as man induced losses we also have gained some species such as the recently arrived Collared Dove. And while certain birds are being lost new birds are being regularly discovered, both as breeding species and as visitors. Although we have a less varied bird fauna than neighbouring Britain we are fortunate in Ireland in one respect — we are not over-run by birdwatchers as the case seems to be there! There is, therefore great scope for the dedicated amateur and many exciting discoveries await us here. There are several organisations concerned with the furtherance of bird-watching and ornithology but their total membership is in the order of thousands rather than tens or even hundreds of thousands, as is the case in more heavily populated Britain. Enthusiastic individuals carry out projects within these groups and engage the help of 'part-timers'. These projects range from small scale studies of areas or species, to national surveys — as in the most successful "Atlas of Breeding Birds of Britain and Ireland" carried out to map the distribution of our breeding birds.

Fortunately attitudes to conservation are changing. People are undoubtedly more aware of the environment, including birdlife. More and more people are appreciating the tranquility of the countryside. It is surely important that we leave enough of the flora and fauna in their natural environment, for the enjoyment of these ever-increasing numbers and for future generations. The sophistication of the modern media, particularly television, which can bring the great outdoors right indoors, has unquestionably helped develop environmental awareness. Books too, are better illustrated and less cluttered with scientific jargon than has been the case in the past. As a consequence wildlife publications can be appreciated by a wider readership than before.

Since Thompson published his three volumes between 1849–51 there has been a number of books on Irish birds mainly updating their status. The primary ones were by Ussher and Warren published in 1900, by Kennedy, Ruttledge and Scroope in 1954, by Ruttledge in 1966, and by Moriarity in 1967, whose useful little paperback describes most species.

'THE GUIDE TO THE BIRDS OF IRELAND' is designed to fill a gap. There has not been a book describing every Irish bird since 1851. There has never been a fully illustrated book on Irish birds and no book before has illustrated our resident birds in full colour. The Guide is intended to be a practical guide, not only to the identification but also the appreciation of the common and not-so-common birds of this country. It is written with an unashamed Irish bias in order that the reader should realise that Ireland has an ornithological identity of its own and is by no means an outlying and unimportant part of the avifauna of Britain and western Europe. It is also written in the hope that it will play some part, however small, in increasing public interest in, and concern for, our wealth of wildlife. Only with that public support will future generations have the pleasures we have of enjoying, free, our bountiful birdlife.

Why watch birds?

Bird-watchers find it difficult to answer this question. There are so many facets to the activity ranging from the appeal of the birds themselves, to the environment in which they are found, that a short answer is almost impossible. Most would not try to analyse birdwatching; they would simply say "It's good fun", and who can argue with that. Birdwatching is, nevertheless, a fascinating, rewarding activity attracting enthusiasts of all ages and from all walks of life. It is no longer regarded as a pursuit for the semi-senile or the overly sentimental as it has been in the past. Nowadays, it provides marvellous common ground for many people and as such is a definite plus in our modern world.

Ornithology, the study of birds, is a branch of the natural sciences. In a broader sense ornithology is part of the study of the environment. The study of the environment provides us with a broad view of the earth in which we live and as a consequence, an objective view of ourselves as its primary inhabitants. In recent years there has been a general awakening to environmental problems world-wide. Due to this concern there has been an upsurge in interest in the natural world. People are realising that the continued survival of wildlife can no longer be taken for granted. Birds, perhaps our most conspicuous wildlife, are the subject of more attention now than ever before. A testimony to this state of affairs is the great number (hundreds of thousands) of people watching birds in Britain and elsewhere.

Unlike most other activities, bird-watching requires almost no elaborate equipment. Once the observer is equipped with a pair of binoculars he has all he needs to identify and enjoy all the birds which are found here. Of course, like other activities, the observer can invest a little, or a lot, depending on how much extra equipment is regarded as necessary. Those who like to be on the spot for the dawn chorus will feel the need for camping equipment and weather resistant outdoor clothing. Some people believe that the only way to watch birds properly is to get in amongst them. Others, whose time and pocket are restricted, can watch from a car window, at lunch breaks or other convenient times. Watching birds feeding or performing their ablutions in the garden can provide endless enjoyment for those at home.

For those who wish to take a less sedentary interest, bird-watching is a stimulating and healthy activity, often taking the observer into the wilder and less populated parts of the countryside. Walking in the country can be much more interesting if it is possible to identify the flora and fauna that make it what it is.

Regular watching makes one realise that there are many more bird species than was originally thought. There is a steady improvement in the performance of the observer due to the increase in his ability to identify more and more species.

To begin with it is necessary to see definite features like the length of the bill, the colour of the breast, etc. After a further period, which varies from one individual to the next, many common species may be identified by their look or 'feel'. In other words, by simply glancing at the birds' shape, flight or flock behaviour, the experienced birdwatcher can identify many birds. It is this skill that enables him to cast his eye through groups of well known birds and pick out rarities. Through watching and noting down aspects of the lifestyle of birds — their feeding, roosting, nesting, migration, and so on, the birdwatcher is well on his way to becoming an expert ornithologist.

By studying birdlife, ornithologists learn the subtlety and delicacy of the natural balance, how vulnerable it is to man's exploitation, and how important it is to retain and protect it for the use, education and enjoyment of future generations. This overall appreciation, which seems to be a natural consequence of wildlife observation and study, is a vital factor in the intelligent management of our countryside in general and our wildlife habitats in particular. Other countries did not realise the wealth that existed in their wildlife before much of it was gone. Let not Ireland follow suit.

How to watch birds

As most birds are small and lively, it takes a quick eye and patience to get any sort of proper view of them. Even then only a small number of birds are approachable to the extent that their patterns and proportions are adequately visible. Of course, putting out scraps in cold weather, and especially the building of a bird table or bird bath in the garden will bring many bird species closer. A parked car is a useful vehicle for the observation of birds in the countryside. By sitting still in a car it is amazing how many birds come close enough to allow satisfactory identification. As soon as the observer steps out of the car he becomes something to be feared and birds retire to a safe distance. Hides are also well tried and successful means of observing birds. They can be awkward to construct and transport to the viewing area and often it is just as convenient to build a make-shift hide out of branches and foliage from the immediate surroundings without, of course, destroying the natural habitat.

Nevertheless, viewing birds with the naked eye has limited possibilities. It is desirable for the bird-watcher to invest in a pair of binoculars at an early stage. Even if he or she decides that birdwatching is not for them later on, binoculars are always a useful item to have. Once furnished with a good pair of binoculars — and of course "The Guide to the Birds of Ireland" — the bird-watcher has all he or she needs to view the myriad of species which occur in Ireland. The less expensive makes are fine instruments which are easily good enough for the majority of observers. For the real enthusiast, however, there is nothing to substitute for either Leitz or Zeiss binoculars. Ideally 8, 9 or 10 magnification should be looked for, with a light factor of at least 5*. A good pair of binoculars will last a lifetime provided they are cared for. It is advisable, at regular intervals, to check the alignment of both images in the binoculars. If they do not coincide exactly, the binoculars are potentially harmful for the eyes and they should be readjusted.

There are a few good telescopes on the market but also many bad ones. A good telescope is one with a wide field of view, plenty of light, good definition and magnification of up to 30X. Because a telescope needs to be held especially steady, either by resting it on immovable objects or mounting it on a tripod, it is of limited use to the bird watchers. It is most useful for scanning waterfowl and waders far out on the estuary or some similar situation. For 'sea-watching' too, telescopes are of assistance, though it is difficult to follow a flying bird with one. Some people become very skilled in identification through a telescope but scrupulous observation is essential, especially where a rarity may be concerned as it is easy to imagine features which do not exist in long distance views of birds. During migration times it is possible to see nocturnal migrants flying across the face of the moon with the aid of a steadily mounted telescope. Naturally to use this method most effectively the moon should be full or nearly so. Students of migration become quite adept at using this method to the extent that it is possible to differentiate between the silhouettes of certain small birds as well as those of ducks, geese, swans and waders.

*Light factor of 5 such as 8 x 40 or 10 x 50 which is the diameter of the objective lens divided by the magnification.

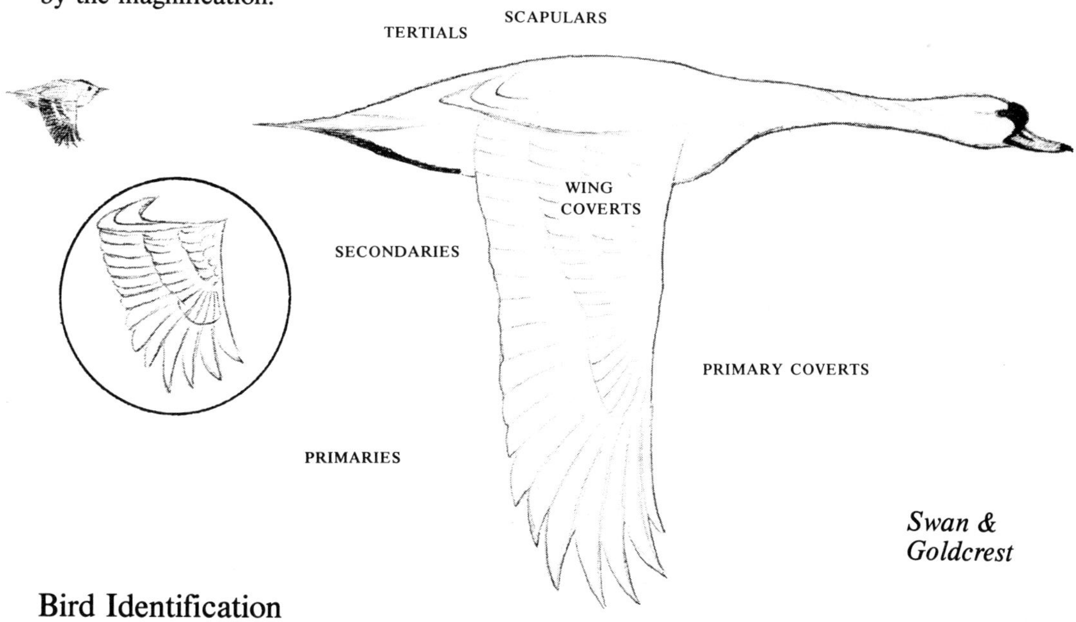

Swan & Goldcrest

Bird Identification

Birds come in all shapes and sizes from the tiny Goldcrest not much larger than a golf ball, to the Mute Swan which is about five feet long. Between these extremities there is a great diversity in size and shape. Some birds have specialised bills and feet to allow them to take advantage of different habitats, and the food found in them. An example is the Snipe, which has an extremely long bill for probing for food and long toes so that it can be supported on the softest of mud. Other birds like the Starling are all-purpose birds, adapted to a great variety of habitats and foods.

Even though a sparrow may look very different from a goose, and a swift may appear to have little in common with a gull, their basic structure is the same and their covering of feathers follows a consistent pattern. All birds have the same feather arrangement shown in the diagrams of Goldcrest and Mute Swan, even though some groups of feathers may predominate over others, in different species.

A basic knowledge of this arrangement is important so that the observer can locate accurately the positions of colours, patterns or distinguishing marks of any bird in the field. Often only fleeting glimpses are obtained. It is especially important in these cases to pin-point features that will aid identification.

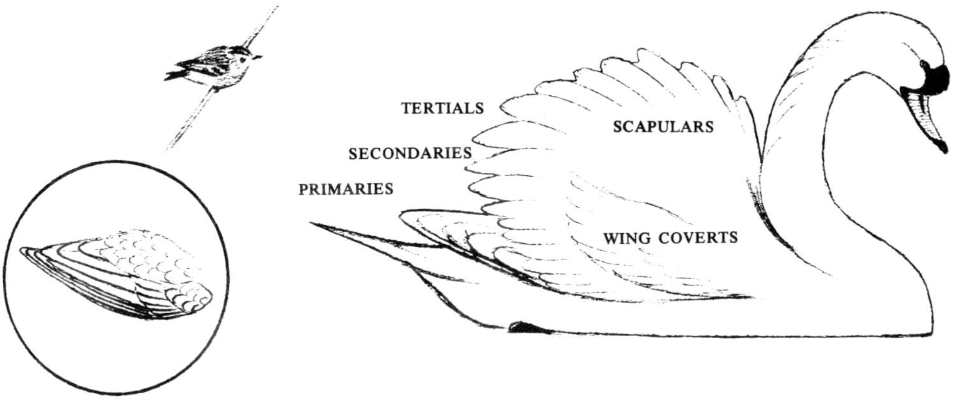

The perched Goldcrest shows certain features which help with positive identification. They are, the vivid stripes on the crown and the white edges to the median and greater wing coverts. In the field the latter show as clear white wing bars. Also note the small bill and moustachial mark. Although the feather arrangement shown in the Goldcrest can also be seen in the Swan above they are of no help in identification. For instance, the wing-coverts are white but so is the rest of the bird, so they are not identification features. However the bill and its black boss, the overall white plumage and the shape and size, are all salient features.

When a bird flies, it does not mean that identification cannot be achieved. On the contrary, it may be as easy or even easier to identify a bird from flight features, which in some cases may be crucial to identification. Colour patches or marks in the plumage or feather patterns may be even more noticable in flight. Consequently, it is important to have a knowledge of the feather arrangements of the flying bird which is consistent from one species to the next.

Although there are obvious diffferences in shape and size it can clearly be seen that there is a consistency in feather arrangement from Goldcrest to Mute Swan.

Not only is shape and size of the flying bird important for satisfactory identification but its mode of flight is also very often relevant. Many small (especially long-tailed) birds fly in an undulating manner, like the Wagtail. Some like the Kingfisher fly in a direct manner. A few like the Snipe fly in a 'zig-zag' manner.

After the appearance of the bird under observation has been established, secondary identification features may be of importance. These are features like, call, song, where the bird is found, what it was feeding on, and so on.

In some cases these features may not be subordinate at all but may be the key features for satisfactory indentification. For instance, the most obvious feature of the Cuckoo is its call "cuck-oo" and the secretive Garden Warbler is most readily identified by its song. The mutilated cones of conifer trees on the ground are often an indicator of the presence of Crossbills in a forest, and berries on the ground beneath a cotoneaster bush maybe a tell-tale sign that the garden has been visited by Waxwings.

Bird Mis-identification:

Even with the best optical equipment, the bird watchers task is not an easy one. There is no substitute for experience, field notes and sketches, for competent identification of Ireland's birds — especially the rarer ones.

It ought to be remembered that light conditions can play havoc with a bird's appearance. When this is coupled with windy conditions, which can disturb the binocular view of the bird under observation and rain which dampens birds, bird-watchers, lenses and occasionally the spirit — it can be seen that it is not all plain-sailing. Foggy weather conditions are notorious for causing red faces among bird-watchers as mist or fog can distort or even magnify a bird's form. This is perhaps most important when seabird-watching. Misty conditions are ideal for bringing oceanic seabirds close to the land on autumn migration. It is quite easy to see how, in these circumstances, a young Gannet could grow into an albatross, through the eyes of an inexperienced bird-watcher.

There are certain birds which continually cause difficulty even in good weather conditions. They fall into two main groups; (a) those which are problematical in themselves and (b) those which are readily confused with other species. Some of those in (a) may indirectly fall into category (b) as well.

Some of the most troublesome birds to the beginner, in that he may not be able to make an identification, or worse, may try to mould them with his imagination into some other, usually rarer species, are the following:

FULMAR — One of the most misidentified seabirds; especially at a distance, it is often confused with gulls.
DUNLIN — In winter or juvenile plumage, it can be mistaken for half a dozen other species.
REEVE (female Ruff) — To the inexperienced observer it can easily be mistaken for rarer waders.
KITTIWAKE — In immature plumage, the flight pattern is similar to that of a few other, rarer gulls.
BLACK GUILLEMOT: In winter plumage it can be misidentified as a grebe, drake smew etc.
SKYLARK — Depending on light, age of bird etc. it can look very variable.
MEADOW PIPIT — Very variable in plumage. Much practice is required with this species.
WHITETHROAT — A confusing bird even for experienced observers.
SPARROWHAWK — This can, and has often been, misidentified for the rare goshawk.
GREENFINCH — The juvenile is not very green and can be difficult.
REEDBUNTING — The female or immature may be mistaken for other rarer species.

Some other species which cause problems, even for the experienced bird-watcher are:
WHINCHAT — The female/autumn plumaged male can be deceptive.
GARDEN WARBLER — A nondescript little bird which usually affords only fleeting glimpses.
CORNBUNTING — If seen away from its known localities, it can be confusing.

The look-alikes are well known to bird-watchers but this does not prevent repeated misidentification, even amongst the experienced. Some of the most regular problem posers are:
FEMALE TUFTED DUCK/FEMALE SCAUP: Even though there are reliable differentiation features these birds are often misidentified.
FEMALE MERGANSER/FEMALE GOOSANDER: The rather common female Red-breasted Merganser can look like the scarce female Goosander.
WHOOPER SWAN/BEWICK'S SWAN: Even at reasonable range it can take time and care to successfully identify these wild swans.
JUVENILE or FEMALE MERLIN/KESTREL: Although these birds are somewhat alike when perched, a little practice can solve the difficulty.
CURLEW/WHIMBREL: Experience of both species is necessary for confidence.
BLACK-TAILED GODWIT/BAR-TAILED GODWIT: (On the ground). Much more difficult to separate than in flight.
GREEN SANDPIPER/WOOD SANDPIPER: Differentiation can be difficult as often only distant views are possible with these wary birds.
ARCTIC SKUA/POMARINE SKUA: The absence of long tail feathers in adult plumage can make identification less than straightforward.
GLAUCOUS GULL/ICELAND GULL: These birds look alike in all plumages.
ARCTIC TERN/COMMON TERN: This pair is almost inseparable except at close range.
JUVENILE ROOK/CARRION CROW: It is unfortunately almost impossible to obtain

experience of the Carrion Crow in Ireland where it is only an uncommon visitor.
FEMALE REDSTART/FEMALE BLACK REDSTART: The difference in habitat is perhaps the best distinguishing feature.
WILLOW WARBLER/CHIFFCHAFF: Experience is required with this pair if the song is not heard.
PIED WAGTAIL/WHITE WAGTAIL: Although they are very alike there are several reliable distinguishing features.

When to watch birds?

On a daily basis, the best time to watch birds is in the early morning. They tend to be at their most active then and an early walk to a wood or a marsh can be quite an experience. Thrushes, finches and others exercise their vocal chords with gusto at the start of the day. Although generally regarded as the sign of male wooing female, birds sing in winter as well as in spring. Certain birds, however, do not become active until the light starts to fade. The dusk-feeding Nightjar, the Woodcock and of course the owls are best looked for at this time. Great clouds of crows, pigeons and starlings can be seen going to roost in trees, buildings or even in reed-beds at this time. At night also it is surprising how many bird species can be identified by listening out for overhead calls. This is particularly rewarding in the latter part of the autumn when thrushes (especially Fieldfares and Redwings) and waders can be heard on migration. The spring is an obvious starting point for bird watchers — the start of the breeding cycle. At this time our resident birds are joined by the summer visitors which have just arrived from their southern wintering quarters. At this time birds are in prime condition, sporting their best and gaudiest plumage for breeding. In addition, they are indulging in courtship, revealing their eye-catching displays. In some species these can be quite remarkable. The Great Crested Grebe, which is a ghostly, inconspicuous, bird in winter is transformed by its elaborate courtship displays in spring. Besides the spectacle of our own birds, fascinating us with their breeding rituals, the spring is also the time that many migrants are passing through Ireland on their way to more northerly homes.

The summer is the time for observing the family life of birds. Marshes are a hive of activity with warblers, buntings, grebes, Coots, and ducks tending to their offspring and doing everything possible to conceal them from intruders, both animal and human. On the quieter sea shores, terns, gulls and some waders are bringing up their families in the most impossible of circumstances. Marauding gulls give no quarter, stealing eggs from the nests of their own kind as readily as from others. The rocky stacks and cliffs hold large communities of Fulmers, Kittiwakes, Cormorants and auks. At night petrels and shearwaters return from daytime fishing expeditions at sea to tend to their young in cliff-top burrows. Only those birds which have two or three broods will have young around them towards the end of the summer and dispersal is usually well under way by this time.

By the beginning of August the south-bound migration has begun. Starting as a trickle, by the end of the month and throughout September, migration is in full swing. Coastal areas have gatherings of Swallows, Swifts, warblers, Wheatears and others awaiting suitable conditions before embarking upon the awesome journey to African wintering grounds. This is the time to observe the migration of shorebirds in our estuaries and elsewhere along our coasts. Sandpipers, gulls and terns, both native and from other Northern European countries, are fattening up for their annual trek. Off the south and west coast, interesting seabird movements are taking place. Offshore islands also provide 'stopping off' points for migrating perching birds, especially when they have the attraction of a lighthouse or when adverse weather conditions force them to seek sanctuary on these islands. Rare visitors from elsewhere in Europe, Asia and America turn up in Ireland during this period and many birdwatchers sift through flocks of commoner species in search of those visitors. It takes an alert and experienced eye to pick them out.

By the end of October most of the passage migration is over and our summer birds have long gone. Now begins a heavy influx of birds into this country from Northern Europe and Britain. Millions use Ireland as wintering quarters. Due to our relatively mild winters and the often severe conditions in continental Europe Ireland is a very important haven for these visitors. They are primarily waterfowl and waders — ducks, geese, swans, plovers, sandpipers and so on. These are accompanied by many land-birds like thrushes, finches and buntings which also pour into Ireland at the same time. Once this immigration is over, at the beginning of winter, there is comparative stability until the early spring. Very cold weather in Britain or the Continent sends additional winter visitors into Ireland which is almost invariably milder. These westerly movements of birds may be quite substantial, especially towards the end of the winter when continental wetlands, wintering refuges for thousands of wildfowl, become frozen over. Irish coastal refuges like Strangford Lough, the Wexford Slobs, or North Bull Island in Dublin Bay which are quiet places in summer, reverberate with the noisy hustle and bustle of thousands of birds in winter. Towards the latter part of the winter, the Shannon estuary, the turloughs of the west and the midland lakes provide vital gathering points for departing waterfowl.

The longer days and the promise of warmer days to come are welcome indications of the start of a new ornithological year. The mass exodus of birds which have overwintered here is underway. It is not uncommon to see these parting visitors in the proximity of newly arrived summer visitors at the end of March — a Sand Martin hawking for insects over a marsh full of north-bound ducks. The first steady trickle of summer visitors reaches Ireland at around the beginning of April. In the following weeks waves of new arrivals, some of which have made the journey many times before, surge into the country, heralding once again the miracle of migration. And so the year has turned full circle. The stage is set yet again for the birds to set up home and, like their counterparts the world over, to propagate their species.

Where to watch birds?

Because Ireland is situated on the western edge of Europe it is a splendid location for watching migrants and for many water birds in particular. To watch waterfowl at their best in the early part of the winter, the north of the country is the place to go. The Lough Foyle region is the first 'stop-off' area for south bound Whooper Swans, Wigeon and geese. The Bann Valley is an important flyway for waterfowl from the north and coastal and inland wetlands fill up gradually from the north of the country southwards. Once of the most magnificent early winter sights is in Strangford Lough where in excess of ten thousand Brent Geese are to be found. They gather in this shallow estuary after a four thousand mile flight from their breeding grounds — a few hundred miles from the North Pole. Their food supply of eel grass sustains the geese for a mere month at Strangford after which they disperse to other estuaries further south.

In mid-winter the coastal estuaries and lagoons hold large numbers of ducks and waders. On the east coast, the estuaries and inlets of Dundalk and Dublin hold large numbers of waterfowl. However, of all the east coast counties, Wexford boasts the most impressive array of water birds with concentrations in Wexford Harbour, Tacumshin and Lady's Island Lakes. On the south coast the estuaries and inlets of Cork and Kerry are most interesting winter resorts for birds. Nowhere on the west coast can compare with the estuary of the Shannon, especially the mouth of the Fergus river, for variety and abundance of wildfowl and waders.

Inland, the lake systems of the midlands as far north as Longford and Cavan hold good numbers of ducks and some geese flocks, while the larger lakes on either side of the Shannon basin and on the river itself are marvellous waterfowl habitats. The Lough Neagh basin holds at least fifty-thousand wintering ducks of some twenty species. At this time also the Greenland White-fronted Geese have attained their winter complement of about six-thousand at the Wexford Slobs where they are joined by large numbers of duck and swans.

Towards the latter part of the winter, the Shannon basin is the place to visit. Almost in the middle of the country, on the callows at Portumna and Little Brosna, huge numbers of waterfowl and waders gather before leaving on the return journey to their northern breeding grounds. The turloughs of Galway and Clare reflect a similar accumulation. Those species involved are mainly Wigeon, Teal, wild swans and geese and amongst the waders, Lapwing, Golden Plover and Black-tailed Godwits.

Lapwings

By the end of March most of this movement is over and it is time to go in search of the first summer visitors — those birds which have wintered in Africa and other warm places and are returning to nest in Ireland. Sand Martins, Chiffchaffs and Wheaters are invariably the first arrivals and even before the start of April, there have been sightings of these species, especially on the south coast. Swallows, warblers, Spotted Flycatchers and other summer visitors pour into the country in April and May and are best observed at east and south coast headlands and islands. At this time migrants, which do not nest in Ireland, may be found at bird observatories like that at Great Saltee Island, Co. Wexford. Birds like Tree Pipits, Yellow Wagtails and rarities from the European mainland turn up, off course, amongst our commoner summer birds. On our marshes and estuaries migrant shore birds like waders, gulls and terns are passing through or arriving to stay for the summer. The coastal lagoons of the east and south coast as well as the western turloughs are good places to see this influx. Notable amongst these localities are Lady's Island and Tacumshin in Wexford, Ballycotton in Cork and Rahasane in Galway.

The nesting season is of course an exciting time for the bird-watcher. A trip to the Wicklow

Bittern and Marsh Harrier

Mountains will bring him or her into the habitat of scarce and specialised species like the Peregrine Falcon, Ring Ouzel and Nightjar. The woodlands have a great variety of breeding species from the finches, tits, crows, warblers to the unlikely Herons. In the oak woods of various counties there is always the possibility of encountering Redstarts and Wood Warblers, two of our scarcest breeders, and the woodland around the lakes and rivers of the midlands have Blackcaps and, in places, Garden Warblers, two of our best songbirds. The vast tracts of bog in the west of the country and their associated lakes have recently revealed that species, not previously known to nest here, do so alongside many of our commoner bog birds like skylarks, meadow pipits, waders and gulls. Lowland, as well as highland rivers and streams have nesting Grey Wagtails, Dippers and Kingfishers. Our lakes have a wonderfully varied summer bird population ranging from grebes and ducks which nest on islands and reedbeds to waders which nest on the water meadows near the shore. Many of Ireland's inshore and offshore islands have 'bird cities' — great masses of auks (Guillemots, Razorbills and Puffins) which nest crammed together like sardines, on cliffs and sea stacks. They are often accompanied by Cormorants, Shags, gulls, Fulmars, Manx Shearwaters and in a few places, Gannets.

After the breeding season is over, migration can once again be observed along our coasts, only now the movement is southwards. Waves of Swallows and martins fly off from coastal headlands, and bushes hide many small birds like warblers waiting for night when they will also fly southwards. At Hook Head, Co. Wexford, or the Old Head of Kinsale, Co. Cork, day and night migrants arrive and leave throughout the autumn. Many nocturnal birds are attracted by the beam from the lighthouses on these headlands. Unusual and rare birds turn up at this time also, especially in September and October. The best places to look for these are south and east coast headlands and islands. Off Cape Clear Island and other south western headlands spectacular seabird movements take place. These are mainly of Gannets, Fulmars, shearwaters, auks, gulls and terns, which are performing large cyclic feeding movements which take them steadily south and west to their Atlantic wintering areas. A similar, though lesser movement can be observed off western and northern promontaries, like Erris Head in Mayo and Malin head in Donegal. Malin Head is also notable for the waves of northern species which pour into Ireland in the late autumn. These are mainly thrushes, finches and buntings.

The American bird species which turn up in Ireland have already been discussed. These are seen in salt marshes, lakes, estuaries all over the country but especially in these habitats in Cork and Kerry. In places like Akeragh Lough, near Tralee, and other well known south and west coast localities, American waders are seen with surprising regularity in the company of sandpipers, shanks and other commoner shorebirds.

How to use the Guide:

Though this book is designed to be of use to the keen bird-watcher it is primarily aimed at the inexperienced or even at the completely uninitiated. It is designed to help quick and accurate identification and also to demonstrate the beauty and variety of our birds. All the common and regularly occurring species have been described and illustrated. In addition those which only turn up in Ireland occasionally are included in the complete bird list on page 166.

Some species have only been seen a few times but others like the Gyrfalcon and the Snowy Owl have been seen many times in the past. There is always the possibility that with increasing observation some of these rarities will prove to be of more regular occurrence than was thought in the past.

The species in the main body of the book may be broken down into four main categories:
RESIDENTS: birds which are found in this country all the year round and raise their young here.
SUMMER VISITORS: birds which come to Ireland to nest, generally from further south.
WINTER VISITORS: birds which come to Ireland for part of, or the whole of the winter. They generally come from further north or from colder countries to the east, where they return to nest in spring.
PASSAGE MIGRANTS: birds which migrate through Ireland on their way to and from wintering or summering grounds in other countries.

It should be emphasised that although some two hundred and nineteen species have been dealt with in the text a good many are scarce migrants or visitors to this country, though nearly all will have been seen a hundred times or more. A few species like the Bearded Tit and the Dotterel have been included in the text even though they are by no means regular visitors to this country. Their inclusion is, I think, justifiable considering that they have nested here in recent years and may be overlooked.

There are three terms used in the text to describe certain scarce or rare passage migrants which may occur in Ireland (mainly on the south coast). They are **DRIFT**, **OVERSHOOT** and **REVERSE** migrants. **A DRIFT MIGRANT** is one which arrives in Ireland after drifting from its normal migration routes. This is mainly due to easterly or south easterly winds. An **OVERSHOOT MIGRANT** is one which has overflown its normal range to arrive in Ireland. A **REVERSE MIGRANT** is one (usually a juvenile bird) which may turn up in this country through disorientation at the beginning of autumn migration. Instead of flying to southern wintering quarters, the reverse migrant heads off to the north or to the north-west.

In the text species are dealt with in the standard Voous sequence (starting with the divers and ending with the buntings). The scientific name, in Latin, follows the species name, and where an Irish name exists this is given below.

Under the heading **IDENTIFICATION** are given the length of the bird (in cms and inches) and those features which, when seen in the field, enable the species to be identified. Such features are listed in approximate order of importance (for example the call of the cuckoo is described before its plumage). If certain features are not reliable or an aid to identification they may be omitted entirely. It is assumed that most observers will be equipped with a pair of binoculars and terms such as 'at close range' may vary from one species to the next and depending on whether or not binoculars are being used. Using binoculars, close range for a soaring Golden Eagle may be over a mile, while for a warbler it may be as little as twenty feet.

Again, under the heading **HABITAT**, the places in which a particular species are found are listed roughly in order of importance. This section provides an important clue to successful identification, but should be treated with caution as it is not unusual to find a species completely removed from its normal habitat (e.g. Treecreeper climbing a wall).

The final section, **STATUS** is intended to be used in conjunction with the distribution maps and should give the observer a fairly good idea of where in Ireland the species in question is likely to be found. I have shown the summer, winter, or normal range of those birds which occur in Ireland for only a part of the year or as visitors and have not discussed the range outside Ireland of those birds which are found here all the year round.

Rare White-tailed Eagles soaring off Slea Head, Co Kerry

The Maps

There are some one hundred and fifty distribution maps which show the range of most of the species mentioned in the text. Those which are not mapped are scarce migrants which may occur anywhere, or are adequately covered in the Status section. Areas shown black on the maps indicate the regions in which the species is common and widespread (in suitable habitat), dotted areas indicate regions of thin distribution (again in suitable habitat); and white areas, regions in which the bird is more or less absent (even in suitable habitat). It is indicated on each of the maps whether the pattern refers to summer, winter or resident distribution. Some of the maps (especially those for the waterfowl) indicate areas of winter concentration of certain species which may be found thinly distributed elsewhere in the country.

The distribution maps are modified on the basis of personal observations from those published in "The Atlas of Breeding Birds in Britain and Ireland", and "Ireland's Wetlands and their Birds" (see further reading).

The Illustrations

The forty eight plates are set out in a way that it is hoped will aid identification. Birds with similarities of family, general appearance, colour scheme or even habitat, are illustrated together where this is considered possible. They have been depicted to show those characteristics which are fundamental to identification, and plumage differences (male/female, adult/immature, winter/summer) are shown where relevant. An attempt has been made in many cases to show typical binocular views of species or small scale impressions of the species in the distance or in flight. These are intended to help the observer gain a feel for the species under observation.

Besides the colour plates a number of black and white wash plates have been included. Two show flight views of all our regular occurring ducks — a necessity in a country noted for its abundance and variety of waterfowl — and others are included where the illustration of the species does not require the use of colour.

There are more than sixty black and white ink drawings throughout the book. Many are of birds that do not require colour to illustrate their features, some are of species which are not included on the colour plates to avoid confusion with commoner species, and some are comparative pictures of species which look alike. The symbol ⊗ beside a bird on a plate indicates that the species or particular plumage shown is rare.

Barn Owl hunting rat

DIVERS and GREBES

Red-throated and Great Northern Divers

RED-THROATED DIVER *Gavia stallata* *Plate 1*

Lóma rua

IDENTIFICATION: 56 cm (22"). In winter plumage (when it is most common in Ireland) it appears ashy grey overall and sits on the water with its bill pointed slightly upwards — a very characteristic feature of the Red-throated Diver. At close range, the dark greyish back is seen to be heavily speckled with white. The summer plumaged bird is seen regularly, mainly on the coast and at the north-western breeding sites. A characteristic of divers is their flight silhouette; they fly as though supporting their head and neck with some difficulty. At the breeding sites, Red-throats call with a high-pitched wail.

HABITAT: Mainly inshore coastal waters. Breeds on small lakes in wild country, near the sea.

STATUS: Common and widespread winter visitor from northern Europe to all coasts, especially the east and south. The species breeds in the north-west of Ireland in small numbers.

Winter

BLACK-THROATED DIVER *Gavia arctica* *Plate 1*

Lóma pibdhubh

IDENTIFICATION: 63 cm (25"). This species occurs almost always in winter when its plumage resembles that of a small Great Northern Diver, looking overall dark above and pale below. At close range the head appears more delicate than that of the Great Northern, and the dark crown and nape are usually slightly paler than the back, but nevertheless contrast strongly with the white face and foreneck. A distinct white patch is often apparent on the side of the swimming bird, near the tail. It is readily distinguished from the winter plumaged Red-throated Diver by the horizontal (not uptilted) carriage of the bill and darker upperparts. In summer plumage it is quite distinctive though beware summer plumage Red-throated Divers viewed in dull light, when the red throat patch may appear black.

HABITAT: Inshore coastal waters, exceptionally inland.

STATUS: Scarce, though annual winter visitor from northern and arctic Europe. It occurs mainly on the north and east coasts.

GREAT NORTHERN DIVER *Gavia immer* *Plate 1*

Lóma mór

IDENTIFICATION: 68–81 cm (27–32"). The only dark above/pale below, goose-sized bird likely to be seen on the open sea around our coasts. A heavy-set bird, the Great Northern Diver has a massive bill which is obvious even at long range. It feeds by diving for fish from the water surface but it does not lunge into the water like the more slightly built Cormorant (see page 40). At close range the head shows a distinctive high forehead and plumage detail on the upperparts is often obvious. In summer plumage this species is unmistakable, but it is infrequent in Ireland in this plumage except where a few wintering individuals linger. Usually seen singly, it occurs locally in loose groups.

HABITAT: Generally inshore coastal waters. In stormy weather it occasionally occurs on the larger inland lakes.

STATUS: Widespread winter visitor and passage migrant mainly from Iceland. May also occasionally be seen in the summer months.

LITTLE GREBE *Tachybaptus ruficollis* *Plate 1*
Spágaire tonn

IDENTIFICATION: 27 cm (10"). The Little Grebe, or Dabchick as it is also known, is a dumpy little diving bird of freshwater. In summer it is a general red/brown colour; in winter, duller and greyer. The only distinctive colouration is the yellow base to the bill. A very active feeder, the Little Grebe may be seen diving continually in the backwaters of ponds and lakes. The high pitched "whinneying" call of the Little Grebe is a typical summer sound at its breeding habitat.

HABITAT: Quieter, less disturbed lake inlets and backwaters. Also ponds, slow-moving rivers and brackish lagoons. Occasionally in salt water in the winter months.

STATUS: Common resident throughout the country. There is evidence also of a passage migration. In some localities over a hundred may be seen together in the winter months.

Summer

GREAT CRESTED GREBE *Podiceps cristatus* *Plate 1*
Foitheach mór

IDENTIFICATION: 48 cm (19"). On its reed bed breeding grounds this bird is obvious, with its beautiful plumage and remarkable head-shaking display. In winter, having lost its summer finery, the Great Crested Grebe becomes a gaunt, dark and pale bird. From a distance, the long neck, dark crown, pale bill and continuous diving are diagnostic. In flight white patches show on both the front and rear of the wings. The much rarer Red-necked Grebe is rather similar in winter plumage (see following description for differences).

HABITAT: In summer, reed-fringed lakes; in winter, mainly coastal estuaries, lagoons, etc.

STATUS: Local resident in small colonies, chiefly in the north and midlands. In winter common and widespread on coastal waters mainly in the east. On one or two estuaries flocks containing hundreds of birds may be found.

Summer

⊗ BLACK-THROATED DIVER
summer
GREAT NORTHERN DIVER
summer
RED-THROATED DIVER
summer
winter
winter
winter
⊗ RED-NECKED GREBE
GREAT CRESTED GREBE
⊗ BLACK-NECKED GREBE
SLAVONIAN GREBE
LITTLE GREBE
summer
summer
⊗ summer
summer
summer
winter
winter
winter
winter
winter

BALEARIC SHEARWATER
under wing
MANX SHEARWATER
SOOTY SHEARWATER
juvenile
⊗ CORY'S SHEARWATER
⊗ GREAT SHEARWATER
FULMAR
adult
GANNET
STORM PETREL
⊗ LEACH'S PETREL

immature
GREY HERON
⊗ LITTLE EGRET
summer
⊗ BITTERN
adult
immature
⊗ SPOONBILL
immature
adult
summer

immature
MUTE SWAN
immature
adult
with
stained
head
WHOOPER SW
immature
BEWICK'S SWAN
immature
female
male
SHELDUCK

imm
GREYLAG GOOSE
GREENLAND WHITE-FRONTED GOOSE
⊗BEAN GOOSE
⊗ PINK-FOOTED GOOSE
GREYLAG GOOSE
GREENLAND WHITE-FRONTED GOOSE
⊗BEAN GOOSE
⊗ PINK-FOOTED GOOSE

⊗ Dark-bellied form
Pale-bellied form
BRENT GOOSE
BARNACLE GOOSE
CANADA GOOSE
Canada Goose with
Greenland White-fronted Geese

female
MALLARD
male
female
TEAL
male
female
GADWALL
male
⊗GARGANEY
female
WIGEON
male
male
SHOVELER
female
female
PINTAIL
male

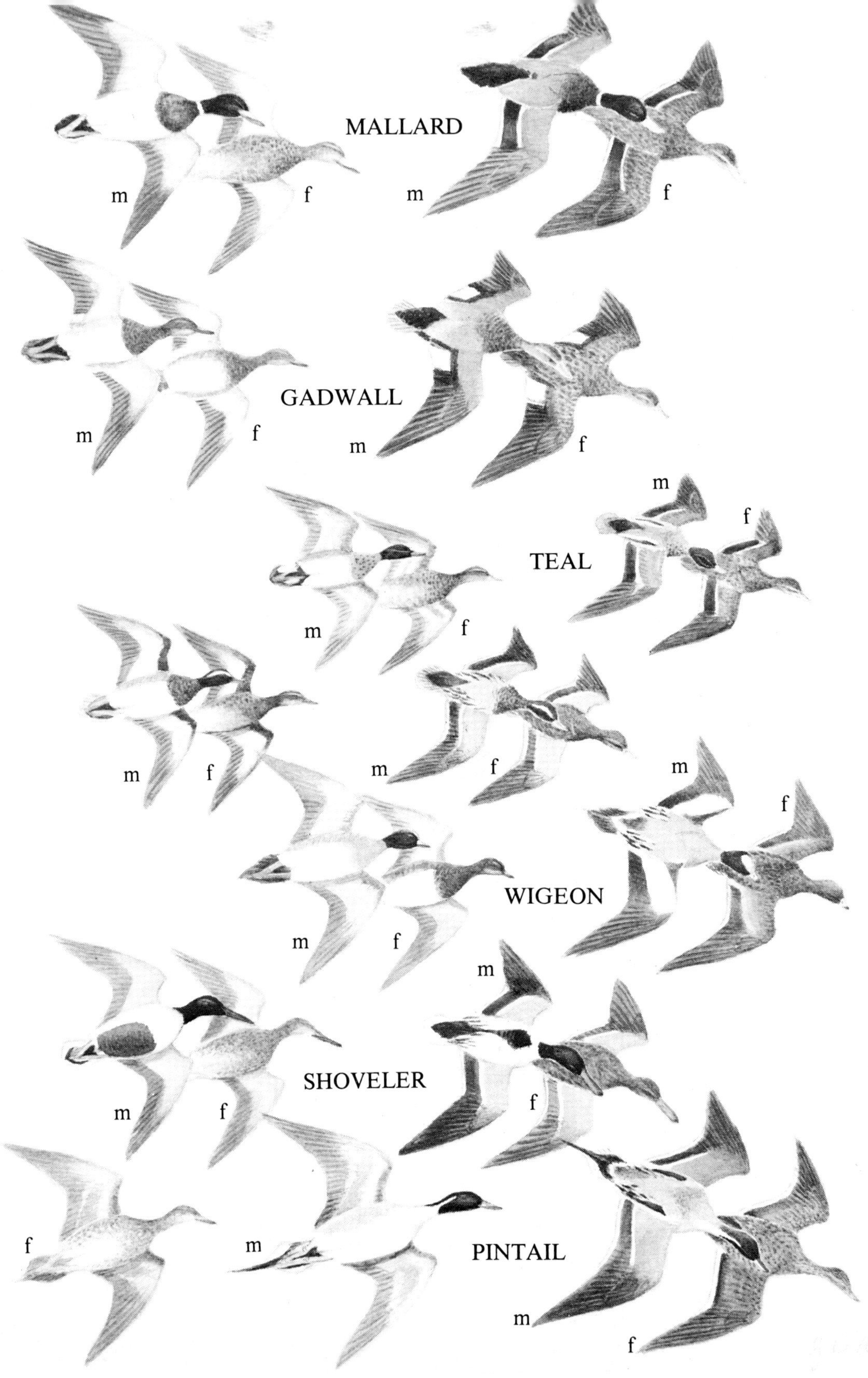
MALLARD
m
f
m
f
GADWALL
m
f
m
f
TEAL
m
f
m
f
m
f
m
f
WIGEON
m
f
m
f
SHOVELER
m
f
m
f
PINTAIL
f
m
m
f

RED-NECKED GREBE *Podiceps grisegena* *Plate 1*

Foitheach pibrua

IDENTIFICATION: 43 cm (17"). This rare grebe occurs mainly in winter plumage in Ireland, when it can be confused with or mistaken for the Great Crested Grebe. It is, however, stockier, with a dark crown extending below the eye, and greyish neck. At close range the bill can be seen to be yellow at the base and dark at the tip. In summer plumage, the front of the neck is brick red, the cheeks white and the crown black. It is likely to be seen in the company of Great Crested Grebes.

HABITAT: Coastal estuaries, bays and lagoons. Exceptionally on inland lakes.

STATUS: Rare winter visitor from northern Europe, mostly after hard weather on the Continent. Recorded on all coasts with the majority in the south and east.

SLAVONIAN GREBE *Podiceps auritus* *Plate 1*

Foitheach cluasach

IDENTIFICATION: 33 cm (13"). The summer plumaged Slavonian Grebe is rare in Ireland. In winter plumage, it resembles a miniature Great Crested Grebe, with clearly demarcated dark crown, white cheeks and fore-neck. The small dark bill is distinctive only at close range. In winter it also resembles the Black-necked Grebe (see following description) and may only be satisfactorily distinguished under ideal conditions.

HABITAT: Coastal estuaries and bays, occasionally on inland waters.

STATUS: Winter visitor from Iceland and northern Europe to a number of traditional localities. A few sometimes linger on into spring. It occurs singly or in pairs but it has been seen in small flocks.

Winter Concentrations

BLACK-NECKED GREBE *Podiceps nigricollis* *Plate 1*

Foitheach pibdhubh

IDENTIFICATION: 30 cm (12"). In winter, resembles the Slavonian Grebe, though less distinctly marked. From a distance, there is much less black/white contrast. At close range the small dark bill looks slightly uptilted and the head less rounded, and more peaked. The black of the crown extends below the eye. In its rarely seen summer plumage this grebe is, like other grebes, unmistakable. It is then mainly blackish, with startling gold-coloured cheek patches.

HABITAT: Estuaries, bays and lagoons mostly on the east and south coasts.

STATUS: As a winter visitor, mainly from central Europe, this grebe is irregular and scarce, though almost annual to Dublin and Wexford. As a nesting species the Black-necked Grebe has bred irregularly in a number of midland and western counties since its discovery there at the turn of the century. It is now either extinct or very rare as a breeding bird, due mainly to the drainage of its breeding habitats.

Black-necked Grebe (○ Summer plumage)

PETRELS and SHEARWATERS

FULMAR *Fulmarus glacialis* *Plate 2*
Fulmaire

IDENTIFICATION: 46 cm (19"). Although like a thick-set gull with rather stiff wings, the Fulmar is, in fact, a member of the petrel family and quite different from gulls at close range. The narrow wings, rump and uppertail are grey, in contrast to the white head and underparts. The bill is yellow and heavy, and structurally complex and the legs are incapable of supporting the fulmar in a standing position. The flight is an alternation of flapping and gliding, often close to the surface of the sea. Fulmars nest colonially, usually alongside Kittiwakes, Guillemots, Razorbills and other cliff-nesting seabirds.

HABITAT: The open sea, often far from land. Nest sites are on coastal cliffs, occasionally some distance inland from the coast proper.

STATUS: Since its arrival in this country at the turn of the century, the Fulmar has spread around all coasts and now nests on most suitable sea cliffs. In the winter it moves out to sea, rarely coming inshore except during storms.

Summer

CORY'S SHEARWATER *Calonectris diomedea* *Plate 2*

IDENTIFICATION: 46 cm (18"). A large shearwater, generally grey-brown above, white below. It can be mistaken for a Fulmar or immature gull at a distance. The flight consists of gliding over the surface of the sea with few wing beats. It looks more relaxed than the Manx Shearwater, the wings being held more 'bowed', less rigid, than our other shearwaters. At closer range, the overall grey-brown upperparts, whitish underparts and the large yellowish bill are the diagnostic features. Compare with the following description of the Great Shearwater.

HABITAT: The open sea. Rarely inshore and usually only in foggy conditions.

STATUS: Annual autumn visitor to the south and south-west coasts from central Atlantic and Mediterranean breeding grounds. It is very scarce elsewhere around the coast. Most are seen after south-westerlies at Cape Clear Island, Co. Cork, where, on occasions, hundreds have been seen in a day.

GREAT SHEARWATER *Puffinus gravis* *Plate 2*

IDENTIFICATION: 46 cm (18"). A large shearwater (about the same size as Cory's) with a rather similar lazy gliding flight close to the surface of the sea. It is distinguished from Cory's by the dark cap on the head in sharp contrast to the white cheeks, and by the pale "V" on the upper tail. These features are only visible from quite close range, however. In calm weather this bird will readily settle on the surface of the sea and will even dive into the water from close to the surface. At close range the bill appears black and there is a dark belly patch which is often visible as the bird shears, showing its underparts.

HABITAT: The open sea, only coming inshore in adverse weather conditions.

STATUS: Annual autumn migrant to south-west Ireland from its breeding ground in the Tristan da Cunha Islands in the South Atlantic. Like some other seabirds it performs large circular migrations. It is generally seen in small numbers but on occasions it has occured in hundreds. Rare elsewhere on the Irish coast.

SOOTY SHEARWATER *Puffinus griseus* *Plate 2*

IDENTIFICATION: 41 cm (16"). This bird is seen most often in the company of Manx Shearwaters. Obviously bigger than the Manx, it is a sooty brown (appearing black) all over, with a quite distinctive silvery central underwing. The flight is also rather different than that of the Manx and Balearic Shearwaters in that it tends, on occasions, to fly higher above the water surface. Like other shearwaters, the Sooty will readily settle on the water in calm weather. From a distance it can appear like a dark phase Arctic Skua (see page 98), but its flight is obviously that of a shearwater and not a skua.

HABITAT: The open sea, although it will come close inshore all along the west coast of Ireland, in autumn.

STATUS: Annual autumn migrant from its breeding grounds in the Southern Hemisphere. Generally only small numbers are seen but, on occasions, it has occurred in hundreds and even thousands. Scarce in spring.

MANX SHEARWATER *Puffinus puffinus* *Plate 2*
Cánóg dhubh

IDENTIFICATION: 35 cm (14"). A distinctive seabird, easily recognised by its black above/white below pattern, as it shears gracefully over the open sea on stiff narrow wings. In certain places Manx Shearwaters may be observed in single file feeding flocks, comprising hundreds of birds. They return from the sea to the nesting burrows at night, when the noise at the colony reaches unbelievable proportions. The Balearic Shearwater, a race of the Manx, is a brownish version, usually paler on the underparts.

HABITAT: By day, the open sea. At night, during the breeding season, colonies on isolated islands and headlands.

STATUS: Occupies breeding colonies all around the coast of Ireland, but especially in the south-west. Some of the colonies hold many thousands of pairs. In autumn, they perform vast circular migrations off the coast, wintering far out at sea. The Mediterranean race of this species, the Balearic Shearwater *P.p. mauretanicus* is a regular, though scarce, passage migrant, mainly to the south-west coast.

Summer

STORM PETREL *Hydrobates pelagicus* *Plate 2*

Guairdeall

IDENTIFICATION: 15 cm (6"). This bird is most likely to be observed as a very small dark form flying low over the open sea. It keeps close to the surface of the water, often hesitating to patter the surface with its tiny webbed feet. The white rump patch is actually only visible at close range. The only common bird with which it could possibly be confused is the House Martin (see page 123) which may occur over the sea on migration. The latter species, however, has white underparts which should confirm identification.

HABITAT: The open sea. Breeding colonies are found on remote rocky islets.

STATUS: Colonies of this, our smallest seabird, occur on islands off the north-west, west and south-west coasts. It is most often seen in autumn, off the south-west coast where it accompanies other migrating seabirds, such as shearwaters.

Summer

LEACH'S PETREL *Oceanodroma leucorrhoa* *Plate 2*

Guairdeall gabhlach

IDENTIFICATION: 20 cm (8"). Slightly larger than the Storm Petrel, the Leach's has a more erratic flight pattern, darting, hesitating and changing direction more readily than the former. A good view reveals pale patches on the upper wing, a distinctly forked tail and less pronounced white rump. It is generally seen in the company of other seabirds, particularly Storm Petrels.

HABITAT: The open sea. However, after severe gales, it has, on occasions, been found in most Irish counties, as a wind blown straggler.

STATUS: Mainly a scarce autumn migrant from the North Atlantic which has been observed at remote headlands and islands following gales. On rare occasions winter "wrecks" cause Leach's Petrels to turn up far inland. There is a long history of reported breeding on one or two islands in the west and south-west, but regular breeding has never been satisfactorily proven.

Gannets: Immature to adult

GANNETS

GANNET *Sula bassana* *Plate 2*

Gainéad

IDENTIFICATION: 90 cm (36"). From a distance the Gannet looks like an outsize seagull with conspicuous black wing-tips. Closer examination shows that the cigar-shaped body, long narrow wings and the habit of diving into the sea for fish are not the characteristics of a gull. Close up the head is seen to be beautifully marked, with a yellowish wash and a white eye set close to the base of the dagger-like bill. The juvenile is sooty, speckled white and immatures have varying amounts of white in their plumage, depending on age.

HABITAT: The open sea, often inshore during the summer months. Wandering juveniles may turn up inland.

STATUS: The huge breeding colony of some 20,000 pairs on the Little Skellig, Co. Kerry has been known for at least 300 years. There are two other smaller colonies — The Bull Rock, Co. Cork, and Great Saltee, Co. Wexford — and there is evidence of nest prospecting off the Mayo coast in recent years. Heavy migration of Gannets may be observed off the west and south coasts in the autumn as birds move out into their Atlantic winter quarters.

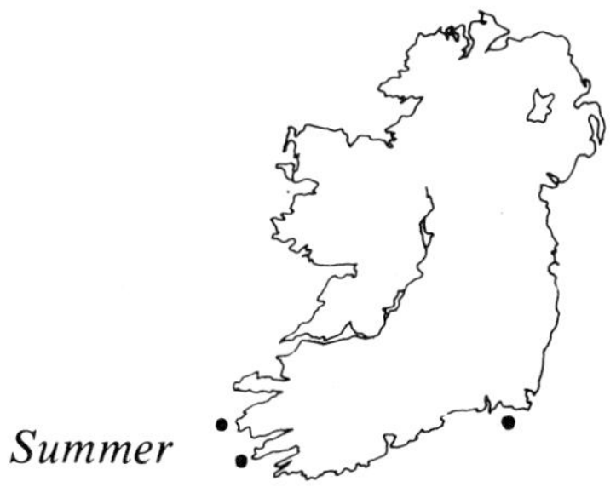

CORMORANTS and SHAGS

CORMORANT *Phalacrocorax carbo* *Plate 27 and 28*
Broigheall

IDENTIFICATION: 90 cm (36"). Our largest black seabird, often to be seen standing upright with wings held outstretched on coastal rocks. Also typically seen swimming with a half submerged body, diving frequently with a lunge from the surface. Cormorants fly low over the water surface with quick wingbeats, or occasionally high in the air in goose-like formation. Adults have white patches on the face and thigh in the summer. Immature birds are brown above, off-white below.

HABITAT: Mainly coastal waters, but also large inland lakes and rivers.

STATUS: The Cormorant is a common and widespread breeder in rocky coastal areas but there are also a few inland colonies in trees. There is some evidence of migration between Ireland and other parts of Europe.

Summer

SHAG *Phalacrocorax aristotelis* *Plate 27 and 28*
Seaga

IDENTIFICATION: 76 cm (30"). Very like a rather small Cormorant, this species is more confined to rocky coastal areas than the former. In summer the adult is greener than the Cormorant, lacks the white patches and has a wispy crest and a bright yellow base to the bill. On the wing, Shags have quicker wing beats and are less inclined to glide than Cormorants. On the ground they look neater than the bigger bird. Juvenile Shags are like small juvenile Cormorants. Shags usually nest under or beside large boulders, not in the open like Cormorants.

HABITAT: Rocky coasts.

STATUS: Common breeder in suitable habitat all around Ireland, though less common on the east coast. Rare inland.

Summer

HERONS

BITTERN *Botaurus stellaris* *Plate 3*
Bonnán

IDENTIFICATION: 76 cm (30"). A rare and secretive member of the heron family, the Bittern usually reveals its presence only at dusk when it is most active. Its flight, like that of the Grey Heron, is slow and ponderous, low over reed-beds. As a means of camouflage the Bittern will point its bill skyward causing it to blend into its reed-bed surroundings. The male Bittern holding territory in the summer emits an incredible resonant "boom" which sounds like a distant foghorn.

HABITAT: Dense and extensive reed-beds and marshes.

STATUS: Rare, though probably annual, visitor from Continental Europe, mainly in winter. The Bittern was a common and widespread resident in Ireland up until the 1840's. Its disappearance was due to drainage of its habitat. If it were not so often shot it could possibly return to nest here again.

LITTLE EGRET *Egretta garzetta* *Plate 3*

IDENTIFICATION: 56 cm (22"). A small, all white heron which could possibly be mistaken only for a Spoonbill (see page 42). A good view of this bird can show it to be remarkably beautiful, with long wispy head, breast and back plumes. The bill and legs are black and the feet yellow. In flight, the neck is tucked back in typical heron fashion and the yellow feet protrude beyond the tail.

HABITAT: Coastal estuaries and lagoons. Also occasionally on freshwater habitats inland.

STATUS: Rare visitor from southern Europe, mainly in spring to the south coast although there are a good many records from the east and north coasts also. Individuals may remain in one locality for long periods. The Little Egret is generally solitary, but has occurred in a small flock.

GREY HERON *Ardea cinerea* *Plate 3*
Corr riasc

IDENTIFICATION: 90 cm (36"). A well known bird of the marshes, often to be seen standing motionless waiting for prey, or flying with great slow-motion wing beats over the reeds. On close inspection the heron is finely marked with black on the head, neck and underparts and a prominent yellow bill. In the wind the long neck feathers and head plume can be seen to best advantage. The flight silhouette is distinctive, with the head tucked back and the long legs protruding beyond the tail. The call is a raucous squawk which may be uttered from the marsh or more often at the nest site.

HABITAT: Generally near fresh water marshes, lakes, rivers, estuaries, even open coastal areas. Herons nest in colonies, usually high in mature trees, but occasionally in lakeside bushes in the west of Ireland. Some even nest on sea cliffs.

STATUS: Resident, breeding in every county of Ireland in colonies of from one or two, to eighty pairs (the largest colony in the country near Lough Erne) although the more usual colony size is about a dozen pairs. There is some winter immigration of Herons into Ireland from Britain.

Grey Heron

SPOONBILLS

SPOONBILL *Platalea leucorodia* — *Plate 3*
Corr leitheadach

IDENTIFICATION: 86 cm (34"). A large white wading bird with long legs and bill. It flies, unlike the herons, with its neck outstretched (see Little Egret page 41). From a distance the bill can be seen to be long, heavy and spatulate. In summer the adult has buffish patches on the nape and breast. The juvenile is like the adult though with black wing tips and a pinkish bill.

HABITAT: Estuaries, salt marshes, lagoons, lake fringes and other shallow water habitats.

STATUS: Rare though probably annual visitor from Europe. They may appear in any month of the year and remain in a locality for a long time. Most of the records are from the south and east coasts. Although usually solitary, Spoonbills sometimes occur in small flocks.

SWANS, GEESE and DUCKS

MUTE SWAN *Cygnus olor* *Plate 4*
Eala bhalbh

IDENTIFICATION: 152 cm (60"). This beautiful bird is known to everyone. The white plumage is relieved only by the orange bill with its black boss. Almost every water body in the country has Mute Swans, swimming with gracefully curved necks and fluffed out back feathers. In flight, the wings produce a monotonous singing with each beat, but otherwise as its name implies, the bird is usually silent. At the nest, however, Mute Swans will hiss and grunt aggressively. The young are a dull brownish grey with less conspicuously coloured bills.

HABITAT: All freshwater habitats, also coastal lagoons and estuaries.

STATUS: Common and widespread resident. In some places flocks of non-breeders, several hundred strong, are to be found. Large numbers collect at tidal estuaries in the winter and in one or two localities more than 1,000 may be found together. Hard weather on the Continent is believed to cause immigration into Ireland.

Winter Concentrations

BEWICK'S SWAN *Cygnus columbianus* *Plate 4*
Eala Bhewick

IDENTIFICATION: 117 cm (50"). The least well known of our swans, Bewick's is a more local winter visitor than the Whooper Swan, (see following description) which is often difficult to distinguish with confidence at a distance, although it appears smaller with a mainly black bill. Close views show the bird to be a smaller version of the Whooper with much less yellow on the bill and a rounder head — the Whooper's head looks quite wedge-shaped in comparison. Bewick's Swan is quieter than the Whooper, but nevertheless has a distinctive honking call which lacks the tuneful quality of the Whoopers'.

HABITAT: Mainly shallow lakes, river callows, agricultural land (fields in grass, stubble and potatoes) where it often associates with geese. Rarely found on salt water in Ireland.

Winter Concentrations

STATUS: Winter visitor in fluctuating numbers, from the Siberian Tundra. When the main wintering quarters in Holland freeze over Bewick's move into Britain and Ireland. The favoured localities in Ireland are the Wexford Slobs and lagoons, the Shannon system and its callows, the Lough Neagh basin and the flatlands of Loughs Foyle and Swilly. Flocks of over a hundred together are notable, but between 500 and 1,000 are regular on the Wexford Slobs in the latter part of the winter.

WHOOPER SWAN *Cygnus cygnus* *Plate 4*
Eala ghlórach

IDENTIFICATION: 152 cm (60"). A well known swan in the north and west of the country. It is most readily identified by its wild and emotive bugling call and its yellow, black-tipped bill visible at considerable range. The Whooper is less naturally graceful than the Mute Swan, carrying its neck more or less erect and rarely fluffing out its back feathers. Many Whoopers have orange staining on the head and neck. The grey coloured young have pink, in place of yellow, on the bill. Whooper Swans do not make the whistling of Mutes with their wings.

HABITAT: Mainly shallow inland waters, also callow land, reclaimed agricultural fields, potato fields, stubble and estuaries.

STATUS: Widespread and fairly abundant winter visitor from Iceland. Most winter in the north of the country and on the Shannon system. It is rarely seen in numbers greater than 500 in a single locality, but over 1,000 have been seen on the flatlands near Lough Foyle in early winter.

Winter Concentrations

BEAN GOOSE *Anser fabalis* *Plate 5*
Síolghé

IDENTIFICATION: F. 76 cm (30") — M. 87 cm (34"). As well as being one of our largest geese, appearing taller on the ground than other similar species, the Bean Goose is also one of the scarcest. The head and neck look slightly darker than the rest of the plumage and from a distance the bill may also appear dark. (See below). At closer range the legs are distinctly orange and the rather long dark bill has an orange patch of variable size. In flight, the Bean Goose lacks the pale forewing of the Greylag and Pink-foot, and has more uniform wings than even the White-front. The call is a nasal honking, but the Bean calls less frequently than other geese in this country.

HABITAT: Mainly with other geese in typical habitat — wet grasslands and other marginal lowlands, such as river callows, turloughs and coastal wetlands.

STATUS: Rare winter visitor from arctic Europe/Asia. It is most often recorded singly or in small groups on the Wexford Slobs.

PINK-FOOTED GOOSE *Anser brachyrhynchus* *Plate 5*
Gé ghobghearr

IDENTIFICATION: F. 61 cm (24") — M. 71 cm (28"). From a distance, the Pink-foot looks somewhat greyer and less brown than similar geese and is decidedly darker on the head and neck (see previous description of Bean Goose). At closer range, the bill appears small and dark with a small pinkish mark. The legs are pink. Pink-feet are noisy in flight, the flock make a high-pitched yelping, quite like a distant pack of hounds. In flight the ash-grey forewings make the birds resemble rather small Greylag Geese, but the dark head and neck, small bill and distinctive call should confirm identification.

HABITAT: Mainly with other geese in typical habitat — as for Bean Goose.

STATUS: Scarce, though now annual, winter visitor from Iceland, occurring most regularly on the Wexford Slobs, usually in small wintering parties. Small off course flocks sometimes turn up in autumn, mainly in the north and east of the country.

WHITE-FRONTED GOOSE *Anser albifrons* *Plate 5*
Gé bháneadanach

IDENTIFICATION: F. 66 cm (26") — M. 76 cm (30"). The Greenland White-fronted Goose, *Anser albifrons flavirostris*, is the race of this goose occurring commonly in Ireland. It is perhaps the best known of our geese with almost half the world population of 12,000 birds wintering on the Wexford Slobs. In general colouration it is brownish with a distinctive white undertail region. From all but very distant views, the prominent feature on this goose is the heavy black belly markings. At closer range, the orange bill and legs are good identification characteristics, as of course is the white "front" to the head. However, this latter feature is not visible at a distance and is absent in the juvenile, where the orange bill and legs alone distinguish it from other similar species. A good way of identifying distant flocks of White-fronted Geese in flight is by their call, which can best be described as a confused high-pitched yelping. The rather pale forewing on the White-front should not be confused with the brighter, more extensive forewings of the Greylag and Pink-footed geese. The European White-fronted Goose, *A.a. albifrons*, which winters in large numbers in Britain and which can be distinguished from the Greenland race by a pink rather than orange bill, is a very rare though annual winter visitor to the Wexford Slobs.

HABITAT: Open low-lying ground near water. To a lesser extent marshes, lakes and bogs.

STATUS: A widespread and locally abundant winter visitor from western Greenland. Half the world population (6,000 birds) winter at the Wexford Slobs. A further 2-3,000 are found in small wintering flocks, mostly in the western half of the country and especially along the callows of the Shannon.

Winter Concentrations

GREYLAG GOOSE *Anser anser* *Plate 5*
Gé ghlas

IDENTIFICATION: F. 76 cm (30") — M. 92 cm (34"). Like most geese on the ground, the Greylag looks rather nondescript. It is overall greyish brown with white undertail region and from a distance the orange bill is visible. The orange bill/pink legs combination is a good identification feature on the ground. In flight, Greylag Geese are easily identified. Much of the upper surface of the wings are chalky grey (the Pink-footed goose which also has grey upperwings, is smaller and has a darker head and neck). Like most geese, Greylags are noisy in flight, calling like farmyard geese, which are themselves descended from domesticated Greylag geese.

HABITAT: Open low-lying ground and agricultural land generally near water, callows, reclaimed slob land. Less frequently lakes, bogs, marshes, etc.

STATUS: Previously a winter visitor, mainly from Iceland, in considerable numbers, but in recent years it has become scarce and local. A few wintering flocks of up to three hundred are still to be found in half a dozen, widely separated localities around Ireland.

Winter Concentrations

CANADA GOOSE *Branta canadensis* *Plate 6*

IDENTIFICATION: F. 92 cm (36") — M. 102 cm (40"). The largest goose occurring in Ireland. This almost swan-sized goose is recognised by its long black neck and head and distinctive white throat patch. The body is generally brown with a white undertail region. In flight the wings appear a fairly uniform brownish-grey and the call is a nasal honking. Canada Geese have been introduced into estates and waterfowl collections in a number of parts of Ireland and those found on lakes and ponds, especially during the summer months, are doubtless of this origin. However, Canada Geese of several different sub-species (genuine wild vagrants from arctic Canada) have been seen at the Wexford Slobs and at other wild goose gaunts in Ireland. They vary in size considerably, but retain the basic plumage pattern of the feral goose. Their honking is rather similar to that of a Bewick's Swan.

HABITAT: Feral birds on lakes, ponds and estates. Wild vagrants on typical goose habitat.

STATUS: Rare vagrant from arctic Canada which occurs annually in small numbers on the Wexford Slobs.

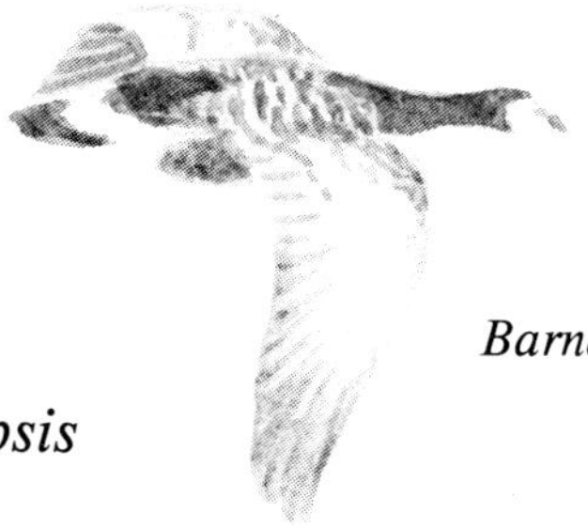

Barnacle Goose

BARNACLE GOOSE *Branta leucopsis* *Plate 6*
Gé ghiúrainn

IDENTIFICATION: F. 58 cm (23") — M. 69 cm (27"). This arguably our most beautiful goose is a bird of the wilder islands and headlands of the west and north of Ireland. Close views are difficult to obtain but are seldom necessary as identification from long range is comparatively easy. Its overall appearance is black and white with an obvious white face and undertail patch. Grey, black and white bands show on the upperparts. The call is a rapidly repeated yelping. Barnacle Geese are gregarious, though the flocks generally number hundreds rather than thousands.

HABITAT: Grassy fields near the sea, mainly on remote islands and promontaries. Occasional on agricultural land, reclaimed slobland estuaries.

STATUS: Local winter visitor from north-east Greenland to the west and north of Ireland, notably Mayo, Donegal and Sligo. Small numbers occur regularly on the Wexford Slobs and on Lambay Island, Co. Dublin.

Winter Concentrations

Barnacle Geese

BRENT GOOSE *Branta bernicla* *Plate 6*
Cadhan

IDENTIFICATION: F. 56 cm (22") — M. 61 cm (24"). A small dark goose of open mudflats. Brent are gregarious, being found at their wintering localities in hundreds and often thousands. At a distance they appear dark — mostly dark grey and black, though with a clear white undertail region. They are dumpy geese with a shortish neck and small head and bill. The legs are dark and a white mark on the side of the adults neck is absent in the juvenile. At low tide the geese feed on the green eel grass, *Zostera*, and other mudflat vegetation, retreating towards the shore with the incoming tide. Brent are noisy birds when feeding.

Large numbers on the mudflats make a continuous "grumbling" which is most characteristic and untypically goose-like. Most of the Brent Geese occurring in Ireland are of the pale bellied form.

HABITAT: Open and exposed estuarine mudflats, roosting at high tide on grassy islands. In recent years Brent have begun to frequent grassy fields near the Wexford coast where they both feed and roost.

Winter Concentrations

STATUS: This Arctic Canadian species winters in abundance in a number of bays and estuaries around Ireland. Huge numbers (up to 15,000) build up in November, at Strangford Lough, dispersing to other localities as their food supply is exhausted. Their chief wintering areas are in counties Down, Dublin, Wexford and Kerry.

Shelduck

SHELDUCK *Tadorna tadorna* *Plate 4*
Seil-lacha

IDENTIFICATION: F. 61 cm (24") — M. 66 cm (26"). A large black and white waterfowl somewhat like a cross between a duck and a goose. At a distance Shelduck show much white, a dark chestband and a black head. At closer range it is a colourful bird with a bottle green head, orange chestband and blood red bill. Apart from the larger size of the male and the prominent knob on his bill, the sexes appear similar. Shelduck are as conspicuous in flight as on the ground and fly with rather shallow wingbeats. The juvenile has a distinctive pale face and foreneck. At the breeding burrows (often old rabbit holes) the anxious adults make whistling and hissing noises, and in courtship flights a cackling call.

HABITAT: In the breeding season beside both fresh water and marine habitats. It favours sandy localities, often nesting among dunes or in disused rabbit burrows. In winter on coastal estuaries, often in association with Wigeon and Brent Geese.

Summer

Winter Concentrations

STATUS: Widespread resident, nesting in every marine county and also on a few of our larger inland lakes. In the autumn Irish Shelducks probably migrate to the North Sea to moult near Heligoland, returning to spend the winter on our coastal estuaries. Flocks may vary from a few birds to over a thousand.

WIGEON *Anas penelope*

Rualacha

Plates 7 and 8

IDENTIFICATION: 46 cm (18"). At close range this duck is eye-catching, the drake largely grey with a red-brown head and buff forehead mark and even the female is distinctive with her rich brown plumage and rounded head shape. However, most views of Wigeon are distant ones, and of large flocks, where the colours may be difficult to discern, but the continual high-pitched whistling of the drakes is a very useful pointer to identification. In flight the drakes show large white wing patches and both sexes show a clear white belly patch while a further flight characteristic is the pointed wings and tail, which give the Wigeon an unmistakable outline even from a long way off.

HABITAT: Open water, both coastal and fresh, the birds being as much at home on estuaries as on lakes and flooded river callows. Wigeon are grazers. They will feed in stubble fields, well removed from water and show an affinity for waterside grassland.

Winter Concentrations

STATUS: Very abundant winter visitor

from north-east Europe and Iceland congregating in thousands on many of our estuaries and lakes. A few pairs have remained to breed in Ireland in recent years, but the species does not nest here on a regular basis.

GADWALL *Anas strepera* — *Plates 7 and 8*
Gadual

IDENTIFICATION: 51 cm (20"). At a distance the bird on the ground or water is rather nondescript. In size and shape they resemble Mallard but the rear-end of the drake is a good identification feature. At closer range the drake is generally greyish with very close, fine markings but the female can only be separated from female Mallard by her yellow bill. In flight, identification is easy — this is our only dabbling duck with a square white patch on the rear wing. The Gadwall quacks noisily, rather like a Mallard.

HABITAT: Lakes, marshes, flooded callows, coastal lagoons, sometimes estuaries. They often prefer cover to open water and readily mix with Teal and Shoveler.

STATUS: Rather local migrant and winter visitor in small numbers, mainly from Iceland. Certain lakes, especially in the south and west of Ireland, may hold up to one hundred. Previously very rare as a breeder, the Gadwall now nests in a number of widely separated localities in this country.

Summer

TEAL *Anas crecca* — *Plates 7 and 8*
Praslacha ghlaseiteach

IDENTIFICATION: 35 cm (14"). The Teal is our smallest duck. It generally remains well hidden and when disturbed, flies off rapidly, in close groups. From fairly close range and in good light the drake can be seen to be quite a colourful bird. The head is copper and green and the body generally greyish with fine markings but perhaps the most obvious features on the water are the white horizontal stripe on the side and the cream coloured undertail patches. The duck is dowdy brown. In flight the speculum of both drake and duck is vivid green. Flocks, well hidden, call nervously — a low ringing sound, not particularly duck-like. The race occurring in Europe is *Anas crecca crecca.* A few individuals of the North American race, the Green-winged Teal *A.c. carolinensis* occur almost annually in winter. The drake differs from our birds by having a vertical white stripe on the side of the breast in front of the wing instead of the horizontal stripe on the side (see Plate 47).

HABITAT: Mainly fresh water marshes, lake shores, etc. Also estuaries, sometimes even coastal bays, though less often on open water than other surface feeding ducks.

STATUS: There is a well distributed, though sparse resident population in Ireland. The majority of the Teal in Ireland in winter are immigrants from Britain and Europe. Flocks of hundreds and even thousands are found in many localities. Wintering numbers are increased during hard weather on the Continent.

Winter Concentrations

MALLARD *Anas platyrhynchos* — *Plates 7 and 8*
Mallard

IDENTIFICATION: 58 cm (23"). Our most familiar wild duck easily identified by the drake's shining green head, white neck ring and black curly upper tail feathers. In flight the colourful blue speculum on the wing is characteristic. Apart from the brown and orange bill and orange legs, the female mallard is dowdy. In eclipse plumage (during the early summer) drakes are mostly brown, like the females. After the breeding season, eclipse plumage drakes gather in flocks to moult. The Mallard is vociferous, uttering a noisy quack on being disturbed.

HABITAT: Marshes, fens, lakes, rivers and almost any freshwater habitat, also estuaries and elsewhere on the coast. The Mallard will feed in stubble fields well away from water, especially in the winter.

STATUS: Very common and widespread resident. The Irish population is mainly sedentary. Large numbers of Mallard are hand-reared by Gun Clubs and released onto ponds and marshes all over the country.

Summer

Winter Concentrations

PINTAIL *Anas acuta* — *Plates 7 and 8*
Biorearrach

IDENTIFICATION: F. 56 cm (22") — M. 66 cm (26"). At a distance a sitting Pintail looks slim and long-necked. The drake has a dark head, white neck and greyish body; the duck is brownish overall and slightly paler than other surface feeding ducks. At close range the drake shows beautiful and subtle plumage with long pointed central tail feathers. In flight the speculum is obscure but a pale trailing edge shows on the wing of both duck and drake. The shape of a Pintail in flight is unique and after some experience identification from long range is straightforward.

HABITAT: Coastal and inland marshes, lagoons and estuaries.

STATUS: Rather local passage migrant and winter visitor from north-east Europe and Iceland. Most of our wintering Pintail are found in a few, widely separated, coastal localities. The majority, a thousand or more, are found in Castlemaine Bay in Kerry and flocks of several hundred birds also occur in Dublin Bay and on the Wexford Slobs. In recent years a few pairs of this species have nested in Ireland in widely separated localities.

Winter Concentrations

GARGANEY *Anas querquedula* — *Plates 7 and 8*

IDENTIFICATION: 38 cm (15"). A small duck, similar to the Teal, but with an obvious curved, white eyestripe on the head of the drake. On the ground or water the female is difficult to distinguish from a female Teal. Identification is relatively easy in flight, however, as both drake and duck Garganey show a distinct light grey forewing, while the underwing has a dark outline and pale inner area. Garganey appear slightly larger when accompanying Teal. They often feed with Shoveler, and are fond of dense aquatic vegetation.

HABITAT: Much as for Teal, but rarely on the coast.

STATUS: Scarce annual migrant from the European Continent, always in small numbers (usually ones or twos). In recent years Garganey have bred with increasing regularity in more than one locality in Ireland.

SHOVELER *Anas clypeata* — *Plates 7 and 8*

Spadalghob

IDENTIFICATION: 52 cm (20.5"). From a distance the Shoveler appears squat and very heavy-billed. The drake shows a lot of white with a black head and dark patch on the side; the duck is dull brown. As with most other drakes, at closer range, the Shoveler is beautifully marked. The dark patch on the side is rust coloured, the head a dark green and the bill is remarkably long and spatulate looking. Identification is relatively simple in flight. Both drake and duck show light blue wing patches and the heavy bill gives the bird a most unusual and distinctive flight silhouette.

HABITAT: Marshes and reedy areas in preference to open water. Most Shoveler are found on marshy lakes, or flooded river callows, but also on coastal lagoons and some estuaries.

STATUS: Passage migrant and winter visitor from Iceland and Europe to many waters. Flocks of over 500 are, however, noteworthy. A scarce breeder in Ireland, it has nevertheless increased in recent years and now nests locally in a number of counties.

Winter Concentrations

POCHARD *Aythya ferina* — *Plates 9 and 10*

Poiseard

IDENTIFICATION: 46 cm (18"). Like the Scaup (see page 56) and Tufted Duck (see page 54) a gregarious species, favouring inland waters. The drake has a grey body with the black 'fore-and-aft' appearance of the Scaup, but in good light the head is bright rust-coloured. In poor light and from a distance, the drake Pochard and drake Scaup can be almost indistinguishable. The female Pochard is brownish-grey with a pale facial pattern. In flight the greyish wings of both sexes show only a paler grey bar, much less vivid than that of both the Scaup and Tufted duck with which they often associate on lakes in winter.

HABITAT: Lakes, large and small, reservoirs. Small groups are found on some rivers, large ponds and, unusually, on estuaries.

STATUS: Abundant winter visitor from Britain and the Continent. There are some to be found on many ponds and reservoirs and huge numbers (thousands) on a few of the larger lakes, notably Loughs Corrib and Neagh. A rare breeder in Ireland.

Winter Concentrations

TUFTED DUCK *Aythya fuligula* — *Plates 9 and 10*

Lacha bhadánach

IDENTIFICATION: 43 cm (17"). Like the Scaup (see page 56) the Tufted Duck is gregarious, but is generally more approachable, being less of an open water species. The drake is a familiar black and white lake bird, with a conspicuous tuft of feathers at the back of the head from which the name derives. The duck is dull brown and lacks the head tuft. There is sometimes a pale ring at the base of the bill, but it is never as extensive as that of the female Scaup. In flight a clear white bar shows on the otherwise dark wings. Tufted Duck dive continually to feed on the lake bed.

HABITAT: Lakes, reservoirs, even ponds and rivers in some areas. In winter, large numbers gather on open water on our larger lakes. Occasionally found on coastal estuaries in small numbers. Breeds on islands in lakes.

STATUS: Abundant winter visitor from Iceland, Britain and Northern Europe, especially to large lakes. The numbers wintering in Ireland are many times greater than the number of breeders, indicating immigration on a large scale. Hundreds are found on many waters and as many as 50,000 on Lough Neagh, on occasions.

Summer

Winter Concentrations

Previously a rare breeder in this country, it is now nesting locally in many counties and quite commonly in the north and west.

Goldeneye

SCAUP *Aythya marila* — *Plates 9 and 10*

Lacha iascán

IDENTIFICATION: 48 cm (19"). The Scaup is a hardy, gregarious diving duck found on open water. Drakes appear light grey with black fore-and-aft; females, dark brown with an obvious white circle around the base of the bill. At closer range the stout grey bill and greenish gloss on the drake's head may be seen. The Scaup is a larger, heavier bird than the Tufted Duck (see previous description). In flight a broad white wing-bar shows on both drake and duck.

HABITAT: Mainly open bays and estuaries. A few of our larger lakes also have wintering flocks.

STATUS: Winter visitor and passage migrant from Iceland, in smaller numbers now than formerly. It is local, but at its traditional wintering sites is found in hundreds and sometimes thousands. The majority occur along the east coast but large numbers are also found on Lough Neagh and in Castlemaine and Tralee Bays in Co. Kerry.

Winter Concentrations

Scaup

EIDER *Somateria mollissima* — *Plate 11*

Éadar lacha

IDENTIFICATION: 61 cm (24"). A beautiful and conspicuous sea duck of our northern coasts. The drake from any distance appears a large, thick set white bird with black patches. The female and immatures are brownish and heavily barred. Eiders have a long wedge-shaped bill and head, a good diagnostic feature at long range. Close up the drake shows subtle pink and green washes to the breast and head. Young drakes are generally dark but have variable pale patches. Groups of eiders bob up and down on the waves even in the most severe conditions. They are reluctant to fly, but when they do so, they are just as distinctive as when on the water. Courting Eider drakes call with an unusual soft cooing.

HABITAT: Rocky coasts with scattered marine islands.

STATUS: A well distributed resident around the northern coast of Ireland from south Donegal to Co. Down. Eiders gather in groups close inshore for the winter months and breed on rocky islets in the summer. Recent records indicate that the Eider may be extending its range southwards.

All Year

LONG-TAILED DUCK *Clangula hyemalis* — *Plate 11*

IDENTIFICATION: F. 41 cm (16") — M. 55 cm (22"). At a distance in winter both male and female Long-tailed Duck show a lot of white in their plumage. The pale head has a distinctive dark cheek patch but the small bill is only obvious at close range as are the long central tail feathers of the male. In flight, this is one of the few ducks with no apparent wing pattern — the wing is uniformly dark.

HABITAT: A coastal species favouring the open sea or bays. Occasionally found in estuaries and even on inland waters.

STATUS: Local winter visitor from arctic Europe (probably Iceland). Found mostly in the northern half of the country and especially on the north-west coast. Long-tails are usually found in pairs or small groups, but over fifty and, on occasions, over a hundred have been seen together.

COMMON SCOTER *Melanitta nigra* *Plate 11*

Scótar

IDENTIFICATION: 48 cm (19"). A hardy, gregarious sea duck, generally quite abundant at its wintering localities. Flocks sit well out from the shore and from a distance show no positive identification features. However, with the aid of a telescope the large pale face patch of the female can be seen and in good light an orange patch is visible on top of the drake's bill. Scoters characteristically cock their tails and often flap their wings when on the water. In flight Scoters appear sooty, with slightly paler underwings. Divers, and perhaps Long-tailed Ducks may associate with Scoters.

HABITAT: The open sea, coastal bays, loughs, and, during the breeding season, island-dotted lakes.

STATUS: Rather local winter visitor from northern Europe gathering in hundreds, sometimes thousands, at traditional winter haunts. Numbers are decreasing, due, at least in part, to the destruction of the mussel beds around our coasts. Large numbers (over five thousand) are still to be found in the Kerry bays. A rare breeder, it nests regularly on two lakes, one in Fermanagh, the other in Mayo.

Summer

Winter Concentrations

Scoters

VELVET SCOTER *Melanitta fusca* *Plate 11*

IDENTIFICATION: 56 cm (22"). A large black sea duck, both male and female show pale marks on the head. In close up (usually through a telescope) the drakes bill is partially yellow and there is a white mark near the eye. The duck's bill is dark and the two white smudges on the face are roughly circular and clearly separate. Immatures and females are alike. In flight, identification is straightforward — Velvet Scoter have a square white patch at the rear base of the wing. This is not usually visible on birds on the water but shows clearly when the wings are flapped. Among a flock of Common Scoter, Velvet Scoter appear larger and bulkier and stand out clearly in flight.

HABITAT: The open sea, sometimes inshore in bays and estuaries.

STATUS: Irregular and local winter visitor from northern Scandinavia, mainly to the east coast. It is usually seen singly or in small parties, but larger groups have occurred.

GOLDENEYE *Bucephala clangula* — *Plates 9 and 10*

Órshúileach

IDENTIFICATION: F. 41 cm (16") — M. 46 cm (18"). A hardy duck of fairly open water, but less gregarious than Scaup, Tufted Duck or Pochard. The drake appears strikingly black and white both on the water and in the air. At close range, the odd head shape and white spot near the bill are visible. The duck is recognisable by its dark brown head, pale neck band and greyish body. Goldeneye have a distinctive profile, they sit low in the water when feeding, their heads appearing outsized. When resting they often sit higher and cock their tails in a characteristic manner. Groups of Goldeneye, up to twenty together, are normal in feeding flocks with females and immatures greatly outnumbering the males. The flock in flight make a curious ringing noise with their wings, which is audible for quite a distance in calm conditions.

HABITAT: Open water, both fresh and salt. Small groups are found on smaller lakes and reservoirs and hundreds may be found on certain estuaries and lakes.

STATUS: Abundant winter visitor from northern Europe, mainly to the northern half of Ireland. Thousands winter on Lough Neagh. Rare in the summer months.

Winter Concentrations

SMEW *Mergus albellus* — *Plate 10*

Síolta gheal

IDENTIFICATION: F. 41 cm (16") — M. 45 cm (17.5"). The majority of Smew seen in Ireland are females or immatures. Smaller than the other mergansers, the duck Smew is most readily identified by its strikingly white cheeks contrasting with a red-brown crown. As with the other members of the family, Smews tend to sit low in the water, and show the same square white wing patch in flight. The drake is a beautiful, toy-like bird with its white plumage finely lined with black, and shaggy head feathers.

HABITAT: Generally fresh water, medium and large lakes and reservoirs. Occasionally on marine loughs and estuaries.

STATUS: Rare, though probably annual winter visitor from northern Europe. It usually occurs singly. Drakes are very rare in this country.

RED-BREASTED MERGANSER *Mergus serrator* *Plates 9 and 10*
Síolta rua

IDENTIFICATION: 58 cm (23"). Mergansers appear slim and streamlined on the water. The drake is a strikingly marked black and white bird with a reddish-buff breast and shaggy back to the head. The bill, often difficult to see at a distance, is bright scarlet and very thin for a duck. The female is duller than the drake with a reddish-brown head and grey-brown body. The flight silhouette is distinctive, being long and streamlined, and both male and female have a large square white patch on the basal half of the wing. The flight is particularly direct, with rapid shallow wing beats. Not usually gregarious though in some localities it has been seen in loose flocks of over a hundred.

HABITAT: Generally inhabits coastal areas in winter, favouring loughs, inlets, bays and even rocky shores. Breeds on islands in marine loughs around Ireland as well as on some of the larger inland lakes.

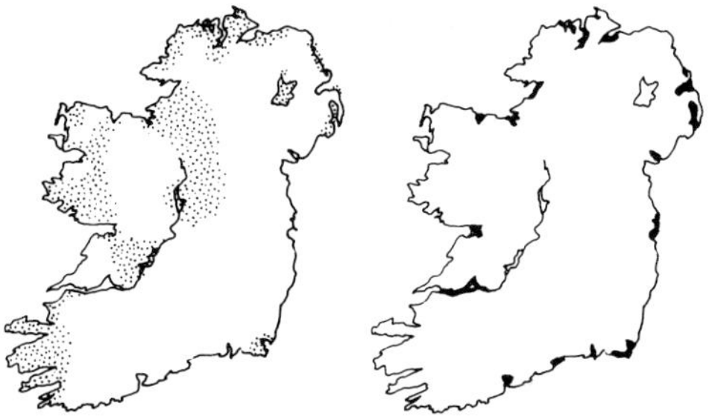

Summer *Winter Concentrations*

STATUS: Fairly widespread resident in this country, being much more abundant in the winter than in summer due to immigration. Breeds in many Irish counties.

GOOSANDER *Mergus merganser* *Plates 9 and 10*
Síolta mhór

IDENTIFICATION: 66 cm (26"). This, our largest member of the merganser family, looks rather similar to Red-breasted Merganser (see previous description) in many respects. The drake has a large dark head (bottle green at close range) and generally white body with a delicate pink tinge. The bright red bill is more obvious than that of the former species. Identification is not as straightforward with females. The female Goosander in general resembles the female Red-breasted Merganser, but is larger, has a different head shape (lacking the wispy crown feathers of the Red-breast) and has sharp demarcation between the rust-coloured head and whitish chin patch and neck. In flight, the wing pattern is similar to that of the Red-breasted Merganser though the Goosander appears larger and heavier.

HABITAT: Much less partial to sea water than the Red-breasted Merganser. In Ireland it most often occurs on medium-sized lakes and reservoirs, though there are many recorded sightings on marine loughs and estuaries.

STATUS: Scarce, though annual winter visitor from Scotland and northern Europe, mainly to the northern half of the country, usually appearing singly or in pairs. There are signs of an increase in recent years. It now nests in at least one locality in north-west Ireland.

Peregrine striking Grouse

EAGLES, HAWKS and HARRIERS

MARSH HARRIER *Circus aeruginosus* *Plate 13*

Cromán móna

IDENTIFICATION: M. 55 cm (21½"); F. 61 cm (24"). Wing span about 122 cm (4'). This rare raptor is a large, dark, gliding bird which is found almost exclusively in reed-bed habitat. The females and immatures are almost totally dark brown except for cream-coloured head and shoulder patches; the male is rusty brown with grey wing patches and black tips. The flight is buoyant and slow. The Marsh Harrier feeds on small aquatic prey which it finds by "quartering" the reed-beds on slightly uptilted wings, flapping only occasionally.

HABITAT: Extensive reed-beds and marshes. Also lagoons, lakes and bogs with reedy and scrubby verges.

STATUS: The story of the Marsh Harrier in Ireland is yet another saga of extermination through shooting, disturbance and drainage of habitat. Once widespread in Ireland, by the turn of the century, the Marsh Harrier had followed the fate of the eagles and was almost gone. At present it is a rare though almost annual visitor, mainly in the spring. The areas most favoured are the coastal marshes of the east and south coasts.

HEN HARRIER *Circus cyaneus* *Plate 13*

Cromán na gcearc

IDENTIFICATION: M. 46 cm (18"); F. 56 cm (21"). Wing span about 87 cm (3½'). Were it not for the re-afforestation of this country in the present century, this harrier would probably not be found here any longer. The man-made forests now provide vital sanctuary for this beautiful bird of prey. The male is an obvious bird with generally pale grey plumage and black wingtips; the larger female is streaked buff below/brown above, has a barred tail and a white rump. They sight their prey by gliding buoyantly, low over the ground on uptilted wings — typically harrier fashion.

HABITAT: The breeding habitat of this harrier is quite restricted — generally between the 500 feet and 1,000 feet contour lines. Its favoured area is young forestry plantations, but it will also nest in moorland heather. In winter, they wander to the lowlands and are found at coastal marshes, lagoons and even low-lying agricultural land.

STATUS: Since its recovery from near extinction in the early years of the present century, the Hen Harrier has extended its range and it now nests in many counties in all provinces. In the past five years, however, they have decreased again and only a few pairs now breed in the southern part of the country.

MONTAGU'S HARRIER *Circus pygargus* *Plate 13*
Cromán liath

IDENTIFICATION: M. 41 cm (16"); F. 49 cm (19"). Wing span about 87 cm (3½'). Quite like a smaller version of the Hen Harrier and identification can be difficult from long range. From closer range, however, there is more black on the wing tips of the male and there is a wing bar. In addition, rusty streaks show on the underparts of the perched male. The female is difficult to distinguish from the female Hen Harrier in the field except by size and by its less obvious white rump patch. In flight the Montagu's Harrier looks proportionately slimmer than the Hen Harrier and flies with a more whipping action of the wing beats.

HABITAT: Although a bird of both hillside and marsh habitats in Britain and Europe, it is found here mainly in young forestry plantations, in similar habitat to that of the Hen Harrier.

STATUS: Rare summer visitor and passage migrant which occasionally nests. The majority of the recordings have been in the southern counties where breeding has occurred in recent years.

SPARROWHAWK *Accipiter nisus* *Plate 13*
Spioróg

IDENTIFICATION: M. 31 cm (12"); F. 38 cm (15"). Wing span about 61-76 cm (2'-2½'). The sexes look quite different. The male is not much bigger than a Mistle Thrush, whilst the female is a good deal larger. The male is blue grey above and light reddish below; the female is grey brown above, whitish below. Both are heavily barred on the underparts. Sparrowhawks rely on stealth to capture their prey, dashing low along hedges, ditches, country lanes, catching small birds by surprise attack. In good weather they will soar in lazy circles above a wood, showing their characteristic shape — shortish, broad wings and long barred tail. They will call near the nest site with a series of monotonous pained notes.

HABITAT: Their favourite habitat is along the edges and less disturbed parts of deciduous woods. Also coniferous plantations, demesnes, and almost anywhere near trees. They readily feed in open country and in winter are to be found at marshes, and even estuaries.

Summer

STATUS: It has recovered from the severe drop in numbers during the pesticide spraying days of the 1960's and is now quite widespread and common. It breeds in every county in suitable habitat. It is still being shot and trapped, however, in some places.

female TUFTED DUCK male

male SCAUP female

male POCHARD female

male GOLDENEYE female

female ⊗SMEW male

male RED-BREASTED MERGANSER female

male ⊗GOOSANDER female

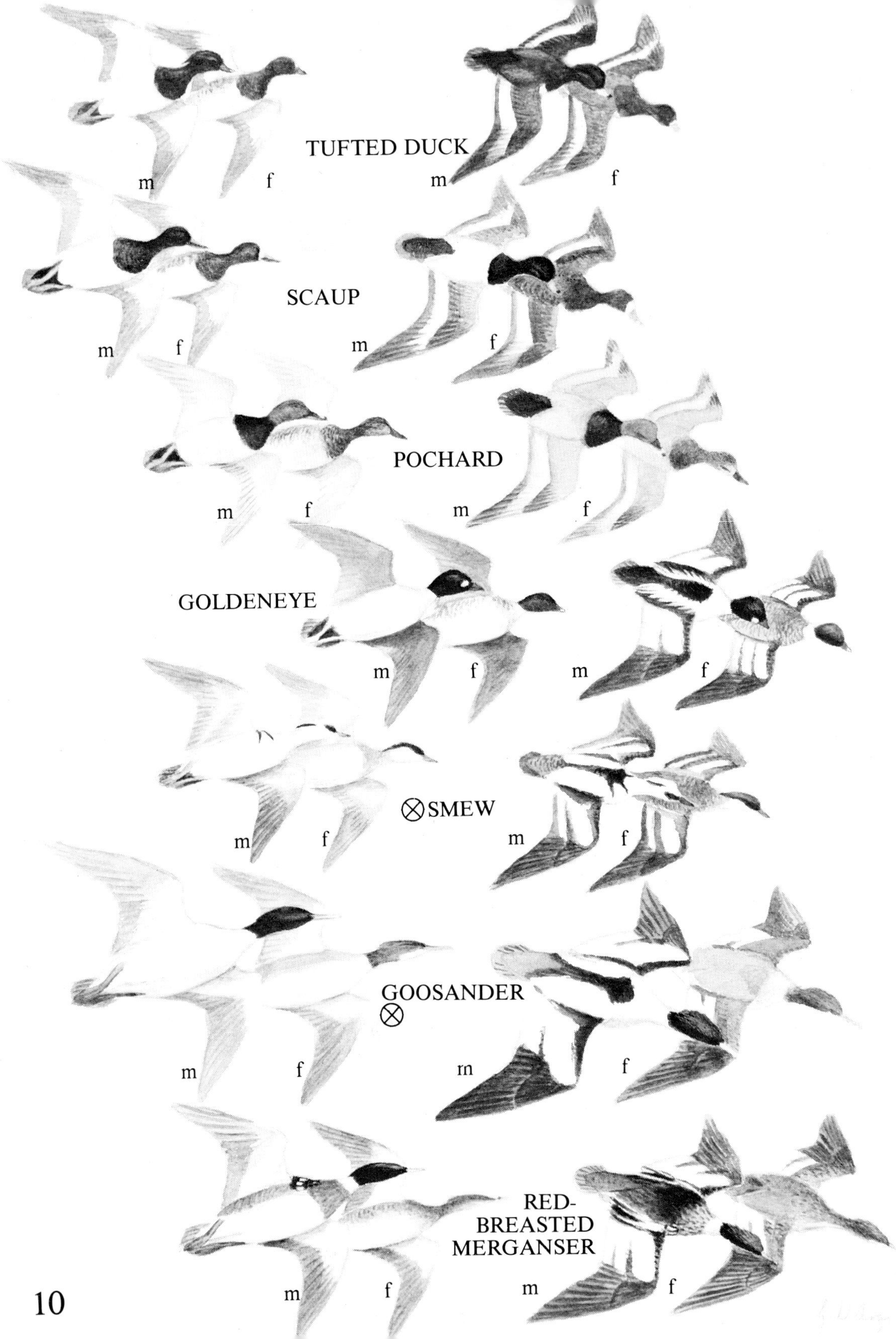
TUFTED DUCK
m
f
m
f
SCAUP
m
f
m
f
POCHARD
m
f
m
f
GOLDENEYE
m
f
m
f
⊗SMEW
m
f
m
f
GOOSANDER
⊗
m
f
m
f
RED-
BREASTED
MERGANSER
m
f
m
f

LONG-TAILED DUCK
male summer
female
male
COMMON SCOTER
female
male
⊗VELVET SCOTER
female
male
EIDER
female
male

immature
adult
⊗ GOLDEN EAGLE
BUZZARD
⊗ OSPREY

SPARROWHAWK
male
female
Sparrow Hawk quartering low over ground
⊗MARSH HARRIER
male
female
HEN HARRIER
male
female
⊗MONTAGU'S HARRIER
female
male
female

KESTREL
male
female
MERLIN
male
female
PEREGRINE
male
juvenile

RED GROUSE

GREY PARTRIDGE
female male juvenile

QUAIL

PHEASANT
female male

WATER RAIL
⊗SPOTTED CRAKE
CORNCRAKE
MOORHEN
adult and juvenile swimming
COOT
Juvenile and chick

BUZZARD *Buteo buteo* *Plate 12*
Clamhán

IDENTIFICATION: M. 54 cm (21"); F. 59 cm (23"). Wing span about 122-137 cm (4'-4½'). From a distance a Buzzard looks like a small eagle. It is stocky, with broad wings fingered at the end and a short tail usually fanned back to the wings. It spends a lot of time on the wing, especially in sunny weather. It soars around in wide circles, the wings characteristically uptilted. From reasonable range the perched Buzzard can be seen to be a bulky, mottled brown bird with yellow on the bill and feet and usually a palish belly patch. In flight, distinctive pale marks show on the elbow at the underwing. A good identification feature is the Buzzard's high pitched "mew" call, which can sound quite cat-like from a distance.

HABITAT: Undisturbed wooded slopes, especially along the northern basalt escarpment. Also cliff faces, wooded river valleys and coniferous plantations.

All Year

STATUS: Resident in the north-east corner of Ireland including Rathlin Island (perhaps their stronghold?) One or two pairs are found elsewhere in the north and it may be spreading. Much suitable habitat exists in Donegal. During the winter, wandering Buzzards may be seen in wild areas, especially in the north and east of the country.

GOLDEN EAGLE *Aquila chrysaetos* *Plate 12*
Iolar fíréan

IDENTIFICATION: M. 80 cm (32"); F. 88 cm (35"). Wing span about 198-229 cm (6½'-7½'). It is shameful that this magnificent bird no longer resides in Ireland. It was relentlessly persecuted by gamekeepers and sheep farmers until it became extinct at the turn of the last century.* Nowadays it occurs as a rare wanderer from Scotland. It is easily recognised by its very large, dark form and soaring flight. From less than a mile it is possible to see the "fingered-ended" wings and squarish tail. The juvenile has a whitish tail with a dark terminal band and whitish patches on the underwings. As the Golden Eagle is a shy bird it is difficult to get within range to see the bird's fine head with large hooked bill, golden nape feathers and large yellow talons. *A pair bred in Fair Head, Antrim from 1953-1959.

HABITAT: Wild, remote areas; mountains; coastal cliffs; islands; possibly extensive forests.

STATUS: Rare and irregular wanderer from Scotland. There have been a number of records in recent years in the north and west. It is within the realms of possibility that it could eventually return to nest in Ireland as much suitable habitat in Scotland is already occupied. Its successful recolonisation would depend, however, on adequate protection being afforded them, and a tolerant public response.

OSPREYS

OSPREY *Pandion haliaetus* *Plate 12*

Coirneach

IDENTIFICATION: M. 51 cm (20"); F. 63 cm (24"). Wing span about 152 cm (5'). A large bird of prey which is nearly always associated with water, as its food is fish. It is most likely to be seen on a prominent perch (often a dead tree) overlooking a lake or river, or flying well above the water surface looking for large fish. It dives feet first into the water to catch unsuspecting quarry just beneath the surface. The Osprey is dark brownish above, white below. There is a thick black mark through the eye and a faint breast band. The strongly hooked bill and unfeathered legs and feet are bluish grey. Care should be exercised on distant flight views as an Osprey can look remarkably like an immature Great Black-backed Gull.

HABITAT: Wood-fringed lakes, large rivers, lagoons and occasionally coastal estuaries.

STATUS: Rare, though fairly regular migrant mainly in autumn. One or two are seen in most years and they have shown signs of the possibility of nesting in at least one locality in recent years.

FALCONS

KESTREL *Falco tinnunculus* *Plate 14*

Pocaire gaoithe

IDENTIFICATION: 36 cm (14"). Our commonest bird of prey, the Kestrel is readily identifiable by its characteristic hovering as though suspended from an invisible line. In normal flight it has an unmistakable long-tailed and pointed-winged shape. The male is beautifully marked with blue-grey head and tail, the latter with a black and white tip, and red brown upperparts, spotted with black. The female is duller and more barred than the male. Although it is generally regarded as a bird of the countryside, the Kestrel has learned to co-exist with man and is often found close to human habitation or even in green belts in our cities. The call often uttered near the nest site is a high pitched kee-kee-kee.

HABITAT: Almost everywhere in rural areas, and also urban fringes, around rubbish dumps, motorway verges, railway embankments, etc.

All Year

STATUS: Widespread resident, being found from the remotest to the heaviest populated areas of the country. There is evidence that some also migrate from Ireland in spring and autumn, and to Ireland in the winter.

MERLIN *Falco columbarius* *Plate 14*
Meirliún

IDENTIFICATION: M. 28 cm (11"); F. 33 cm (13"). This small lively falcon preys on a variety of small and medium-sized birds which it catches on the wing. It is most likely to be seen in autumn or winter at coastal or marshy areas, where it can readily feed on waders and other small birds. The silhouette is quite like that of a diminutive Peregrine, though the tail is distinctly barred (in the female) or dark tipped (in male) and the underparts are heavily streaked. The male is slate grey on the upperparts, light rufous on the underparts. The female and immature are brownish above, buffish below.

HABITAT: The Merlin nests in mountain moorland; extensive blanket bog with rocky outcrops; also occasionally moorland lakes; inland cliff faces; sometimes old nests in trees. In autumn and winter there is considerable local migration and immigration, Merlins being fairly commonplace in low lying regions like marshes and estuaries.

Summer

STATUS: Sparsely distributed resident in suitable habitat over the whole of Ireland. Widespread local movement to lowlands takes place in autumn. There is undoubtedly immigration of Merlins from Iceland and the Continent as records from islands and light stations will testify, and the number of Icelandic Merlins obtained here points to winter immigration from there.

PEREGRINE *Falco peregrinus* *Plate 14*
Fabhcún gorm

IDENTIFICATION: M. 38 cm (15") F. 48 cm (19"). Perhaps our most majestic bird of prey, killing its prey on the wing by "stooping" at speeds of 160 Km/h. and more. From a distance the Peregrine looks stocky with a medium length tail. The wings taper to a point but are broader than those of our other falcons. In flight, the wingbeats are rapid and shallow. The "stoop" is a nose dive with closed wings, the prey being killed instantly by the violence of impact with the Peregrine's talons. From a reasonable distance the slate grey of the upperparts and the whitish, barred underparts may be seen. Easily the most distinctive feature is the dark head and thick moustachial marks. The cere on the bill and the talons are bright yellow and are visible on the perched bird from a reasonable distance. As in most birds of prey, the female is larger than the male. The immature is browner than the adult and the underparts are heavily streaked, not barred. The call is an agitated yek-yek-yek.

HABITAT: The breeding sites are precipitous cliffs in wild and remote areas, both on the coast and inland. In autumn and winter they wander to the lowland marshes, estuaries and other coastal areas where food (mostly waders, ducks and pigeons) is plentiful. Some Peregrines have shown a recent trend to take up winter residence on cathedral steeples in more than one town and prey on local feral pigeons.

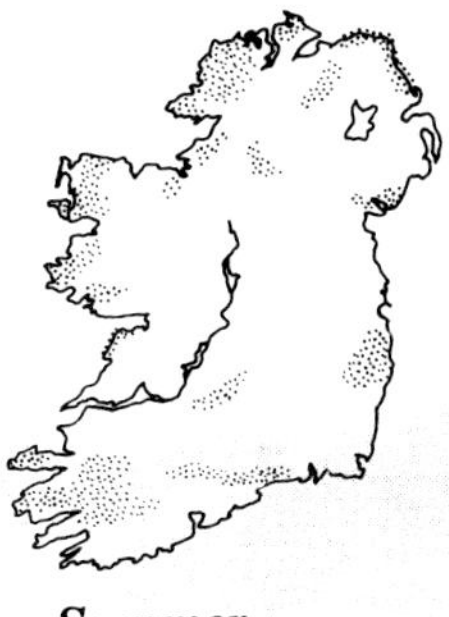

Summer

STATUS: The Peregrine population has recovered from a long term decrease which almost exterminated it in the 1960's, when the numbers of breeding pairs may have dropped to less than 20 from a possible 150. Present surveys indicate that numbers have increased significantly. Like all birds of prey Peregrines are still very vulnerable to pesticides (which affect their breeding success) to illegal egg-collectors and falconers, and to disturbance by rock climbers.

Peregrine hunting feral pigeon

GAME BIRDS

RED GROUSE/WILLOW GROUSE *Lagopus lagopus* *Plate 15*

Cearc fhraoigh

IDENTIFICATION: 38 cm (15"). The Red Grouse, *Lagopus lagopus scoticus*, is the subspecies of the European Willow Grouse found in Ireland. In common with the Dipper (see page 127), the Coal Tit (see page 147) and the Jay (see page 150) it is considered that the Irish Red Grouse is a unique variety. In the male, the overall colouration is a deep reddish brown, lighter yellow-brown in the female. The usual view of Grouse is of a dark, heavy game bird, exploding into the air, close to the observer in open moorland. A chance view of the bird on the ground shows it to be remarkably camouflaged against a heathery background, with only the red wattle and white feathered feet giving the bird away. Grouse are quite noisy during the breeding season and their crowing sounds can sound almost human.

HABITAT: Found mainly on heathery moorland above 1000 feet altitude, but also on some low lying raised bog areas.

STATUS: Thinly and locally distributed on moorland of most of the counties of Ireland. It is probably commonest in the Wicklow range. Re-stocking by gun-clubs in the past has been unsuccessful in halting a gradual decline and there has been some introduction of the British race over the years. The decline is primarily due to decreasing heather (its primary food plant) and changing hill management.

All Year

GREY PARTRIDGE *Perdix perdix* *Plate 15*

Patraisc

IDENTIFICATION: 30 cm (12"). A secretive game bird, formerly common, but now sadly only local in Ireland. Unless disturbed, or observed by chance in the open, the Partridge goes un-noticed. The best time to find them is in the early morning when the covey feeds in the open. Later they tend to retire to the undergrowth. They are plump greyish birds with fine markings and a red-brown belly mark. On being flushed they utter a distinctive rattling note and fly off swiftly on whirring wings. The covey may consist of a pair or over a dozen individuals.

HABITAT: Less accessible agricultural fields with overgrown verges, especially in the western half of the country. Also bogs, fringes of marshy areas, commonages. Occasionally also found on mountain sides, at altitude.

All Year

STATUS: Local resident in suitable habitat, scarce in the east. Generally decreasing throughout the country, probably largely due to modern agricultural methods.

QUAIL *Coturnix coturnix* — *Plate 15*

Gearg

IDENTIFICATION: 18 cm (7"). The Quail is our tiniest game bird and also our scarcest. It generally remains hidden until it is flushed, when it jumps up suddenly and flies off with a typical stiff-winged flight. It usually returns to cover quickly. It is plump, Starling-sized and generally rich brown in colour with buff snipe-like stripes on the back. In the hand the Quail is finely marked with a distinctive black and white face and throat pattern. Perhaps the best indicator of the presence of the Quail is the call of the male in the breeding season — a characteristic "quip-ip-ip", uttered from the dense cover of a grain field.

HABITAT: Cultivated grain fields in the lowlands during the breeding season. On migration, on rough ground near the coast, notably islands and headlands.

Summer

STATUS: Formerly a widespread summer visitor to Ireland. Nowadays it is very scarce, its strongholds being the cultivated areas of Kildare and Meath. It occurs elsewhere as a sporadic breeder and as a fairly regular spring migrant in ones and twos, at island observatories on the south coast.

PHEASANT *Phasianus colchicus*

Plate 15

Piasún

IDENTIFICATION: F. 60 cm (24"); M. 92 cm (36"). Although it is widespread and common, the Pheasant is not a native Irish bird, it was probably first introduced at the end of the 16th Century. The male is a well known game bird, copper-brown with very long pointed tail streamers. The cock bird is gorgeous with a metallic sheen on its body and bottle green head. There is usually a white neck band and a red wattle round the eye. In contrast, the female is a dull grey brown bird, mottled and barred. On being flushed, pheasants rise noisily, making for nearby cover with rapid, shallow wingbeats. The male calls from the undergrowth with a loud, raucous crow, often accompanied by audible wing flapping.

HABITAT: Rough ground almost anywhere in the countryside. Marshy and low-lying scrubland, bog, unkempt fields, woodland.

STATUS: Widespread and common resident which, as numbers deplete, is repeatedly re-stocked by gun-clubs.

All Year

Water Rail

RAILS and CRAKES

WATER RAIL *Rallus aquaticus* *Plate 16*
Rallóg uisce

IDENTIFICATION: 28 cm (11"). A bird much more often heard than seen, its pained screeching from dense marsh and fen is perhaps the best indicator of its presence. When flushed, a water rail flies low with dangling legs and settles again quickly. Such a chance view reveals it to be reddish brown above, slate grey below. The flanks are barred vividly black and white, the bill is long and red and the undertail is white. The best time to look for Water Rails is in the evening when they occasionally emerge from cover and walk nervously along the muddy fringes of the fen. They will call in the evening and throughout the night.

HABITAT: Dense reed-beds, fens, marshes. In winter they may be found in scrub cover in low lying and flooded areas.

STATUS: A surprisingly common resident in this country. It is undoubtedly overlooked because of its secretive nature, but it is found in every county. The number of Water Rails killed at light stations around our coasts testifies to the heavy autumn migration to Ireland from Iceland, Britain and the European Continent.

All Year

SPOTTED CRAKE *Porzana porzana* *Plate 16*
Traonach ballach

IDENTIFICATION: 23 cm (9"). Like the Water Rail, this is a secretive bird of fens and marshes but unlike the former it is a rarity here. In overall appearance it is duller than the Water Rail with a buff, not white, undertail. At close range the plumage can be seen to be profusely speckled with white, and the short bill is orange and yellow. The call, which is uttered at night, is a series of short sharp notes, sometimes described as sounding like whipcracks.

HABITAT: Dense reed-beds, fens and marshes. Some of the migrants which turn up in Ireland are killed at lighthouses on coastal islands.

STATUS: This bird may once have nested regularly in Ireland in view of the number of instances of birds shot in the breeding season in various parts of the country in the 19th century. At present, the Spotted Crake is a rare passage migrant chiefly in the autumn, and is noted mainly in the southern coastal counties.

CORNCRAKE *Crex crex* *Plate 16*
Traonach

IDENTIFICATION: 27 cm (10.5"). The grating call of the Corncrake, very much a traditional part of the Irish scene, is sadly decreasing. The bird is more often heard than seen and as many country folk know, it will call as readily by night as by day. Corncrake can be attracted towards the observer by imitating their call with a pair of serrated bones, and using this method it is often possible to catch a glimpse of this otherwise elusive species. The Corncrake is a dumpy brownish bird, heavily streaked and barred. In flight, it shows red-brown wing patches and the legs dangle. Although a migrant, covering thousands of miles each year, it is reluctant to fly on being disturbed, and such flights as do occur are invariably brief.

HABITAT: Previously rough grassy fields and agricultural areas, but now only the less disturbed of these. Also certain rough ground, occasionally sand dunes and coastal islands.

STATUS: Formerly widespread and common summer resident, nesting all over the country, even in close proximity to human habitations. Now, at least in part due to modern agricultural methods (silage cutting, removal of hedgerows, etc.) the Corncrake is nowhere common, though there are still many nesting pairs west of the Shannon. East of the Shannon it is found in scattered localities, but it is decreasing or absent from much suitable habitat. It has been known to winter in this country on occasions.

Summer

MOORHEN *Gallinula chloropus* *Plate 16*
Cearc uisce

IDENTIFICATION: 33 cm (13"). Also known as the Waterhen (a name more indicative of its habitat), this is decidedly a bird of damp areas. Easily identified by its overall dusky appearance, white undertail patches and bright red and yellow bill. Moorhen are very often seen dashing into marshy cover on long green legs showing a glimpse of white undertail. When swimming, the birds nod their head continuously and jerk their tails backwards and forwards. The calls, usually uttered from dense cover, are a variety of shrill squawks.

HABITAT: Reed fringed lakes, ponds and rivers, marshes, ditches. Also brackish lagoons, etc. In winter it is found away from cover and may be seen on estuaries, in open fields and even at roadsides.

STATUS: Common and widespread resident in Ireland. There is also evidence of some immigration.

COOT *Fulica atra* — *Plate 16*
Cearc cheannann

IDENTIFICATION: 38 cm (15"). A duck-sized, sooty water bird with a most distinctive white bill and forehead shield. The Coot can be identified even at a considerable distance by its blunt-ended appearance. When taking to the wing, the Coot patters noisily over the water surface on its lobed toes and shows white trailing edges to the wings. The juvenile has a pale face and foreneck. In early winter Coots form huge flocks on open water. Coots call with a loud "koot', usually from cover.

HABITAT: Reed fringed lakes, ponds, reservoirs. In winter, open water on large lakes and lagoons. Occasionally in loughs and estuaries in hard weather.

STATUS: Abundant and widespread resident. Very large early winter flocks are found on the larger lakes, especially Lough Corrib, where over 10,000 accumulate. There is evidence of migration to and from this country.

Summer

Woodcock 'roding'.

WADERS

OYSTERCATCHER *Haematopus ostralegus* *Plate 17*
Roilleach

IDENTIFICATION: 43 cm (17"). A common shorebird, whose black and white plumage, orange bill and pink legs make it quite unmistakable. In flight it is equally striking, with a broad white wing bar and monotonic high-pitched piping call — a common sound off the seashore. At high tide, large numbers of Oystercatcher gather in flocks above the waterline dispersing again at low tide to probe for food on the mudflats.

HABITAT: In winter, coastal regions. Both rocky and muddy shores are frequently used and huge flocks are found in our estuaries. In summer the Oystercatcher breeds chiefly on shingle beaches on the less disturbed headlands and islands but also on the sandy shores of a few inland lakes.

Winter Concentrations

STATUS: Very common. Large numbers winter in Ireland mainly on muddy estuaries. As a summer resident it breeds mainly in the north and west, but also in scattered localities around the coast. Nesting occurs fairly regularly at a number of inland lakes, mainly Loughs Neagh and Erne. Non-breeding flocks are to be found around the coast throughout the summer.

Oystercatchers

Avocets

AVOCET *Recurvirostra avosetta*
Abhóiséad

IDENTIFICATION: 15 cm (18"). The Avocet is a striking bird even from a distance with its elegant black and white plumage, long blue-grey legs and fine black, up-tilted bill. In flight, the pattern is equally distinctive with black and white wing patches, the legs protruding beyond the tail. As body size is similar to that of the Black-headed Gull, it can be difficult at times to distinguish an Avocet among a flock of small gulls at a distance. The call is a high-pitched "kleek" or "klook".

HABITAT: Estuaries, mudflats, coastal lagoons.

STATUS: Rare autumn or winter visitor from European coastal areas. Most sightings are from the south and east coasts, especially counties Cork, Wexford and Dublin. In 1938 two pairs nested in Co. Wexford, but this proved to be a once only occurrence as nesting has not been repeated in Ireland.

RINGED PLOVER *Charadrius hiaticula* *Plate 18*
Feadóg chladaigh

IDENTIFICATION: 20 cm (8"). This small native shorebird can be readily identified by its black breastband. From close range it is seen to be a plump brown and white wader with short orange and black bill, orange legs and black head markings. The flight is swift, the wings showing a central white bar. In common with other plovers, this bird has a typical run/stop/run behaviour on the ground. The juvenile has brown instead of black on the head and breast. The call is a soft liquid piping.

HABITAT: Sea shores, beaches, mudflats, some sandy inland lakes.

STATUS: Common passage migrant and winter visitor. Breeds on sandy and shingly shores along much of our coastline, and also at some of the larger lakes in the central lowlands.

Summer

Winter Concentrations

DOTTEREL *Charadrius morinellus* *Plate 18*
Amadán móinteach

IDENTIFICATION: 22 cm (8.5"). Most Dotterel seen in this country occur in the rather dull autumn plumage when they resemble small winter plumaged Golden Plover. The white eyestripes are, however, still evident and there is a trace of the pale breastband. The stance is usually more upright than that of the Golden Plover and the behaviour of running a few steps, then stopping and stretching the neck is typical of the Dotterel. At close range the yellow legs may be seen. Summer plumage is unmistakable, with rusty underparts, striking white eyestripe and thin black and white breastband. The call is a trilling piping. The species is included here, having recently been added to the list of Irish breeders.

HABITAT: Open grassy areas, often near water. Occasionally on islands on migration. The breeding habitat is mountain moorland.

STATUS: Rare passage migrant, recorded mainly on the south and east coasts in autumn. It is usually seen singly, but small flocks have occurred on a number of occasions. In recent years the Dotterel has been proved to breed in Ireland.

GOLDEN PLOVER *Pluvialis apricaria* *Plate 18*
Feadóg bhuí

IDENTIFICATION: 28 cm (11"). A very gregarious wader, which spends the winter here in huge flocks. From a distance the flock appears to be comprised of closely packed, yellow-

Golden Plovers

brown birds with large heads and short bills. They seldom permit close approach and will take to the wing readily. In flight, the flock performs spectacular aerobatics in unison showing silvery undersides one moment and golden uppersides the next. Close up, winter-plumaged Golden Plover are buffish beneath and brownish above, the upperparts finely flecked with bright yellow. In summer plumage the belly is black and the face either mottled or black depending on the race of the bird. The Golden Plover's call is a plaintive, descending whistle.

HABITAT: Open lowlands often near water. Some of its favourite habitats are: callows, estuaries, marshes, turloughs, golf courses. They often associate with Lapwing in winter. They nest on mountains generally above 1,000 feet, but also on blanket bog in the west of Ireland.

Summer

Winter Concentrations

STATUS: Very abundant passage migrant and winter visitor, mainly from northern Europe and Iceland. The Irish winter population may be a quarter of a million birds. In some localities over 10,000 birds may be found together. The Golden Plover is much more common as a winter visitor in Ireland than in Britain. Some birds breed in a few counties, though very sparsely, and the population is sadly decreasing.

GREY PLOVER *Pluvialis squatarola* *Plate 18*

Feadóg ghlas

IDENTIFICATION: 28 cm (11"). In this country the Grey Plover is seen mostly in winter plumage as greyish shorebird with fairly long black legs and short black bill. At close range it looks fairly plump with a rather square head, large dark eye and finely speckled upperparts. In flight, it shows white wing bars and rump and the best feature is clear black "armpits" (patches at the bases of the underwings). The summer-plumaged bird is striking with black face and underparts, fringed broadly with white and grey upperparts. The call is a soft piping which falls and rises at the end.

HABITAT: Sandy and muddy estuaries, coastal lagoons, etc. It occasionally occurs inland at lake shores, on migration.

STATUS: Passage migrant and winter visitor generally in small numbers. In some localities, however, it is found in hundreds. It is not unusual to see Grey Plovers in summer plumage in their favoured haunts.

Winter

LAPWING *Vanellus vanellus* *Plate 17*

Pilibín

IDENTIFICATION: 30 cm (12"). A common and widespread member of the plover family, the Lapwing is well known for its black and white plumage, peculiarly rounded wings and its "pee-weet" call note. Close up such features as the greenish sheen to the upperpart the orange undertail patch and the remarkable upstanding head plume, may be seen. Lapwings fly with rather jerky wingbeats, uttering their thin nasal cry. They gather in large flocks in winter.

HABITAT: Open low lying ground, generally near water. Favoured areas are callows, marshes, agricultural fields, golf courses, mudflats.

STATUS: Very abundant winter visitor and passage migrant, found in thousands in many areas all over Ireland. Winter immigration is from Britain and the Continent. The Lapwing is also a widely distributed breeding bird in this country, nesting in every county.

Summer

Winter Concentrations

JACK SNIPE

SNIPE

WOODCOCK

LAPWING

OYSTERCATCHER

RINGED PLOVER
GOLDEN
PLOVER
winter
Southern race in summer
Northern race in summer
GREY PLOVER
winter
summer
⊗DOTTEREL
winter
summer

summer
KNOT
winter
summer
winter
PURPLE SANDPIPER
winter
summer
TURNSTONE
winter
summer
⊗ RED-NECKED PHALAROPE
GREY PHALAROPE

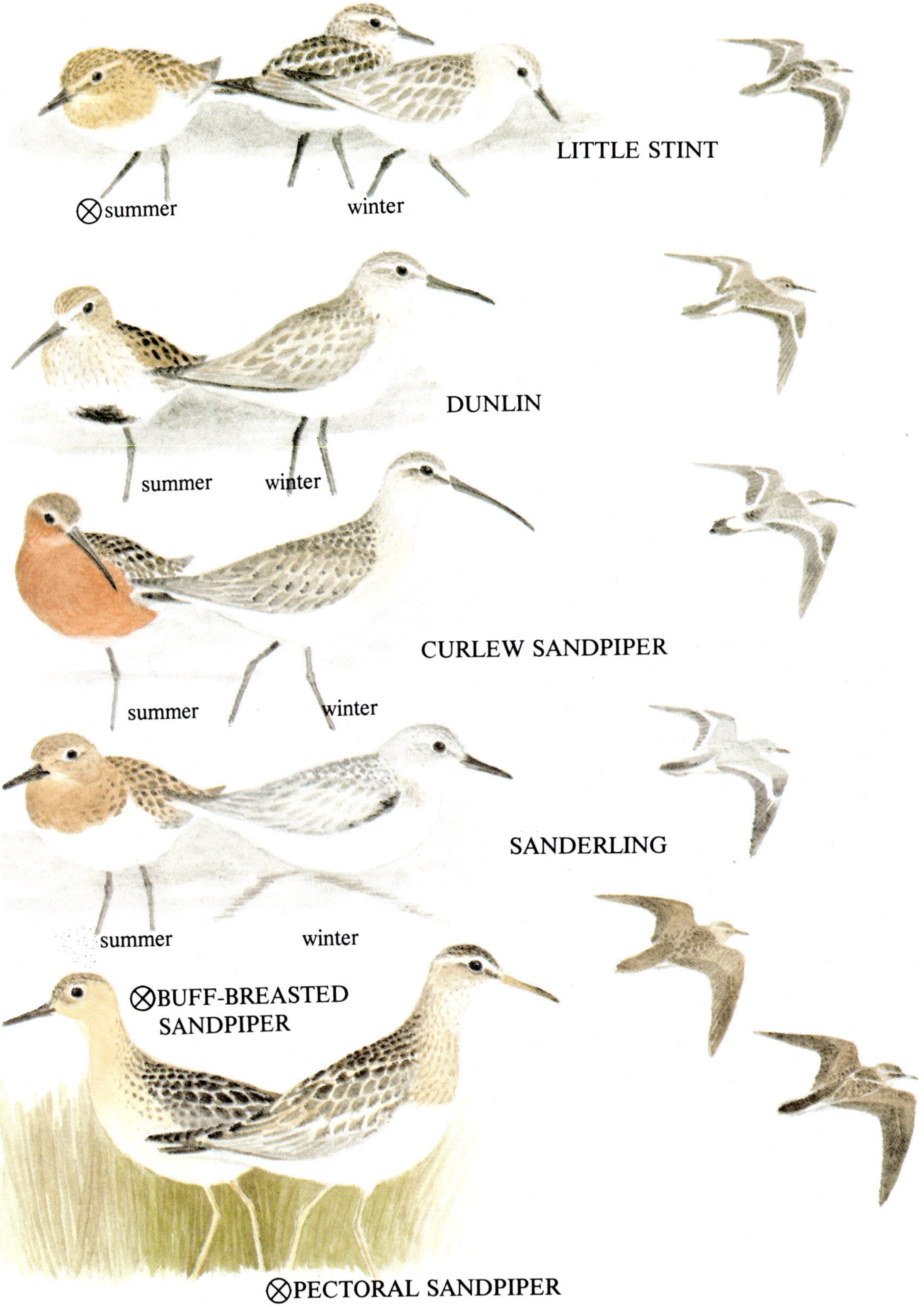
LITTLE STINT
⊗summer
winter
DUNLIN
summer
winter
CURLEW SANDPIPER
summer
winter
SANDERLING
summer
winter
⊗BUFF-BREASTED SANDPIPER
⊗PECTORAL SANDPIPER

CURLEW
WHIMBREL
BAR-TAILED GODWIT
BLACK-TAILED GODWIT
winter
summer
winter
summer

GREEN SANDPIPER
COMMON SANDPIPER
WOOD SANDPIPER
RUFF
female
male
GREENSHANK
REDSHANK
winter
⊗ summer
SPOTTED REDSHANK

Immature Herring Gull
GREAT SKUA
Pale phase
Dark phase
immature
POMARINE SKUA
Pale phase
immature
ARCTIC SKUA
Dark phase
LONG-TAILED SKUA
⊗

adult
winter
immature
winter
summer
BLACK-HEADED GULL
adult
winter
juvenile
summer
winter
LITTLE GULL
adult
juvenile
COMMON GULL
adult
immature
KITTIWAKE
adult
winter
immature
⊗ SABINE'S GULL
winter
summer

Lapwings

KNOT *Calidris canutus*
Cnota

Plate 19

IDENTIFICATION: 26 cm (10.5"). Hugh numbers of Knot come to Ireland to spend the winter on our estuaries. In winter plumage the knot is ashy grey, about the size of a Golden Plover. In flight, it is fairly uniformly greyish with a vague pale wing bar and rump. The bill and legs are short and dark. In the seldom seen summer plumage the underparts are brick red. Knot are more usually seen in large flocks than singly. These flocks perform spectacular aerobatics in unison showing alternatively grey upperparts and silvery underparts.

HABITAT: Coastal mudflats. Smaller numbers may be found in a more restricted habitat (lagoons, small inlets, rock shores or even occasionally inland).

STATUS: Abundant passage migrant and winter visitor mainly from northern Greenland and Arctic Canada. In some areas flocks may be over 10,000 strong, and cover acres of mudflat, especially on Strangford Lough and the North Bull. A few Knot are regularly seen inland on migration.

Winter Concentrations

SANDERLING *Calidris alba*

Plate 20

Luathrán

IDENTIFICATION: 20 cm (8"). Sanderling resemble "clockwork-toy" shorebirds as they run about the tideline busily feeding in small groups. As their name implies, they are often found on sandy shores and are recognisable from a distance by their silvery plumage and their active behaviour at the water's edge. In close up, the winter-plumaged Sanderling is a neat little Dunlin-sized wader with black bill and legs. The upperparts are grey, speckled white and there is a blackish shoulder mark. The head and underparts are generally white, with fine dark marks and there is often a buffish smudge on the side of the breast. In flight, the white wing bar is obvious, as is the short sharp call note "wit-wit". The russet, summer-plumaged bird is much less common in this country.

HABITAT: Mainly sandy shores. Also on rocky coasts at high tide and occasionally on salt marshes and mudflats. Rarely on sandy lake shores.

STATUS: Winter visitor and passage migrant from arctic Asia and Greenland to favoured beaches around the Irish coast. Sizeable flocks are seen on the east and west coasts. It is uncommon inland though it probably occurs annually at Lough Neagh, on migration.

Winter Concentrations

LITTLE STINT *Calidris minuta*

Plate 20

Gobadán beag

IDENTIFICATION: 14 cm (5.5"). This is our smallest sandpiper. In the company of Dunlin, (a bird with which it often associates) the Little Stint appears about one-third smaller. In addition, it is a more active feeder than the Dunlin — more like the Sanderling in behaviour. At close range the Little Stint usually looks paler than the Dunlin. The brownish upperparts have pale edges to the feathers and there is a buffish breast smudge. The bill and legs are black and both are considerably shorter than those of the Dunlin. A pale "V" shape on the back of the immature is a good identification feature. In flight, the wing pattern is Dunlin-like, but the Little Stint can readily be picked out of a flying flock by its small size and its flight call, "tit-tit". Winter plumage Little Stints are greyish, and look rather like miniature winter plumage Sanderling from a distance.

HABITAT: Muddy coastal areas. Much less frequently inland.

STATUS: Regular passage migrant from arctic Asia, mainly in the autumn and usually in small numbers. In some years it is much more abundant than in others. Most are seen on the east coast of Ireland. Scarce in spring.

PECTORAL SANDPIPER *Calidris melanotos* *Plate 20*
Gobadán broinnstríocach

IDENTIFICATION: 20 cm (8"). The Pectoral Sandpiper is probably the most regularly occurring American sandpiper in Ireland. Rather like a Dunlin, but larger, the Pectoral has Snipe-like markings on the upperparts and a distinct cut-off between the streaked breast and white underparts. The legs are yellowish and the bill which is shorter and straighter than a Dunlin's is horn coloured with a darkish tip. There is a clear eyestripe which tends to highlight the dark cap. This species is often quite tame, allowing close approach before flying off. The flight is fast and rather Snipe-like and the call is a short trill — "kerrik kerrik" (quite like the chirp of a Skylark from a distance).

HABITAT: The Pectoral Sandpiper shows a preference for wet grassy areas at the edge of mud rather than the open flats. It has been seen in a wide variety of habitats such as salt marshes, lagoons, lake shores and turloughs.

STATUS: Probably an annual autumn visitor from North America in very small numbers. In some years only one or two are seen, but in others, dozens turn up. Most records are from coastal areas, especially in the south and south-west, but there are many records for inland counties. The larger influxes often correspond with periods of westerly gales.

CURLEW SANDPIPER *Calidris ferruginea* *Plate 20*
Gobadán crotaigh

IDENTIFICATION: 19 cm (7½"). This is one of a number of species which can look very Dunlin-like in winter plumage and at a distance it can be difficult to separate one of these birds from among a flock of Dunlin. It is, however, slightly slimmer and taller and with a good view it can be seen to be paler, with a long down-curved black bill and a whitish eyestripe. The bill is gently and evenly curved over its length and not kinked downward near the tip like that of a Dunlin. The reddish summer-plumaged Curlew Sandpiper is unusual in Ireland. In flight, identification becomes much easier as the rump is white, without the central dark band of the Dunlin. In addition, the flight call, a trilling "treep", is quite different from the call of the Dunlin.

HABITAT: Estuarine mudflats, salt-marshes. Occasionally inland at lake shores, turloughs etc.

STATUS: Regular autumnal passage migrant to Ireland from arctic Asia. In some years it is scarce, but in others, quite widespread flocks of hundreds have been seen at some coastal localities. The Curlew Sandpiper is uncommon in spring, but it is at this time that the red-plumaged bird is likely to be seen.

PURPLE SANDPIPER *Calidris maritima* *Plate 19*
Gobadán cosbhuí

IDENTIFICATION: 21 cm (8"). Perhaps the best guide to the identification of this species is the habitat in which it is found. It is strictly a bird of the rocky coastline. The Purple Sandpiper is a plump, dark little wader, heavily marked on the breast and whitish on the undertail. The legs are a dull yellow/orange and the bill is a similar colour, darker at the tip. In flight, the pattern is typical of many small waders — dark central tail and rump feathers and a thin pale wing-bar. In its feeding habits it is most methodical, foraging amongst rock and seaweed and avoiding the breaking waves. It is generally found in small groups, often accompanied by Turnstones (see page 95).

HABITAT: Rocky coasts, especially where there are seaweed-covered rocks exposed by the tide. Sometimes on shingly beaches.

STATUS: Widespread winter visitor from arctic Europe and Iceland. It is probably more common on the east coast than elsewhere, but is nowhere abundant. Groups of 10 to 30 are normal but over 100 together have been recorded in Mayo.

DUNLIN *Calidris alpina* *Plate 20*
Breacóg

IDENTIFICATION: 17-19 cm (6.5-7.5"). The Dunlin is perhaps our most abundant small shorebird. It is recognisable as a gregarious little wader, greyish brown above, and white below, often found in large numbers on estuarine mudflats. The winter-plumaged Dunlin looks quite nondescript and greyish, though with black legs and a longish, slightly downcurved black bill. The summer-plumaged bird has a black belly patch and red-brown upperparts. In flight, Dunlin shows a thin pale wing-bar and a dark band down the rump and tail. The call is a thin buzzing trill. The Dunlin is the commonest of a number of small brownish or greyish sandpipers. To identify any of the others reliably, it is important first to be familiar with the variety of plumages and shapes of the Dunlin.

HABITAT: Estuarine mudflats, salt marshes and other coastal areas. Inland on lake shores and turloughs. At breeding grounds, on marshes, both coastal and inland, and at some bog lakes.

STATUS: Widespread and abundant winter visitor. There is heavy immigration from northern Europe. The southern race of the Dunlin is a thinly distributed breeder in Ireland, nesting in many counties, mainly in the western half of the country. Mayo is the Dunlin's breeding stronghold in Ireland.

Summer *Winter Concentrations*

Dunlin

BUFF-BREASTED SANDPIPER *Tryngites subruficollis* *Plate 20*
Gobadán broinndhonn

IDENTIFICATION: 20 cm (8"). This rare North American visitor to Ireland is quite similar to a small female Ruff (see following description), though it is generally a warmer buff on the underparts. At closer ranges it appears smaller and finer than the reeve with a small rounded head, large dark eye, pale eye ring, fine dark bill and yellow legs. There are varying intensities of buff colour on the underparts, depending on plumage wear or age and many of the birds occurring in Ireland are largely creamy on the underparts. The dark centre/pale edges of the feathers of the upperparts give a scaly appearance but the upperparts appear uniform brownish in flight, somewhat resembling a Golden Plover. The underwing is shiny white in flight. Buff-breasted Sandpiper favour the drier, grassy areas of marshes and are often very tame. The flight call is a dry trilling "treep" somewhat resembling the flight call of the Curlew Sandpiper (see page 83).

HABITAT: In this country it occurs mainly on marshes, but may be well away from the water. Sometimes it is encountered in grassy callows or meadows and may be in the company of Golden Plover.

STATUS: An almost annual visitor from North America. Next to the Pectoral Sandpiper (see page 83) it is probably our most regularly occurring transatlantic visitor. Usually seen singly, there are records of small flocks in more than one place. Nearly all the records are in autumn and most are from Kerry, Wexford or Derry.

Ruff

RUFF *Philomachus pugnax* *Plate 22*
Rufachán

IDENTIFICATION: F. 25 cm (10") — M. 32 cm (12.5"). A variable plumaged wader about the size and shape of a Redshank. Although the female (reeve) is considerably smaller than the male, their plumage outside of the breeding season is generally similar. In good conditions the bird looks generally buffish brown with pale feather edges on the upperparts, a shortish dark bill and legs which can be almost any colour, but are generally greenish yellow. It is readily distinguished from the Redshank by its flight pattern — a thin pale wing bar and white patches to either side of the dark tail and rump. The flight looks more leisurely than that of other similar sized waders. In addition, Ruffs seldom call on being flushed — a useful identifying feature, considering most waders utter a characteristic flight call. The beautiful summer-plumaged male only expands its ruff during display, rarely seen in this country. This ruff can be a wide range of colours and patterns.

HABITAT: Coastal and freshwater marshes. Occasionally lakes, river callows, even mudflats and cultivated fields well away from water.

STATUS: Passage migrant, mainly in the autumn from the European Continent. In recent years it has summered and overwintered in a number of places. Flocks of a hundred or more have been recorded in the autumn, but only small numbers in spring. It is most common along the south and east coasts and in the north.

JACK SNIPE *Lymnocryptes minimus* *Plate 17*
Naoscach bhídeach

IDENTIFICATION: 19 cm (7.5"). The Jack Snipe is like a smaller version of the common Snipe (see next description), though with a much shorter bill. It usually rises without calling, flies off with less conviction than its commoner relation, and returns quickly to cover. If a view is obtained of the bird on the ground it will appear duskier than the common Snipe, having a purple sheen to the upperparts, and a different head pattern: it lacks the pale central crown stripe of the common Snipe.

HABITAT: Similar habitat to the common Snipe, but perhaps more frequently in areas of shorter marsh vegetation.

STATUS: Regular, though thinly distributed, passage migrant and winter visitor from northern Europe. Although it is to be found all over the country, the Jack Snipe is usually found singly or, exceptionally, in small groups.

Jack Snipe (top) and Snipe

SNIPE *Gallinago gallinago* — *Plate 17*
Naoscach

IDENTIFICATION: 27 cm (10.5"). The Snipe is one of our best known marsh birds, familiar to shooter and laymen alike. It usually appears as a rather small, richly marked, long-billed bird, exploding into the air from almost under foot. Sometimes careful stalking is rewarded with a view of the bird on the ground. Clear dark and pale stripes are visible on the head and back and the feathers are heavily flecked and edged pale. The overall effect is a marvellous camouflage. The flight is very fast and zig-zagging and an unmistakable rasping call is invariably uttered. At the breeding areas displaying Snipe make a noise in flight caused by air rushing through the outer tail feathers which sounds like the bleating of a kid goat. They also give a distinctive call — "chucka-chucka".

HABITAT: Wet ground, extensive and confined, especially marshes and bogs. It may even be found well away from water on occasions, in arable fields, bracken, etc. In mild weather Snipe are sometimes found on open mudflats while hard weather drives them to springs and ditches.

Summer

STATUS: Very abundant passage migrant and winter visitor. In some areas, and especially prior to hard weather, it may be found in hundreds. Ringing recoveries indicate that Snipe from northern Europe and Britain winter in Ireland. The Snipe nests in marshy habitats in every county.

WOODCOCK *Scolopax rusticola*
Creabhar

Plate 17

IDENTIFICATION: 33 cm (14"). The Woodcock is a strange counterpart of the Snipe, found in wooded habitat. Good views of the bird on the ground are difficult to obtain as it sits, superbly camouflaged, among dead vegetation. It is usually seen as a plump rich brown bird deftly winging through the trees. In the evening the Woodcock becomes more active and may be seen flying over the trees with owl-like wingbeats, uttering its peculiar call. This is best witnessed in the breeding season when the Woodcock performs its 'roding' display. The call sounds like the sudden swish of a rope through air followed by a deep croak. The Woodcock is a heavily barred and mottled red-brown bird with a long probing bill. It is a favourite game bird. There is definite proof that when threatened the Woodcock will fly off, carrying its young.

HABITAT: Woodlands, both deciduous and coniferous. Also scrub bracken and scrub-covered marshy areas where it feeds at night.

Summer

STATUS: Well distributed resident which has perhaps increased due to re-afforestation. As a passage migrant and winter visitor large numbers come to Ireland from Continental Europe and smaller numbers from northern Britain. During periods of severe cold, Woodcock move around within Ireland as well as into Ireland from elsewhere.

BLACK-TAILED GODWIT *Limosa limosa* *Plate 21*
Guilbneach earrdhubh

IDENTIFICATION: 41-46 cm (16-18"). This is a long-legged, long-billed wader, almost the size of a Curlew (see page 90). In winter plumage it is grey brown, paler beneath and with an obvious pale eyestripe. The summer-plumaged bird is russet with black bars showing on the white flanks. The bill is virtually straight, very long and pinkish with a dark tip. The flight pattern is most distinctive. There is a black tail, white rump and clear white wing bar. The long legs extend a couple of inches beyond the tail in flight. Black-tailed godwits are quite noisy in the spring, calling a hard "wicka-wicka-wick".

HABITAT: Mainly coastal estuaries and mudflats, but also the callows, lakes and turloughs associated with the major river valleys.

Summer

STATUS: Regular passage migrant mainly from Iceland. The largest numbers move through Ireland in early spring, following the line of the Shannon valley, where thousands may occur. As a winter visitor it has greatly increased in recent years with hundreds and sometimes thousands wintering on estuaries in the south and south-west.

BAR-TAILED GODWIT *Limosa lapponica* *Plate 21*
Guilbneach stríocearrach

IDENTIFICATION: 35-44 cm (14-17"). The Bar-tailed Godwit is a long-legged, long billed wader similar to the previous species though slightly smaller in overall size, leg and bill length. In winter plumage it is ashy coloured; in spring and autumn, browner. In the uncommon summer plumage it is a deep reddish brown. The winter plumaged bird looks like the Black-tailed Godwit, but is distinguished by its slightly upturned bill, and more Curlew-like markings on the upperparts. In flight, identification is easy: the wing pattern is like that of a Curlew and the bird lacks the black tail and white wing bar of the Black-tailed Godwit.

HABITAT: More exclusively coastal than the Black-tail. Loose flocks are found on mudflats in loughs and estuaries. It is uncommonly found inland.

STATUS: Abundant and gregarious winter visitor and passage migrant from Lapland and Siberia. Flocks may linger until summer in certain localities where individuals in the beautiful summer plumage may be seen.

Winter Concentrations

WHIMBREL *Numenius phaeopus* — *Plate 21*

Crotach eanaigh

IDENTIFICATION: 46-46 cm (16-18"). The Whimbrel is rather like a small version of the Curlew (see following description). It appears somewhat greyer from a distance and has a shorter, less down-curved bill. At close range it is possible to see the dark cap on the crown, with a pale central stripe. In flight, Whimbrel look very like small Curlew. Migrating Whimbrel are perhaps most readily identified by their call, a tremulous whistle, descending in pitch, which is completely different from the Curlew's.

HABITAT: Coastal and freshwater marshes, open mudflats. Migrating Whimbrels will follow flightlines such as major river valleys and coastlines.

STATUS: Regular spring passage migrant from western Mediterranean and African wintering grounds to Iceland, where they breed. Small parties stop off in Ireland, gathering at migration roosts which may be several hundred strong. In the autumn only a trickle of Whimbrels pass through this country on their way south. Summering and wintering here is uncommon, though a few regularly winter on the south coast.

CURLEW *Numenius arquata* — *Plate 21*

Crotach

IDENTIFICATION: 53-58 cm (21-23"). A large brown wading bird with a long down-curved bill. The Curlew's call is as familiar as is its appearance. From a distance it appears overall buffish-brown, but at closer range it is heavily streaked and speckled. The undertail region and rump are white and the tail is barred. Besides the characteristic clear whistle "cur-lew" rising in pitch at the end, there is an extended liquid trilling, uttered mainly at the breeding site.

Migrating Whimbrel

HABITAT: The Curlew may be found almost anywhere in open country, but especially on marshes, mudflats and river callows. In the breeding season many are found on moorlands and mountain plateaux. In hard weather large flocks gather on cultivated fields.

STATUS: Widespread resident, nesting in every county. As with other common waders, there is a heavy winter immigration into this country. Curlews are also passage migrants through Ireland in spring and autumn.

Summer *Winter Concentrations*

SPOTTED REDSHANK *Tringa erythropus* *Plate 22*
Cosdeargán dorcha

IDENTIFICATION: 30 cm (12"). Outside of the breeding season the Spotted Redshank is rather like a longer-billed, longer-legged, version of the Redshank (see following description). The main differences show in flight where the wings lack the white trailing edges, the white rump extends well up the back and the red legs project well beyond the tail. A close view of the winter plumaged bird shows it to be greyer than the Redshank with a white eyestripe and redder legs. The rare summer plumage is unmistakable. The bird is almost totally black with white speckles on the upperparts. The call, a "tiu-wic", is quite different from that of the Redshank.

HABITAT: Coastal and less frequently inland marshes. Occasionally mudflats.

STATUS: Regular, though local autumn passage migrant from Lapland and Siberia, mainly to the east and south coasts. In some areas, notably Wexford, flocks may occur, with over 100 at times on the Wexford Slobs. Outside autumn, they are uncommon and the black summer plumage is rare.

REDSHANK *Tringa totanus* *Plate 22*
Cosdeargán

IDENTIFICATION: 28 cm (11"). A medium-sized brownish wader, the Redshank's best field mark is the orange-red legs. In flight, it shows white trailing edges to the wings and a white rump. A good view of the bird on the ground shows it to be heavily speckled brown with a red, black tipped bill and a pale eye-ring. The call is a clear whistle 'tiu-oo-oo" and variations on this theme.

HABITAT: In winter, mainly coastal. Large numbers are found on mudflats, estuaries, bays, salt marshes, even rocky coasts. It breeds on marshes, both coastal and inland, callows and bogs.

STATUS: Abundant and gregarious winter visitor, passage migrant and thinly distributed resident. Many of the winter visitors are from Iceland. The Redshank nests sparingly in all the provinces, but locally in Leinster.

Summer

Winter Concentrations

GREENSHANK *Tringa nebularia* *Plate 22*
Ladhrán glas

IDENTIFICATION: 33 cm (13"). This wader is rather similar to the Redshank (see previous description) though slightly larger and greyer. At close range the greyish-green legs and long, slightly-upturned bill may be seen. In winter plumage the Greenshank looks very pale, especially about the head. In summer, it is darker and more speckled. In flight the dark wings contrast with the white wedge formed by the lowerback, rump and tail, giving an overall black and white appearance. The call is a distinctive whistle — either "tu-tu" or "tu-tu-tu".

Redshank

HABITAT: Coastal mudflats, marshes and lagoons, also inland on migration.

STATUS: Passage migrant and regular winter visitor from northern Europe. It is not unusual to see loose flocks of over fifty Greenshanks in favoured localities. Only small numbers are found here in summer. Greenshank may breed in one or two places in the west of Ireland.

Winter Concentrations

Green and Wood Sandpipers

GREEN SANDPIPER *Tringa ochropus*

Plate 22

Gobadán glas

IDENTIFICATION: 23 cm (9"). A small, solitary wader, the Green Sandpiper has a striking flight pattern and call. In flight it looks very black and white, with both the upper and undersides of the wing and the tip of the tail black. The flight is fast, jerky and rather snipe-like. The flight call is a clear, mellow whistle "tu-weet-a-weet-weet". On the ground, where views tend to be distant ones, the Green Sandpiper looks somewhat like a tiny Greenshank. The bill is rather long and straight and there is a whitish eye-ring and eyestripe (between the bill and the eye).

HABITAT: The favoured habitats are quiet, undisturbed marshy areas, both inland and coastal. Also reservoirs, lagoons and large drainage ditches.

STATUS: Scarce passage migrant from north-eastern Europe in the autumn, rare in spring. It is generally seen singly though groups have been recorded. In recent years isolated birds have wintered.

WOOD SANDPIPER *Tringa glareola*

Plate 22

Gobadán coille

IDENTIFICATION: 20 cm (8"). The Wood Sandpiper is similar to the Green Sandpiper (see illustration below), and rather like a tiny Redshank with yellowish, not red, legs. The legs appear longer than those of the Green Sandpiper and the bill shorter. In flight, there are several differences; the white rump is less distinct; the underwings are pale; and the feet project beyond the tail. A good view will show the upperparts to be finely speckled and there is a clear eyestripe. The call is a clear whistle "chee-weep-eep", but lacks the loudness and clarity of the Green Sandpiper's.

HABITAT: Marshes, both brackish and freshwater.

STATUS: Regular, though sparse passage migrant from north-east Europe, mainly in the autumn and principally to eastern and southern counties. Although it is usually seen singly, there have been reports of small groups.

COMMON SANDPIPER *Actitis hypoleucos* *Plate 22*
Gobadán

IDENTIFICATION: 20 cm (7.5"). The Common Sandpiper is a small, neat, brown and white wader. Its movements are perhaps the best identification features. When on the ground it continually wags the end of its body up and down rather like a wagtail. Also, in flight, (which is generally close to the water surface), the wings are "shivered" on each downbeat, in a distinctive fashion. The plumage is "mousey" brown above, white below, with a brownish smudge on the breast. The bill is thin and straight and the legs yellow-green. In addition to the characteristic flight, the wing pattern is also distinguishable from those of Green and Wood Sandpipers, as there is a wing bar and no white rump. The call is a series of descending whistles, thin though mellow, and quite unlike the other sandpipers.

HABITAT: On migration, waterways, both inland and coastal. At the breeding sites, mountain rivers, lakes and reservoirs. Occasionally low-lying areas and marine islands, especially in the west.

STATUS: Widespread breeder in the north and west of Ireland, scarce in the east. Regular passage migrant in the spring and early autumn. Sometimes seen in loose flocks of fifty or more. Our Common Sandpipers winter in Africa, though a few regularly overwinter in Ireland, especially on the south coast.

Summer

TURNSTONE *Arenaria interpres* *Plate 19*
Piardálaí trá

IDENTIFICATION: 23 cm (9"). This interesting little shorebird is associated mainly with rocks and seaweed. As the name implies, it is often to be seen busily turning stones and shells searching for food along the shoreline. The winter-plumaged Turnstone is fairly dull, mottled brown black and white, with orange legs. In breeding plumage, however, the bird is transformed into a striking wader with bright orange and black upperparts and an almost totally white head. In flight, the Turnstone is easily identified with its clear white wing bars and tail pattern. The call is an unmusical series of staccato notes which are uttered on taking flight.

HABITAT: Generally rocky and seaweed covered shores. Also shingly beaches, tidal mudflats, etc. It has also been found far inland on lake shores, on migration.

STATUS: Common and widespread passage migrant and winter visitor from Greenland, and northern and Arctic Europe. Some Turnstones regularly summer in Ireland when they can be seen in full summer plumage.

RED-NECKED PHALAROPE *Phalaropus lobatus* *Plate 19*
Falaróp gobchaol

IDENTIFICATION: 19 cm (7½"). In winter this little Arctic wader is generally greyish in colour with whitish underparts/dark eyestripe; in summer it is marked with white and orange red on the neck. As with other Phalaropes, the female is more brightly coloured than the male, a phenomenon extremely rare in the birdworld. The most certain identification feature is the very fine and delicate bill, as Greys and Red-necks can look otherwise alike in winter plumage. In flight, the pattern is similar to the Grey, but it looks smaller and darker and the flight is more buoyant.

HABITAT: In winter, the open sea. At breeding stations, remote coastal marshes.

STATUS: This bird, once a rare breeder in more than one locality in the west, is sadly, very close to extinction in Ireland. It also occurs as a rare autumn visitor from northern Europe, turning up mainly after storms at the south-western extremity of Ireland.

GREY PHALAROPE *Phalaropus fulicarius* *Plate 19*
Falaróp gobmhór

IDENTIFICATION: 21 cm (8"). This is a strange ocean-going wader, more at home on the surface of the sea than wading among the shallows. In this country it occurs in winter plumage when it appears as a white and ashy-plumaged bird, with a dark smudge through the eye. At close range the base of the bill and the legs appear yellowish. It feeds in a distinctive manner, spinning on the surface of the water — the whirlpool so formed bringing up small food items to the surface. In flight, the wing pattern is like that of the Sanderling (see page 82) though less striking and the flight call is also quite similar. The red summer plumaged bird is very rare in Ireland. Phalaropes may be extraordinarily tame, allowing approach to within a few feet.

Grey Phalarope

HABITAT: In winter the open sea, only coming inshore during gales. In these "wrecks" Grey Phalarope may turn up anywhere around the coast and even occasionally inland.

STATUS: Irregular autumn passage migrant from the Arctic. Most are seen after storms at sea when many are forced inshore. Large numbers, sometimes hundreds, are occasionally seen at migration stations, especially Cape Clear Island, Co. Cork. The species has been recorded from several inland counties.

SKUAS

POMARINE SKUA *Stercorarius pomarinus* *Plate 23*

Meirleach pomairíneach

IDENTIFICATION: 54 cm (21"). This species is slightly smaller than the Great Skua (see page 99) with less conspicuous wing patches. Pomarine and Arctic Skuas are alike in that they have two plumage phases. The dark phase is dusky overall; the pale phase is dark capped, white cheeked, and has pale underparts. Immatures are overall dark, heavily mottled. The Pomarine is only slightly smaller than the Great Skua and is also heavily built. The wings are proportionately longer and more angled than the Great Skua's. With a good view it is possible to see that the central tail feathers extend beyond the rest. They are, in fact, twisted and blunt-ended. This is not the most reliable of features, however, as they are often broken off and are absent in the immatures. Conclusive identification takes some experience.

HABITAT: The open sea, sometimes close inshore during passage migration.

STATUS: A regular though scarce passage migrant from arctic Asia. It is almost as regular in spring, especially in May, as in the autumn. Generally seen singly or in pairs, Pomarine Skuas have been seen in loose groups and may be accompanied by other skuas.

ARCTIC SKUA *Stercorarius parasiticus* *Plate 23*

Meirleach artach

IDENTIFICATION: 46 cm (18"). This, the commonest of the skuas, is like a scaled-down Pomarine. As the Pomarine is roughly the size of a Herring Gull, so the Arctic is roughly the size of a Common Gull. The white wing flashes are less distinctive than both those of the Great and Pomarine Skuas. The flight is somewhat gull-like normally, but is positively falcon-like in attack. Arctic Skuas will attack almost any seabird in the pursuit of food, though they show preferences for Kittiwakes and terns. The pointed central tail feathers are only visible from close range and are absent in the immatures. Although they will readily settle on the surface of the sea, skuas of all species are most often seen in flight in this country.

HABITAT: As for Pomarine Skuas.

STATUS: Regular passage migrant from northern Europe. Passage is heaviest in autumn when loose marauding flocks (sometimes dozens) have been seen. Besides the coastal migration, small numbers of Arctic Skuas have been seen migrating along the Shannon and other major river valleys in Ireland.

LONG-TAILED SKUA *Stercorarius longicaudus* *Plate 23*
Meirleach earrfhada

IDENTIFICATION: 54 cm (21"). This is the smallest and the rarest of the skuas which turn up in Ireland. It is roughly the size of a Black-headed Gull, but has a buoyant, tern-like flight. The colour scheme is like that of a pale-phase Arctic Skua, but it is rather neater, with whiter underparts and neat black cap unlike other skuas. Hardly any pale flash shows on the wings. The very long central tail feathers are an unreliable identification feature as they are only visible in good conditions, or may have broken off. The immature is like a small Arctic Skua with a tern-like flight. It is slightly greyer than other immature skuas and shows no white on the wings.

HABITAT: As other skuas, though many of the records are from inland counties.

STATUS: Rare, though nearly annual visitor, mainly in the autumn from Scandinavia or the Arctic. Most of the records are from the north or west coasts.

GREAT SKUA *Stercorarius skua* *Plate 23*
Meirleach mór

IDENTIFICATION: 56 cm-64 cm (22"-25"). This is a large, dark, heavily built seabird, somewhat like a large gull. It is usually seen flying near the surface of the sea with steady powerful wingbeats. The overall sooty plumage is relieved only by conspicuous white flashes on the wings. On sighting a quarry, this parasitic seabird accelerates with consumate ease to overtake and harry its victim. It usually feeds on food which the victim carries, or else it makes it regurgitate recently swallowed food. It occasionally also kills the victim. Also known as the Bonxie, the Great Skua will attack any seabird, including the Gannet. The attack call is gutteral and audible from quite a distance. In calm conditions it will readily settle on the sea.

HABITAT: The open sea, sometimes close inshore during passage migration.

STATUS: Regular passage migrant to Irish coastal waters from northern Europe, and the Arctic. Most occur in the autumn, but there is a thin spring passage as well. The largest numbers are seen on the south and west coasts. It is usually seen singly or in pairs.

GULLS and TERNS

Arctic Tern

LITTLE GULL *Larus minutus* *Plate 24*

Faoileán bideach

IDENTIFICATION: 28 cm (11"). At a glance this gull looks like a small Black-headed Gull, but closer scrutiny will reveal fairly obvious distinctions. Apart from being a good deal smaller, the flight is buoyant and butterfly-like on rather round-tipped wings which are strikingly sooty on the undersides. Like the Black-headed Gull, the dark head of summer gives way to a small dark cheek mark in the winter. The hood is however black, not dark brown, and it is more extensive than that of the Black-headed Gull. From close range the red bill and legs can be seen. The immature has the same black zig-zag pattern on the upperparts as the immature Kittiwake, but it is very much smaller and has a different flight.

HABITAT: Generally coastal regions. Favoured areas are coastal lagoons, saltmarshes and estuaries. It occurs less frequently on inland lakes and reservoirs.

STATUS: Passage migrant and winter visitor from continental Europe. In some years it is more abundant than others. In recent years it has been regular in spring and autumn to some localities on the east and south coasts. Occasionally hundreds occur.

SABINE'S GULL *Larus sabini* *Plate 24*

IDENTIFICATION: 33 cm (13"). This is a small rare gull with a rather tern-like flight and a most distinctive wing pattern. In all plumages there is a white triangle on the rear of the wings and a forked tail. Immature Kittiwakes and immature terns can be mistaken for this species at a distance. Only in summer plumage has the adult the dusky hood. Like most dark-hooded gulls, the head is white in the winter, with a dark mark behind the eye. The immature plumage is similar to the adult in winter, but with a black tip to the forked tail. From close range the bill and legs may be seen to be blackish, the bill with a yellow tip in the adult.

HABITAT: This is a high arctic species which winters at sea in the Atlantic. There have been inland occurrences in Ireland after storms.

STATUS: Rare autumn visitor from its Atlantic wintering grounds. The majority of the occurrences are from the south-western corner of Ireland.

BLACK-HEADED GULL *Larus ridibundus* *Plate 24*

Faoileán ceanndhubh

IDENTIFICATION: 39 cm (15"). The Black-headed Gull is our commonest small gull.

Perhaps the most consistent identification feature is the white forewing which this species shows in all plumages*. In summer the adult's hood is dark brown (appearing black at a distance) and is replaced by a dark mark behind the eye in winter. The immature is marked with brown and black on the upperparts and has a black-tipped tail. The rather fine bill and legs are red in the adult; the immature's bill is yellowish with a black tip.

HABITAT: This is an adaptable species which may be found in a wide variety of habitats. It breeds in large colonies on freshwater lakes, bogs and marshes. In the winter months it is perhaps most abundant in coastal regions, especially estuaries, saltmarshes, lagoons, etc.

STATUS: Very abundant resident nesting colonially, mainly in the northern half of Ireland, though some of the largest colonies are in the midlands. There is substantial immigration into Ireland in the winter.

Summer

*There are one or two other very rare gulls with this feature, but the likelihood of seeing them in Ireland is small.

COMMON GULL *Larus canus* *Plate 24*

Faoileán bán

IDENTIFICATION: 43 cm (17"). The name of this gull is misleading. It is in fact much less common here than the Herring Gull. From a distance it is rather like a scaled-down Herring Gull. In flight, the black wing tips look bigger than those of the Herring Gull. There are also larger white spots on the black tips. From closer range the head looks quite rounded and the bill is proportionately smaller than the Herring Gull's and is greenish-yellow. The legs are also greenish. The flight is lazy and graceful and the call is a distinctive "mew". The juvenile is easily distinguished from a juvenile Herring Gull by size and a broad black band on the white tail.

HABITAT: Outside the breeding season, it is found generally in coastal areas, but it breeds in colonies on inland lakes and bogs. It also nests regularly in small numbers, on a few marine islands.

STATUS: The Common Gull is a rather localised lake breeder in Ireland. It is virtually restricted to the north-west. In winter it is found in gatherings on our coasts, though more locally on the south coast. There is evidence of winter immigration from elsewhere in Europe.

Summer

LESSER BLACK-BACKED GULL *Larus fuscus* *Plate 25*

Droimneach beag

IDENTIFICATION: 56 cm (22"). This gull, sometimes considered a subspecies of the Herring Gull, is superficially like it in many ways. It really only differs in the colour of the back and wings which are much darker than the Herring Gull's — probably intermediate in darkness between Herring and Great Black-back. The wing tips always look blacker than the rest of the upperparts in the Lesser, while back and wingtips of the larger Great Black-back look equally black. On the ground, the legs of the Lesser are bright yellow, not pink as with the other large gulls. In the field the juvenile is almost indistinguishable from the juvenile Herring Gull. The rare Scandinavian Lesser Black-back is overall black on the back, like the Great-back, but the size and the yellow legs confirm identification.

HABITAT: Generally inland. It breeds colonially on some of the larger lakes in the northern half of the country. Others breed on a few of the extensive bogs. There are colonies on a few marine islands. Autumn accumulations take place in our coastal estuaries and bays.

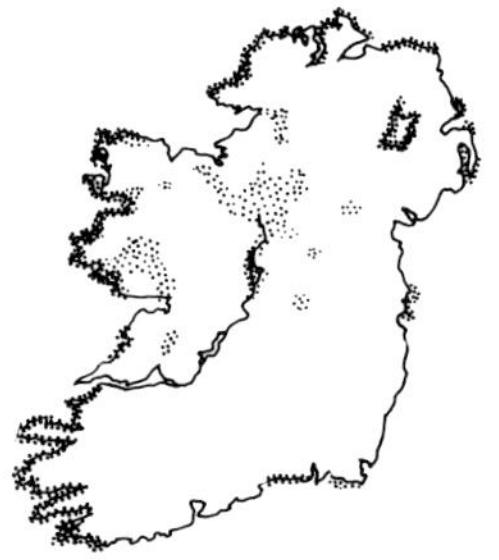

Summer

STATUS: Summer visitor and passage migrant in Ireland. It winters mainly in the Mediterranean and in North Africa. Winter occurrences in Ireland are rare but increasing. The Scandinavian form is a rare, though probably annual visitor which has been recorded in most of our coastal counties.

HERRING GULL *Larus argentatus* *Plate 25*

Faoileán scadán

IDENTIFICATION: 56–66 cm (22–26"). This is our commonest large gull. It is the typical "seagull" with its white head and underparts, light grey back and wings and black wing tips. The bill is yellow with a red spot; the legs are pink. The immature plumage ranges from the overall dark brown juveniles to the progressively paler immatures. In the final year of immaturity the bird is almost identical to the adult except for the black tipped, pinkish bill. The flight is unhurried and graceful and the call is an often repeated high-pitched yelping.

HABITAT: Although it is perhaps most often associated with the coast, this species is highly adaptable and may be found almost anywhere; lakes, rivers, rubbish dumps, over cities, etc.

STATUS: Very abundant resident breeding on coastal cliffs, islands, etc. It also nests on some inland lakes and bogs and even on some city buildings. There is evidence of winter immigration into Ireland from elsewhere in Europe.

Summer

ICELAND GULL *Larus glaucoides* *Plate 25*
Faoilean íoslannach

IDENTIFICATION: 56-66 cm (22"-26"). This is a Herring Gull-sized whitish gull. As with the Glaucous Gull, this is a pale bird in all plumages, with white wing tips. Iceland and Glaucous Gulls will stand out against other gulls because of their rather uniform paleness. The plumage changes with age are similar to those of the Glaucous Gull. Differentiation between Glaucous and Iceland is best done on a proportional basis, as they can look very alike. The most reliable feature is the closed wings of the Iceland, which project well beyond the tail of the sitting bird. Other, closer range features are the "milder facial" expression and less sinister-looking bill. In flight, the wings look long and the proportions are those of the Herring Gull.

HABITAT: As Glaucous Gull though rare inland.

STATUS: Scarce visitor from the high arctic. The name is misleading as the Iceland gull breeds in Greenland, whilst the Glaucous does so in Iceland. Less regular than the Glaucous, it is however, recorded in most winters.

GLAUCOUS GULL *Larus hyperboreus* *Plate 25*
Faoilean glas

IDENTIFICATION: 64-81 cm (25-32"). This is a large whitish gull, the size of a Great Black-back. In all plumages it is pale and the wing tips are white, not dark as in all the commoner gulls. The juvenile plumage is creamy buff, finely barred, becoming progressively paler with age, until adult plumage is attained. The adult's back and wings are very pale grey. In the immature the bill is pinkish with a black tip, whilst the adult's bill is yellow with a red spot. The bill looks long and sinister but less heavy than the Great Black-back's. From close range the Glaucous Gull has a "nasty" facial expression and the closed wings don't project beyond the tail of the sitting bird. (See Iceland Gull). The flight is heavy and lazy and the wings look broad.

HABITAT: Mainly coastal areas. Favoured localities are harbours, quays, rubbish dumps or among other gulls in estuaries. Inland occurrences are unusual.

STATUS: Scarce annual visitor from the Arctic, mainly in the winter or early spring. Most are seen in the north and west, but there are records for all coasts. Although it occurs mostly singly, small groups have been seen together.

GREAT BLACK-BACKED GULL *Larus marinus* *Plate 25*

Droimneach mór

IDENTIFICATION: 74 cm (29"). This is our largest gull. The adult is readily identified by its white body and black wings and back. The massive bill is visible even from considerable range. In the adult the bill is yellow with a red spot near the tip; the legs are pink. The upperparts of the immature are mottled dark brown, but the head and underparts are whitish, speckled darker. The bill is all dark in the juvenile, dark tipped in the immature bird. The Great Black-backed Gull flies with casual grace. At the breeding colonies the call is deep and guttural.

HABITAT: Breeds on coastal islands, headlands and on some larger lakes. Outside the breeding season many are found on inland waters.

STATUS: This species nests colonially all round Ireland. Most nest on rocky coasts and marine islands, but some nest on islets in lakes in the west. Large numbers congregate on estuaries and loughs in the winter, where a thousand or more have been seen together.

Summer

KITTIWAKE *Rissa tridactyla* *Plate 24*

Saidhbhéar

IDENTIFICATION: 41 cm (16"). This species could be described as the coastal counterpart of the Common Gull. It is only rarely found away from the sea. In overall appearance it looks rather like a Common Gull, but in flight the wings are more angled and pointed and the tips are black (looking as though they were dipped in ink) lacking the white spots of the Common Gull. The immature has a strong upper pattern of black wing bars, neck mark and tail tip. The flight is buoyant with strong wing beats quite different from the lazy flight of the Common Gull. At the breeding colonies, Kittiwakes often repeat their own name — a nasal 'Kit-i-wak'.

HABITAT: A sea-going species, which nests on rocky cliffs and islands all around our coasts. In winter most move out to the open sea, coming inshore during storms.

STATUS: Abundant summer resident of the Irish coastline. Scarce inshore in winter and rare inland.

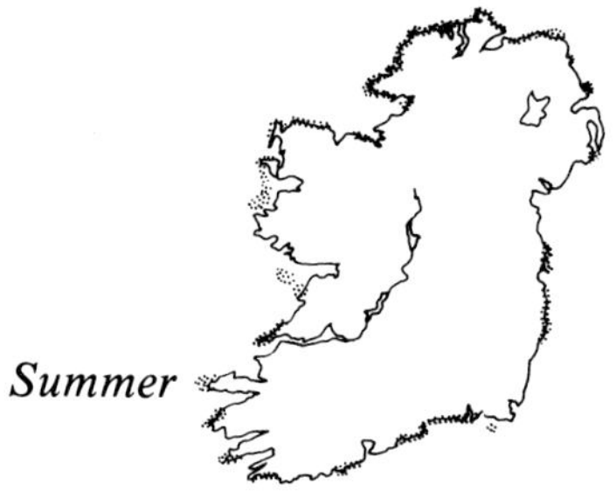

Immature Kittiwake and Little Gull

SANDWICH TERN *Sterna sandvicensis* *Plate 26*

Geabhróg dhúscothach

IDENTIFICATION: 41 cm (16"). This is our largest tern. It flies with powerful beats on long angled wings. The overall whitish appearance, slightly forked tail and loud raucous call are salient features. From a view of the bird on the ground the black cap has a distinctly shaggy look at the back. The legs and bill are black, the latter with a yellow tip. The loud call sounds like "kru-ick, kru-ick".

HABITAT: The sea coast and one or two of the larger lakes in the west.

STATUS: Summer visitor from coastal West African wintering grounds. It nests in colonies of varying size but usually smaller than those of the Common or Arctic Terns. The range is mainly on the north and west coasts, but there are some inland colonies, notably on Lough Erne.

Summer

Sandwich Tern

ROSEATE TERN *Sterna dougallii* *Plate 26*

Geabhróg rósach

IDENTIFICATION: 38-43 cm (15"-17"). The most graceful of the terns, the Roseate looks whiter than other terns, has longer tail streamers and a distinctive call. On the ground, from reasonable range the delicate pink flush on the underparts, the red legs (decidedly longer than other similar terns) and the red-based black bill, can be seen. However it is the general whiteness of the plumage, the long tail streamers and the harsh "kru-it, kru-it" call which are hallmarks of the Roseate Tern at a distance or in flight.

HABITAT: Almost entirely coastal, nesting on marine islets.

STATUS: Scarce and local summer visitor, wintering mainly in coastal West Africa. The Roseate Tern is becoming scarcer in Ireland, its remaining nesting colonies being found scattered along the east and west coasts. The largest colony (over 1,000 pairs) is in Co. Down. A substantial proportion of the entire world population is found in Ireland.

COMMON TERN *Sterna hirundo* *Plate 26*

Geabhróg

IDENTIFICATION: 36 cm (14¼"). All our sea terns are light grey above, white below, with a black cap on the head. They are all very buoyant and graceful in flight and dive into the sea for the small fish on which they feed. The Common Tern has a deeply forked tail, bright red legs and black-tipped red bill. Common Terns and Arctic Terns are very alike, but can be separated when seen in good light. In flight, the wings of the Common Tern are opaque to bright sunlight. On the ground the underparts are clear white and the legs are a little longer than the Arctic Tern's (see Arctic Tern). The juvenile plumage is mottled with brown, the black cap is incomplete and the bill is dark. The call of the Common Tern is an extended, grating, "kerr-agh".

HABITAT: Coastal areas and the larger lakes, especially in the west.

STATUS: Summer visitor which winters in the southern hemisphere. There are numerous nesting colonies on coastal sandy islets, rocky islands and on many inland lakes. It is least common on the south coast. The colonies range from a few pairs to hundreds of pairs and are often amongst other tern species or Black-headed Gulls.

Summer

ARCTIC TERN *Sterna paradisaea* *Plate 26*

Geabhróg artach

IDENTIFICATION: 37 cm (14½"). This species is very similar to the Common Tern and is probably best distinguished in the air by the translucent primary feathers on the wings (the Common Tern has only the basal primaries translucent). On the ground the underparts, which are tinged grey, can be seen to contrast with white cheeks. In addition, the bill does not have a black tip and is a slightly deeper shade of red and the legs are a little shorter than the Common Tern's. The call is very like that of the Common Tern, but to the experienced ear it sounds less extended.

HABITAT: Mainly coastal. Less common on inland waters than the Common Tern.

STATUS: A rather local summer visitor, wintering in the southern hemisphere. Although it nests all around Ireland it is scarce on the south coast. Most of the breeding colonies on the lakes in the west have decreased, and indeed, the colonies fluctuate in number and location from year to year.

Summer

LITTLE TERN *Sterna albifrons* *Plate 26*

Geabhróg bhídeach

IDENTIFICATION: 25 cm (10"). By far the smallest of the sea terns, the features to look for are the slight fork in the tail, the white forehead/black cap combination and the yellow legs and black tipped bill. As with other terns, the juvenile plumage is mottled and white triangles show on the wings. The jerky wing beats of the flying bird are faster than those of other terns. Although it has something of the harsh quality of the other terns, the call of the Little Tern is higher pitched and much quieter.

HABITAT: The seashore, especially shingly beaches. Very rare inland.

STATUS: Local summer visitor from the West African coast. Most of the colonies are on the east and north west coasts. The colonies are small and scattered and are often on beaches used by bathers. They are consequently vulnerable to human disturbance.

Summer

BLACK TERN *Chlidonias niger*
Geabhróg dhubh

IDENTIFICATION: 24 cm (9½"). This is a small marsh tern which feeds from the water surface. The best feature is the light, flipping flight with regular dipping to the water surface to catch insects. Only in breeding plumage is this bird blackish. The majority of those seen here are either immature or winter plumaged adults when they are dull greyish above, white below, with a partial black cap and dark shoulder mark. The rump and tail are never white as in the sea terns. In this country it is generally silent, unlike the sea terns.

HABITAT: Generally coastal marshes, lagoons, sometimes estuaries or elsewhere on the coast. Also inland on the major river valleys and lake systems.

STATUS: Regular autumn migrant from continental Europe in small numbers. Rare in spring and in summer plumage. It has bred in Ireland.

Black Terns.

AUKS

GUILLEMOT *Uria aalge* *Plate 27 and 28*
Foracha

IDENTIFICATION: 42 cm (16½"). At a glance, both of our largest auks look somewhat alike. The Guillemot is, however, velvety brown instead of black on the upperparts; the bill is dagger-like; overall the bird is larger and less stocky than the Razorbill. In winter the face and throat turn whitish as with other auks, but the Guillemot retains a dark line through the eye. In flight, it is similar to the Razorbill, and identification from a distance is difficult, unless the bill can be seen. The "bridled" Guillemot is a form of the common bird which has a pale line round the eye and running back from it, visible in summer plumage. The sounds of a colony of breeding Guillemots is a weird gargling, conjuring up ideas of witch's laughter.

HABITAT: Coastal cliffs, marine islands with cliffs, sea stacks. Outside the breeding season, the open sea.

STATUS: Abundant breeder in large colonies, on suitable cliffs around the Irish coasts. Some of the colonies have thousands of pairs (mainly on the west coast but also on Great Saltee Islands off the south-east). Like the Razorbills the Guillemots leave Ireland and spend the winter off the coast of Iberia and in the Mediterranean.

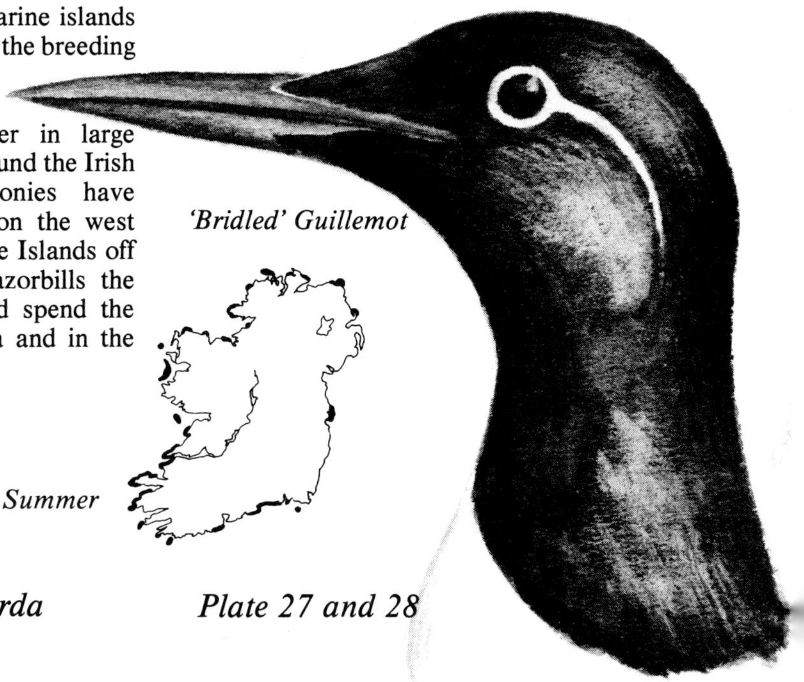

'Bridled' Guillemot

Summer

RAZORBILL *Alca torda* *Plate 27 and 28*
Crosán

IDENTIFICATION: 41 cm (16"). This is a stocky, penguin-like seabird, which is most likely to be seen on or near its breeding colonies, around our coasts. When standing on the rocky ledges on which it nests it is quite upright, showing white underparts, black upperparts and small wings. The effect is quite penguin-like though, unlike a penguin, the Razorbill flies, with whirring wings. The webbed feet, used primarily for swimming, are also used as landing gear and as rudders when the bird is in flight. A close view is needed to see the stout black bill with fine white lines on it. With the onset of winter the face and throat become white, and the bill loses its markings. The juvenile is like a winter plumaged adult with a smaller bill. The call of the breeding colony is a curious low growling.

HABITAT: Coastal cliffs, marine islands with cliffs and precipitous stacks. They prefer overhanging rocks and crevices rather than the exposed ledges on which the Guillemots nest. After the breeding season the Razorbill's habitat is the open sea.

Summer

STATUS: The Razorbill breeds in large colonies all around our coasts. Some of these colonies have thousands of breeding pairs, especially on the north and west coasts. Most of our Razorbills winter in the open sea off Iberia and in the Mediterranean.

BLACK GUILLEMOT *Cepphus grylle* *Plate 27 and 28*

Foracha dhubh

IDENTIFICATION: (34 cm) 13½". This is a smallish auk with a striking difference between summer and winter plumage. The summer plumage is black with a large white wing patch, whilst the winter plumage is whitish with grey barring. The bill is blackish and dagger-like, the legs and webbed feet are bright red. The white wing patch is very obvious in the flying bird both in summer and winter. At the breeding site the call is a thin whistle and the birds shows a bright red inside to the bill when calling.

HABITAT: Rocky coasts, especially islets, skerries, old piers and quays, where it nests in holes.

Summer

STATUS: This is a rather local breeding bird which does not nest in large colonies like other auks. It is found on all coasts, but is perhaps commonest in the west and south west. During the winter Black Guillemots disperse, but do not tend to migrate to the south like the other auks.

LITTLE AUK *Alle alle* — *Plate 27 and 28*

Falcóg bheag

IDENTIFICATION: 20 cm (8"). This bird is rather like a tiny Razorbill. There is really no mistaking it as it is only the size of a Starling and has a very small bill. As with the other auks it is mostly black above, white below. In winter plumage (the plumage in which it is most likely to be seen in Ireland), the face and throat are white. It flies close to the surface of the sea, like other members of this family, and on rapidly whirring wings. The underwings are distinctly dusky, in contrast to those of the other auks. It is rare in summer plumage in this country.

HABITAT: Generally on the open sea, but storms drive it inshore occasionally.

STATUS: Irregular winter visitor from its Arctic breeding grounds where it is found in countless millions. During severe conditions at sea, Little Auks may be driven inshore and hundreds have been picked up dead all over Ireland, even far inland.

PUFFIN *Fratercula arctica* — *Plate 27 and 28*

Puifín

IDENTIFICATION: 30 cm (12"). The Puffin is a stocky, rather comical-looking member of the auk family. In summer plumage it is one of the most striking of our birds with its black back, white belly, orange legs, pale grey face and large multicoloured bill. In winter it is much less colourful, but retains its peculiar appearance. The bill sheds its coloured outer shell becoming a dull replica of the summer splendour and the head takes on a more auk-like, less clownish appearance. Puffins in flight are easily identified, even at a distance, due to their distinctive dumpy or neckless look.

HABITAT: The grassy plateau or slope immediately above sea cliffs or on marine islands is where the Puffin excavates its nesting burrows. Outside the breeding season it is found on the open sea.

STATUS: Abundant summer resident at its breeding stations which are to be found locally on all coasts. The biggest colonies, which may be in excess of 10,000 pairs, are found in the south west. It only occurs inshore occasionally, in the winter, usually after storms. Puffins have been found far inland after gales.

Summer

PIGEONS and DOVES

ROCK DOVE *Columba livia* *Plate 29*
Colm aille

IDENTIFICATION: 34 cm (13½"). City street pigeons are descendants of the Rock Dove which have been hand reared and released. The wild bird is like the slate grey feral variety with the white patch on the lower back and black wing bars. Compared with the feral bird it is, however, of cleaner appearance and much less approachable. Due to the interbreeding of wild and feral doves, the true indigenous Rock Dove is becoming increasingly scarce. It is a favourite quarry of the Peregrine on the sea cliffs.

HABITAT: Exclusively rocky coastal areas, especially the more remote stacks of the west and north.

STATUS: Common and widespread on the western and northern coastal islands and cliffs. It is a rather local resident on the east and south coasts. The feral form is common on the east coast, and inland — particularly around towns while the true wild species is confined to the outer coasts.

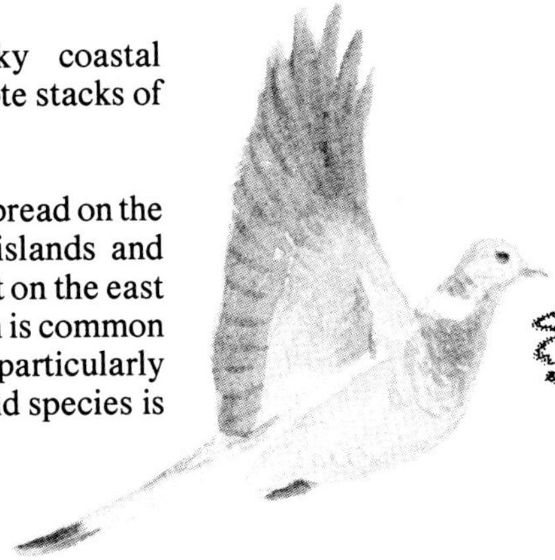

All Year

STOCK DOVE *Columba oenas* *Plate 29*
Colm gorm

IDENTIFICATION: 33 cm (13"). This bird is rather like a small Woodpigeon without the prominent white wing patches. It is an overall slatey grey pigeon with a blackish outside edge to the wings and two short broken black wing bars. From fairly close range it is possible to see the greenish sheen on the side of the head, purplish sheen on the breast and lack of white on the neck. It is shyer and much more local than the Woodpigeon but may be found accompanying it on arable land.

HABITAT: Open agricultural land, fields, parkland. Favoured breeding habitats are old buildings and ruined castles and occasionally in holes in old trees.

STATUS: Widespread though rather local resident in Ireland. It is scarcest in the north-west and commonest in the fertile agricultural areas of the east and midlands.

All Year

adult
juvenile
GREAT BLACK-BACKED GULL
adult
juvenile
LESSER BLACK-BACKED GULL
adult
juvenile
HERRING GULL
adult
juvenile
⊗ ICELAND GULL
adult
juvenile
GLAUCOUS GULL

COMMON TERN
ARCTIC TERN
ROSEATE TERN
SANDWICH TERN
immature
LITTLE TERN

PUFFIN
GUILLEMOT
SHAG
RAZORBILL
CORMORANT
BLACK GUILLEMOT

juvenile
adult
juvenile
adult
SHAG
CORMORANT
Diving
SHAG
CORMORANT
RAZORBILL
BLACK GUILLEMOT
GUILLEMOT
PUFFIN
⊗LITTLE AUK
RAZORBILL
GUILLEMOT
⊗LITTLE AUK
BLACK GUILLEMOT
PUFFIN

WOODPIGEON
STOCK DOVE
ROCK DOVE
Feral pigeons
TURTLE DOVE
adult
juvenile
COLLARED DOVE

LONG-EARED OWL
Short-eared Owl
being mobbed
by Jackdaw
SHORT-EARED OWL
BARN OWL

SWALLOW
SAND MARTIN
HOUSE MARTIN
SWIFT

⊗WAXWING
KINGFISHER
JAY
female
male
⊗ GOLDEN ORIOLE
⊗HOOPOE

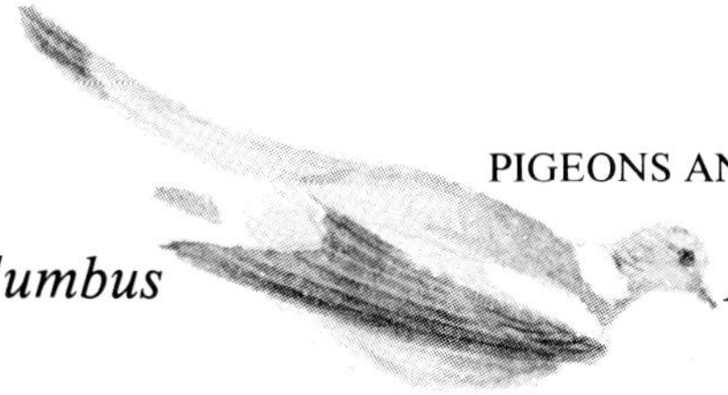

WOODPIGEON *Columba palumbus* *Plate 29*
Colm coille

IDENTIFICATION: 41 cm (16"). This is our commonest, most widespread, and largest pigeon. It is easily recognised by its large size, smallish head, conspicuous white wing flashes and overall soft grey plumage. Close views (which this bird readily affords) show it to be plump, short-legged, to have sheens of green and pink on the head and breast and a white mark on the sides of the neck. The grey tail has a thick dark band at the end. The juvenile lacks the white neck marks of the adult. When flushed the Woodpigeon rises with urgent flaps of the wing, which often make an audible smacking noise, and the tail is fanned back in a semi-circle. The Woodpigeon utters an unmistakable soft "cooing" throughout the year but most intensely in the summer.

HABITAT: Almost anywhere in the country, especially open arable fields and woods. Many are found in city greenbelts and parks and even suburban gardens.

STATUS: One of our commonest birds having reached pest proportions in many parts of the country. There appears to be a winter immigration from Britain or further east.

All Year

Woodpigeon display flight

COLLARED DOVE *Streptopelia decaocto* *Plate 29*
Fearán baicdhubh

IDENTIFICATION: 31 cm (12"). A well known Irish bird, but only since about 1960. This beautiful dove is an overall greyish buff colour, lightest on the head. The black and white neck mark, dark bill and red eye are diagnostic. When it takes to the air this dove shows dark wing tips and base to the undertail and white outer fringes to the uppertail. In flight it has a distinctive bent-winged profile. Collared Doves feed readily on the ground near buildings and roads. The breeding call is a cooing, rising and falling in intensity. The flight call is a nasalised "h-nnnn".

HABITAT: Near human habitation in the country, especially in or near villages. Recently it has become so common as to be found in the centres of our towns and cities.

STATUS: This species is essentially southern Asiatic in origin. About fifty years ago it began a remarkable western extension of its range in which it spread from Asia Minor, through Europe from south east to north west, arriving in Ireland about 1960. Since then it has become a common member of our avifauna. It is a resident in all provinces though is still quite local in some of the midland counties.

TURTLE DOVE *Streptopelia turtur* *Plate 29*
Fearán

IDENTIFICATION: 27 cm (11"). The Turtle Dove is similar in shape and size to the Collared Dove, but is much more richly coloured. Basically it is chestnut brown with large black spots on the upperparts, whitish with a pinkish tinge on the underparts. The head and tail are soft greyish, the former with distinctive white and black neck markings, the latter with black and white bands at the end. The juvenile is duller and greyer than the adult. At the breeding site it utters a soft cooing.

HABITAT: As a migrant it is found in trees and shrubbery on coastal islands, promontories, occasionally even inland. At nesting sites, in woods and large suburban gardens. gardens.

STATUS: regular spring migrant, in small numbers, from south of the Mediterranean mainly to the south and east coasts. It is less regular in the autumn. It nests irregularly, but sometimes in a number of localities on the south and east coasts, occasionally far inland.

Cuckoo

CUCKOOS

CUCKOO *Cuculus canorus*
Cuach

IDENTIFICATION: 33 cm (13"). The Cuckoo is one of the few species which is usually identified by its call which, as everyone knows, is the repetition of its name. The muffled "cuck-oo" of the male bird is very much a part of our countryside on a summer's day. However it is less often seen. In flight the Cuckoo looks rather hawk-like with long pointed wings and long tail. From a good view it can be seen to be a medium-sized grey bird with barring on the white underparts. The tail is long and rather rounded at the end and is heavily marked with white on the underside. It is moved strangely from side to side by the calling male. The feet and eyes are bright yellow. The behaviour of the female depositing her eggs into the nests of other species is well known, as are the photographs of the oversized young being fed by overworked foster parents.

HABITAT: Almost anywhere in the countryside from pasture land to bogs, from mountain sides to marine islands and sand dunes.

Summer

STATUS: Summer visitor to Ireland from African wintering grounds. Cuckoos arrive in April and depart in August. They are widespread in this country, but are sadly decreasing not only here but throughout Europe.

OWLS

BARN OWL *Tyto alba* *Plate 30*
Mulchán

IDENTIFICATION: 36 cm (14"). This nocturnal bird is perhaps most frequently seen illuminated by car headlights. At night it looks ghostly white, with a wavering, moth-like flight. Sometimes it is possible to get a good view of a barn owl standing on a post or near a ruin in the late evening or early morning. It stands upright showing whitish underparts, soft grey and buff upperparts and a most distinctive flat, heart-shaped face with dark eyes. The effect is rather cat-like. The nocturnal call is an extended screeching or shrieking.

HABITAT: It nests in and is generally found near old buildings, ruined mansions, castles, farm outbuildings. It hunts far and wide at night often in cultivated country areas, but also near human habitation even venturing into towns occasionally.

STATUS: Formerly a widespread, if thinly distributed resident. In recent years it has decreased so that it is very scarce in many counties. However it appears to be well established in the midlands and in Kerry.

All Year

LONG-EARED OWL *Asio otus* — *Plate 30*

Ulchabhán fadchluasach

IDENTIFICATION: 36 cm (14"). Like the Barn Owl, this is another nocturnal species, rarely seen in daylight, unless disturbed from its roost. It is a dark brown owl, heavily mottled and barred, with pronounced flat facial disc and staring eyes. The "ears" are not ears at all, but simply upright tufts of feathers on the top of the bird's head. At night, in car headlights, it looks less pale than the barn own and is less frequently found near human habitation. The call is a drawn out, quivering "ho-oo-oo".

HABITAT: This is a woodland species found thinly distributed in both deciduous and coniferous woods. Small groves of trees are favoured as nesting sites.

STATUS: Our commonest owl, it is resident in all counties and is increasing, due mainly to the recent re-afforestation of this country. It has taken readily to the artificial environment of the spruce forests.

Summer

SHORT-EARED OWL *Asio flammeus* — *Plate 30*

Ulchabhán réisc

IDENTIFICATION: 36-38 cm (14"-15"). A diurnal owl of open, treeless country. It is an overall buffy-brown bird, heavily mottled above and streaked below with tiny "ears" (head tufts) that are only visible from very close range. The flat facial disc is pale and the staring yellow eyes are highlighted by dark surrounding feathers. The distinctive features of this owl in flight are the large size, the flat-faced appearance, the dark and pale marks at the joints of the wings and the slow motion flapping on stiff wings. It is often mobbed or harassed by other birds which recognise it as a predator.

HABITAT: Mainly coastal flatlands — marshes, sand dunes, open rough ground. It is less frequently encountered inland, on open ground, mountains, bogs, etc.

STATUS: Regular winter visitor and passage migrant in varying numbers. In some winters it is very scarce. In recent years it has bred in the west of Ireland. A number of pairs have successfully reared young and it is possible that if undisturbed, this owl could become established as a new resident bird of prey.

NIGHTJARS

NIGHTJAR *Caprimulgus europaeus*
Tuirne lín

IDENTIFICATION: 27 cm (10½"). This is a bird of the dusk — a crepuscular species, which sits inactive by day and hunts moths and other insects at dusk. Consequently it is not often seen except by a patient observer (in the breeding area). It is most often detected by its call, which is a seemingly unending churring noise, uttered at dusk; it is often described as a purring trill. It does not sound as though it is being made by a bird at all, having a mechanical quality, as it rises and falls in pitch (see Grasshopper Warbler). The resting bird is remarkably camouflaged and is virtually indistinguishable from the lichen-covered stones or rotten branch on which it lies during the day. The displaying male sports white spots on wing and tail and hovers during courtship, smacking the wings together with a whip-crack. In flight it has a hawk-like appearance with long wings and tail and flies swiftly and erratically.

HABITAT: Bracken-covered and heathery hillsides and commonages with trees. Also undisturbed raised bog at the edge of some conifer plantations. On migration, on islands at lighthouses.

STATUS: Formerly a widespread summer visitor, which winters in Africa, nesting in all four provinces. Following a decline, the Nightjar is now very scarce and thinly distributed.

Summer

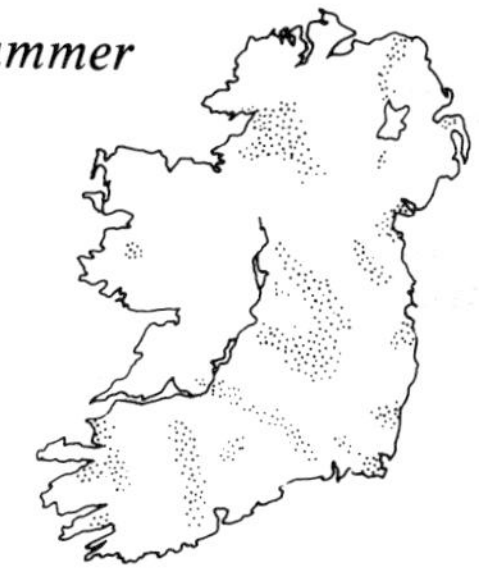

Nightjar

SWIFTS

SWIFT *Apus apus* — *Plate 31*
Gabhlan gaoithe

IDENTIFICATION: 18 cm (7"). The Swift looks like one of the swallow family with its fast, agile flight on sickle-shaped wings and forked tail. It is, in fact, unrelated. These dusky birds are well known for their frantic, "follow-my-leader" antics amongst the high buildings of towns and cities. Small groups fly at breath-taking speed among the roof tops, calling with high-pitched screaming. They look black from a distance but are in fact dark brown with a small pale chin patch. Almost all of their time is spent on the wing. They only land to nest which is normally in holes in masonry, near the tops of tall buildings.

HABITAT: The Swift's habitat is the open sky. They nest in high buildings, but have bred at cliff sites. Insects which they catch on the wing are the Swifts' food. Large numbers accumulate over marshes or over lake-side scrub to feed.

Summer

STATUS: Abundant summer visitor from African wintering grounds. It nests in buildings in all counties, arriving in May and leaving mainly in August. Post-breeding accumulations of many thousands of birds are found in certain areas, notably the Lough Neagh basin.

KINGFISHERS

KINGFISHER *Alcedo atthis* *Plate 32*
Cruidín

IDENTIFICATION: 18 cm (7"). This is one of our best known and most beautiful birds. Most views of it are brief — an electric blue flash near the surface of a river. If one is fortunate enough to see a Kingfisher perched or fishing from close range, it is seen to be a beautiful, brightly coloured bird about the size of a Starling. The upperparts are blue, or greenish-blue, depending on the light. The rump is pale blue, the underparts orange and the cheek and chin patches white. The bill and head are long and look outsized. The feet are bright red. The tail is disproportionately short. Fishing is carried out from an overhanging branch or by hovering skilfully in one spot above the water. By plunging into the water the Kingfisher catches small fish which it either eats itself or carries into the nest hole for the young. This is invariably a tunnel in the sand bank of a river.

HABITAT: Usually the larger, slow moving rivers. Less often on smaller watercourses, canals, even at lakesides, reservoirs or ponds. In winter they have been noticed at the coasts near estuaries, lagoons, etc.

STATUS: Widely distributed resident probably commoner than supposed. It breeds in every Irish county, but is scarce in some.

HOOPOES

HOOPOE *Upupa epops* *Plate 32*
Húpú

IDENTIFICATION: 31 cm (12"). This beautiful bird, which has the look of an escapee from a tropical aviary, turns up regularly as a wild visitor to Ireland. From almost any range it looks exotic, with its pinkish plumage, black and white wings and tail, "Indian-headress" style crest and downcurved bill. In flight, it appears predominantly black and white with heavy barring on the upperparts, and wings that are very rounded. It flies in a casual dipping fashion, and on alighting disappears rapidly into ground cover. The call is a low "poo-poo-poo" which has been corrupted into the bird's name.

HABITAT: Most are seen on rough ground near the sea, especially on islands, headlands, sand dunes, and in coastal gardens.

STATUS: Scarce though regular on migration, overshooting from Continental Europe, mainly in the spring. One or two are recorded in most years, but occasionally dozens turn up. The majority occur on the south coast, but there are records for most Irish counties.

WOODPECKERS

WRYNECK *Jynx torquilla*

Cam-mhuin

IDENTIFICATION: 16 cm (6.5"). This member of the woodpecker family is a rare drift migrant to Ireland. Its normal habitat is broad-leaved woodland, but in this country it occurs mainly near the coast. It is a small greyish brown bird, about the size and shape of a skylark. From close range it can be seen to be heavily barred and marked with black which provides it with perfect camouflage against a woodland background, but make it rather conspicuous on open ground. A clue to its woodpecker lineage is the arrangement of the toes — two in front and two behind. The name is derived from its peculiar habit of twisting and stretching its neck.

HABITAT: Wrynecks are found in a variety of habitats in this country, but rarely in trees. They turn up on rough ground on coastal islands and occasionally on the mainland (among sand dunes, on stone walls etc.).

STATUS: Rare autumn drift migrant, very rare in spring. In recent years it has occurred almost annually. The majority of records are from the south coast, especially Saltee Island in Wexford and Cape Clear in Cork.

Wryneck

GREAT SPOTTED WOODPECKER *Dendrocopos major*

Morchnagaire breac

IDENTIFICATION: 23 cm (9"). Although there are no woodpeckers resident in Ireland, one or two Great Spotted Woodpeckers are identified most winters in this country. Their salient feature is their black and white plumage with red patches on the head (absent in the female) and undertail and the loud, sharp call note, and their habit of drumming dead wood in a "machine gun-like" fashion are also obvious. They feed by walking up tree trunks and rooting out insects from the bark. The flight is swift and dipping.

HABITAT: Woods and forests, both deciduous and coniferous. Also occasionally in small copses and even gardens.

STATUS: There is evidence that this woodpecker was once widespread in Ireland as its bones have been found at more than one prehistoric site. The existence of the Irish name also suggests its former habitation here. Today it is an irregular winter visitor from northern Europe. It is absent in some years, but in others as many as 29 have been identified.

Great Spotted Woodpecker

LARKS

SKYLARK *Alauda arvensis* *Plate 33*
Fuiseog stairiceach

IDENTIFICATION: 19 cm (7.5"). The Skylark is probably one of our best known birds. The varied and long-winded song from a tiny fluttering form, high in the air, is a familiar part of the open countryside. With careful stalking it is fairly easy to get a good view of this ground-feeding bird. It is mainly sandy brown with neatly outlined feathers on the upperparts and bold streaking on the breast. There is a small crest on the back of the head which can be raised and lowered at will. Skylarks are rather reluctant to fly, preferring to scurry away on being approached. When they do take to the wing they show conspicuous white outer feathers on the tail and a pale trailing edge to the wings. The call is a distinct "chirrup".

HABITAT: Almost any open rough ground, devoid of trees. Their favourite habitats arc open moorland, bogs, golf courses, commonages and sand dunes.

STATUS: Abundant and widespread resident, winter visitor and passage migrant. Although it is found in suitable habitat in all parts of Ireland, a decrease has been noticed in recent years. There is very substantial immigration into Ireland from northern Europe in the winter months.

All Year

SWALLOW and MARTINS

SAND MARTIN *Riparia riparia* *Plate 31*

Gabhlán gainimh

IDENTIFICATION: 12 cm (4.5"). This bird is somewhat like a brown counterpart of the House Martin (see page 123). The obvious differences are the lack of a white rump and the brown breast band. It is also slightly smaller than the House Martin and has a less forked tail. The calls are unmusical twitterings uttered on the wing and a "tirrup", less distinctive than the call of the House Martin. Although a common summer visitor, the Sand Martin is not as well known in Ireland as the House Martin.

HABITAT: Sand Martins are usually found near fresh water. They breed colonially in banks in sand and gravel quarries, in river banks and in sandy cliffs, sometimes far away from water. In some areas they nest in the peat face of cut away bog.

Summer

STATUS: Widespread and locally common summer visitor from African wintering grounds. It is one of our earliest summer visitors, often arriving in March, but the majority arrive in early April. Most depart in September.

SWALLOW *Hirundo rustica* *Plate 31*

Fáinleog

IDENTIFICATION: 19 cm (7.5"). The arrival of Swallows in the spring is a sure indication to many people of the coming of warmer weather. On the wing the Swallow is swift and lively, with pointed wings and a very deeply forked tail. It is blue-black above, creamy below with rusty coloured patches on the head. A row of white spots show on the tail when it is fanned open. The juvenile bird lacks the long tail streamers of the adult. A group of Swallows utter a pleasant twittering when on the wing and the call is a shrill "cheer-eet". When about to depart on autumn migration, lines of Swallows are often seen on telegraph wires, near the coast.

HABITAT: At breeding sites, farm buildings, human habitations in the country, occasionally caves. Flocks of swallows will feed near marshes and lakes and many roost in large reedbeds. On migration large numbers of Swallows are found near the coast.

STATUS: Widespread summer visitor from South African wintering grounds. Most arrive in Ireland in April and depart by September. Ringing experiments have shown Swallows to return to the same nest in subsequent years.

Summer

HOUSE MARTIN *Delichon urbica* *Plate 31*
Gabhlán binne

IDENTIFICATION: 13 cm (5"). The House Martin is somewhat like a Swallow (see previous description) without the long tail streamers. The most obvious difference is the white rump patch which is easy to see on the bird in flight. Further differences are white underparts from the throat to the undertail and the white feathered feet (only visible from close range). Most House Martins nest under the eaves of houses, constructing a neat mud bowl with a small hole at the top. The call, a hard "tirrup", is quite different from that of the Swallow.

HABITAT: Nests under the eaves of houses in villages and towns, usually in small colonies. It also nests on sea cliffs and under some bridges.

STATUS: A rather local but nevertheless widespread summer visitor from its African wintering grounds. Most House Martins arrive towards the end of April and depart in September. They often accompany swallows in pre-migration flocks.

Summer

Swallows

PIPITS and WAGTAILS

TREE PIPIT *Anthus trivialis* *Plate 33*
Riabhóg choille

IDENTIFICATION: 15 cm (6"). In size, shape and plumage pattern this pipit is very similar to the Meadow Pipit (see following description). It is however a light brown or sandy coloured bird lacking the olive tinge of the latter. From fairly close range it looks neater than the Meadow Pipit with a clear distinction between the streaked buffish breast and the white belly. Leg colour is a delicate flesh pink, not pinkish brown, and from really close range, or in the hand, the claw on the hindtoe is much shorter than that of the Meadow Pipit. The call is confirmation of identification. It is a "teeze", quite different from the Meadow Pipit's "seep".

HABITAT: Although the Tree Pipit is found in trees in its breeding range, as a migrant in Ireland it occurs mainly on coastal islands and headlands with low vegetation. It often shows a preference for perching on top of bushes and walls rather than entirely on the ground.

STATUS: A widespread and common breeder in Britain and Europe, it winters in the Mediterranean area. In Ireland however it is only a passage migrant in small numbers mainly to the east and south coasts and especially to Co. Wexford. It has recently been found in likely breeding habitat in this country.

MEADOW PIPIT *Anthus pratensis* *Plate 33*
Riabhog mhóna

IDENTIFICATION: 15 cm (5.5"). This is probably the commonest open country bird in Ireland. It is the small streaked brownish bird which flies up out of the grass uttering its distinctive "seep-seep" call. The white outer tail feathers are another distinctive feature. It can be difficult to get a good view of a Meadow Pipit, as the rather olive-tinged, brownish plumage is heavily streaked both above and below, breaking up the bird's outline on the ground. The plumage can vary considerably, some Meadow Pipits looking much darker than others. In spring and summer the singing Meadow Pipit performs a delightful gliding flight to the ground, looking like a paper aeroplane. On migration they are often seen with wagtails.

HABITAT: Open rough ground from lowland and coastal marshes to the high mountain tops. In winter and on migration, flocks of Meadow Pipits are found on open lowland meadows, callows and saltmarshes.

STATUS: Abundant and widespread resident all over the country. There is heavy

All Year

migration of Icelandic Meadow Pipits through Ireland in spring and autumn and our own resident population undertakes local migrations at the same time.

ROCK PIPIT *Anthus spinoletta* *Plate 33*
Riabhóg chladaigh

IDENTIFICATION: 17 cm (6.5"). This is a larger, darker pipit than the Meadow Pipit (see previous description). It is a dusky grey-brown above, paler below and is indistinctly streaked darker. The outer feathers on the tail are not white as in both Meadow and Tree Pipits, but greyish. The bill is longer and sturdier than those of the other pipits, and the legs are dark. Perhaps the best identification feature is the Rock Pipit's habitat. It is strictly a coastal species often to be found in the company of other shorebirds feeding amongst the tangle of seaweed and rocks. The call is a single or double "jeet" rather like that of the Meadow Pipit but more noticeable.

HABITAT: Coastal habitats of all types, favouring cliffs, rocks and seaweed. It may also be found at sewage farms, ruined buildings, etc. near the shore.

STATUS: Widespread and common resident all around our coasts. There is evidence of local seasonal movements but apparently no overall migration pattern.

All Year

YELLOW WAGTAIL/BLUE-HEADED WAGTAIL *Motacilla flava*
Glasóg bhui/Glasóg cheannghorm *Plate 34*

IDENTIFICATION: 17 cm (6.5"). The Grey Wagtail is often mistakenly called the Yellow Wagtail on account of its yellow underparts but the real Yellow Wagtail (*Motacilla flava flavissima*) is merely a scarce migrant in this country. The Yellow Wagtail's plumage is green above, yellow below with much yellow on the head, and the dark tail has white outer feathers. The female is a duller version of the male. In the autumn the upperparts can look rather more brown than green. The Blue-headed Wagtail (*M.f. flava*) is sub-specific with the Yellow Wagtail. In spring plumage it is unmistakable with its blue-grey head, and white eyestripe and throat. The female is slightly duller. In the autumn the Blue-head can be difficult to distinguish from the Yellow due to the faded plumage of both, but the whitish eye-stripe and throat of the Blue-head are usually diagnostic. "Flava" wagtails (a collective term used to describe all subspecies of the Yellow Wagtail/Blue-headed Wagtail) call with a high pitched "ts-eeer", especially in flight. They frequent grassy areas rather than fast flowing waters.

HABITAT: Mainly coastal areas, especially flat open land such as marshes or low meadowland. The breeding habitat is open meadows, mainly beside lakes.

STATUS: Regular passage migrant in small numbers mainly to the east and south coasts. Up until 1940 the Yellow Wagtail nested here in a number of widely separated localities, but since the collapse of these colonies there has been only sporadic breeding in Ireland.

Pied Wagtail

GREY WAGTAIL *Motacilla cinerea* *Plate 34*
Glasóg liath

IDENTIFICATION: 18 cm (7"). Without doubt our most attractive resident wagtail. The fast dipping flight, flash of yellow plumage and sharp call note are features which reveal the presence of Grey Wagtails. This bird is rarely found far from water, and is typically on fast flowing streams and rivers. At close range the Grey Wagtail looks slimmer and more delicate than other members of the family. It has the long black, white-edged tail of the other wagtails, but is blue-grey above and yellow below, brightest under the tail. The male in summer has a white eye-stripe and black throat patch. After breeding, the male's plumage becomes less striking and resembles that of the female. The calls are varied, the commonest being a sharp metallic "tissik" from the flying bird.

HABITAT: Almost always near running water. Nearly every mountain river and sizeable stream holds Grey Wagtails. Many move to lake shores, lowland rivers and even the coast in winter. It has been noticed increasingly in cities, farmyards etc., away from its normal watery habitat.

STATUS: Widespread resident in suitable habitat throughout the country. As a passage migrant small numbers are noticed chiefly on our coasts.

All Year

PIED WAGTAIL/WHITE WAGTAIL *Motacilla alba* *Plate 34*
Glasóg shraide/G. bhán

IDENTIFICATION: 18 cm (7"). Known widely as "willy" wagtail, the Pied Wagtail (*Motacilla alba yarrellii*) is unmistakable with its black and white plumage and continually wagging tail. The female is dull greyish on the back and the juvenile is duller still with blackish markings on the throat and a yellowish tinge to the head. In autumn the male's black throat becomes less extensive and the back becomes greyish. The White Wagtail (*M. a. alba*) is an altogether paler form than the Pied. The back is a pearly grey, not dull greyish as in female and autumn-plumaged Pied Wagtails, and the black bib is separated from the grey of the upperparts. The calls are many and varied, the most usual being a sharp "chissick".

HABITAT: A wide variety of habitats, and often close to human habitation. Favoured localities are roadsides, farms and damp areas. The White Wagtail is found mainly in coastal areas, especially on salt marshes, headlands and islands. Inland sightings are frequently on river callows.

STATUS: The Pied is a widespread and common resident throughout Ireland. There is a also considerable passage migration especially in the autumn. The White Wagtail is regular on passage migration especially to the east coast. Arrivals and departures are noted, often in abundance, at Great Saltee, Co. Wexford.

WAXWINGS

WAXWING *Bombycilla garrulus*
Sciathán céarach

Plate 32

IDENTIFICATION: 20 cm (7.5"). Anyone who has seen Waxwing at close range must agree that they are among the most captivating of all our wild birds. When they are intent on feeding on a berry tree they will often allow close approach. Starling-sized birds, they have a soft velvety plumage and an obvious, swept-back crest on the head. The predominating colours are pinkish brown and grey, with intricate yellow, white and red markings on the wings and a yellow tipped, black tail. At a distance Waxwing are a lot less obvious and in flight they closely resemble Starlings. Gregarious by nature, small flocks of Waxwing will eat berries, their staple diet, until they are almost too fat to fly. They call with a pleasant trilling, resembling the sound of tiny bells.

HABITAT: The bushes, scattered trees and hedgerows of open countryside. As they become more confiding, Waxwing will move into gardens to feed on cotoneaster, rose and other shrub berries.

STATUS: Irregular winter visitor mainly to the east and north of the country from north-east Europe. The invasions which occasionally occur are often due to a poor berry crop on the rowan trees in northern Europe. Flock sizes are usually small but over a hundred have been seen together on occasions.

DIPPERS

DIPPER *Cinclus cinclus*
Gabha dubh

Plate 37

IDENTIFICATION: 18 cm (7"). This is a bird with a most distinctive lifestyle. Its dark, white-breasted form standing on a rock in a stream or river is very conspicuous. Besides its pied appearance (there is, in fact, a reddish-brown band beneath the white bib, though this is less obvious than in British Dippers and is one of the features that make the Irish Dipper a distinct race), it is a particularly dumpy bird, similarly proportioned to a large wren, and has a most characteristic dipping action when standing on a rock — hence the name. The patient observer may see the Dipper launch itself head first into the fast-flowing water in pursuit of food. It "flies" underwater or walks along the bottom holding on with its strong claws. The usual call is a loud "zit-zit-zit" or "clink-clink" and the song is loud and rather Wren-like. The young Dipper is greyish brown and does not have the striking white bib of the adult.

HABITAT: Mainly fast flowing and rocky streams in the hills and mountains. However, Dippers are found on low lying streams and rivers in quite a number of areas. It is sometimes seen on rocky shores near the mouths of rivers, especially in the winter.

All Year

STATUS: Widespread resident in suitable habitat all over the country. It is however scarce or absent from much of the midlands. In winter many Dippers move to low-lying waterways.

WRENS

WREN *Troglodytes troglodytes* *Plate 43*
Dreoilín

IDENTIFICATION: 9 cm (3.5"). This minute bird is as well known as any of our birds. Most people recognise the Wren as an elusive little creature, flittering about near the base of gorse bushes or flying short distances near the ground. It is reddish brown in colour and is heavily barred. The tail is often cocked up vertically giving the Wren a perky look. Both the "chick-chick" call note and the vigorous song, usually emanating from the undergrowth, are very loud for such a tiny bird. The ubiquitous Wren is found in suitable habitat from mountain tops to sea level.

HABITAT: Low vegetation and cover of all kinds. Favoured areas are bracken, gorse, brambles, especially near stone walls.

STATUS: Very abundant and widespread resident. It is found in every part of the country from the lowest to the highest. There is a suggestion of migration due to the occurrence of Wrens at light-stations. The hunting of the "ran" was an age-old St. Stephen's Day tradition in Ireland, though generally not practised in the North. It is now illegal and has almost died out.

SKYLARK

juvenile MEADOW PIPIT adult

TREE PIPIT ⊗

ROCK PIPIT

juvenile
female
male
PIED WAGTAIL
WHITE WAGTAIL
GREY WAGTAIL
male
female
YELLOW WAGTAIL
⊗ BLUE HEADED WAGTAIL

ROBIN
juvenile
adult
male
REDSTART
female
WHEATEAR
female
male
female
male in autumn
male
BLACK REDSTART

SPOTTED FLYCATCHER

⊗ male

female
autumn male

PIED FLYCATCHER

STONECHAT

female male

WHINCHAT

male

female
autumn male

STARLING

adult juvenile

BLACKBIRD

male female

RING OUZEL

male female

DIPPER

SONG THRUSH

REDWING

MISTLE THRUSH

FIELDFARE

GARDEN WARBLER
SEDGE WARBLER
WHITETHROAT
male
GRASSHOPPER WARBLER
BLACKCAP
male
female
⊗ REED WARBLER

WOOD WARBLER
CHIFFCHAFF
WILLOW WARBLER
juvenile
adult
⊗ ICTERINE WARBLER
⊗ MELODIOUS WARBLER
⊗ YELLOW-BROWED WARBLER
GOLDCREST
female
male
⊗ FIRECREST
female
male

DUNNOCKS

DUNNOCK *Prunella modularis* *Plate 43*
Donnóg

IDENTIFICATION: 15 cm (5.5"). The Dunnock or Hedge Sparrow is a rather shy and retiring little bird which is nevertheless common and widespread. Almost every area of gorse or thick vegetation has its resident Dunnocks. It is a rich brown bird with heavy darker streaks on the upperparts and a slate grey head and breast. At first sight, however, it simply looks dark and rather nondescript. It feeds on or near the ground on insects of all kinds and really only makes its presence known in spring when it will sing from the top of a gorse bush or bramble patch. The song is rather brief and high pitched and the simple call is a rather monotonous "peep".

HABITAT: Favoured habitats are thick, tangled low vegetation such as brambles, bracken, hedgerows, but also scrub, gardens, woodland and even open rough ground with stone walls.

STATUS: Abundant and widespread resident bird in Ireland, the Dunnock is found in every corner of the country. There is evidence of small scale migration in spring and autumn.

All Year

THRUSHES and CHATS

ROBIN *Erithacus rubecula* *Plate 35*
Spideog

IDENTIFICATION: 14 cm (5.5"). A favourite Christmas card bird, the Robin hardly needs a description. Few gardeners can have missed the company of this bird in the course of digging or planting. Indeed, many will recount how a redbreast hopped to within a few feet or perched on top of the fork, keeping a vigilant and bright eye out for insect food in the turned ground. The breast and face are a deep orange-red, fringed by a light bluish-grey band, the remainder of the underparts being white. The upperparts are warm brown. Young Robins are brown, with pale speckling. The cocky stance, with pouted breast and cocked tail are indications of the aggressiveness of this little bird. It will defend its breeding territory against all-comers, man and beast alike. The call is a sharp "tick-tick" and the song a rather rich warbling.

HABITAT: Woodlands, both hardwood and softwood, scrub and scattered trees; parkland, orchards and gardens. It shows a preference for the proximity of human habitation and will nest in garages, greenhouses, etc.

All Year

STATUS: One of our most widespread and common resident birds, the Robin nests in every part of the country. There is a passage migration of Robins in the autumn, most noticeable on the east coast.

BLACK REDSTART *Phoenicurus orchruros* *Plate 35*
Earrdeargán dubh

IDENTIFICATION: 15 cm (5.5"). The male in summer is, as the name suggests, a black version of the Redstart (see following description). It has the reddish tail feathers of the Redstart, but is otherwise much less colourful. A whitish patch shows on the closed wing. Males in summer plumage are, however, scarce in this country and the majority of Black Redstarts seen here are females, young, or autumn-plumaged males. These vary from dark grey brown to dusky grey but all have the reddish tail feathers. The female and young Common Redstart always look a paler, warmer brown and show a pale eye-ring. Like the Redstart, the tail is shivered, not unlike a wagtail's. Less likely to call than the Redstart, it sometimes utters a short, thrush-like "tsip".

HABITAT: As a migrant the Black Redstart is rarely found far from the coast. Its favourite habitats are rocky areas, quays, lighthouse buildings and ruins near the coast. It is rarely found in wooded habitat.

STATUS: Regular, though thinly distributed passaged migrant and occasional winter visitor. Scarce in spring or in summer plumage. The majority are seen on the east coast though it has been recorded from around most of the coastline.

REDSTART *Phoenicurus phoenicurus* *Plate 35*
Earrdeargán

IDENTIFICATION: 14 cm (5.5"). The male Redstart is a handsome bird with its light blue-grey back, orange breast, reddish tail, and black, white and grey head pattern. The female is warm brown above, off white below, but has the reddish tail of the male. There is a faint pale eye-ring on the soft brown head of the female. At the breeding sites, Redstarts are shy and elusive, their presence being most readily detected by the male's song. The tail is noticably "shivered" while singing. The call is a clear "hui, chick-chick". In the autumn, the plumage of the male is considerably duller than in spring.

HABITAT: Very attracted to mature oakwoods for nesting sites, but has also been found in other hardwoods and occasionally conifers.

STATUS: Rare summer visitor wintering in Africa. This bird was probably indigenous to Ireland before the decimation of the oakwoods. There has been sporadic breeding for the past hundred years, but there is evidence in recent years of more widespread and regular nesting, particularly in Wicklow. Redstarts occur annually on passage migration at bird observatories.

WHINCHAT *Saxicola rubetra* *Plate 36*
Caislín aitinn

IDENTIFICATION: 13 cm (5"). Like the Stonechat (see following description), the Whinchat is an obvious little bird standing on top of bushes, walls, posts, etc. in an upright posture. It re-affirms its presence frequently by tail and wing flicking and by uttering its call note. The male in breeding plumage is generally paler than the Stonechat with dark cheeks and a thick white eyestripe. The breast is warm buff, the brownish back is heavily streaked and there are small white wing patches. One of the best features for identification is the white tail patches. In the less striking female, autumn male and young birds the general paleness and the white sides to the uppertail are the best identification features. The call is a "tick, tick" and "u-tick" and the song is brief and jumbled.

HABITAT: Less disturbed rough areas: bracken-covered hollows on the sides of hills and mountains, young forestry plantations, gorsey and brambly areas on or near raised bog.

Summer

STATUS: Scarce and local summer resident which winters in Southern Europe and North Africa. Whinchats breed in many counties but their main range is in a band running across the midlands from Wicklow to Sligo. They have increased in recent years, possibly due in part to reafforestation. A regular, though thin, passage migration is noticed annually at bird observatories on the south and east coasts.

STONECHAT *Saxicola torquata* *Plate 36*
Caislín cloch

IDENTIFICATION: 13 cm (5"). A Robin-sized bird, the Stonechat is perky and readily shows itself off by perching on top of posts, bushes, etc. It perches in a rather upright fashion and frequently flicks its wings and short tail. The summer male is brightly coloured with its orange breast, black head with white neck patch, and white rump and wing patches. The female, young and winter male are rather dull-coloured versions of the summer-plumaged male, but there is a vague similarity in pattern. The call is a distinctive "whit-chick, whit-chick" and the song, which is always delivered from a prominent perch, is jumbled and rather jangling. It is reminiscent of those of other small birds such as the Dunnock and Corn Bunting (see page 165).

HABITAT: Open ground, especially near the sea. The favourite habitat is gorse. It is widespread also on heather covered areas with low vegetation and sheep-cropped grassy areas with stone walls.

All Year

STATUS: Abundant and widespread resident, most common in coastal areas. Although well distributed inland in Ireland, it is scarce or absent from a large part of the inland areas of the north and east. There is evidence of some migration to and from this country. Many Stonechats are killed off in severe winters.

WHEATEAR *Oenanthe oenanthe*
Clochrán *Plate 35*

IDENTIFICATION: 15 cm (5.5"). The name "wheatear" is the key to this bird's identification. "Wheat" and "ear" are corruptions of old words for "white" and "rump" and indeed this is the bird's most striking feature. Like other members of the thrush family the Wheatear is an obvious bird standing on top of walls, stones, etc. and flying away on approach showing its rump and tail pattern. A perky, active bird, the Wheatear stands very upright, often flicking its tail up and down. It flies with a dashing, undulating flight. The male in summer is brightly coloured with grey upperparts, black wings and eye-stripe and white underparts, washed yellow/orange on the breast. The female and male out of breeding plumage are brown on the upperparts, white and buff below. The call is a loud "chup" or "whit-chup" and the song is brief and jangling, sounding rather like a snatch from a Skylark's song.

HABITAT: It breeds mainly on rocky mountain slopes, screes and corries and locally on lower ground, especially rocky coastal areas and islands. On migration, open ground near the coast is favoured.

Wheatear

STATUS: Fairly widespread summer visitor to the coastal areas of Ireland. It winters along with the rest of the world's wheatears, in Africa. It is most abundant on the western seaboard and is local on the east and south coasts. Over the remainder of the country it is local and thinly distributed being commonest in the mountain ranges. As a passage migrant it is regular at headlands, and islands all around Ireland.

Summer

RING OUZEL *Turdus torquatus* *Plate 37*
Smólach broinnean

IDENTIFICATION: 25 cm (10"). The Ring Ouzel is a regrettably scarce mountain counterpart of the common Blackbird. In shape and size it resembles the commoner bird, but it has a very obvious white breast patch. The male, though black, has pale feather edges on the wings and sides and a dull yellow, not orange, bill. Like the female Blackbird, the female Ring Ouzel is brownish but has the pale breast patch. The juvenile is heavily marked with pale feather edges and lacks a clear pale patch on the underparts. Ring Ouzels are shy birds and fly away swiftly, dashing amongst the craggy rocks on being approached. The call is Blackbird-like and the song contains many Blackbird-like sequences. The presence of Ring Ouzel is most readily detected by the far carrying piped "peu-peu-peu-peu" emanating from the rocky mountain sides.

HABITAT: Exclusively on the scree slopes and corries of mountains. The remaining breeding Ring Ouzels show a preference for boulder-strewn and craggy escarpments with scattered bushes.

STATUS: Scarce summer visitor, wintering in the Mediterranean area. It now breeds in very few counties and there are no more than a few pairs in any. Its strongholds are probably Leitrim and Wicklow. This species has declined dramatically over the past century and may well be gone completely from Ireland in a few years. As a migrant it has been noticed in spring and autumn at bird observatories especially on the south coast.

Summer

BLACKBIRD *Turdus merula* *Plate 37*
Lon dubh

IDENTIFICATION: 25 cm (10"). Like the Song Thrush, the Blackbird is one of our most familiar garden birds. It is completely black with a striking orange bill, and an orange eye-ring which is visible from close range. A Blackbird, on being disturbed, will fly away rapidly, uttering its startled alarm call note. The female Blackbird is dusky brown and lacks the male's orange bill and eye-ring. In some, the breast and throat are very pale and mottled and the bird is sometimes mistaken for a thrush by the inexperienced observer. Like the Song Thrush, the Blackbird's song is unmistakable. It is a marvellous combination of fluty notes, without the range of the Thrush, but richer and throatier.

HABITAT: Mainly close to human habitation; gardens, parkland and woodland. On migration, on remote islands and headlands.

STATUS: Widespread and abundant resident. It is found in suitable habitat in every part of the country from the lowlands to the highlands. There is heavy immigration into Ireland from Britain and Northern Europe.

All Year

FIELDFARE *Turdus pilaris*

Sacán

Plate 38

IDENTIFICATION: 26 cm (10"). This northern thrush is about the size and shape of a Mistle Thrush but is readily distinguished from reasonable range by the soft grey back to the head and rump patch. In contrast to these grey patches, the tail is blackish and the back is rich brown. The underparts do not have the clear spotted effect of the Song and Mistle Thrushes. The breast and flanks are washed buffish and are heavily marked black, and the remainder of the underparts are whitish. In flight, the Fieldfare resembles the Mistle Thrush from a distance, with its white underwings, but the flight call is an unmistakable "chack-chack". Like the Redwing, Fieldfares are fond of gathering into feeding flocks.

HABITAT: Open countryside, especially large fields with hedgerows. Flocks feed on haw and other berries in hedges and copses. Windfall apples in orchards are also favoured.

STATUS: Widespread and generally abundant winter visitor from Scandinavia. They arrive in numbers in November, departing again in April. They are more abundant in the northern half of the country where flocks of hundreds or even thousands are found in places, especially after hard weather elsewhere in Europe.

SONG THRUSH *Turdus philomelos*

Smólach

Plate 38

IDENTIFICATION: 22 cm (8.5"). This is the familiar garden bird which is often seen "listening" for worms on the lawn or smashing open snails on a stone. Basically it is warm brown above, whitish below, with a profusion of black spots and a buffish wash on the breast.

In flight, the underwings are buff coloured and the call note is a thin "tsip". The song, for which this bird is named, is loud, melodious and interspersed with short, sharp, often repeated notes. It is undoubtedly one of our best songbirds.

HABITAT: Gardens, lawns, hedgerows. Also a wide range of country habitats, though often near human habitation. On migration Song Thrushes occur in the open near the coast or on islands.

STATUS: Widespread and common resident all over the country. There is a movement of our Song Thrushes out of Ireland at the end of the summer which is followed by an immigration from Northern Britain in autumn and winter. In cold winters there is very heavy movement of thrushes into Ireland.

All Year

REDWING *Turdus iliacus* — *Plate 38*

Deargán sneachta

IDENTIFICATION: 21 cm (8.5"). The Redwing could be described as the northern counterpart of the Song Thrush. It is about the same size, though somewhat shorter-tailed. The upperparts are darker brown, the underparts are more heavily streaked than those of the Song Thrush. The most obvious identification features, however, are the thick pale eye-stripe and the dark reddish patch on the side, against the closed wing, and on the underwing in flight. Redwings call with a characteristic thin "seeer" which often reveals their presence on migration as they pass overhead at night.

HABITAT: The open countryside and woodland edges. It often accompanies Fieldfares in mixed flocks.

STATUS: Widespread winter visitor from Northern Europe and Iceland. In some years it is less abundant than in others, but it is generally common. Hundreds and even thousands occur at headlands and islands especially in the north and west during autumn migration.

MISTLE THRUSH *Turdus viscivorus* — *Plate 38*

Liatráisc

IDENTIFICATION: 28 cm (11"). This is the larger of our two resident thrushes. Both are brownish above, spotted below, but the Mistle Thrush, besides being larger, is paler and greyer on the upperparts. The tail is fairly long and the tips of the outer feathers are white. When it takes to the wing, the underwings are whitish, not buffish as in the Song Thrush, and the flight call is a harsh chatter. It has the name of "storm cock" for its defiant singing, often in a gale, and is famous for the defence of its nest. Mistle Thrushes will attack any bird, animal or even man in the nesting vicinity.

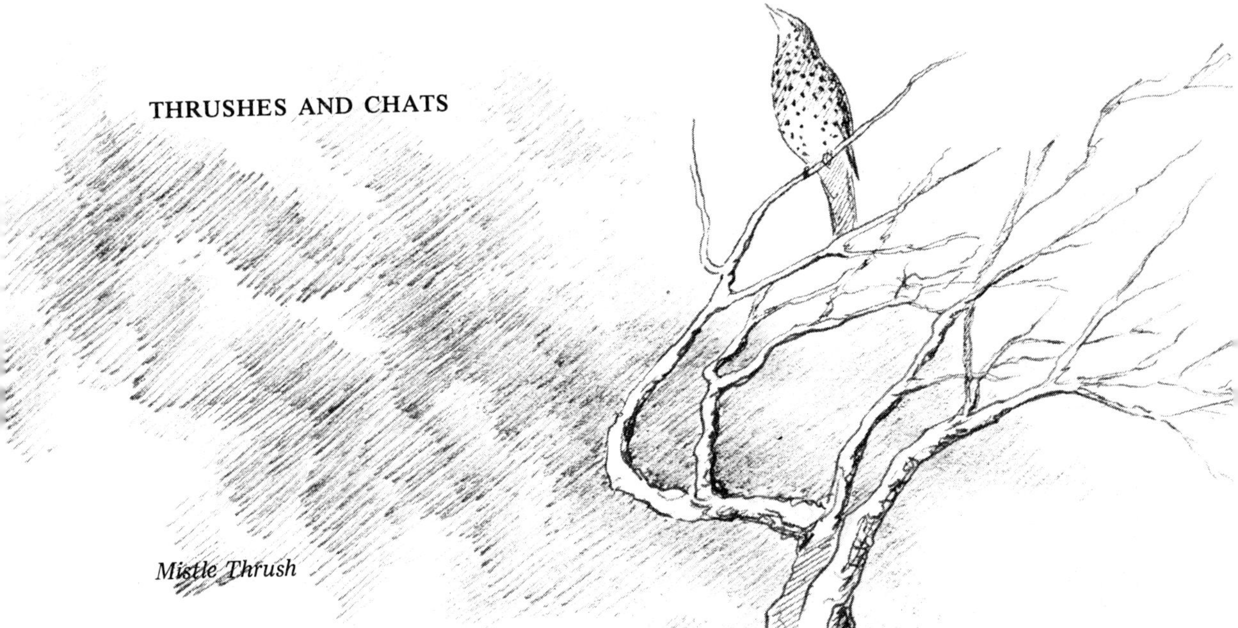

Mistle Thrush

HABITAT: Woodland edges and open country with scattered trees. Parkland, orchards and large gardens are also favoured. It is even found in wild and remote rocky areas with little cover.

STATUS: Widespread and fairly common resident found in all counties since its first appearance in Ireland in 1800. There is heavy winter immigration of Mistle Thrushes into Ireland from northern Britain.

All Year

WARBLERS

GRASSHOPPER WARBLER *Locustella naevia* *Plate 39*

Ceolaire casarnaí

IDENTIFICATION: 13 cm (5.5"). This is one of our most secretive warblers — much more often heard than seen. The song, emanating from dense marsh vegetation or undergrowth, is a long continuous trilling, sounding very like a fisherman's reel. The only other native bird with which it could possibly be confused is the Nightjar, which is found in a different habitat and has a louder song which is not heard during the day. Glimpses, which tend to be few and far between, reveal a dull greyish brown warbler, streaked heavily above, lighter below. The tail is vaguely barred and has a rather rounded end. It is much less reddish-brown and lacks the striking head pattern of the Sedge Warbler, a bird which occupies similar habitat.

HABITAT: Marshy areas especially fens. Also dense vegetation at lake shores and occasionally well away from water, in areas like willow scrub and young conifer plantations.

Summer

STATUS: Widespread though somewhat local summer resident, wintering in Africa. It is thinly distributed over most of the country and is perhaps commonest in the North Midland's lake district. Grasshopper Warblers are regularly seen and caught at Irish bird observatories on migration.

SEDGE WARBLER *Acrocephalus schoenobaenus* *Plate 39*
Ceolaire cíbe

IDENTIFICATION: 13 cm (5"). This is our commonest "reed warbler", sometimes called the "Irish Nightingale". The song, which is rich, loud and varied, and also the fact that it will sing readily at night, has prompted the name. Most extensive reedy or marshy areas in the country have a population of breeding Sedge Warblers which sing out enthusiastically from cover. An active little bird, the Sedge Warbler usually only affords brief glimpses as it flits nimbly through the reeds. It is rich brown above, vaguely streaked, and has a noticeable reddish-brown rump. The underparts are buffish white. There is a strikingly pale eye-stripe which contrasts with the dark crown. In flight the tail is noticeably round-ended. The call is a hard "pit-pit" and a "churr".

HABITAT: Marshy areas of all kinds. The favoured habitat is dense and extensive reed-beds, but it is found also in all kinds of rough and tangled vegetation, usually near water.

Summer

STATUS: Widespread and abundant summer resident, wintering in Africa. It breeds in wet plaçes in all counties. There is evidence of a decline in the numbers of Sedge Warblers (a decline reflected generally amongst many summer birds) in the past decade or so. Large numbers of Sedge Warblers are caught and ringed at our bird observatories, especially on the south coast.

REED WARBLER *Acrocephalus scirpaceus* *Plate 39*
Ceolaire giolcaí

IDENTIFICATION: 13 cm (5.5"). The Reed Warbler is unlikely to be seen here, other than at bird observatories, as it is only a rare migrant to this country. It is warmer brown than our other warblers with buffish white underparts. The tail is round-ended and the bill is fairly substantial for a warbler. It could really only be mistaken for the Garden Warbler which is similarly warm brown, but slightly greyer, has a rounded head with no trace of an eye-stripe, and generally occupies a different habitat. The call is a hard "churring" and the song, which is almost unknown here, is a vigorous chattering interspersed with fluty bursts.

HABITAT: On migration the Reed Warbler is not confined to reeds, it is often seen in other marshy vegetation and even in dry undergrowth.

STATUS: Rare passage migrant, mainly in autumn. The vast majority of records come from the south coast bird observatories. It has nested successfully once or twice. Due to the fact that one or two other European species (not found here) resemble the Reed Warbler, most field records are classified as Reed-type warblers or technically, unstreaked *Acrocephali*.

ICTERINE WARBLER *Hippolais icterina* *Plate 40*
Ceolaire ictireach

IDENTIFICATION: 13 cm (5"). This species is greenish above, yellowish on the underparts and there is a faint yellowish eyestripe. It is considerably yellower than any of the other warblers which occur here and can be distinguished from the yellow-breasted Wood Warbler by the fact that its yellowish underparts extend to the undertail region. The very similar Melodious Warbler is slightly smaller, deeper yellow and lacks the pale panelling of the Icterine's closed wings. The long and rather prominent bills of both these species are flesh-coloured at the base and are one of their best identification features. A good field identification feature of the Icterine is its rather ostentatious feeding behaviour as compared with the skulking and secretive melodious Warbler. The call is an irritated sounding "tee" and a clear "hooeet".

HABITAT: On migration it occurs mainly on coastal islands and headlands where it is found in low vegetation, bushes, wire fences, walls, etc.

STATUS: Rare though annual autumn migrant from continental Europe mainly to the south coast, especially Co. Cork. There has been a scattering of other occurrences around the rest of the coast. It is a vagrant in spring.

MELODIOUS WARBLER *Hippolais polyglotta* *Plate 40*
Ceolaire binn

IDENTIFICATION: 13 cm (5.5"). The Melodious Warbler is a counterpart of the Icterine, from south-west Europe. It is very like the Icterine in appearance, but is more shy and retiring. many Melodious Warblers that occur in this country cannot be identified properly until they are caught for ringing. Like the Icterine Warbler the colour pattern is greenish above, yellowish below, but the upperparts are slightly more brown than those of the Icterine and the underparts are deeper yellow. The best identification feature is the wings. Melodious have shorter, more rounded wings than Icterine Warblers and lack the pale panelling on the closed wing of the latter. The legs are greyish, less blue, and the bill is longish like that of the Icterine. The Melodious shares the "hoo-eet" call of the Icterine but has a characteristic "tit tit" and other sharp call notes.

HABITAT: When it occurs in this country it is usually found in low vegetation on coastal islands and headlands — gardens, shrubbery, etc.

STATUS: Rare autumn visitor from south-west Europe which occurs mainly along the south coast. In recent years it has been seen almost annually though less often than the Icterine.

Whitethroat

Lesser Whitethroat

LESSER WHITETHROAT *Sylvia curruca*

Gilphíb bheag

IDENTIFICATION: 13 cm (5.5"). This is a rare relative of the common Whitethroat in this country. It resembles the commoner bird, but is greyer on the upperparts and has a distinctive dark patch on each side of the head. The tail is shorter and it looks generally smaller and slighter than that of the Whitethroat. In habits this species is less ostentatious than the Whitethroat. The call is a sharp "tic, tic" like that of the Whitethroat.

HABITAT: On migration it favours low, dense vegetation like garden bushes, overgrown hedgerows, etc.

STATUS: Rare drift migrant from Britain and Continental Europe occurring in the autumn mainly at bird observatories on the southern Irish coast. In recent years the Lesser Whitethroat has been recorded almost annually in Ireland.

WHITETHROAT *Sylvia communis* *Plate 39*

Gilphíb

IDENTIFICATION: 14 cm (5.5"). A more obvious warbler than the Blackcap or Garden Warbler, the Whitethroat tends to show itself more, both in feeding and in display. The male is brown above (orange brown on the wings), whitish below with a pinkish breast. The head is grey, contrasting with the very white throat. The female is a duller version, lacking the grey head and pink breast. Both sexes show distinctive white outer tail feathers. The song is a brief warbling, ending harshly, which is uttered by the male in a short gliding flight from the top of a bush. The call is a "whit, whit, whit" and a deep "churring".

HABITAT: Tangled vegetation, brambles, gorse, broom. Thick vegetation around lakes and marshes. Overgrown hedgerows.

STATUS: Formerly widespread and well distributed summer resident in Ireland, wintering in southern Africa. In the last decade there has been a dramatic decline in numbers so that now it is a local breeding bird in this country (also in Britain). Migration is noted along the coasts mainly in the spring. Large numbers of Whitethroats have been seen in the past moving through Great Saltee Island, Wexford, in spring (up to 500 in a day).

Summer

GARDEN WARBLER *Sylvia borin* — *Plate 39*

Ceolaire garrai

IDENTIFICATION: 14 cm (5.5"). Even more retiring than the Blackcap, the Garden Warbler is most often identified by its song. This is rich and melodious like the Blackcap's, but is lower pitched and is usually sustained for a longer period. Both male and female are alike in plumage — overall greyish brown, paler on the underparts. There are no distinctive features to aid identification, but the head is quite rounded in shape and the bill is short compared with other warblers. The legs are greyish. The Garden Warbler has a hard "tack" call similar to that of the Blackcap.

HABITAT: Thick woodland with scrub usually beside lakes or rivers. Parkland with thick woodland. On migration in gardens and undergrowth.

STATUS: Local summer resident which winters mainly in Africa. The range in this country is confined to the midlands and is almost invariably adjacent to fresh water. Its stronghold is probably around Lough Erne. As a migrant it is noticed, generally in the autumn, at bird observatories mainly on the south and east coasts.

Summer

Garden Warbler

BLACKCAP *Sylvia atricapilla* *Plate 39*
Caipín dubh

IDENTIFICATION: 14 cm (5.5"). Like other warblers, it is difficult to get a good view of the Blackcap. This pleasantly marked but shy bird spends most of its time in dense foliage and only the patient observer is likely to see it. The male is an ashy grey warbler, brownish on the wings and tail with, as the name implies, a neat black cap on the head. The female is greyish brown, darkest on the upperparts and has a reddish-brown cap. Male Blackcaps sing from the cover of foliage their rich melodious song which is one of the finest of our songbirds'. The call is an aggressive "tack-tack".

HABITAT: Open woodland with mature hardwoods. Scrubland with scattered trees, parkland and large gardens. Blackcaps will visit bird tables.

Summer

STATUS: Fairly widespread though still rather local summer resident, wintering in southern Europe and North Africa. In recent years, however, wintering is of regular occurrence in Ireland, especially in the eastern counties. Blackcaps, formerly rare breeders in this country, have increased and extended their range in recent years. Many are reported annually from bird observatories, chiefly on the south coast.

YELLOW-BROWED WARBLER *Phylloscopus inornatus* *Plate 40*

IDENTIFICATION: 10 cm (3.5"). This Siberian leaf warbler has been noticed so many times in Ireland recently that it can no longer be considered a vagrant. It is smaller than the Willow Warbler/Chiffchaff, almost Goldcrest-sized and has the Goldcrest's double pale wing-bars. It is generally greenish above, yellowish-white below and has a long thin creamy eyestripe, more obvious than the Willow Warbler's. The call, though similar, is louder than Willow Warbler's or Chiffchaff's.

HABITAT: It is only seen here during the migration period, when it is noticed in gardens, bushes and low vegetation, on coastal islands, headlands, etc.

STATUS: Rare autumn visitor, probably of annual occurrence. The majority are seen on headlands and islands off the north and south coasts. Most have been recorded on Cape Clear Island, Co. Cork.

WOOD WARBLER *Phylloscopus sibilatrix* *Plate 40*
Ceolaire coille

IDENTIFICATION: 13 cm (5"). A larger leaf warbler than the Willow and Chiffchaff, the Wood Warbler is also more brightly coloured. The upperparts are greener than the others and the eyestripe, throat and breast are light yellow. There is a clear demarcation between the yellow of the breast and the white of the remainder of the underparts. Although young Willow Warblers can look yellowish on the underparts, they do not have white on the belly, and are smaller. If a good view is obtained the wings may be seen to be very long, almost reaching the end of the tail on the perched bird. The singing Wood Warbler has to be heard to be believed: its song is a long series of mellow notes which start slowly and accelerate into a descending trill, during which the whole bird shivers enthusiastically. The call is a clear "pee-oo".

Summer

HABITAT: Hardwoods, especially oakwoods in wooded valleys or hillsides. It is more fond of tree canopy than the other warblers, though it is found in low vegetation and gardens on migration.

STATUS: Rare and irregular summer resident which winters in Africa. It probably nests annually in a few places, especially in Co. Wicklow, but singing males have been located much more often than nesting has been proved. In recent years they have been recorded mainly in the north and east. It is occasionally seen in spring or autumn at coastal migration stations.

CHIFFCHAFF *Phylloscopus collybita* — *Plate 40*
Tiuf-teaf

IDENTIFICATION: 11 cm (4.5"). This little warbler is so like the Willow Warbler that positive identification in the field by visual means alone is difficult. Like the former species, it is generally greenish in colour, but tends to have more brown and less yellow in the plumage. In addition, the pale eyestripe is less noticeable and does not extend much beyond the eye in the Chiffchaff. The legs are nearly always dark coloured, whereas the Willow Warbler's are usually flesh coloured, but this is not the most reliable of features. The most conclusive identification feature is the song, after which this bird is named. The notes of the song are deliberate "chiff-chaff, chiff-chaff" and separate, and may continue for some time. The call is "hoo-it" like that of the Willow Warbler.

Summer

HABITAT: Much more fond of the canopy of mature trees, especially hardwoods, than the Willow Warbler. After nesting and on migration it is found in bushes, scrub, undergrowth and gardens.

STATUS: Widespread and abundant summer resident, which winters in southern and south-western Europe and North Africa. It tends to arrive earlier and leave later than the Willow Warbler and is noted in lesser numbers at coastal migration stations. Chiffchaffs winter annually in a few places in Ireland.

WILLOW WARBLER *Phylloscopus trochilus* *Plate 40*
Ceolaire sailí

IDENTIFICATION: 11 cm (4.5"). This is our commonest "leaf" warbler, so named because in size, shape and colour it can look like a small leaf. Huge numbers of Willow Warblers pour into Ireland every spring, stay to rear a family and return south again in the autumn. The Willow Warbler is a tiny active bird, which is difficult to pin down. Like other, less common leaf warblers, it is overall greenish brown above, yellowish white below and depending on the light, time of year and age of bird, it can look predominantly brownish, greenish or yellowish. There is a clear, thin eyestripe, the bill is small and the legs are usually flesh coloured. Juvenile Willow Warblers can look very yellow on the head and underparts. The call is similar to that of the Chiffchaff. It sounds like a soft "hoo-eet" and the song is a descending warbling. (See Chiffchaff, above).

Summer

HABITAT: Favoured areas are willow scrub and low-lying marshy areas with scattered small trees. It is however found in a wide range of areas especially on migration (woods, gardens, undergrowth on headlands, islands, etc.).

STATUS: Widespread and abundant summer resident which winters mainly in Africa. There is a large migration especially along the south and east coasts. In the spring thousands pass through the Saltee Islands, Co Wexford.

GOLDCREST *Regulus regulus* *Plate 40*
Cíorbhuí

IDENTIFICATION: 9 cm (3.5"). This is our smallest bird — smaller even than the Wren — but less often seen as it spends most of its time in the tops of conifer trees. At a glance it looks like a leaf-warbler, being of similar size and having greenish plumage, but a good view will reveal it to be quite different. There is a double pale wing-bar and a striking pattern on the top of the head. This is an orange-yellow cap (yellow in the female) bordered with black. Goldcrests are dumpier birds than warblers, having perhaps a more tit-like shape. In fact, they associate with tits in the winter when they forage for insects in small groups. The call is a thin but characteristic "si, si, si" usually heard coming from high up in conifer trees.

HABITAT: Usually conifer trees of all kinds, but in the winter it is found in all sorts of cover, nearer the ground, including garden vegetation.

STATUS: A widespread and abundant resident all over Ireland. There is a large immigration from Britain and continental Europe in autumn and winter, which has been recorded mainly on the east and south coasts. Hundreds have been seen on single days in the autumn on Saltee, Co. Wexford.

All Year

FIRECREST *Regulus ignicapillus* *Plate 40*

Lasairchíor

IDENTIFICATION: 9 cm (3.5"). This tiny bird is identical in size and shape to the common Goldcrest. At a glance, the plumage is also very much the same. The best distinguishing feature is the clear whitish eyestripe between the eye and the black bordered red cap (orange yellow in the female). The red in the cap is not reliable as the male Goldcrest can have a reddish cap. The Firecrest is greener above, whiter below then the Goldcrest and has a buffish smudge on the sides of the breast. Otherwise it is very like the Goldcrest and great care needs to be exercised in the field to distinguish the two species. The call is a more obvious squeaking than the Goldcrest's and the "zc-zc-zc-zc" notes rise in pitch. It sounds rather like the Long-tailed Tit's call.

HABITAT: In Ireland it is most likely to be seen on coastal islands and headlands where it will secrete itself in all kinds of low vegetation in gardens, etc.

STATUS: Rare autumn migrant from continental Europe. In recent years it has been recorded nearly every autumn on the south coast, especially at Cape Clear Island, Co. Cork.

FLYCATCHERS

SPOTTED FLYCATCHER *Muscicapa striata* *Plate 36*

Cuilire liath

IDENTIFICATION: 15 cm (5.5"). This, our only breeding flycatcher, is a rather dull representative of a generally gaudy family. It is nevertheless a bird of some personality, characterised by its distinctive feeding habits. It sits on a protruding branch of a tree, post or other prominent perch and flies out at regular intervals to catch passing insects. It has mousey-brown upperparts, creamy white underparts and vague dark spots or streaks on the breast. The square-ended tail has pale outer feathers and there is a pale eye-ring. The posture of the Spotted Flycatcher is a good identification feature. It generally sits very upright on its perch, in a rather hunched attitude with its legs tucked up beneath its body, and after returning from catching a fly it flicks its wings and tail enthusiastically. The call, which is most often heard when the adults are with their young, is a "zit" or "zit-chick".

HABITAT: A woodland species which is especially fond of sunny clearings or edges of mature deciduous woods (oaks, beeches, etc.). Also parkland with mature trees, orchards, farmland and gardens.

STATUS: Widespread though rather local summer visitor, wintering in Africa. It is found in suitable habitat in every county and is noticed at bird observatories around the Irish coast, on spring and autumn migration.

Summer

RED-BREASTED FLYCATCHER *Muscicapa parva*

Cuilire bídeach

IDENTIFICATION: 11 cm (4.5"). This rare little flycatcher is smaller and rounder in shape than even the Pied Flycatcher (see next description). Like other members of the family it catches insects by flying out from prominent perches. The colourful, somewhat robin-like plumage of the male is virtually unknown in Ireland. The majority which turn up here are immatures (see illustration) which are grey-brown on the head and upperparts and off white below. By far the best characteristic is the prominent white sides to the base of the dark tail. The bill and legs are small neat and black and the dark eye has an obvious pale eyering. The call is a short clicking trill 'dit–derrrrit' recalling the wren's.

HABITAT: On migration in the autumn on coastal islands and headlands. It is often seen in low vegetation, on walls, in small trees in gardens, etc.

STATUS: Rare though probably annual visitor on autumn migration, which turns up mainly at the bird observatories on the south coast of Ireland. It breeds in north-eastern Europe and winters in southern Asia. There is a scattering of records from other coastal observation points around Ireland.

Red-breasted Flycatcher immature plumage

PIED FLYCATCHER *Muscicapa hypoleuca* *Plate 36*
Cuilire alabhreac

IDENTIFICATION: 13 cm (5"). On autumn migration (when most Pied Flycatchers are seen in this country) this bird is dull brown above and whitish below. There is a conspicuous white patch on the wing and white outer tail feathers. Only in spring and summer is the male black and white, when it is virtually unmistakable. A smaller bird than the Spotted Flycatcher, the Pied is also more rounded in shape, stands less upright, does less flycatching from an elevated perch and spends more time on or near the ground. Its actions are jerky and tit-like but with many of the wing and tail-flicking actions of the Spotted Flycatcher. The call is a sharp repeated "tzit" and other similar notes.

HABITAT: Nearly always coastal islands and headlands. Often found on open ground or near low vegetation. It is very rarely seen in breeding habitat (oakwoods) in Ireland.

STATUS: Regular autumn migrant in small numbers to the east and south coasts. Scarce elsewhere and in spring. On Cape Clear Island, Co. Cork over thirty have been seen on a good day. This species was thought to be a rarity until the establishment of the bird observatories proved it to be a regular visitor.

Great Tit

TITS

BEARDED TIT *Panurus biarmicus* *Plate 41*
Meantán croiméalach

IDENTIFICATION: 17 cm (6.5"). This is a recent and most welcome addition to the Irish bird list. Its survival here is dependent on the survival of undisturbed reed beds, large enough to support it. Its presence is usually detected by its call note — a twanging "ping". Small groups of these birds feed busily in tall reeds, flying short distances with a distinctive, undulating flight and moving acrobatically among the reed tops. The shape of the birds is equally distinctive. They look rather like heavily built Long-tailed Tits with heavier tails. At close range the colour scheme is seen to be basically brown above with white wing patches, long brown tail and buffish white underparts. The head of the male is light blue-grey and there are very distinctive black moustachial marks. The female and young are duller without the head pattern of the male.

HABITAT: Exclusively dense reedbeds.

STATUS: Unknown in Ireland until 1966,

the Bearded Tit has occurred a number of times since then, mainly on the east coast, but also on Cape Clear Island on more than one occasion. It has nested successfully in more than one locality on the east coast and looks as though it may establish itself as a regular breeder in at least one reedbed, if given adequate protection.

LONG-TAILED TIT *Aegithalos caudatus* *Plate 41*
Meantán earrfhada

IDENTIFICATION: 14 cm (5.5"). This tit is quite unlike the other members of the group in shape as well as in its plumage. The tail is remarkably long, longer than the 6 cm long ball of feathers that is the bird's body. The colour scheme is crimson-pink, black and white. There are conspicuous black and white head stripes and white outer edges to the tail. The usual call is a series of thin buzzing notes, very characteristic of the feeding flock. In winter, flocks of a dozen or more can be seen moving along hedgerows in the search of food.

HABITAT: Woodland, mainly deciduous, but also coniferous. Also scattered trees, scrubland and hedgerows.

STATUS: Thinly distributed, though widespread resident in this country. Long-tailed Tits are very vulnerable to prolonged cold and are greatly reduced in numbers following hard winters.

Summer

COAL TIT *Parus ater* *Plate 41*
Meantán dubh

IDENTIFICATION: 11 cm (4.5"). This is an active little bird, about the same size as the Blue Tit, but quite different in appearance. It has the bold black cap and white cheeks of the Great Tit, but a clear white patch on the back of the head is the best distinguishing feature. The plumage is brownish grey above, yellowish-buff below, unlike the green and yellow of the Great and Blue Tits. The juvenile Coal Tit has the white parts of the adult tinged yellow. The Coal Tit has a variety of calls, many of them reminiscent of those of the Great Tit, especially a series of scolding notes. The song is a clear 'si-to, si-to", often repeated.

HABITAT: More of a woodland bird than either the Great or Blue Tit. It is probably commonest in conifer plantations.

STATUS: Fairly common and widespread resident in all counties. The Irish Coal Tit, a distinct race from the British bird, is found everywhere in Ireland, bar the north east, where the British race occurs.

Summer

BLUE TIT *Parus caeruleus* *Plate 41*
Meantán gorm

IDENTIFICATION: 11 cm (4.5"). Although there is a superficial resemblance to a small Great Tit, several obvious differences exist between the two species: the top of the head is sky blue in the blue Tit not black as in the bigger bird; the black on the chin does not extend down the belly in a thick line; and the Blue Tit's upperparts are bluer/less green than those of the Great Tit. The Blue Tit is a particularly active little bird. Its behaviour at a bird table is well known, as it hangs acrobatically upside down to feed on peanuts on pieces of string. Like the Great Tit it will steal the creamy top off the milk, before the bottles can be taken in from the doorstep. The call is nasal and quivering and quite unlike that of the Great Tit.

HABITAT: Similar to Great Tit. Very likely to nest in boxes.

STATUS: Common and widespread resident in all parts of Ireland. Due to the frequency of occurrence at bird observatories all around our coasts, it appears that there is some migration of Blue Tits, especially in the autumn.

All Year

GREAT TIT *Parus major* *Plate 41*
Meantán mór

IDENTIFICATION: 15 cm (5.5"). This is the largest members of the tit family, roughly the same size as a sparrow. The most obvious features are the white cheeks on an otherwise black head and the black of the chin extending down the belly in a thick line. The underparts are yellowish, the upperparts greenish. Like the other tits, the Great Tit is a lively little bird which feeds readily at bird tables and will take a drink from a milk bottle at the front door. The calls of the Great Tit are varied but tend to be loud and aggressive. The song sounds like "teacher-teacher-teacher".

HABITAT: Woodland and parkland. It is also a familiar garden bird and is found in gardens even in city centres. It nests in holes in walls and will readily use nest boxes.

STATUS: Widely distributed resident found in suitable habitat throughout the length and breadth of the country. There is some evidence of immigration from the Continent.

All Year

TREECREEPERS

TREECREEPER *Certhia familiaris* *Plate 43*
Snag

IDENTIFICATION: 13 cm (5"). It would be excusable at first glance to mistake this little bird for a mouse, as it is usually seen creeping quickly yet methodically up the trunk of a tree looking for insects in the bark. Starting near the bottom, the Treecreeper moves up the tree in a spiral, sometimes venturing onto the thicker branches, and then flies onto the next tree to repeat the performance. The upperparts are brownish, heavily streaked darker, and the underparts are white. The tail is rather long and stiff and is used to prop the bird against the tree. The bill is thin and downcurved. A thin high pitched squeaking is the characteristic call of the Treecreeper. In winter, Treecreepers often join foraging flocks of tits, moving through woodland in search of insects.

HABITAT: Mixed woodland, with a preference for hardwoods. They are sometimes seen looking for insects on walls.

STATUS: Common and widespread resident in suitable habitat. It does not appear to be a migrant in significant numbers.

Treecreeper

All Year

ORIOLES

GOLDEN ORIOLE *Oriolus oriolus* *Plate 32*
Óiréal

IDENTIFICATION: 24 cm (9.5"). The male of this rare species is unmistakable with its yellow and black plumage. The female and immature are much duller — generally greyish green with streaking on the underparts. Due to the shy and retiring nature of the bird it is very difficult to obtain good views and females and immatures must often go undetected in thick foliage. A good feature to note is the rather substantial, pinkish bill of both sexes. The flight is fast and dipping, the bird disappearing quickly into cover on alighting. A yellow rump shows in flight on all Golden Orioles. The call is an unusual noisy screeching uttered from cover.

HABITAT: In this country, it is usually seen in shrubby vegetation in gardens, near the coast.

STATUS: Rare though almost annual spring or summer visitor to the south coast, especially counties Cork and Wexford. It has been recorded at one time or another from most Irish counties.

CROWS

JAY *Garrulus glandarius*
Scréachóg

Plate 32

IDENTIFICATION: 35 cm (14"). The presence of this unlikely-looking crow is often detected by a loud, raucous, squawk from the cover of trees. It is reluctant to show itself however, and most views are of a medium-sized pinkish bird with a white rump flying off into cover. The patient observer may be rewarded with a view of one of our most beautiful birds. It is an overall pinkish brown with a black moustachial mark, black patches on the wings and a black tail. There is white on the wings as well as on the rump and a patch of bright blue near the shoulder. When calling or in an agitated state the Jay raises and lowers the crown feathers in a rough crest. It will occasionally mimic the calls of other birds. The Irish Jay is considerably brighter and pinker than birds found in Britain and on the continent and is considered to be a discrete sub-species.

HABITAT: Woodland, both deciduous and coniferous. Occasionally in large gardens and orchards.

STATUS: Fairly widespread, but thinly distributed resident. It is increasing and is found most commonly in the midlands, east and south east. It is still scarce in the north, west and south west. It does not appear to migrate.

All Year

MAGPIE *Pica pica*
Snag breac

IDENTIFICATION: 46 cm (18"). The black and white plumage, long wedge-shaped tail and harsh chattering call, make identification of the Magpie very easy. In good light the blue sheen on the wings, green sheen on the tail, and crow-like head and bill can easily be seen. Apparently always on the move, the Magpie does not easily afford scrutiny. It dashes efficiently about gardens on short flights, often raising and lowering its tail on alighting. On longer flights, however, the Magpie looks by no means competent, its white-tipped wings flapping energetically to keep the bird airborne. It is unpopular with many because of its egg-stealing activities.

HABITAT: Trees and large bushes both in town and country. It is probably most abundant in suburban areas. It carries out cleaning up operations on roadsides and motorways where carrion can be found. The solitary nest can easily be recognised — a large globe-shaped bundle of twigs with an entrance hole at the side.

Opposite Page: Crows. From left: Jackdaw, Hooded Crow, Raven, Rook, Chough.

Magpie

STATUS: The species was first noticed in Ireland about 1676 when it appeared in Co. Wexford. Since then it has spread throughout the country and now breeds in every county wherever there are trees. There is no real evidence of migration.

All Year

CHOUGH *Pyrrhocorax pyrrhocorax* *Plate 42*
Cág cosdearg

IDENTIFICATION: 41 cm (16"). This is the rarest member of the crow family found in Ireland, being generally confined to rocky coastal areas. It is a glossy, sleek bird, slightly larger than a Jackdaw with bright red legs and a thin, red, slightly downcurved bill. Choughs are quite shy and will not allow close approach. They have a very distinctive flight silhouette — the wings are broad and rounded and their ends deeply "fingered". In the breeding season they perform dramatic aerobatic displays, often dropping from a height with closed wings. The call is an unmistakable "kee-ow", a far carrying sound in the rugged coastal areas which the Chough frequents.

HABITAT: Rugged and undisturbed coastal cliffs and islands. Small numbers are also found inland in mountainous areas in parts of the West.

STATUS: The Chough, though rather localised and mainly restricted to the west coast, is commoner in Ireland than elsewhere in Northern Europe. Lesser numbers are found along the south and north coasts, but Choughs are almost entirely absent from the eastern seaboard.

All Year

JACKDAW *Corvus monedula* *Plate 42*
Cág

IDENTIFICATION: 33 cm (13"). Our smallest crow, the Jackdaw is readily identified by its grey nape and loud "chack, chack" call. At close range the white eye is visible, a feature which gives the Jackdaw a decidedly sinister or mischievous appearance. It is an adaptable species, being found in close proximity to human habitation, and will often allow close approach before flying off. The flight is rather hurried, with quick wing beats. Jackdaws appear to strut about on the ground — they walk with distinctive jerky strides.

HABITAT: They breed in old buildings, ruined castles, walls, often close to occupied houses. Also on sea cliffs, quarries, old trees and in churchyards.

STATUS: Abundant and widespread resident nesting in all counties in a wide variety of habitats. There is some evidence of migration.

All Year

ROOK *Corvus frugilegus* *Plate 42*
Rúcach

IDENTIFICATION: 48 cm (19"). Although the Rook is a member of the crow family it is often wrongly called the Crow in Ireland. The true crow is the Carrion Crow (see following description) — rare in Ireland. The Rook is roughly the same size and shape as the Carrion Crow but has a bare whitish patch at the base of the bill. This feature is absent in the juvenile and the observer needs to exercise caution with juvenile Rooks which can look quite like Carrion Crows. Rooks have untidy flank feathers and are altogether less neat than the sleek, greenish-glossed Carrion Crow. The call is an extended "caw". It is altogether a more gregarious bird than the rather solitary Crow.

HABITAT: Rooks nest communally in the tops of fairly high trees, often near roads. They feed in flocks in open fields. They are most often associated with agricultural land.

STATUS: Common and widespread resident breeding in colonies in all counties. There is evidence of migration between the continent of Europe and Ireland.

All Year

HOODED CROW/CARRION CROW *Corvus corone* *Plate 42*
Feannóg/Caróg dhubh

IDENTIFICATION: 51 cm (20"). The Carrion Crow (*Corvus corone corone*) and the Hooded Crow (*C. c. cornix*), also known as the Grey or Scald Crow, are not separate species but are considered so closely related as to be sub-specific. Both are identical in shape and size, but the Carrion is completely glossy black whilst the Hoodie is greyish on the back and belly. The Carrion Crow is rare in this country but the Hoodie is very widespread and common. They both call with a harsh "graugh". The latter is notorious amongst gamekeepers and sheep farmers for some of its predatory habits but it performs a useful function in the removal of carrion from roads and the countryside. The juvenile Rook, which lacks the pale patch of the adult's bill, is often mistaken for the Carrion Crow, but the bill shape is different and there are other differentiating features (see previous description of Rook).

HABITAT: The Hooded Crow is primarily a bird of the uplands, especially mountainous areas, but it is widespread though thinly distributed in much of the lowlands. It is found all around the Irish coastline and in winter it forages for food on estuaries and near towns. The Carrion Crow favours wooded, or open lowland country.

STATUS: The Hooded Crow is almost unknown in England and Wales, but a common and widespread resident in Ireland. The Carrion Crow, conversely, though widespread and common in Britain is rare in Ireland. It does however breed in a number of places in the northeast and occurs occasionally elsewhere.

All Year

RAVEN *Corvus corax* *Plate 42*
Fiach dubh

IDENTIFICATION: 64-69 cm (25-27"). This, our largest crow, is an inhabitant of the wilder and more remote parts of the country. It is much larger than the other crows but size alone is not the most reliable of features when viewing a solitary bird in open country. The best identification feature is the wedge-shaped tail which can be picked out even at long range. Close up this glossy black bird shows fingered ends to the wings, a massive bill and a shaggy throat. The call is also a distinctive feature — a loud, resonant croak. Ravens nest early. They may be at the nest site when there is still snow on the ground. They perform spectacular aerial displays, calling with a series of unusual notes near the nest. Intelligent and courageous birds, Ravens will defend their young against all intruders. They are carrion eaters and provide a useful service in clearing up dead animal remains in the country.

HABITAT: The wilder, more remote areas. Mountains, sea cliffs, forestry plantations, occasionally they will nest in ruined castles. In winter they wander to the coasts.

STATUS: A rather local resident which is however found in much of the suitable habitat in Ireland. It is commonest in the western coastal counties and in Wicklow. It has increased considerably in the present century.

All Year

STARLINGS

STARLING *Sturnus vulgaris* *Plate 37*
Druid

IDENTIFICATION: 22 cm (8.5"). Starlings are probably as much a part of our towns and villages as are cats and dogs. Their unpleasant screeching calls and clever mimicry are known to many. Large flocks stream over the rooftops on the way to and from their roosting places. The summer-plumaged Starling is a glossy blackish bird with purple and greenish sheens. In winter the plumage becomes duller and is covered with small pale speckles. The yellowish bill of the summer bird becomes dull in the winter. Young Starlings are greyish brown, with a whitish chin, becoming progressively darker and speckled with age until adult plumage is attained in the second year. The song of the Starling, which is often sung all the year round, is a highly individual composition. It comprises snatches from the songs of other birds and their calls.

HABITAT: Almost anywhere in the proximity of man. It resides and breeds in buildings, occupied and unoccupied, old ruins, trees, etc. It roosts in tall buildings, shipyards, trees, reedbeds, etc.

STATUS: Widespread and abundant resident, especially near human habitation. It is least abundant in the west. There is very heavy winter immigration mainly from northern Europe.

All Year

Starling

SPARROWS

HOUSE SPARROW *Passer domesticus* *Plate 43*
Gealbhan binne

IDENTIFICATION: 15 cm (6"). Everyone knows the House Sparrow. Its contented chirping greets us first thing in the morning. It has become so much associated with man's habitation that it is noticeably absent from open country where there are no houses. Due to the pollution in our cities, it is necessary to go to country villages or farms to see what clean House Sparrows really look like. The male is heavily streaked brown on the back, greyish white on the underparts and face. The nape is red brown, the cap dark grey and the chin and upper breast is black. Females and young are dull grey brown, lacking the distinctive head markings of the male. The calls are a variety of single and double chirps and cheeps. Sparrows love to dust bathe in little groups along the sides of country lanes.

HABITAT: Seldom far from human habitation, but also in hedges and fields near farms, and along roadsides.

STATUS: Widespread and very abundant resident throughout the country. It is scarce in open barren country in the west.

All Year

Tree Sparrow

TREE SPARROW *Passer montanus* *Plate 43*

Gealbhan crainn

IDENTIFICATION: 15 cm (5.5"). At a glance, this scarce little bird looks rather like a neat House Sparrow. It would be better named "ruin sparrow" rather than Tree Sparrow, as in Ireland it is found mainly in ruined buildings rather than trees. If a good view is obtained it can be seen to be more neatly marked than the male House Sparrow with a chestnut coloured cap, white cheeks with a distinctive black mark and a small black chin mark. It is generally lighter coloured than the male House Sparrow and male and female are alike in plumage. Tree Sparrow chirping is sweeter than the House Sparrow's, sounding like a high pitched "cheup". They are altogether less confiding than the commoner bird.

HABITAT: Although found in old trees in Britain and occasionally in Ireland, their main habitat is ruins of all kinds especially near the coast. They will occupy old buildings from small outhouses to large ruined castles.

All Year

STATUS: Local resident which has increased and extended its range in recent years. It is found in a good number of places along the northwest, north and east coasts and in a number of inland localities, notably around Lough Neagh.

FINCHES and BUNTINGS

CHAFFINCH *Fringilla coelebs* *Plate 44*

Rí rua

IDENTIFICATION: 16 cm (6.5"). This is our commonest finch, being found in a wide variety of habitats all over the country. The white outer tail feathers and white shoulder patches are the best identification features. The male is quite gaudy with plum-coloured face and breast, blue grey cap and nape, brown back, greenish rump and yellow feather edges on the wing. The female and young are dull brown above, light greyish brown below, but have the greenish rump and white wing and tail patches of the male. The call is an unmistakable "pink, pink" and the song is rather unremarkable except that it sounds as if it is brought to a hurried end.

HABITAT: Gardens, woods, scattered trees, orchards, parks, roadsides and almost anywhere in proximity to man. In autumn and winter flocks of Chaffinches occur in open fields, on barren headlands and elsewhere on the coasts.

STATUS: Widespread and abundant resident. There is very heavy passage migration and winter immigration of Chaffinches into Ireland. These come largely from central Europe and Scandinavia and though identification of subspecies is not reliable in the field, they look brighter and more richly-coloured than our own birds. During hard weather in continental Europe large flocks are found in stubble fields and woods throughout Ireland.

BRAMBLING *Fringilla montifringilla* *Plate 44*
Breacán

IDENTIFICATION: 15 cm (6"). This is the northern European counterpart of the Chaffinch and is decidedly like it in many ways. The white rump patch is the best field mark (the only other white-rumped finch likely to be seen in similar circumstances is the Bullfinch). In addition, the Brambling has an orange, not pinkish-red breast, and there is orange on the Brambling's wing and shoulder. The head and back of the female and winter male are dull grey brown, but the summer plumaged male has a black head and back. Bramblings are usually seen amongst other seed-eaters, and most often amongst Chaffinches where their orange breasts and white rumps reveal their presence.

HABITAT: When accompanying winter flocks of finches, they are usually found in or near woods, especially beeches. Small groups also turn up in fields and stubbles inland or near the coast, and occasionally on raised bogs.

STATUS: Fairly regular winter visitor from its Scandinavian breeding grounds. It occurs throughout Ireland, but especially in eastern coastal counties. The numbers are usually small but flocks of hundreds have been seen. Summer-plumaged birds are scarce in this country.

GREENFINCH *Carduelis chloris* *Plate 44*
Glasán darach

IDENTIFICATION: 15 cm (6"). There are only two fairly common greenish finches in this country, the Greenfinch and the Siskin. The Greenfinch is the larger and more widespread of the two. It is a stocky finch with a stout pinkish bill and with striking yellow flashes on its slate grey wings and tail. Only the male in breeding plumage is really green. The plumage of the female and male outside the breeding season is brownish green and the yellow flashes are more subdued. The young are greyer and are vaguely streaked. Greenfinches call with a nasal "dwee". Outside the breeding season Greenfinches gather with other finches into nomadic feeding flocks, sometimes numbering up to a hundred or more birds.

HABITAT: Mainly countryside hedgerows, orchards, large gardens, the edges of plantations. In the winter, farmyards, stubble fields, granaries.

STATUS: Widespread and fairly common resident. It is most abundant in good farming country with plenty of hedgerows. There is evidence of passage migration especially in the autumn.

Goldfinch

GOLDFINCH *Carduelis carduelis*
Lasair choille

Plate 44

IDENTIFICATION: 13 cm (5"). Those who have seen this bird from close range would probably agree that it is our most attractive finch. The dark red, black and white head and the bright yellow wing patch render it unmistakable. The body colour is pale brown, buffish white below. The colouring of the young is much more obscure with no distinct head markings, and there is dark streaking on the greyish brown plumage. Even the call of the Goldfinch is pleasant. It is a liquid note "plwick" which may be extended into twittering especially when the small party are feeding together. Feeding Goldfinches are a treat to watch as they cleverly extract the seeds from the tops of thistles and other wild plants, going about their business with jaunty flights and tit-like movements.

HABITAT: Goldfinches' favourite habitats are rough, untilled fields with high weeds, especially thistles. They nest in uncultivated corners of farms, orchards or unkempt large gardens.

STATUS: A widespread though somewhat thinly distributed resident. It has increased recently, and in some places winter gatherings of dozens or more are to be found. There is a small scale migration, especially on the south-east coast in the autumn.

SISKIN *Carduelis spinus*
Siscín

Plate 44

IDENTIFICATION: 12 cm (4.5"). This is the smaller of our two green-coloured finches. It occupies a different type of habitat to the Greenfinch, being more or less confined to conifer plantations. Due to their high canopy habitat it is difficult to get good views of Siskins. They are usually viewed as tit-sized greenish birds flitting from tree to tree in search of cones. Their constant twitterings and yellow wing and tail flashes are good features. Good views can sometimes be obtained in winter, especially when Siskins feed on ground weeds. The male is green, yellowish on the underparts and rump, with bright yellow sides to the tail and a double yellowish wing-bar. There is black on the crown and chin. The female is greyer and streaked below; the young are brownish and more heavily streaked.

HABITAT: The breeding habitat is in conifer plantations. In the winter our resident population, supplemented by winter visitors, wander to alder and birch trees in the lowlands. They will fly down to feed on seeds in rough ground when the occasion permits.

All Year

STATUS: Resident, breeding rather locally in most counties. Recent afforestation has caused considerable increase in our population especially in Kerry and Wicklow. Following winter immigration Siskins, often accompanied by Redpolls, are frequently found in scrub woodland.

LINNET *Carduelis cannabina* *Plate 45*
Gleoiseach

IDENTIFICATION: 14 cm (5.5"). This is a common finch of rough ground areas. Little parties of Linnets are a common feature of rough hillsides and uncultivated land near the sea. The summer-plumaged male is rich brown above, off-white below with a greyish head. There are red patches on the forehead and upper breast. The female is generally duller and greyer and streaked both above and below. The young are like the female but slightly browner. Linnets in the field show white edges to the tail and to some of the flight feathers on the wing. These are good distinguishing marks even when the Linnets are in dowdy winter plumage. The flight call is an unmusical twitter with an occasional "twee-ee". The song is a pleasant jangling usually uttered from the top of a bush or fence.

HABITAT: In the summer the breeding habitats are marginal lands such as gorse-clad commonages, rough hillsides, dunes and other coastal areas. In winter Linnets gather in flocks, some of which may be large, and feed in stubble fields. They often accompany larks and buntings.

All Year

STATUS: Common and widespread resident in suitable habitat. There is heavy passage migration through Ireland to and from western Europe. This is most noticeable in autumn along the east coasts and to the north. There is also some winter immigration.

TWITE *Carduelis flavirostris* *Plate 45*
Gleoiseach sleibhe

IDENTIFICATION: 14 cm (5.5"). Often loosely described as the upland counterpart of the Linnet, the Twite is much more than that. It is the only European representative of a group of species which are found on the high Asiatic plateau. It is very like the Linnet in shape, size, overall colour, and outside the breeding plumage in call and song. It takes an experienced eye and a good view to identify a flock of Twites in winter. If a good view is obtained, the Twite's bill can be seen to be yellow, not the dull horn-colour of the Linnet's. In summer the best feature is the pinkish rump of the male and the clear buff-coloured throat in both male and female. Otherwise, with their warm brown, heavily streaked plumage and white edged flight feathers, they look like female Linnets. The tail looks marginally longer than that of the Linnet. One of the calls from which the name is derived sounds like "twa-it".

HABITAT: Mainly wild, barren and rocky coasts and islands. They favour exposed cliff tops and mountains near the sea, but are found well inland in some places. In winter they wander in flocks and may be found on rough ground near the sea, well removed from their breeding areas.

STATUS: Thinly distributed resident along the western and northern seaboard of Ireland. It is rare elsewhere. There is evidence of migration to the north coast, probably from Scotland.

REDPOLL *Carduelis flammea* *Plate 45*
Deargéadan

IDENTIFICATION: 13 cm (5"). This little streaked brown finch is rarely found far from trees, and is usually seen flitting about in the topmost branches. Consequently close views are not easy to come by. Redpolls twitter continually whilst feeding, sometimes flying off spontaneously and returning as a close flock. The calls are a variety of trills and single notes uttered rapidly. If a good view is obtained the pinkish breast and rump of the male may be seen. Both sexes have a bright red forehead and black chin, again only visible under good conditions. There are several northern races of the Redpoll, rare visitors to this country, which are identified by their larger size, overall paler and greyer appearance, whitish wing bars and rumps. It is difficult to ascribe one of these birds to a specific race on field characters alone.

HABITAT: Redpolls are found in conifer plantations, birch, alder and willow scrub and orchards. After the breeding season they join nomadic feeding groups of other finches, notably Siskins and will feed on seeds in ground vegetation.

BLUE TIT

COAL TIT

GREAT TIT

⊗BEARDED TIT

male female

LONG-TAILED TIT

RAVEN
HOODED CROW
⊗ CARRION CROW
adult ROOK juvenile
JACKDAW
CHOUGH

TREE SPARROW

HOUSE SPARROW
male female

TREECREEPER

DUNNOCK

WREN

female
BRAMBLING
both in winter
male
CHAFFINCH
female
male
SISKIN
male
BULLFINCH
male
female
female
CROSSBILL
female
male
GOLDFINCH
GREENFINCH
juvenile
adult

TWITE
female
male
male
summer
female
LINNET
Northern
race
REDPOLL

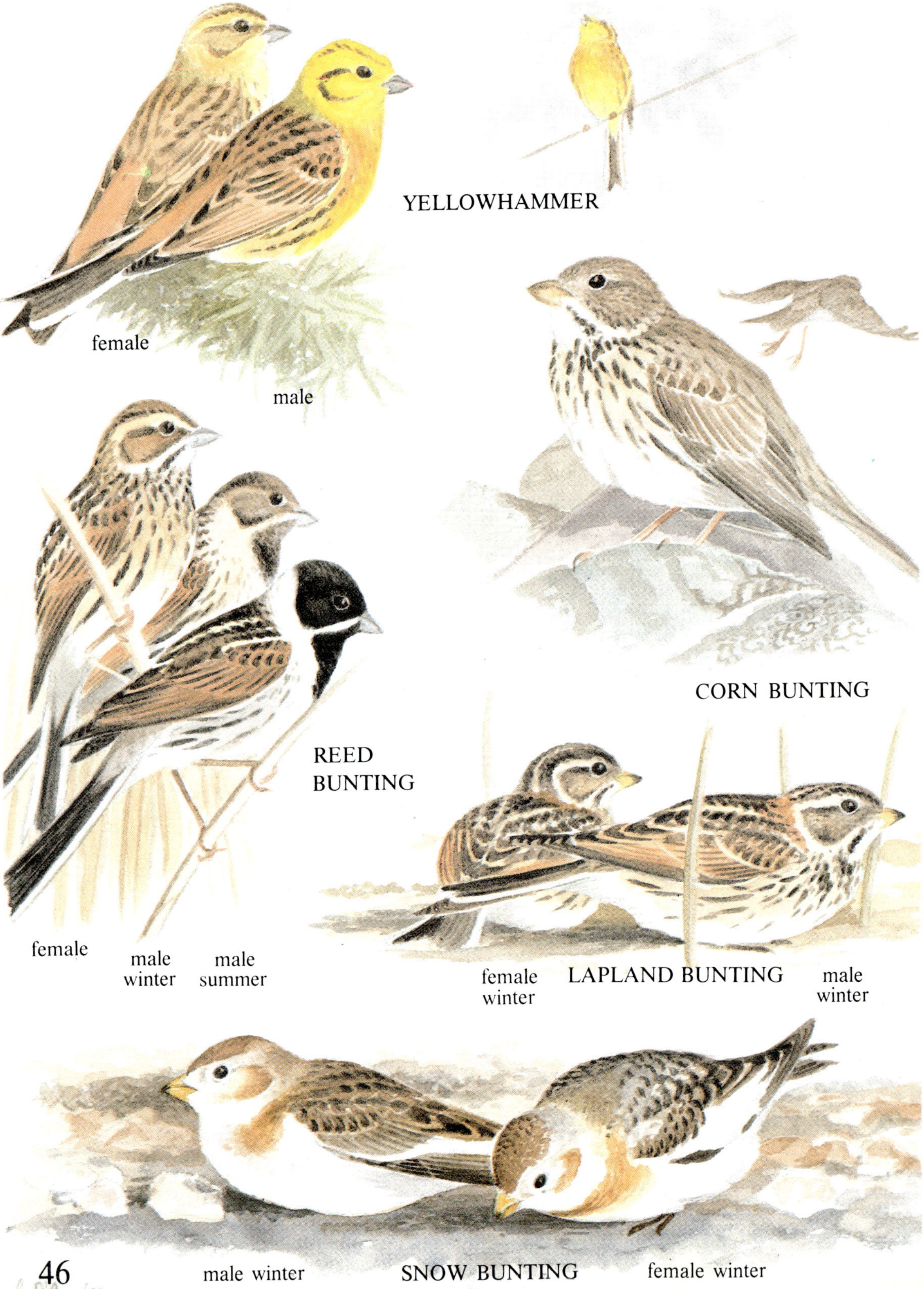
YELLOWHAMMER
female
male
CORN BUNTING
REED
BUNTING
female
male
winter
male
summer
female
winter
LAPLAND BUNTING
male
winter
male winter
SNOW BUNTING
female winter

⊗SNOW GOOSE
⊗Blue Phase
⊗AMERICAN GREEN-WINGED TEAL
male
⊗BLUE-WINGED TEAL
male
⊗AMERICAN WIGEON
male
female
male
⊗ RING-NECKED DUCK

⊗DOWITCHER
winter
⊗LESSER
YELLOWLEGS
⊗BAIRD'S SANDPIPER
⊗WHITE-RUMPED SANDPIPER
⊗WILSON'S PHALAROPE
⊗LESSER
GOLDEN PLOVER
winter

STATUS: Widely distributed and fairly common in suitable habitat. With the Irish programme of conifer afforestation, there has been a noticeable increase in the population of Redpolls in this country. The race occurring in Ireland is the Lesser Redpoll (*Acanthis flammea cabaret*). The Mealy Redpoll (*A. f. flammea*) which breeds in Northern Europe has occurred more often than the other northern races, but is nonetheless a rare visitor in autumn and winter.

All Year

CROSSBILL *Loxia curvirostra*
Crosghob

IDENTIFICATION: 14-17 cm (5.5-6.5"). Although a member of the finch family, the Crossbill has its bill unusually adapted to extract seeds from the cones of conifer trees. Periodically, they erupt from their main range on the European continent and a fraction sweep into Britain and Ireland, remaining to breed in gradually diminishing numbers until another invasion replenishes the stock. The presence of a flock in a conifer plantation may be detected by the loud "jip-jip" call note and the birds unusual preoccupation with the cones on the trees. The males are reddish, the females greenish, with the dark wings and short tails highlighting the paler rumps. Crossbills are large, stocky finches with large heads and bills, but the actual criss-cross of the tips of the bill can only be seen from very close range.

HABITAT: Coniferous forests. During eruptions they are sometimes found in isolated stands of pines. The presence of Crossbills may be detected by stripped cones on the ground, beneath the trees.

Crossbill

STATUS: Rare and irregular visitors from continental European pine forests, which arrive in flocks, some staying to nest in our conifer plantations. Invasions may be five or twenty five years apart and usually lead to the establishment of small resident populations which dwindle and disappear after a few years. The Crossbill has shown no real signs of breeding on a permanent and regular basis in this country.

BULLFINCH *Pyrrhula pyrrhula*
Corcrán coille

Plate 44

IDENTIFICATION: 15 cm (6"). It is unfortunate that this gorgeous bird is so shy. Its presence is best detected by its soft call or by a glimpse of its white rump, as it flies into cover. No other smallish bird (apart from Wheatear and Brambling) has such a striking white rump, visible in flight. The male is a dumpy finch with soft pinkish red underparts, blue grey upperparts and black wings, tail and cap. The female is dull grey above and brownish grey below but has the black tail, wings and cap of the male. There is a white patch on the rump and wings of both sexes. The juvenile has no black cap. Bullfinches call with a distinctive low whistle "be-oo".

HABITAT: Woodland clearings with underbrush, scrub, orchards, undisturbed hedgerows and large gardens.

STATUS: Widespread resident, probably a lot commoner than supposed. It is scarce or absent only in the extreme west of Connaught. There is only a suggestion of migration from the coastal bird observatories.

All Year

LAPLAND BUNTING *Calcarius lapponicus* *Plate 46*
Gealóg laplannach

IDENTIFICATION: 15 cm (6"). At first sight this northern visitor is rather like a Reed Bunting (see page 164). It is, however, stockier, with a shorter tail and only likely to be seen on the ground in this country. It is often associated with other ground feeders, especially Skylarks. The overall plumage pattern is like that of the female Reed Bunting, buffish brown with heavy dark streaks on the crown and back and lighter streaks on the underparts. There is often a rusty smudge on the sides of the neck and a dusky smudge on the breast. The white outer feathers on the tail are less obvious than on a Reed Bunting. A good feature from close range is the dull yellowish bill. The male in summer plumage has more black on the breast than the Reed Bunting and has a rusty back to the head, but this plumage is almost unknown in Ireland. The flight call is a most distinctive "trrrick — teu".

HABITAT: Mainly stubble and other fields, near the shore and on some remote headlands and islands. It is probably overlooked amongst Skylarks and other seed-eaters.

STATUS: Scarce autumn passage migrant from Northern Scandinavia (and possibly Greenland) occurring mainly on the north and northwest coasts and usually in small numbers. Exceptionally, flocks of over a hundred are seen. A few occasionally occur on migration at south coast observatories and on the east coast in winter.

SNOW BUNTING *Plectrophenax nivalis* *Plate 46*
Gealóg shneachta

IDENTIFICATION: 17 cm (6.5"). This is another open country, ground feeding bunting usually found near the coast in this country. It is gregarious, liking to stay in flocks of its own kind. A flock on the wing is a remarkable sight as the birds look largely white and dance lightly in the air, like snowflakes. From a distance they look like a wind-blown skiff of snow. Once on the ground they disappear against a sandy or stony background. The plumage is variable but is generally greyish brown above with dark mottling and buff on the head and sides of the breast. The female shows little white on the closed wing, but the male has a large white wing patch, showing clearly. The tail is dark with white outer feathers. The male in summer is largely white with a blackish back, wing tips and central tail, but this plumage is usually only seen in spring in this country. The call of the flock on the wing is a variety of trills, cheeps and a characteristic whistled "teu", reminiscent of other bunting calls.

HABITAT: Mainly coastal areas especially less disturbed flat areas with enough ground feeding to sustain the flock. Occasionally flocks are found on mountains, especially near the coast. Rarely elsewhere.

STATUS: Winter visitor mainly from Iceland. The majority are found on the north and west coasts where flocks of hundreds are sometimes seen. Smaller flocks overwinter at a number of localities on the east coast. As a migrant, it is noticed in spring and autumn mainly on the west and north coasts.

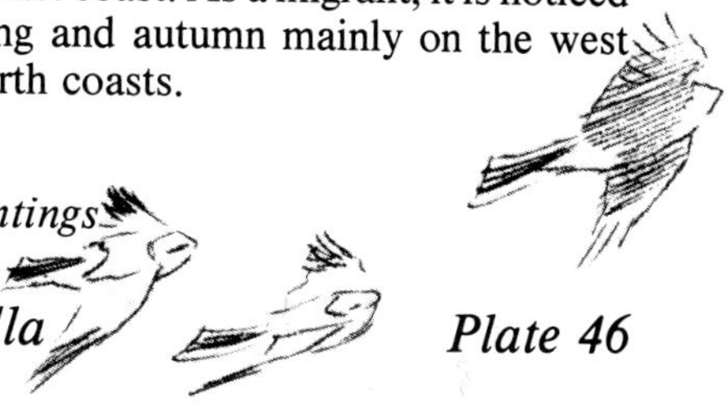

Snow Buntings

YELLOW HAMMER *Emberiza citrinella* *Plate 46*
Buíóg

IDENTIFICATION: 17 cm (6.5"). The yellowish plumage and particularly the yellow head of the male is the outstanding feature of this bunting. When singing from the top sprig of a gorse bush in bloom it is, however, remarkably inconspicuous. A close view of the male shows it to be largely yellow on the head and underparts, though with dark streaks, especially on the breast. The rich brown back is also heavily streaked and the rump is a bright red-brown. The female is duller, with a subdued yellow head and underparts. Both sexes have conspicuous white outer tail feathers which show most clearly in flight. The song is a series of fast notes followed by an extended note on a different pitch and popularised as "a little bit of bread and no cheeeese". The call is a loud "chick".

HABITAT: Very much a bird of rural areas the yellowhammer is most abundant on quiet roadside hedgerows. Also commonages, rough ground, especially gorse-covered.

STATUS: Widespread and fairly common resident. It is found in most open country, but is strangely absent from some suitable habitat, mainly in the north. It appears to have decreased recently. There is a suggestion of some autumn or winter immigration.

All Year

Ortolan Bunting

ORTOLAN BUNTING *Emberiza hortulana*
Gealóg ortoláin

IDENTIFICATION: 17 cm (6.5"). The Ortolan is a rare bunting from the European mainland which in recent years has been recorded more or less annually in Ireland. The male is quite unlike any of the common buntings, with grey-green head and breast, yellow throat and rusty underparts. The female and young birds are rather like other female buntings — they are generally brown, heavily streaked above, faintly streaked below. The outer tail feathers are white like other buntings. The best identification feature in all plumages is the semi-circular pale mark on the side of the head. This is bordered by a dark moustachial streak. Other reliable features are the pale eye-ring and the pinkish bill and legs. The call on being flushed sounds like "pwit" and is most distinctive.

HABITAT: Rough ground, stubble fields etc., often amongst other seed-eaters. It is likely that it has been overlooked.

STATUS: Rare drift migrant, almost entirely in the autumn. In recent years it has been recorded more or less annually particularly at Cape Clear Island, Co. Cork. The great majority of sightings of the Ortolan Bunting have been on the south coast of Ireland.

REED BUNTING *Emberiza schoeniclus* *Plate 46*
Gealóg ghiolcaí

IDENTIFICATION: 15 cm (6"). This is our commonest bunting. It is found in moist habitats all over the country. Reed buntings readily reveal their presence. They will stand on the tops of reeds, or waterside bushes, and call or sing to one another. The male in summer plumage is easy to recognise with its black head and throat, split by a white mark from the bill to the sides of the neck. The upperparts are red-brown, heavily streaked darker. Female and young Reed Buntings are rich brown above, paler below with heavy dark streaking both above and below. The dark cheeks are separated from the rest of the head by a thick buff line. Reed Buntings have conspicuous white outer tail feathers. The call is an arresting whistle "tsiu", and the song begins slowly but has a buzzing finish.

HABITAT: Mainly reed-beds and lake and riverside vegetation but is found in a variety of habitats sometimes far removed from water. In winter Reed Buntings feed with other finches in hedgerows and in fields.

All Year

STATUS: Widespread and abundant resident found throughout the country from the lowlands to the highlands wherever watery situations are to be found. There is evidence of migration.

CORN BUNTING *Emberiza calandra* *Plate 46*
Gealóg bhuachair

IDENTIFICATION: 18 cm (7"). This bunting like so many other brownish streaked birds, lacks identification features. Unlike many of these, however, the outer feathers of the tail are not white. Also it is rather large and dumpy in shape and has the stout bill of a bunting. In flight the legs are sometimes dangled and the flight is rather reluctant. Perhaps the best identification feature is the song, which is a most distinctive jangling, resembling the vigorous shaking of a bunch of keys. This may be sung from a post, a wall, or telegraph wires, etc.

HABITAT: Cultivated country near the coast particularly small holdings and rough tillage. Some of the western islands have small populations.

All Year

STATUS: Scarce and local resident which has declined dramatically in the past fifty years, vacating all its inland haunts. It is now confined to a number of separate coastal districts around Ireland though it is locally quite common in Mayo. There is scant evidence of migration.

LIST OF IRISH BIRDS

This is a list of all the birds of Ireland up to the time of writing — new species are being added almost annually. The 219 species recorded more than one hundred times in the past, or now recorded annually, are dealt with in the text of this book and are printed in medium type in the list below. The remaining 169 species or subspecies, printed in italics, occur less frequently and for their identification it will be necessary to consult other texts. Symbols to the left of these species give some indication of their rarity status. Species seen on only a few occasions and which are truly accidental in this country are given a solid circle ●; species seen up to 25 times and quite likely to recur are given on open circle ○; and those which have occurred between 25 and 100 times are given no symbol. It must be emphasised that many of these birds are difficult to identify in the field and painstaking notes and sketches are often necessary for their satisfactory identification. For the scientific acceptance of occurrences of all species preceeded by an asterisk in the list, such notes should be submitted to the Rarity Records Panels of the Irish Wildbird Conservancy or the Northern Ireland Ornithologists' Club for vetting. An observer should not feel too disappointed if a submitted rarity record is rejected as a great deal of experience is necessary to successfully identify many of these rare species.

Red-throated Diver
*Black-throated Diver
Great Northern Diver
● **White-billed Diver*
Little Grebe
Great Crested Grebe
*Red-necked Grebe
*Slavonian Grebe
*Black-necked Grebe
○ **Black-browed Albatross*
Fulmar
● **Bulwer's Petrel*
*Cory's Shearwater
Great Shearwater
Sooty Shearwater
Manx Shearwater
**Little Shearwater*
● **Wilson's Petrel*
Storm Petrel
*Leach's Petrel
● **Madeiran Petrel*
Gannet
Cormorant
Shag
● **Frigatebird*
*Bittern
**American Bittern*
**Little Bittern*
**Night Heron*
○ **Squacco Heron*
● **Cattle Egret*
*Little Egret
Grey Heron
● **Purple Heron*
**White Stork*
**Glossy Ibis*
*Spoonbill
Mute Swan
Bewick's Swan
Whooper Swan
*Bean Goose
*Pink-footed Goose
White-fronted Goose
—Greenland White-fronted Goose
—**European White-fronted Goose*
● **Lesser White-fronted Goose*
Greylag Goose
**Snow Goose*
*Canada Goose
Barnacle Goose
Brent Goose
**Ruddy Shelduck*
Shelduck
Wigeon

**American Wigeon*
Gadwall
Teal — European Teal
— **American Green-winged Teal*
Mallard
○ **Black Duck*
Pintail
*Garganey
**Blue-winged Teal*
Shoveler
**Red-crested Pochard*
Pochard
**Ring-necked Duck*
○ **Ferruginous Duck*
Tufted Duck
Scaup
Eider
○ **King Eider*
Long-tailed Duck
Common Scoter
**Surf Scoter*
*Velvet Scoter
Goldeneye
● **Hooded Merganser*
*Smew
Red-breasted Merganser
*Goosander
○ **Honey Buzzard*
● **Black Kite*
○ **Red Kite*
○ **White-tailed Eagle*
● **Griffon Vulture*
*Marsh Harrier
Hen Harrier
*Montagu's Harrier
**Goshawk*
Sparrowhawk
*Buzzard
**Rough-legged Buzzard*
● **Spotted Eagle*
*Golden Eagle
*Osprey
● **Lesser Kestrel*
Kestrel
● **Red-footed Falcon*
Merlin
**Hobby*
**Gyrfalcon*
Peregrine
Willow/Red Grouse — Red Grouse
Grey Partridge
*Quail
Pheasant
Water Rail
*Spotted Crake
● **Sora Rail*
○ **Little Crake*
● **Baillon's Crake*
Corncrake
Moorhen
Coot
● **American Coot*
**Crane*
● **Sandhill Crane*
○ **Little Bustard*
● **Great Bustard*
Oystercatcher
○ **Black-winged Stilt*
*Avocet
○ **Stone-curlew*
● **Cream-coloured Courser*
● **Collared Pratincole*
● **Black-winged Pratincole*
○ **Little Ringed Plover*
Ringed Plover
○ **Killdeer*
○ **Kentish Plover*
*Dotterel
**Lesser Golden Plover*
Golden Plover
Grey Plover
● **Sociable Plover*
Lapwing
Knot
Sanderling
**Semipalmated Sandpiper*
● **Western Sandpiper*
Little Stint
○ **Temminck's Stint*
○ **Least Sandpiper*
**White-rumped Sandpiper*
**Baird's Sandpiper*
*Pectoral Sandpiper
● **Sharp-tailed Sandpiper*

Curlew Sandpiper
Purple Sandpiper
Dunlin
○ **Broad-billed Sandpiper*
● **Stilt Sandpiper*
*Buff-breasted Sandpiper
Ruff
Jack Snipe
Snipe
**Great Snipe*
● **Short-billed Dowitcher*
**Long-billed Dowitcher*
Woodcock
Black-tailed Godwit
Bar-tailed Godwit
● **Eskimo Curlew*
Whimbrel
Curlew
● **Willet*
○ **Upland Sandpiper*
Spotted Redshank
Redshank
Greenshank
○ **Greater Yellowlegs*
**Lesser Yellowlegs*
○ **Solitary Sandpiper*
Green Sandpiper
Wood Sandpiper
Common Sandpiper
○ **Spotted Sandpiper*
Turnstone
**Wilson's Phalarope*
*Red-necked Phalarope
Grey Phalarope
Pomarine Skua
Arctic Skua
*Long-tailed Skua
Great Skua
**Mediterranean Gull*
● **Laughing Gull*
Little Gull
*Sabine's Gull
● **Bonapart's Gull*
Black-headed Gull
○ **Ring-billed Gull*
Common Gull
Lesser Black-backed Gull
Herring Gull
Iceland Gull
Glaucous Gull
Great Black-backed Gull
○ **Ross's Gull*
Kittiwake
○ **Ivory Gull*
● **Gull-billed Tern*
● **Caspian Tern*
● **Royal Tern*
Sandwich Tern
Roseate Tern
Common Tern
Arctic Tern
● **Bridled Tern*
Little Tern
○ **Whiskered Tern*
Black Tern
**White-winged Black Tern*
Guillemot
● **Brünnich's Guillemot*
Razorbill
Black Guillemot
*Little Auk
Puffin
**Pallas's Sandgrouse*
Rock Dove
Stock Dove
Woodpigeon
Collared Dove
Turtle Dove
● **Great Spotted Cuckoo*
Cuckoo
● **Black-billed Cuckoo*
○ **Yellow-billed Cuckoo*
Barn Owl
○ **Scops Owl*
**Snowy Owl*
● **Little Owl*
Long-eared Owl
Short-eared Owl
Nightjar
● **Needle-tailed Swift*
Swift
○ **Alpine Swift*
● **Little Swift*
Kingfisher

● *_Belted Kingfisher_
○ *_Bee-eater_
○ *_Roller_
Hoopoe
*Wryneck
● *_Green Woodpecker_
*Great Spotted Woodpecker
*_Short-toed Lark_
○ *_Lesser Short-toed Lark_
○ *_Woodlark_
Skylark
○ *_Shore Lark_
Sand Martin
Swallow
● *_Red-rumped Swallow_
House Martin
○ *_Richard's Pipit_
○ *_Tawny Pipit_
● *_Olive-backed Pipit_
*Tree Pipit
Meadow Pipit
○ *_Red-throated Pipit_
Rock Pipit
Yellow Wagtail
Grey Wagtail
Pied Wagtail
Waxwing
Dipper
Wren
Dunnock
○ *_Rufous Bush Robin_
Robin
○ *_Nightingale_
○ *_Bluethroat_
Black Redstart
Redstart
Whinchat
Stonechat
Wheatear
● *_Pied Wheatear_
● *_Black-eared Wheatear_
● *_Rock Thrush_
● *_White's Thrush_
● *_Swainson's Thrush_
Ring Ouzel
Blackbird
Fieldfare
Song Thrush
Redwing
Mistle Thrush
○ *_American Robin_
● *_Cetti's Warbler_
○ *_Fan-tailed Warbler_
● *_Pallas's Grasshopper Warbler_
Grasshopper Warbler
○ *_Aquatic Warbler_
Sedge Warbler
● *_Blyth's Reed Warbler_
*Reed Warbler
● *_Great Reed Warbler_
● *_Olivaceous Warbler_
*Icterine Warbler
*Melodious Warbler
○ *_Dartford Warbler_
○ *_Subalpine Warbler_
*_Barred Warbler_
Lesser Whitethroat
Whitethroat
Garden Warbler
Blackcap
○ *_Greenish Warbler_
● *_Arctic Warbler_
● *_Pallas's Warbler_
*Yellow-browed Warbler
● *_Dusky Warbler_
○ *_Bonelli's Warbler_
*Wood Warbler
Chiffchaff
Willow Warbler
Goldcrest
*Firecrest
Spotted Flycatcher
*Red-breasted Flycatcher
Pied Flycatcher
*Bearded Tit
Long-tailed Tit
Coal Tit
Blue Tit
Great Tit
Treecreeper
*Golden Oriole
*_Red-backed Shrike_
● *_Lesser Grey Shrike_
*_Great Grey Shrike_

**Woodchat Shrike*
Jay
Magpie
Chough
Jackdaw
Rook
Carrion/Hooded Crow
Raven
Starling
**Rose-coloured Starling*
House Sparrow
Tree Sparrow
● **Red-eyed Vireo*
Chaffinch
Brambling
○ **Serin*
Greenfinch
Goldfinch
Siskin
● **American Goldfinch*
Linnet
Twite
Redpoll
○ **Arctic Redpoll*
○ **Two-barred Crossbill*
Crossbill
● **Parrot Crossbill*
○ **Scarlet Rosefinch*
Bullfinch
**Hawfinch*
● **Black-and-white Warbler*
● **Yellow-rumped Warbler*
● **Blackpoll Warbler*
● **American Redstart*
● **Ovenbird*
● **(Summer/Scarlet) Tanager*
● **Fox Sparrow*
● **White-throated Sparrow*
● **Slate-coloured Junco*
*Lapland Bunting
Snow Bunting
Yellowhammer
● *Cirl Bunting
*Ortolan Bunting
● **Rustic Bunting*
○ **Little Bunting*
● **Yellow-breasted Bunting*
Reed Bunting
● **Black-headed Bunting*
Corn Bunting
● **Rose-breasted Grosbeak*
● **Bobolink*

FURTHER READING

de Buitléar, É. The Irish Names of Plants and Animals, Government Publications Office, Dublin. (In press).
D'Arcy, G. 1978. Birds at Lough Beg, Blackstaff Press, Belfast.
Hutchinson, C. D. 1975. The Birds of Dublin and Wicklow, Dublin.
Hutchinson, C. D. 1979. Ireland's Wetlands and their Birds, I.W.C., Dublin.
Kennedy, P. G. 1953. An Irish Sanctuary — Birds of the North Bull, 3 Candles, Dublin.
Kennedy, P. G., R. F. Ruttledge, C. F. Scroope. 1954. Birds of Ireland, Edinburgh.
Jeffrey, D. W. (ed), 1977. North Bull Island, Dublin Bay, R.D.S., Dublin.
Irish Naturalists Journal. 1937 onwards. Published by Ulster Museum, Belfast.
Irish Birds. 1977 onwards. Published by the Irish Wildbird Conservancy, Dublin.
Moriarity, C. 1967. A Guide to Ireland's Birds, Mercier, Cork.
Mitchell, F. 1978. The Irish Landscape, Collins, London.
O'Gorman, F. (ed.) 1979. The Irish Wildlife Book, Coughlan, Dublin.
Merne, O. J. 1975. The Birds of Wexford, Wexford.
Perry, K. W. 1975. The Birds of the Inishowen Peninsula, Craigavon.
Perry, K. W., S. W. Warburton. The Birds and Flowers of the Saltee Islands, Belfast. (no date given).

Roche, R., O. J. Merne. Saltees, Islands of birds and legends, O'Brien Press, Dublin. (no date given).
Ruttledge, R.F. 1966. Ireland's Birds, Witherby, London.
Ruttledge, R. F. 1975. A list of the birds of Ireland, Dublin.
Sharrock, J. T. R. 1969. Scarce migrant birds in Britain and Ireland, Poyser, Berkhamsted.
Sharrock, J. T. R. 1973. Natural history of Cape Clear Island, Poyser, Berkhamsted.
Sharrock, J. T. R. 1976. The Atlas of Breeding Birds in Britain and Ireland, Poyser, Berkhamsted.
Thompson, W. 1849–51. The Natural History of Ireland. Vol 1–3 Birds, London.
Voous, K. H. 1978. List of Recent Holarctic Bird Species, B.O.U., London.
Ussher, R. J. and R. Warren. 1900. The Birds of Ireland, Gurney and Jackson, London.
Waters, J. J. 1853. The Natural History of the Birds of Ireland, Dublin.
Whilde, T. 1977. Birds of Galway and Mayo, Galway.

USEFUL ADDRESSES

Official Agencies:
Forest and Wildlife Service, Upper Merrion Street, Dublin 2.
National Parks Division, Office of Public Works, St. Stephen's Green, Dublin 2.
Irish Biological Records Centre, Foras Forbartha, St. Martin's House, Waterloo Road, Dublin 4.
Department of the Environment, Custom House, Dublin 1.
Nature Reserves Division, Department of the Environment, Stormont, Belfast.
Forestry Service, Department of Agriculture, Dundonald House, Belfast.

Voluntary Bodies:
The Irish Biogeographical Society, c/o Department of Botany, Trinity College, Dublin 2.
Irish Deer Society, Garrihan, Sandyford, Co. Dublin.
Irish Wildbird Conservancy, South View, Church Road, Greystones, Co. Wicklow.
Irish Wildlife Federation, 8 Westland Row, Dublin 2.
National Association of Regional Game Councils
National Trust (Northern Ireland Committee), 82 Dublin Road, Belfast.
Royal Society for the Protection of Birds, Belvoir Park Forest, Belfast.
An Taisce, 41 Percy Place, Dublin 4.

Observatories:
Cape Clear Bird Observatory, Baltimore, Co. Cork.
Copeland Bird Observatory, c/o Department of Extramural Studies, Queen's University, Belfast.

ENGLISH INDEX

The Index lists only the primary entry to each species

Plate numbers Italic

IRISH INDEX

LATIN INDEX

CW01677863

MEN OF PROPERTY

Knight Frank & Rutley
20
20

MEN OF PROPERTY

Knight Frank & Rutley

THE BUILDING OF
A PARTNERSHIP

Alan Jenkins

QUILLER PRESS
LONDON

First published in 1986 by
Quiller Press Ltd
50 Albemarle Street,
London W1X 4BD

ISBN 0 907621 75 9

Typeset by Galleon Photosetting, Ipswich
Printed and bound in Great Britain by W. S. Cowell Ltd, Ipswich

Contents

Acknowledgements

As author, I would like to thank a large number of people for their help in preparing this book. First, Mr George Baker, FRICS, without whose organization of archives, meticulous filing of press cuttings, and tireless research at the British Library and elsewhere the task would have been much more difficult. Second, all those partners and staff, both active and retired, who spared the time to be interviewed and answered my layman's questions with patience and good humour – particularly the Senior Partner Mr Alan Shelley and Mr W. H. Yates; the late Mr S. K. H. Goodenough and Mr G. J. Akroyd; two retired Senior Partners, Messrs Peter Oldfield, OBE, and Geoffrey Gay; and Mr William Cunningham.

The account of the firm up to 1966 written by Mr Ronald Browne, FRICS, was especially valuable for the light it threw on the 1920s and 1930s. I am indebted to Sir Robert Frank, Bart., for the loan of correspondence and for information about his father, Sir Howard Frank, Bart., GBE, KCB, and to Lady Coningham, OBE for further details of the Frank family. Mr Anthony Coleridge, of Christie, Manson & Woods Ltd, gave me information about his father, the late Mr Guy Coleridge, MC, and Mrs Jean Heller supplied biographical details of her late husband Mr G. P. Heller, and of her father Lt.-Col. William Gibson, DSO, OBE, MC. I have also to thank the Keeper of the Library of the Victoria & Albert Museum for permission to examine all the Knight Frank & Rutley 'chattels' auction catalogues 1896–1970.

To the Senior Partner and others I should like to express my gratitude for reading the typescript and correcting a number of errors.

Among books consulted, the most useful were:

The Diary of John Holt (Henry Young & Sons, Liverpool 1948)
The War of Nigerian Unity (Sir Rex Niven) Evans Bros. 1970
The Property Boom (Oliver Marriott) Hamish Hamilton 1967
Sotheby's (Frank Herrman) Chatto & Windus 1980
Under the Hammer (Jeremy Cooper) Constable 1977
The Crystal Palace (Patrick Beaver) Hugh Evelyn 1970
The Phantom Major (Virginia Cowles) Collins 1958
A Silver Plated Spoon (John, Duke of Bedford) Cassell 1959

A.J.
1986

Picture Acknowledgements

Quiller Press would like to acknowledge the following:

1. Illustrated London News – pp. 20, 34, 82, 119, 169.
2. Imperial War Museum – pp. 55, 56, 130, 138.
3. Greater London Record Office and History Library – pp. 31, 64, 70, 129, 147, 154.
4. Photo Source – pp. 136, 139.
5. National Trust – p. 182.
6. National Portrait Gallery, London – p. 192.
7. BBC – p. 91.
8. BBC Hulton Picture Library – p. 77.
9. Pitkin Pictorials Ltd – p. 51.
10. St Brides – p. 100.
11. Yesterday's News – p. 114.
12. Country Life – p. 152.

The remainder are from Knight Frank & Rutley's own archives.

I
20 Hanover Square

I first met Knight Frank & Rutley when I was fourteen. It was in a dentist's waiting room, and I was trying to stop my hands trembling as I leafed through old copies of *Country Life*, knowing that I was going to have four teeth out because I had too many. Furthermore, I was going to have to wear a plate to push my jaw out, and that was going to make school games difficult. These fears were temporarily dispelled by advertisements of gorgeous stately homes and even castles, beautifully photographed and romantically described, with a strong feeling for history.

Knight Frank & Rutley: the names sounded sturdy and reliable. One of my hobbies, about this time, was collecting firms with frivolous names, which are plentiful in the estate agency world: Doolittle & Dally of Shrewsbury; Giddy & Giddy of Maidenhead; Reason & Tickle of Brighton; Bidwell & Sons of Cambridge, and Button, Menhenitt & Mutton of Wadebridge, Cornwall. These highly estimable practices somehow did not have the same ring of confidence as Knight Frank & Rutley. Knight Frank & Rutley sounded so *British*. A recent opinion poll has shown that they are among the four best-known names in property. In the 1930s, when there were more but smaller property firms, it was enough for Flanagan and Allen to invent an estate agency called 'Knife Fork and Cutlery' to produce a gale of laughter because everyone in the audience knew whom they meant.

As I grew up, I felt I had known Knight Frank & Rutley all my life. They perhaps represented something unattainable. I imagined them as a cosy club of old Etonians buying and selling castles, or at least Elizabethan mansions, for (and to) other old Etonians. Knight Frank & Rutley are by no means ashamed of their undoubted pre-eminence in the country house market, and – yes – they do have some old Etonians; but they would like it better known that they do other things as well, and in sixty-five different countries.

Today they describe themselves as the most comprehensive property service in the world. They could, if they were boastful people, make all of the following claims: 'We sold the Crystal Palace in 1911.' 'We sold Stonehenge in 1915.' 'We sold Chartwell to Winston Churchill – *and* his town house in Hyde Park Gate.' 'We sold the Wembley Exhibition . . .' 'We sold the contents of the old German Embassy in 1945.' And it is not easy to know how to reply when a partner barely on the threshold of middle age tells you: 'I suppose I must have sold £100 million pounds worth of country estates since I've been here.'

Between April 1896, when they opened for business, and the mid 1980s (the approximate compass of this book), they have handled well over 100,000 properties of all sizes. They have been called 'the Rolls-Royce', even 'the Cartiers' of the property world. Knight Frank & Rutley found most of the land for Broadcasting House to be built, and have recently acted for the BBC in the purchase of the 'new Broadcasting House' at the White City. They have for twenty-five years been surveyors to The All-England Lawn Tennis and Croquet Club at Wimbledon. They are also surveyors to Lords. A few years ago they launched the first (and so far the only) international property investment group, which is quoted on the Amsterdam Stock Exchange. They have sold or bought almost every habitable island (and even one or two unhabitable ones) off the coast of Britain. They carried out, a few years ago, what is believed to be the biggest-ever valuation for a client whose properties were worth £12,000 million.

You begin to see what they mean by *comprehensive*. They are neither the biggest nor the oldest firm of property consultants. Jones Lang Wootton are bigger in the United Kingdom. Cushman Wakefield are bigger in America. Savills, who can trace themselves back to the eighteenth century, and Strutt & Parker are both older. Knight Frank & Rutley employ about 1300 people throughout the world, 300 of them in Britain. Their autonomous overseas offices nowadays yield a large percentage of all their business – in Belgium, France, New York, Nigeria (six offices), Zimbabwe, Hong Kong, Singapore, Botswana and Australia. Their commercial departments have become much larger than their residential, a trend which has been going on for the last twenty years. They have experience of working in (as some of them like to say) 'every continent except Antarctica', but if ever some smart developer starts a leisure complex at the South Pole, one feels that Knight Frank and Rutley will soon be there.

The overwhelming atmosphere of their headquarters at 20 Hanover Square, in the West End of London, is of stability. Quiet suits, conservative ties, hair worn shortish, very few beards; and young men call you Sir. Many of them look like Guards officers in mufti (some of them are). You get the impression that people enjoy working here, and that most will stay for ever. Even Oliver Marriott, stern critic of the property world in his book *The Property Boom*, doffs his cap to Knight Frank & Rutley and can find only one word for them: 'prestigious'. The word implies ethical principles about which Knight Frank & Rutley are stricter than some. The partnership deeds state that no partner may deal in property or even own property shares. It is clearly understood that this is a profession first and a business second (not that profit is by any means a dirty word) and that its job is to represent buyers or sellers, without having any personal interest in a deal.

They do not like to drop names, but interrogation reveals that they have, over the years, numbered among their clients various landowning Dukes, Rosa Lewis of the Cavendish Hotel, the Astors, the Beatles, Cabinet Ministers of both right and left persuasions, Lord Samuel, Lord Weinstock, Noël Coward, Lord Forte and Adam Faith.

Some idea of the complexity of the contemporary property scene may be gathered from a quick tour of Knight Frank & Rutley's departments at 20 Hanover Square, and at nearby 3 and 5 Hanover Square. 'Development' can mean finding a site for an industrial estate or an office block in Epsom or Paris, or helping to plan a new shopping centre in Aberdeen. It can involve, at the beginning, a feasibility study; and later on, arranging finance, assembling the professional team, managing the project and eventually letting or selling the completed building, for either occupation or investment. All this will demand expert knowledge of property legislation, planning and taxation.

Knight Frank & Rutley (Nigeria) were project managers for the new town of Agbara, about 40 km from Lagos. Knight Frank & Rutley (London) did the same kind of job for the British Government at Wickhams Cay in the Virgin Islands. Beside the Nile in Cairo, a very large office, shopping and residential development, Cairo Plaza, has arisen as a four-storey podium, dominated by two thirty-storey towers, the whole providing 57,000 square metres of space. Knight Frank & Rutley advised on the feasibility and financing.

Surveying is the basic skill of the property world, and it has to be a continuing process. From the initial feasibility report through the selection of a contractor to the supervision and cost control of the building operation, Knight Frank & Rutley accept complete responsibility. They prepare regular fire insurance reviews, and even offer a specialist service for interior design, decoration and furnishing.

Knight Frank & Rutley, acting for leading industrial companies, property companies and investing institutions, acquire, sell and let industrial property, advise on rent reviews, negotiate lease renewals and arrange valuations of factories, warehouses, depots and garages. For their clients BP the London office have sold research laboratories in Surrey, a complex of research and office buildings, and for BP, we shall see in a later chapter, they brought off one of the biggest property transactions of all time.

The value of property is affected by an increasing number of influences: inflation, recession or its opposite, interest rates – so that regular revaluation is needed. For balance sheets, company mergers and takeovers, new issues, for clients who may be banks or insurance companies, trusts, pension funds, commercial valuations are a basic function of the business. In an enormous range of valuation tasks, it is an advantage if plant, machinery, land and buildings can all be valued by the same firm.

'Office rents,' it is often said, 'are one of the barometers of the economy.' Knight Frank & Rutley's Offices Department is divided into City, West End and Suburban and Provincial. It both finds accommodation for clients, according to their specific requirements, and markets office space. It negotiates rent reviews and lease renewals; and for this it is especially necessary to have a detailed knowledge of rental agreements in each particular district.

The last twenty years have seen a revolution in the pattern of shopping – the self-service supermarket, the hypermarket outside towns, the traffic-free shopping precinct; all these things have affected the value of shop property. That Knight Frank & Rutley's specialized Shops Department buys and sells shops goes without saying. It also advises retailers and landlords, at home and abroad, on all aspects of shop property, especially now that investors, both private and institutional, are increasingly interested in it – and this can mean rent reviews, lettings, disposals and negotiations involving the Landlord and Tenant Act.

Hotels, perhaps even more than offices, are an indicator of the economy. For their clients Trust House Forte, the firm have undertaken a wide variety of tasks. They search for suitable properties and sites, negotiate purchases; prepare reports and valuations for mortgages, debenture, balance sheet and Stock Exchange purposes. Grosvenor House Hotel, Park Lane, is one of many properties valued for Trust House Forte; and for Princess Properties International, formerly one of the D. K. Ludwig group of companies, the firm revalued the Acapulco Princess Hotel, one of the great luxury hotels of the world with over 700 bedrooms and conference facilities for 2500.

Knight Frank & Rutley have a large number of clients interested in investing in property; pension funds, insurance companies, property unit trusts, property companies and private clients. This market is becoming more international: Knight Frank & Rutley's Paris office bought, for their clients, Bovis, a large office block, Chantecoq, while it was still being built, and also became its letting agents.

In the management of urban property, the nitty-gritty of management goes far beyond the collection of rent. Many owners of such property lack the expertise to look after valuation, rating, planning law, intricate insurance problems, and ensuring that tenants honour their obligations. Repairs, engaging staff, rent revision – these headaches are better dealt with by professionals.

Within the collective experience of Knight Frank & Rutley is a vast knowledge of town and country planning, with its maze of legislation. Compensation, compulsory purchase, planning applications, appeals and ways of dealing with 'trade disturbance' – we shall see them all deployed, later on, in the long task of moving Covent Garden Market to Vauxhall.

We shall see that, in the ninety years of their existence, Knight Frank & Rutley, as estate agents, began with country houses, estates and farms, and these have largely constituted their public 'image'.

Institutional investors are increasingly interested in farms; there are still an astonishing number of people (some foreign) who want to buy grouse moors, deer forests and fishing rights.

It would be false modesty to deny the firm's pre-eminence in this field. But they do not merely buy and sell country estates and farms: they manage them too. Not every man who invests in a farm knows how to run it. Even those who do are often grateful for advice. Knight Frank & Rutley can do this internationally through their agricultural services, which operate abroad (particularly in Africa). These services are being used for internationally sponsored agricultural projects in the developing countries. Budgeting, costing, cropping, stocking; maintenance and modernization of farm buildings . . .

In the United Kingdom, managing estates may involve everything from farm management and profitability to sporting facilities, care of timber, drainage schemes, rent revisions and collection, taxation advice, even 'provision of facilities for tourists' if the estate is attached to a stately home. 'On-going' managements of thousands of acres are usually carried out from the firm's branches in Hereford, Hungerford, Shrewsbury and Sherborne.

'London Residential', the department concerned with some of the most spectacular house and flat properties in the West End and an area roughly defined by the borders of the former Greater London Council, lives appropriately near Sloane Square. The firm says candidly that it deals in properties 'in the most exclusive and expensive parts of London'. Later on in this book we shall see that it is possible to pay over £1,250,000 for a town house in Belgravia – never mind a mansion in Regent's Park.

The story of Knight Frank & Rutley is really one view of the social and commercial history of Britain and Europe in the twentieth century. It is worth while looking at land ownership from medieval times onward, in order to see how and why estate agents became, with increasing specialization and professional qualification, 'property consultants'.

By the seventeenth century the great ducal estates were being built up by the simple process of buying out small squires, crippled by the detested Land Tax (four shillings in the pound, at its worst) which financed the wars of William III and Marlborough. The Dukes of Bedford, two of whom would one day become clients of Knight Frank & Rutley, were archetypes of this kind of landowner. Yet they would farm more efficiently, grow more food – until the Empire came, with huge imports of cheap food from abroad, especially duty-free grain from America. Then followed the agricultural slump of the 1870s and the first signs of the breaking-up of great estates. In 1894 Sir William Harcourt, the Gladstonian Liberal Chancellor of the Exchequer, introduced a memorable budget which equalized the Death Duties on real and personal property. Suddenly we can see the topicality, in *The Importance of Being Earnest* (1895), of Lady Bracknell's observations on land, as she interrogates Jack Worthing about his suitability to marry Gwendoline. She is relieved to hear that his income comes from investments and not from land: 'What between the duties expected of one during one's lifetime, and the duties expected from one after one's death, land has ceased to be either a profit or a pleasure. It gives one position and prevents one from keeping it up. That's all that can be said about land.'

From about 1880 the old belief in the 'safety' of landowning had begun to decline. So had rents. Stately homes were already changing hands – from aristocrats to businessmen who had made their pile. Fabulously wealthy landowners like the Dukes of Westminster and Bedford were becoming professional, assisted by professional advisers. In the 1750s Samuel Driver called himself 'seedsman, nurseryman and surveyor'. In the 1820s it was possible for Jonathan Savill, founder of another great firm of property consultants, to describe himself as 'architect, builder, land agent and surveyor' without having any qualification to write after his name. His son Alfred, some thirty years later, called himself 'land agent, surveyor and auctioneer'. Both might have added the word 'valuer', but this was not yet recognized as a separate function.

Howard Frank auctions Peasmarsh Place near Rye on 23 October 1912. In 1910 Knight Frank & Rutley had offered over 93,000 acres for sale – roughly 35 per cent of the total sales in Britain for that year.

Country estates, in the latter half of the eighteenth century, were often managed by 'surveyor-stewards': they were known in Scotland as 'factors' or (in the case of the Dukes of Argyll) 'chamberlains'. Farmers and land surveyors (who used to be known as 'measurers and mappers') tended to do their own valuation. By the 1820s lawyers were doing a good deal of land agency and estate management (especially for absentee landlords): hence the term 'attorney-steward'. One of the great stimulants of valuation was the Railway Boom of the 1840s, when land had to be valued for compulsory purchase.

Professionalization began loosely with the Land Surveyors' Club of 1834. In 1868 came the Institution of Surveyors which, after the periodic changes of name and a Royal Charter, became in 1946 the Royal Institution of Chartered Surveyors. Auctioneers and Valuers also had their professional bodies. Auctioneering has changed a great deal since the great James Christie, 'King of Epithets', who in the 1770s had something of the oratorical style of the Victorian music-hall Master of Ceremonies. The founder of Christie's used to invite offers in such words as 'the inexhaustible munificence of your superlatively candid generosity must harmonize with the refulgent brilliance of this little jewel . . .' His main rival was George Robins, to whose performance Thackeray devotes most of Chapter XVII of *Vanity Fair*.

Today an auctioneer really knows what he is selling, avoids rhetoric and has all the answers ready. We shall see that Howard Frank, in particular, had a considerable influence on the technique of auctioneering. In other ways larger than life, Frank was a model of brevity on the rostrum. On the threshold of the twentieth century he and his two partners were entering a partly-professionalized world of property: it was as if that world were waiting to receive them.

II
9 Conduit Street

The twentieth century was four years away; the old Queen, now seen only as a tiny figure in black, riding in her carriage at Windsor or Osborne, was approaching her Diamond Jubilee; the South African War would soon begin to destroy the self-confidence of the British Empire; there was a craze for riding bicycles; a very few people drove motor-cars at a speed-limit of 14 miles per hour; a certain Signor Marconi had just shown that something called wireless telegraphy was possible; and everybody was singing songs from *The Geisha*, a musical comedy at Daly's Theatre starring Marie Tempest.

On Saturday, 11 April 1896, the auction and estate page of *The Times* carried the following advertisement:

> 'MESSRS KNIGHT FRANK & RUTLEY, Auctioneers, Surveyors and Valuers, the Conduit Street Galleries, 9 Conduit Street W1, undertake the SALE by public AUCTION or private Treaty, of TOWN and COUNTRY properties, Ground-rents, Reversions, Life Policies, Annuities, Negotiations of Mortgages, Partnerships, Arrangement of Compensation Claims, the letting of Furnished Mansions, Flats, Business Premises etc.' They also 'begged to announce . . . that their handsome, well-lighted GALLERIES are now OPEN for the reception of PICTURES, Plate, Jewellery, Books, Prints, Bronzes, China and other Art Property, choice Furniture, private Cellars of Wine, etc intended for sale by public auction. Valuations for probate or other purposes.'

Within a few weeks their advertisements admitted stamps, medals, coins, sporting guns, fishing rights and musical and scientific instruments. The original letterheads show no telephone number, though there was a telegraphic address: GALLERIES, London. The telephone arrived in 1900: 1942 GERRARD. There were no typewriters until well into Edward VII's reign: were not typewriters rather vulgar?

9 Conduit Street (now the London headquarters of Christian Dior) was built in 1779 by James Wyatt and is believed to have been 'the first stucco-ed house in London'. It seems to have set one aspect of Knight Frank & Rutley's style: the preference for living in eighteenth-century houses.

John Frederick Horace Knight, 38, was an auctioneer, specializing in *objets d'art* and old furniture. Howard George Frank, 25, had had a brief training with Eiloart & Inman, a firm of estate agents now incorporated in Daniel Watney, Eiloart, Inman & Nunn, of Charterhouse Square, EC, and a few years with Alexander Turner of 199 Piccadilly (afterwards the site of Lyons' Popular Cafe), with branch offices in Guildford, Weybridge, Reading and Howard Frank's home town, Tunbridge Wells. William Rutley, 42, was an expert in valuing antiques, especially paintings.

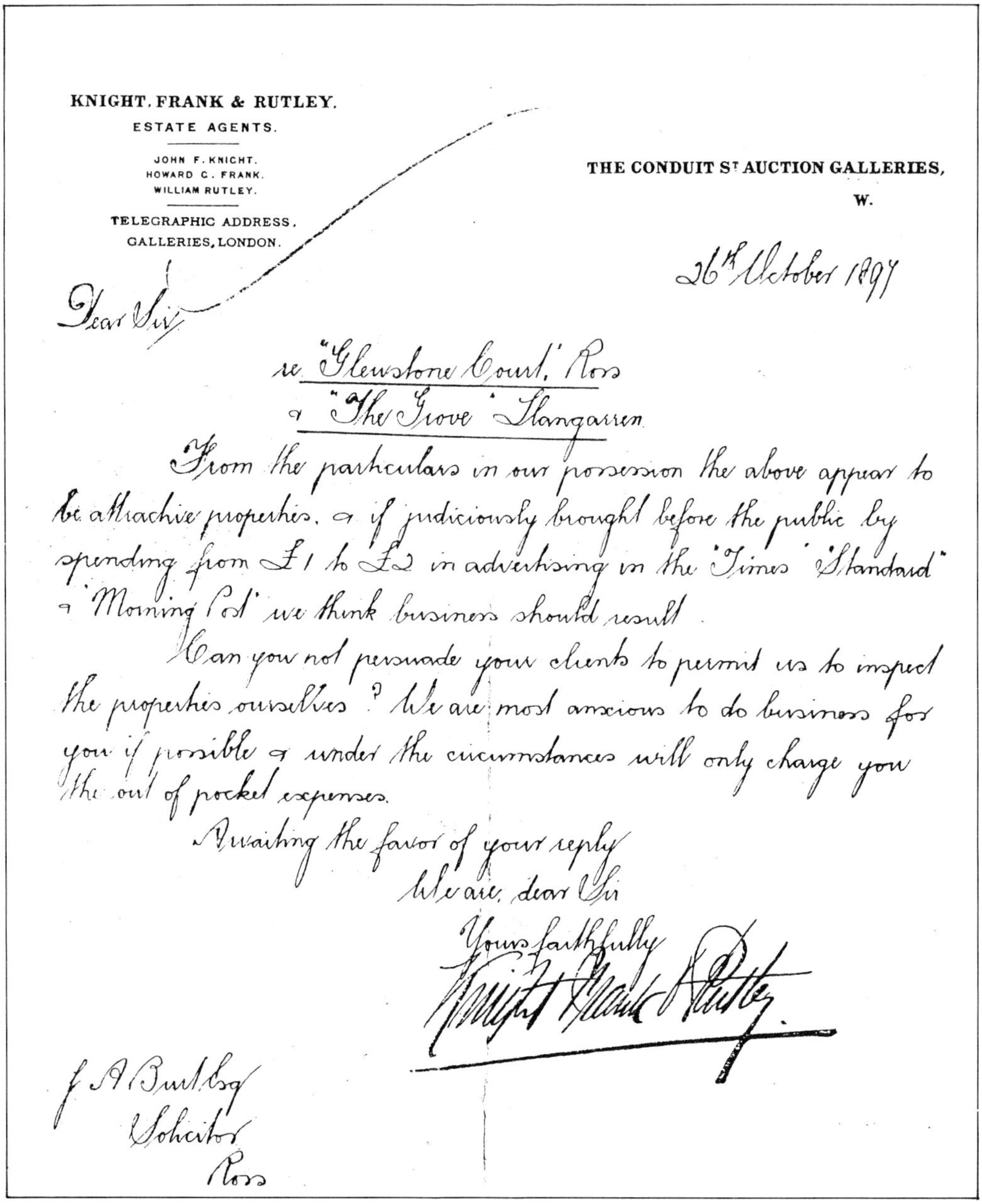

KNIGHT, FRANK & RUTLEY.
ESTATE AGENTS.
JOHN F. KNIGHT.
HOWARD C. FRANK.
WILLIAM RUTLEY.
TELEGRAPHIC ADDRESS, GALLERIES, LONDON.

THE CONDUIT St AUCTION GALLERIES,
W.

26th October 1897

Dear Sir

re "Glewstone Court," Ross
& "The Grove" Llangarren

From the particulars in our possession the above appear to be attractive properties, & if judiciously brought before the public by spending from £1 to £2 in advertising in the "Times" "Standard" & "Morning Post" we think business should result.

Can you not persuade your clients to permit us to inspect the properties ourselves? We are most anxious to do business for you if possible & under the circumstances will only charge you the out of pocket expenses.

Awaiting the favor of your reply
We are, dear Sir
Yours faithfully
Knight Frank & Rutley

J A Burt Esq
Solicitor
Ross

An early letter from the Conduit Street Auction Galleries. Already the value of advertising was being stressed as a means to obtaining instructions.

We do not know precisely how the three partners met. Oral tradition, which is remarkably circumstantial, says that they used to spend fishing holidays together at Rose Cottage, Shaldon, on the south bank of the river Teign, and that the idea of going into partnership was John Knight's. The firm was to be called Rutley Frank & Knight, and it is referred to as such in the original articles of partnership of 3 October 1895, which were valid for fourteen years.

The Conduit Street Galleries. At the turn of the century the greater part of the business was conducted in the auction rooms. John Knight was an auctioneer specialising in objets d'art and old furniture. William Rutley was an expert in valuing antiques, especially paintings.

The firm's capital was £5400: Rutley and Frank provided £2500 each and Knight £400. No partner was to receive more than £400 a year in profits, and after five years any accumulated profits were to be used for repaying capital, on which there was no interest. The partners from the start planned for expansion: they had acquired 23a Maddox Street at the back of No. 9 and within three years had taken No. 10 as well. The rent was £750 a year, of which they recovered £102 by sub-letting office space to other firms. 'Restoration and fitting' cost them over £1000 and in the first year of trading they spent £1800 on advertising and printing. From the outset they established a bold, not to say lavish, style of publicity.

The first-ever sale at Conduit Street Galleries, on 23 April 1896, was the contents of a house called Weybourne in Portmore Park, Weybridge, for a total of £270 13*s*. The 'chattels' side of the business made a profit from the outset; but the estate agency, started from scratch, was doing likewise within three years. This was due to the immense drive of the youngest partner: not for nothing was Howard Frank called 'Pusher' by his staff. That staff, by 1900, was still less than twenty strong, but it included Arthur Knight, John's son, who had joined in 1896 as a youth of 17, and Frank Capon, who joined in 1900 at the age of 31. Arthur Knight, later a partner, became a famous auctioneer of the contents of mansions and of art collections. Frank Capon had trained for thirteen years with Ralph Clutton at Reigate, where he had gained a great deal of experience in farms, timber and land agency. He became the firm's chief surveyor and agricultural valuer. We have very few records of the firm's first estate transactions: in 1901, however, a register kept in copperplate handwriting

The jewels of 'the Wagnerian King'. Some of the jewels belonging to King Ludwig of Bavaria, the mad king, which were sold in the Conduit Street Galleries in October 1903.

shows property No. 707, a house named Heath Gate, on Rushall Common, Tunbridge Wells, as having been sold on 2 February.

Howard Frank's dominating height – 6 ft 3 in. – added to a totally authoritative manner and unhesitating directness of approach made him a formidable figure in business. He could not afford to be wrong, and seldom was. As an auctioneer his opening remarks were brief and to the point. The skill lay in gently forcing bidders to make up their minds. And he had an original touch of showmanship: instead of the traditional hammer he used a short blackthorn shillelagh or knobkerry.

His was anything but a rags-to-riches story. The family wealth came from Livett Frank & Sons, founded in 1840 by Howard's grandfather, an artist's colourman who branched out into manufacturing paint, varnishes and 'oils of every description'. They were ship's chandlers, sail-makers, ship painters, suppliers of all ships' stores, and the mainstay of their work was Admiralty contracts, to service which they had depots at Victoria & Albert Docks, London, and at Southampton and Gosport. Their London offices were at 22 Borough High Street, SE, and 52 Leadenhall Street, EC.

The Frank family motto, unexpectedly modest for the flamboyant personality of young Howard, was *Non Omnibus Nati* ('We are not born to all things', which has been frivolously mistranslated by his children as 'Not born in a bus'). The family

Howard Frank was quick to appreciate the value of showmanship. He soon discarded the traditional auctioneer's hammer in favour of a silver-bound blackthorn shilleglagh.

home was on an estate in Tunbridge Wells called Blackhurst (it is now a home for nurses). Howard, son of Frederick Frank's first marriage, was educated at Marlborough College and afterwards, instead of going to university, spent a year or two at Château de Prangins, a sort of male finishing school at Königsfelt in the Black Forest. In the year of his firm's foundation, 1896, he had married a Tunbridge Wells girl, Mabel Helen Arnold. They began their married life at Northaw, Potters Bar, where Howard could indulge his passion for horses: at this time he owned a gelding, Roderick Dhu, a prize-winner said to have been 'the finest mover in harness ever seen'.

A new magazine, *Country Life*, had been started in 1897 by a country-loving businessman, Edward Hudson, to give his printing works something to do. Hudson glamorized the country, made successful businessmen long to live in it, secure in the knowledge that by selling up and buying land one could become at least a sort of gentleman. From its outset Howard Frank cultivated a special relationship with *Country Life*, paying record prices for key advertising positions. A landmark was Howard Frank's first full-page in the magazine (27 August 1898) resplendent with photographs (a rarity in those days), which also gives a clear idea of the country property market in which the firm was to become pre-eminent. 'OVERLOOKING THE WYE . . . Elizabethan MANSION . . . grounds of indescribable beauty . . .' And, to remind us of the recent gold and diamond rush in the Transvaal, 'TO WEALTHY SOUTH AFRICANS AND CITY MEN – NORTH OF LONDON – To be SOLD, A FREEHOLD RESIDENTIAL ESTATE . . . suitable for those desirous of entertaining largely . . .' The firm also seeks clients who require 'management of landed estates'.

By 1902 the property department was already overtaking the 'chattels' side of the business. But 1903 was a year of disaster which might have destroyed the firm altogether had not the three partners shown exceptional courage and wisdom. It would have been a bad year anyway: they were discovering how usefully a steady bread-and-butter income from valuations could improve a balance-sheet. Nevertheless, the partners could barely afford their own salaries of £400 a year. Far worse was to follow.

On 12 October *The Times* and other papers carried an advertisement announcing an auction, at Conduit Street Galleries, of jewellery, all the main pieces of which were listed. The sale was to take place 'on Friday, 16 October at one o'clock precisely'. Those who came on 'day prior', Thursday, were not all buyers. Some were highly professional thieves. Let the *Morning Post* of Saturday, 17 October, take up the story in its flatulent way:

GREAT JEWELLERY ROBBERY
Heavy Loss

> 'An extensive robbery of jewellery, amounting in value from £8000 to £10,000, took place during Thursday night at the premises of Messrs Knight Frank & Rutley, auctioneers, Conduit Street.
>
> Several firms had placed collections of valuables in the hands of the auctioneers for sale yesterday, and these were on view to intending purchasers throughout Thursday, while a sale of furniture was also conducted on the premises during the day. Messrs Knight Frank & Rutley's galleries were, therefore, practically open to the public and no difficulty would have been experienced by either an individual thief or an organised gang of thieves in making themselves fully acquainted with the interior of the premises and the whereabouts of the jewels . . .
>
> Detective Inspector Drew of Vine Street station thought the thieves had hidden on the premises overnight and used duplicate keys to unlock the safes.'

It is clear that the firm's insurance cover was quite inadequate. Although they had some theoretical measure of protection in the phrase 'at owner's risk', their reputation, after only seven years' existence, was in jeopardy. The partners decided to raise enough money to pay every vendor not only the reserve price, but a percentage to cover 'possible auction expectations'. In a letter to *The Times* dated 16 October (the morning the robbery was discovered), they offered a reward of £500 for information leading to the conviction of the robbers and the recovery of the goods, which they listed.

The compensation money was raised at least partly by two loans from William Rutley, some of which was still outstanding at his death six years later. It is believed that Howard Frank's father, Frederick Frank, also came to the rescue.

All through his life, Howard Frank was adept at extracting advantage from adversity and personal credit from the threat of disaster. It is not difficult to detect his power of decision and swiftness of action in the affair of the robbery. In the long run the publicity did the firm nothing but good.

There is no evidence that any of the stolen goods were recovered, and the end of the next financial year (August 1904) showed another substantial loss. But honour

The Great Jewel Robbery – the accused in court. On the night of Thursday, 15 October 1903 almost the entire collections of jewellery which were due to be auctioned the next day were stolen from the gallery. Although the culprits were quickly brought to book, the haul was never recovered.

had been saved, and a loyal client (Messrs Jones & Son, of 19 Long Acre) wrote to the *Morning Post* praising the firm and reaffirming their trust in them.

The estate market was in the middle of a short depression, of which the 1903 results had been a symptom. Yet by 1906 the firm's turnover had grown by nearly 50 per cent. Both property and chattels did well, but the expansion of the property side was spectacular, helped by a new branch office at Tattenham Park, Tadworth, Surrey. The growing professional reputation of Howard Frank in handling landed estates was recognized, in 1905, by his election to the Council of the Royal Agricultural Society; and the following year John Knight became a Fellow of the Auctioneers' and Estate Agents' Institute.

Even during the property recession years, the firm was handling some quite big deals, for example the Staughton Manor estate in Huntingdonshire, 'comprising the manor house and the picturesque village of Great Staughton'; Joyce Grove estate, Nettlebed, Oxfordshire, 'of about 2000 acres with a fine Mansion on the Chiltern Hills'; Orcop Grange, Herefordshire; and in London, business premises at 223 and 223a Regent Street, and the town mansion of the Earl of Caledon, 5 Carlton House Terrace, acquired for Anthony J. Drexel, the American banker. Lord Caledon, one of the great landowners of the day, owned 30,000 acres, most of them in Co. Tyrone.

The Earl of Chesterfield's Holme Lacy estate, between Hereford and Ross-on-Wye, was the outstanding estate sale of 1909. It was to feature more than once in the firm's affairs. The estate was re-sold in 1922 and Holme Lacy House was again on the firm's books in the summer of 1985.

In 1907 a young man of 27, Herbert Davis Kelleway, joined the firm as manager of the Country Department. A future partner, he was to become the son-in-law of A. J. Burrows, of Ashford, Kent, who would one day join forces with Knight Frank & Rutley and become Senior Partner. Another future partner, Charles J. Woosnam, joined in the same year: he was a specialist in furniture auctions and valuations.

Lord Chesterfield.

Frank Capon, whose earthy personality contrasted oddly with Howard Frank's, was the indispensable backroom man who inspected and surveyed properties, prepared valuations and sale 'particulars', and clerked the auctions – but never conducted them.

It is possible that John Knight resented the mercurial rise of his younger partner Frank, whose estate sales did not always bring in chattels to be sold. Knight had, after all, a considerable reputation: as Sotheby's was known for rare books, so Knight was known for antique furniture. Towards 1908 the two firms had a number of meetings to discuss a possible merger. Sotheby's (then known as Sotheby, Wilkinson & Hodge, with premises in Wellington Street, and Tom Hodge as sole proprietor) had already offered themselves to another firm of auctioneers specializing in books, Hodgsons of Chancery Lane, for only £6500. It was suggested that Knight Frank & Rutley might like to come in on the deal. But in February 1908 J. E. Hodgson politely turned the whole scheme down.

In July negotiations were re-opened. Tom Hodge now wanted Hodgson to pay £10,000 for a third share in Sotheby's: Knight Frank & Rutley impatiently offered *their* third share in cash on the nail. The two bookmen looked uneasily at each other, as if they were frightened of the man nicknamed 'Pusher'. One could not imagine them in partnership. The talks fell through, both Hodgson and Hodge had motor-car accidents, Hodge went to Llandrindod Wells to take the waters, and the merger was not mentioned again for four years.

This was one of William Rutley's last appearances: on Saturday, 6 March 1909, he died at the early age of 55. 'Mr Rutley's speciality was the valuation of works of art and objects of antiquity of nearly every description,' said *The Times* in its obituary. 'To this work he brought a natural aptitude, which had been cultivated by a careful study in the art galleries of Europe, and developed in the course of a long and busy career.' The *Estates Gazette* praised his 'wide culture and exceptionally fine taste' and his 'quiet and unassuming disposition'. He had been on the rostrum at a jewel sale only the day before his death, which was due to a heart attack.

Ever since the Great Jewel Robbery, the amount spent on publicity had been double what it was before 1903, and absorbed 25 per cent of the firm's gross income. Not until 1909 was this percentage reduced, for by then the firm's profitability was assured until war broke out in 1914. Property sales between 1903 and 1909 had quadrupled – a tribute to the power of advertising. And not only advertising: property sales made news in their own right, and Howard Frank was a master of what we now call public relations.

The outstanding estate sale of 1909 was that of the Earl of Chesterfield's Holme Lacy, between Hereford and Ross-on-Wye. The auction was held not at Conduit Street but at the Mart in Tokenhouse Yard, EC. Howard Frank may have had a reputation for not wasting words on the rostrum, but he was almost emotional when he offered Holme Lacy on 29 July 1909. For one thing, it appealed to his strong sense of history. Walter de Lacy had settled there soon after the Norman Conquest. It had passed into the Scudamore family, one of whom had been the patron of the poet Spenser, who had immortalized him as 'Sir Scudamore' in *The Faerie Queene*. Charles I had been entertained there during the Civil War. Pope had been inspired by it to write a poem, *Man of Ross*.

'Unquestionably one of the most beautiful seats in England,' the estate comprised 5596 acres, 250 of which were a deer park; nine miles of salmon fishing on the Wye; eighteen farms and 'several villages'; 749 acres of woods with excellent shooting; and a rent-roll of £7000 per annum. The mansion, only 200 years old and thus not 'noble', yet 'notable', was enriched with Grinling Gibbons carvings; more practically, there were four bathrooms and twenty servants' rooms.

Howard Frank was in no hurry to use his shillelagh. The estate, he emphasized, had not been placed on the market merely to test its value: Lord Chesterfield, Lord Steward of the Royal Household, firmly intended to sell. The land was some of the best in the country: in his experience, the best land was the cheapest in the long run. Moreover, this was a class of property which would not be seriously affected by the Budget (we shall see in a moment that this was a shrewd card to play). Would someone offer him a quarter of a million? '£130,000,' said a voice. This was followed by a bid of £150,000, which the auctioneer accepted only as a starting point. Further advances of £5000 a time brought the sum to £200,000; thereafter by thousands, with two bids of £500, to £210,000. Howard Frank's sales talk – 'an old English home . . .

Holme Lacy, 1985.

which must give endless enjoyment' – was of no avail. He then sprang a surprise: he could not accept £210,000 – before the sale an offer had been made for the greater part of the estate which Lord Chesterfield thought he ought to accept, if the reserve for the whole of the property was not reached. His instructions, therefore, were to enter into a contract for the sale of the house, the park and 3396 acres to Sir Robert Lucas-Tooth (Chairman of the Bank of New South Wales in London). 'I am glad to think,' he added, 'that the property will remain in the hands of an Englishman.' Loud cheers. Holme Lacy House today is a hospital.

The Budget Howard Frank referred to was of course Lloyd George's famous attack on the landowning class, the 1909 Finance Bill, regarded at the time as worse than Communism, which imposed four new duties on land: on its increment value, on reversion, on undeveloped land and on mineral rights. To see this in its context, it is worth remembering that income tax in 1909 was only a shilling in the pound up to £3000, and thereafter 1*s* 3*d*. Controversy raged for several years afterwards. A Land Defence League (eventually called the Land Union) was formed to resist the Bill. The result was the 1910 Finance Act and the constitutional crisis in which the House of Lords lost the right to veto money bills because Prime Minister Asquith threatened to swamp them with newly-created Liberal peers; and a Duke was seen to leave the Upper House in tears.

David Lloyd George, whose 1909 Finance Bill was seen as an attack on the land-owning class. It imposed four new duties on land at a time when income tax was only one shilling in the pound. It was to have a significant effect on the development of Knight Frank & Rutley's estates business.

That Knight Frank & Rutley, or at least Howard Frank himself, planned to expand internationally is clear from some of the firm's advertisements, one of which offered an enormous ranch at Laswanermoor in Queensland – 800,000 acres (about four-fifths the size of Kent), with 21,000 head of cattle and 600 horses.

There was a connection with shipping through the family firm of Livett Frank, and there is some evidence that Howard Frank wanted to create a special Shipbroking Department. Moreover, he was beginning to add yachting to horses as a hobby. So it is not entirely surprising to find him, in the summer of 1909, trying to sell on behalf of Cammell Laird & Co. Ltd., one of the symbols of the great age of conspicuous spending, 'the magnificent twin-screw steam yacht *Valiant*', one of the several ocean-going yachts built for William Kissam Vanderbilt of New York.

The *Valiant*, built by Lairds of Birkenhead in 1893, was certainly magnificent. She was 312 ft long and of 2200 tons, with 'every convenience and luxury' – cold stores, refrigeration machinery, distilling plant producing 500 gallons of water daily, and electric light. At her top speed of 17 knots she burnt 60 tons of coal per 24 hours. The whole had cost Mr Vanderbilt £140,000. Yet something had gone wrong: after sixteen years it was valued at only a quarter of its original cost. Knight Frank & Rutley were asking only £35,000.

The accommodation at 9–10 Conduit Street (which also housed the Incorporated Estate Agents' Institute, to whose Council Howard Frank had recently been elected) was too small for a rapidly growing firm. It was not only the expansion of staff on the property side: 'chattels' took up an enormous amount of space and required porters to handle them, and on days before as well as during sales the premises were thronged with people. The firm had taken additional storage space at 47–57 Marylebone Lane, an inconvenient distance away, and 'sales of contents' were now often held on owners' own premises (in country house sales this could sometimes fetch higher prices). That this was part of a larger plan was clear from the firm's advertisements in the autumn of 1909: Marylebone Lane store was called 'Temporary Auction Galleries, pending completion of new Galleries at 20 Hanover Square'. The conversion of No. 20 took thousands of pounds and nearly a year. In November the *Estates Gazette* reported:

> 'Casual pedestrians in Hanover Square, during the last six months, have seen nothing to indicate the enormous work involved in the reconstruction of the back portion of No 20, where Mr. Vincent Harris, the well-known architect, has had a hundred men working practically day and night. On the Bond Street side, in Dering Yard, a different scene has been presented. A huge steam crane and gangs of navvies speedily removed all traces of this portion of the structure and excavations on a large scale followed to make space for the hydraulic lifts, strong rooms, basement sale gallery and warehouses which have been erected. The firm now have under one roof probably the most comprehensive premises in the profession.'

Knight Frank & Rutley moved their estate and professional departments into Hanover Square, still only half converted. The noise of the steam crane and the navvies must have been almost unbearable. In the autumn of 1910 all was ready for the rest of the move, when the Royal Society of Medicine (owners of No. 20) went out and the remaining staff from Conduit Street took possession.

III
Edwardian Twilight

The pedigree of Hanover Square must have pleased Howard Frank's sense of history. Sir John Summerson, in his *Georgian London*, thinks it was planned by Richard Lumley, the first Earl of Scarborough, who in 1713 acquired two acres of freehold land on the east side of what is now George Street, and then a much larger area to the north, as far as Oxford Street. Most of the Square was built between 1715 and 1720. No. 20 has been attributed to the architect James Wyatt, which seems unlikely, as he was not born until 1746. A more probable candidate is Nicholas Dubois. Either Wyatt or his brother may have decorated part of the interior.

The Square's earliest residents, recorded in the Rate Books for 1725, included the Dukes of Montrose, Roxburghe and Bolton; Lords Hillsborough, Falkland, Carpenter, Dunmore, Londonderry and Coventry; the Dashwood family and Sir Theodore Jansen, MP (a Governor of the Bank of England and Director of the disastrous South Sea Company). Other residents at various times were Lord Cowper (Lord Chancellor), Lord Rodney, Lord Palmerston, the Marquess of Salisbury, an Earl of Harewood and Prince Talleyrand, who spent some years in what is now the National Westminster Bank.

By the end of the century Hanover Square was at the height of fashion. We know almost everyone who lived at No. 20 (making allowance for the fact that the square was built gradually and the houses were unnumbered until 1835). The first was the Earl of Dunmore (whose twentieth-century descendant Lady Elisabeth Murray married a Senior Partner of Knight Frank & Rutley). He occupied the house for thirty years, and was followed by the Earl of Shelbourne, who died in 1765, leaving his widow in residence until 1780. The next five years are blank; but in 1785 Mrs Elizabeth Coke (of the family of the Earls of Leicester of Holkham in Norfolk) began her fifteen years' tenure. She was followed by Earl Talbot, and then Sir Simon Clarke, who died in 1830. His executors continued in ownership, and in 1835 the house was numbered 19: this was changed four years later to 20.

The next occupant, who was there for eighteen years, beginning in 1842, was Lieutenant-General the Earl of Lucan, the unfortunate commander whose inability to understand Lord Raglan's written order at the Battle of Balaclava led to the Charge of the Light Brigade. He was followed by Earl Poulett in 1862 and by his Dowager Countess. When she died in March 1877 the Earl's Trustees offered No. 20 for sale by auction.

It seems that there were no takers, or none willing to bid high enough, and the house remained unoccupied for the next twelve years, until 1889, when the Royal Society of Medicine and other non-residential tenants moved in.

The arrival of Knight Frank & Rutley at No. 20 was marked by a special issue of

Lieutenant-General The Earl of Lucan lived at 20 Hanover Square from 1842 to 1860. It was from there that he went to the Crimea where he issued the disastrous order which led to the Charge of the Light Brigade.

the *Estates Gazette*, which published a long article with photographs, not only of the new sales rooms, but of Howard Frank, John Knight and his son Arthur. 'The firm now have under one roof probably the most comprehensive premises in the profession . . . the separate offices for the town and country estate departments, the auction room inquiry section, the country house and delivery branch, are all admirable in every way.'

On the first floor was the new sale gallery (it had once been the Winter Garden), which was to be used for auctions of real estate. 'A private consulting room in rear of the rostrum is an innovation which clients and their solicitors attending such sales will appreciate.' On the upper floors were offices in which the actual management of country estates was carried on. The Jewel Room, 'particularly well lighted', was next to the chief Sale Room where auctions of furniture and works of art were to take place – 'a handsome hall rebuilt on classic lines' with 'large pillars' giving 'spaciousness' enhanced by 'a good ventilation and heating system'.

The Senior Partner's Room (the old dining room, said to be haunted) has changed little since Howard Frank's time: its Adam style has been preserved; the room looks out on to the square, and still contains the same large desk, the same long table for

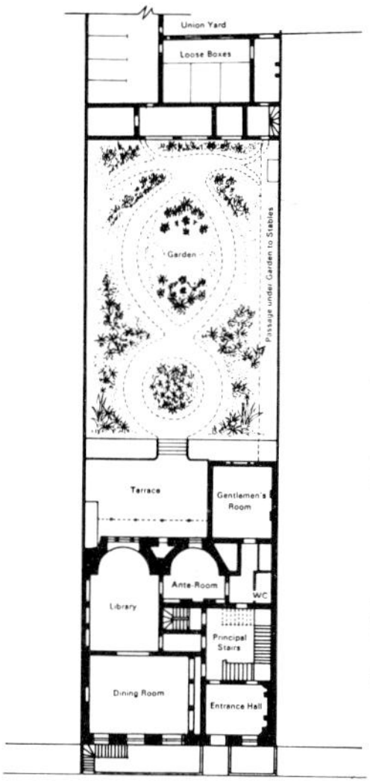

Ground Floor Plan 1877

HISTORY OF No. 20

BUILT IN 1720 AND ATTRIBUTED TO JAMES WYATT

In 1877 Sale Particulars describe the property as :

'An exceedingly desirable Town Mansion with large garden, extensive stabling and coach house premises'.

These original Sale Particulars are held in No. 20.

1975 - European Architectural Heritage Year - Knight Frank & Rutley were awarded a Commendation in recognition of :

'Structural repair and restoration, both inside and out, of an 18th century five-storey town house, for continued use as offices'.

The houses were un-numbered in Hanover Square until 1835, when number 20 appears in the rate book as number 19.

In 1719, only 2 or 3 houses were built on the West side of the Square, number 20 was not one of them.

Previous Occupants of No. 20

1720-1750	The Earl of Dunmore
1755	The Earl of Shelburne
1765-1780	Lady Shelburne
1785-1810	Mrs. Elizabeth Coke
1815	Earl Talbot
1820-1830	Sir Simon Clarke
1835	Numbered for the first time as No. 19 The Executors of Sir Simon Clarke
1839	Numbered for the first time as No. 20
1840-1841	Unoccupied
1842-1860	Lieutenant General The Earl of Lucan K.C.B.
1862-1864	Earl Poulett
1865-1877	Dowager Countess Poulett
1878-1888	Unoccupied
1889	Royal Medical Society and others
March 1910	Knight Frank & Rutley

It is worth noting that the Earl of Lucan lived in number 20 from 1842 throughout the time of his activities in the Crimea.

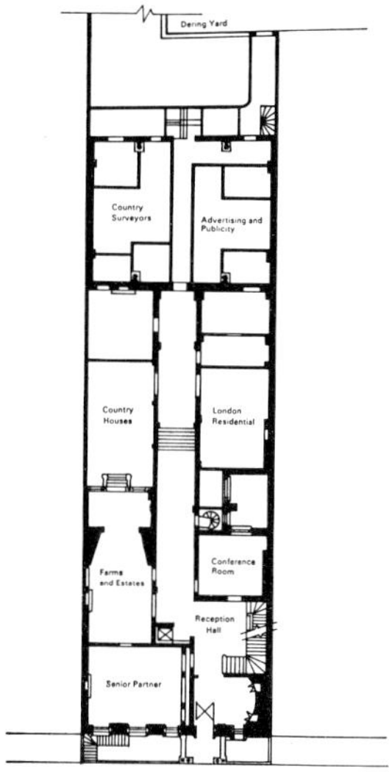

Ground Floor Plan 1976

Plan of 20 Hanover Square.

partners' meetings, the same glass-fronted bookcase now full of historic catalogues and 'particulars', auctioneers' copies of great property sales and leather-bound copies of enormous valuations. The two most thoroughly-thumbed books on Howard Frank's desk were *Burke's Peerage* and *Who's Who.*

Having settled the staff in their new home, Howard Frank gave them a dinner at the Trocadero Restaurant, Piccadilly Circus, in October. He followed the Loyal Toast (and it was to a new King, George V, who had just succeeded but not yet been crowned) with a toast to 'The Staff', seizing the occasion to reel off an array of progress figures: 'During the past three years the firm has sold 113,730 acres of agricultural properties pure and simple, realizing £2,603,594.' In 1910 the firm had offered over 53,000 acres, and already had 32,550 acres to offer for 1911. As the total sales of land for the whole of Britain in 1910 (according to *The Times*) were 104,626 acres, realizing £2,844,270, Knight Frank & Rutley had enjoyed an astonishingly high proportion (roughly 35 per cent) of the market.

Howard Frank then made a surprise announcement: the firm would shortly be opening offices in New York and Winnipeg. There was 'a feeling of insecurity among capitalists in the United Kingdom, who had been putting a good deal of their money abroad'. Almost certainly Asquith and Lloyd George had thoroughly frightened them. No records survive to show what happened in New York and Winnipeg, but

John Knight at the time of the move from Conduit Street to 20 Hanover Square.

we do know that a number of younger sons and adventurers like Mortimer Frewen went out to try their hands at ranching. The firm 'were not competing in any way with agents and valuers in America', Howard Frank went on soothingly, they 'would be associated with one of the best firms in New York'.

The reputation of Howard Frank within the profession was now very high, even allowing for the almost fulsome tributes accorded to him by the *Estates Gazette*, which in October 1910 presented its readers with a full-page photograph of him. He was a man of ideas (he kept one notebook for them by his bedside, another on his desk and a third in his carriage, or in his car, for he was one of the earliest motorists). He had built up a large business in fourteen years, and he was still only 39. He had been twice invited to stand for Parliament, and had refused, saying that he did not want to toe any party line. He had been elected to the Council of the Royal Agricultural Society. He had somehow found time, in addition to showing his horses in Britain and Holland, to travel all over the world, visiting Canada, America, Egypt, Ceylon, Samoa, Hawaii, Australia and New Zealand.

In 1910 the *Estates Gazette* seemed mesmerized by him.

'In their first few weeks at Hanover Square,' said the *Gazette*, 'the firm have made their mark. The antique furniture in the Meinertzhagen collection and the fine old pictures on November 4 brought the buyers in crowds, and within the last few days a collection of Greek, Roman and ancient English gold and silver coins, catalogued with meticulous accuracy, and further collections of fine jewels, silver and Russian sables have attracted other classes of buyers.'

There were Sir Walter Gilbey's collections at Cambridge House, Regent's Park, and the Hon. H. D. Curzon's at Salisbury; the Jones Parry pictures and silver at

Madryn Castle, near Pwllheli, Caernarvonshire; Sir Francis Seymour Haden's collection of furniture at his Hampshire home; and the contents of Lord Chesterfield's Holme Lacy (the house itself, we have seen, had been sold in 1909).

The entire contents of Madryn Castle ('Genuine Early Tudor Castle . . . first-rate shooting . . .') disposed of in a two-day sale, included 'ancient Welsh MSS of Giraldus Cambrensis and the Mabinogion', sixteenth-century coins and medals, a Holbein portrait of Henry VIII, porcelain of many countries, embroidery that had once belonged to Queen Anne, and all the great craftsmen of English furniture. The Madryn estate was withdrawn from auction, having been bought privately by the Smallholdings Committee of the Caernarvon County Council. The Faskally estate of 17,458 acres in Perthshire, near Pitlochry, also attracted wide publicity because it included the Pass of Killiecrankie, scene of a famous victory over the English in 1689. Faskally House is today a Forestry Training School, and the river Tummel is now part of a hydro-electric scheme.

Totting up his sales for 1910, as he loved to do (eventually taking advertising space to announce them), Howard Frank arrived at totals of 58,598 acres for a turnover of £767,000.

He had been elected, in November, President for the following year of the Incorporated Estate Agents' Institute. Typically, he responded in the New Year by giving a Smoking Concert at No. 20 for Institute Members and their guests, nearly 200 of them: 'The programme was an excellent and varied one, and Mr Arthur Knight superintended its presentation with such effect that there was never a dull moment.'

For several years an amalgamation between the Estate Agents' and the Auctioneers' Institute had been under discussion. How else could registration of all who were dealing in real property be completed? At the IEAI Annual Dinner Howard Frank had, as his Presidential guest speaker, the Rt. Hon. Walter Long, MP, whose Wiltshire estates he helped to manage, and parts of which he was about to offer for sale. Mr Long, a former President of the Board of Agriculture, cricketer, huntsman, adamant opponent of Votes for Women, and the future Viscount Long of Wraxall, spoke on 'The Land Question'. He had obviously been badly scared by Lloyd George. It was easy enough, he said, to change your money investments, but what could you do if your wealth was tied up in land? He obstinately believed that in every country in the world land was the first and the most important security . . .

Howard Frank delayed his announcement of the amalgamation until the Annual General Meeting in November, and it came into effect early in 1912. Meanwhile, he had been re-elected President of the IEAI. He had also been made a Fellow of the Surveyors' Institution in October 1911.

Country mansions were being sold, but they were also being bought. For country house life was changing. The reign of Edward VII, both at Court and in the country, had seen a new alliance between landowners and businessmen. Peers now sat on the boards of companies. Sometimes their sons became bankers or stockbrokers. You could have a house in the country for entertaining your friends without having a

Knight Frank & Rutley were to offer the Chequers Court Estate for sale in 1910. The house was left in trust by the owners to be available as the official country residence of the Prime Minister of the day. Its first occupant was David Lloyd George.

burdensome amount of park- or farm-land which might take sixty staff to run. You could even let your country house (as was to happen in the 1920s) to a Society hostess for the season. The new buyers were often new-rich, with new motor-cars; yet some of them learnt to give the friendly leadership required of the squire and his relations.

For others, country houses were competitive. Ballrooms were added or enlarged. A billiard room was always a selling point. Rooms were added for up to forty guests, some bringing their own servants. More stables, more garages, more bathrooms (in many stately homes there was only one, most people and their guests still using slipper baths, laboriously filled from jugs of hot water). A country house, a sporting estate, a grouse moor – these became success symbols.

It wasn't *all* Lloyd George's fault. And yet there is a certain irony in one of the properties offered by Knight Frank & Rutley in 1910 and 1911. Chequers Court estate, Butler's Cross, near Wendover, Bucks., contained an Elizabethan-Gothick mansion with 1800 acres, 'the outlying portions' of which, comprising farms, a mill, cottages and small-holdings, 'magnificent building sites' and 'valuable agricultural land', were to be sold off. But not the house, which belonged to Lord and Lady Lee of Fareham, who had lived in it since 1909. They set up a Trust which provided that Chequers, on their death, should be 'available as the official country residence of the Prime Minister of the day . . . even if his income should be limited to his salary'. In 1917 they decided to make it available in their lifetime. And who was the first Prime Minister to take advantage of it, in January 1921? David Lloyd George.

IV
Saving the Palace

It began as the Hyde Park Glass-House Exhibition of 1851 ('Crystal Palace' was a mocking nickname invented by *Punch*). As early as 1844 Mr F. Wishaw, Secretary to the Society of Arts, suggested to his Council that it should take the lead in promoting international commerce by a great Exhibition to be held in London. By 1849 the Prince Consort had been made President of the Society and was warmly enthusiastic about the scheme. It eventually became identified with him, and would at last bring him popularity.

From the outset *The Times* opposed the project. It had all been got up by 'City jobbers'. It would ruin Hyde Park; if there had to be an exhibition, could it not be built on the derelict Isle of Dogs? In Parliament the loudest critic was Colonel Charles de Laet Waldo Sibthorpe, MP for Lincoln. The Exhibition was 'one of the greatest frauds, greatest humbugs, greatest absurdities ever known'. London would be filled with foreigners, who would be the only people to benefit from it.

The Palace was designed by Joseph Paxton, seventh son of a Bedfordshire schoolmaster, who had worked his way up from a gardener to be manager of the Duke of Devonshire's estates at Chatsworth where he had constructed a glass conservatory 300 ft long by 40 ft wide, covering nearly an acre of ground.

Opposition to the plan continued right up to the opening of the Exhibition. The sun's rays, streaming through the glass, which would act as a lens, would roast the public alive. The rabble of foreign visitors, it was thought (the Prince complained), were 'certain to commence a thorough revolution here, to murder Victoria and myself, and to proclaim the Red Republic in England'. One writer even saw danger in the arrival of the Queen, 'in circumstances of unparalleled pomp', to open the Exhibition: surely the salvo of artillery that greeted her would 'shiver the glass roof of the Palace', and 'thousands of grand ladies who were to be in their seats by 10 a.m. would be cut into mincemeat'.

The nave of Paxton's 'cucumber frame' was 1608 ft long and 312 ft wide, with wings each 574 ft long. The central transept was 387 ft wide and 175 ft high. It was estimated that the entire building contained 9642 tons of iron, 1,650,000 square feet of glass, and 50 miles of hot water piping. It had cost £170,000 to build, and miraculously made a profit of £180,000.

The Times, having seen the 100,000 exhibits, suddenly changed its tune: the Palace begot 'a sense of mystery' which made one feel 'near the Throne of God'. Napoleon III and the Empress Eugenie came to see it and, not to be outdone, determined to have an International Exhibition in Paris. When it was all over, the Queen knighted Paxton, Mr Fox of Fox & Henderson (the building contractors) and even Herr August Manns, the Prussian bandmaster who conducted the Palace Band.

Crystal Palace: The Fountains.

What was to become of the Crystal Palace now? Sir Joseph Paxton, a man of vision and a good negotiator, raised £500,000 to move it to Sydenham Hill, then in open country. It was bought from Fox & Henderson for £70,000, and the Crystal Palace Company issued shares to raise £1,300,000, the estimated cost of removing and

Crystal Palace: The Clock.

re-erecting the colossal structure at Sydenham. At a time of high unemployment it provided work for 7000 men. It was to be in every way bigger and better than it had been in Hyde Park. There were to be Medieval, Grecian, Roman, Romanesque, Byzantine, Pompeian, Chinese, Renaissance, Assyrian and Egyptian Courts; a Hall of Fame; a Concert Room with 4000 seats and a Grand Orchestra for up to 4000 musicians with, in the middle, a Grand Organ with over 4500 pipes. All this was described as 'educational'.

Outside were two glass towers 284 ft high, designed by I. K. Brunel, for central heating and for pumping water to the fountains in the surrounding gardens: each had a capacity of 300,000 gallons. The Gardens contained a sort of educational 'adventure playground' with statues of prehistoric animals. There was a Grand Maze and an underground Grotto; a cricket ground, a Maxim Flying Machine and a Cycle Track.

By 1900 the Palace's popularity was waning: it seemed to be running out of ideas. It had tried hard. The first Zoëtrope (moving pictures) had been demonstrated there. There had been triennial Handel Festivals, so that the Palace's theme-song, in the minds of many Londoners, was the Hallelujah Chorus. There had been balloon ascents. Blondin, the great tightrope walker, had cooked an omelette while on a wire stretched across the central transept 170 ft above the ground. There were rose shows, cat and dog shows, circuses, horseless carriage shows, concerts, massed military bands, mass meetings of Temperance Leagues; and, every Thursday night, fireworks which could be seen from all over South London.

In 1911 the show of the year, celebrating George V's Coronation, was the Festival of Empire, featuring a South African diamond mine, an Indian tea plantation, a Canadian logging camp – it may have inspired the British Empire Exhibition at Wembley thirteen years later. It was the biggest-ever Palace show; and it was put on in the year of the Palace's bankruptcy.

The news that the Palace was to come under the hammer caused instant controversy. Long before the actual auction announcement, however, Howard Frank, with his flair for public relations, was mobilizing public opinion. The firm's brochure – 'auction particulars' is too prosaic a term – was lavish even for a Coronation Year production. Its generous layout and typography were years in advance of its day. Printed on handwoven paper, it contained fifty-two pages of photographs and engravings and sixty-four pages of text running to more than 20,000 words. Today it might cost more than £25 a copy. 'Its weight is approximately 3¼ lb, apart from the substantial cardboard case,' *The Times* reported wonderingly, 'its size is 16½ in. by 11 in., and . . . a second edition of the particulars will be issued shortly containing the conditions of sale.'

The auctioneers were to be Howard Frank, of course, and John Roy Lancaster of Horne & Co. The property was to be offered as a going concern, 'a freehold estate of 200 acres, 3 roods, 22 poles,' as one lot. The Introduction stressed the 'high moral and educational tone' enjoyed by the Palace's original Charter. 'It would be in the nature of a public calamity if this radiating centre of information, enlightenment and entertainment at Sydenham were not somehow or other preserved to the nation which it has served so long and so supremely well.'

It was 11 September when *The Times* broke the news, and the auction was to be held at 20 Hanover Square on 28 November. Was there not a risk that this 'Home of

Science, Art, Literature and Music' could fall victim to unworthy commercialism? Would not the land alone tempt speculative builders if the property were to be broken into several lots? There was just over ten weeks in which to do something.

Those ten weeks were to generate many articles and letters to the press. The Lord Mayor of London, Sir Thomas Strong, called a meeting at the Mansion House for 23 October, of 'all public bodies and persons interested in the acquisition of the Crystal Palace and its grounds for the use of the public for ever'. The Mayor of Hampstead, William Woodward, wrote the first letter to *The Times*. He was worried about speculative builders. The Palace was now in a 'heartrending' state of neglect. It was in danger of being given over to 'football matches and other attractions for vulgar mobs'. Surely the money to save it could be raised somehow? What about a subscription of one guinea each from a million people?

By the beginning of October it was known that more than 200 acceptances had been received to the Lord Mayor's invitation – from local government representatives all over south-eastern England. It was now believed that £300,000 was needed to save the Palace, £210,000 of it to buy the property.

At this point the two auctioneers, Howard Frank and Roy Lancaster, wrote a joint letter to *The Times* adding fuel to the controversy. They were worried about letters they had received which seemed to imply a belief 'that the interests involved are so vast that the chances of the property being acquired for national purposes are remote'. Could the property be broken up to advantage? 'Assuming the Crystal Palace itself to be razed to the ground' (with hindsight, there is a terrible irony here) 'there would be left about 100 acres . . . which might be dedicated to the public for ever . . . the area surrounding this open space would at once become more valuable and would readily let. We should be pleased to submit plans of a scheme to this end.' The rumours of speculative building were causing a depreciation in property values in Sydenham. 'We hope and believe that the Palace will be bought for the nation. Our duty, however, is to sell to the highest bidder.'

This letter was dated a week before the Mansion House conference. Meanwhile 'Save the Palace' schemes had multiplied. Lord Strathcona and other notables had already contributed gifts totalling £7000. At the meeting Mr Francis Fox of Fox & Henderson, who had surveyed the Palace structure, said that it was 'good for another 60, 80 or 100 years'. The Lord Mayor moved a resolution that the building and its grounds should be acquired for the public: seconded by Lord Plymouth, carried unanimously. A committee was appointed.

On 31 October, in a half-page advertisement, among several large Scottish sporting estates, Knight Frank & Rutley announced the auction, as they were bound to do; but they must have been reasonably certain by this time that the property would be withdrawn. On 9 November *The Times*, under the headline THE CRYSTAL PALACE SAVED, announced that Lord Plymouth, who was Lord Lieutenant of Glamorgan, mayor of Cardiff, an authority on Constable, and owned 30,500 acres including his own St Fagan's Castle, had provided a deposit of £20,000. It was now a matter of applying to the Court of Chancery for sanction to arrange a private sale.

Crystal Palace: The Great Fire.

Nine days later *The Times* reported: 'We are authorized to state that the contract for the Sale of the Crystal Palace, entered into by Mr Howard Frank (Messrs Knight Frank & Rutley), representing the Vendors, and Lord Plymouth, was £210,000. The sale by auction, which was to have taken place at the Estate Room, Hanover Square, on 28 November, has accordingly been cancelled.'

It was the largest item in the firm's sales for 1911, a record year in which 93,269 acres had been offered and total turnover was £1,780,000.

So the oratorios and the circuses, exhibitions and fireworks and brass band contests continued until 6 p.m. on 30 November 1936, when a fire, believed to have started in a staff lavatory, fanned by a north-west wind, spread and engulfed the whole building. Next morning's papers front-paged the Palace and the first rumblings of the Abdication crisis. The glow of the blaze in the night sky was visible fifty miles away in Brighton. Only the two towers survived. Ninety fire engines and 380 firemen rushed to Sydenham Hill, impeded by car-loads of sight-seers choking all the main streets of South London: they included the Duke of Kent.

Next day the solitary figure of Queen Mary was seen walking through the reeking ruins, prodding things with her umbrella, amid the ashes of the Victorian Age.

V
Before the Storm

Before 'wireless', long before television, before the cinema, before even the gramophone had been perfected, people blessedly made their own amusements and their own music. Young people formed concert-parties, pierrot-troupes and amateur dramatic societies: for one thing, it was a convenient way to meet the opposite sex. Any firm that prided itself on being a 'happy family' had its own social life based on one of these things. Knight Frank & Rutley had a Social Club and also a Concert Party called 'The Nuts'.

The Knight Frank & Rutley Club, in 1912, held Smoking Concerts in the Estate Room, and sometimes sent a show on the road, 'entertaining over 800 tenants and friends' at rent audits as far away as the Lyman estate in Cheshire. Its seasonal events happened mostly in the winter – smoking concert, whist drive, debate, Ladies' Night.

We have a surviving programme of The Nuts, who announced their artists in the new modern way without any Mr or Miss – a trick they had certainly learnt from Harry Pélissier's *Follies*, a seaside concert party which had been promoted to the West End and had had two long runs at the Apollo Theatre. 'Beatrice Keys will sing a Quaker Song . . . Eric Butler will sing a Burglar Song . . . Bruce Ker will sing about "Paper Bag Cookery" . . .' And Beatrice Keys closes the show by singing *My Moon*, the most famous of the Pélissier songs, a big romantic number sung by everyone in 1912 and now totally forgotten.

It was about this time that Howard Frank started a Shipping Department for 'the purchase, sale, construction and chartering of steam and sailing yachts'. There is little evidence that this venture developed very far, except as a means of exchanging business with Livett Frank & Son; but yachting was to become a passion with him in the 1920s.

For the present, his main interest outside business was horses. Since about 1907 he had been buying, selling and showing hackney horses. He would have been the first to admit that the reputation for being a good judge of horseflesh, like belonging to the yachting fraternity, besides being enjoyable, enabled him to move in the sort of circles which were likely to bring in top-class estate business. He was one day to own Tissington Kit-Kat and Cock Robin, and a world champion named Lighthouse (its owner, we shall see, was at that time living in a lighthouse). Now, in 1912, 'Mr Howard Frank again figures in the list of prize-winners at the International Horse Show at Olympia, having at the sixth meeting this week . . . carried off the second prize for novice pair of horses (over 15 and not exceeding 15.2 hands) with Buckingham and Lilian, and the fourth prize for novice pony (over 13 and not exceeding 14 hands) with Apollo,' as the *Estates Gazette* faithfully reported. By the end of 1914 he was President of the Hackney Horse Society, on whose Council he had served for the past ten years, having meanwhile won other prizes at Cardiff, Dublin, Bath and the Hague.

At the annual dinner in April of the newly-amalgamated Auctioneers' and Estate Agents' Institute, and at the opening meeting of the 1912–13 Session, the speeches, one of them by Howard Frank's friend and client, Walter Long, MP, were predictably about the steady fall in values of gilt-edged securities as well as land (there was a Forsyte-ish cry of 'Consols are too cheap!'); of rising prices; of the headlong break-up of estates – surely it was time to make the public aware that bricks and mortar were still the safest investment? Walter Long had just sold a large part of his own estate in Wiltshire, and had reason to be grateful to Howard Frank. Writing from the House of Commons, he said: 'I desire, without any delay, to thank you for all the trouble you have taken and to express my great admiration of the skill and tact with which you have conducted the various complicated negotiations . . . In my opinion the work of your office has been most admirably performed. I have today seen and passed the account which seems to be thoroughly reasonable.'

The 'Land Question' would not go away. One of Lloyd George's proposals in 1909–10 had been a valuation of *all* land in England and Wales, and there was a good deal of popular support for this. The necessary work of valuation by the Inland Revenue was to take ten years, and towards the end of the War the scheme would be largely repealed. Meanwhile, for the victims – the big landowners – it looked like a tax on wealth, and many began to sell. The trend, in these years, was to divide estates and sell them off in lots, beginning with 'outlying portions'. Frequently an estate would be bought as a whole by a speculator and then resold in lots, so that an estate could come on the market twice in a year or two.

More than 200 auctions of estates were held between 1911 and 1914, representing nearly 600,000 acres and £7,500,000 worth.

In its '1912 Brochure', a publication rivalling the Crystal Palace particulars in lavishness, the firm described fifty of the larger estates on offer either under the hammer or privately. It gives us a good idea of the class of business Knight Frank & Rutley were both seeking and getting; and if, among all the resounding names, we notice a few that seem to have been on the books rather a long time, let that stand as a tribute to the patience and persistence which often earn the estate agent his commission. Six Mile Bottom, five miles from Newmarket, with 6640 acres, was a 'modern house' with seventeen bedrooms, a garage for two cars but only two bathrooms (an insight into pre-1914 priorities). Never mind – it had its 'own railway station'. It was sold before auction to Sir Ernest Cassel, Bt, Edward VII's favourite financier and Edwina Mountbatten's grandfather. Another property near Newmarket, Exning House, was 'a fine Georgian residence' with thirty bedrooms, no fewer than seven bathrooms and 900 acres.

Ogbeare Hall, in Devon, dating back to the fifteenth century, had just over 3000 acres, and lent itself to the full historical treatment – Tudor dining room 36 ft

The entrance hall at Six Mile Bottom. The Estate with 6640 acres was sold in 1912 to Sir Ernest Cassel Bt, King Edward VII's favourite financier and Edwina Mountbatten's grandfather.

long, armour, French tapestry; twenty bedrooms – and one bathroom. Not far away Membland Hall, ten miles from Plymouth, had bedrooms and bathrooms in a ratio of twenty-three to six.

Miserden Park, near Cirencester, 'one of the most beautiful properties in England'; Beeches Hall, Norfolk; Finedon Hall, Northants; Llanerchydol estate, Montgomeryshire; the Rûg estate, Merioneth . . .

Cowley Manor, near Cheltenham, offered a 64 ft ballroom with enormous cut-glass chandeliers as a special attraction; also 'stabling for 19 horses . . . and Fully Appointed Motor Garage for 5 cars and pit'. The pit was important: chauffeurs

Kildalton House, Islay. The firm was to build a great reputation in the Western Isles, many times going back to the same island. Mr Iain Ramsay's Kildalton and Oa Estate with 54,500 acres was sold in June 1914. Islay House came on the market in the summer of 1984.

spent half their time under the car. Hemsted, which included what is now the Bedgebury National Pinetum, Europe's largest collection of conifers, and '41 farms convertible into private houses', was bought by Sir Harold Harmsworth, Bt, a director of Amalgamated Press (part of the estate has been, since 1923, Benenden School). Rolleston, near Market Harborough, offered 'hunting six days a week . . . with the Quorn, Cottesmore, Mr Fernie's, Pytchley and Belvoir'.

More and more Scottish properties, many of them famous sporting estates, were coming on to the market (and we shall soon see that Howard Frank's eyes were looking to north of the Border for future expansion). The 54,500 acres of the Kildalton and Oa estate, forming the southern part of the Isle of Islay, contained a mansion in a deer park of nearly two square miles – five-and-a-half miles of a salmon fishing on the river Laggan, a yacht anchorage and a rent-roll of £9955 a year . . . But it was the shooting bag that was really impressive: over the last seven years it had averaged 800 grouse, 150 blackcock, 600 woodcock, 350 snipe, 2000 pheasants, 200 partridges, 250 wild duck and widgeon, 1000 rabbits . . . Or what about Blair Drummond in Perthshire? A Scottish Baronial mansion of no great age (1873) with 7180 acres and capital sporting facilities. Or Lord Colebrooke's 'historical Abington and Crawford estates' between Edinburgh and Carlisle – 27,000 acres with grouse moors of 20,000 acres, two shooting lodges (one of them with *eight* bathrooms) and a

The Soldier, Slochd-Mahol-Doraidh, on the Kildalton and Oa Estate.

'motor house for 5 motors'. Or the island of Gigha, with a mansion, fourteen farms and a private eighteen-hole golf course . . .

The '1912 Brochure' ended, for good measure, with a number of fruit farms in British Columbia, 'on the Thompson river two miles from the city of Kamloops', reached by the Canadian Pacific main line: to the homesick settler, good fishing and shooting were promised, social clubs and a mild climate. And the very last page offers two yachts, a steam vessel of 1400 tons and a gaff-rigged yawl of 200 tons.

Throughout the spring and summer of 1912, the gentle dialogue with Sotheby's, broken off in 1908, had been resumed.

At Sotheby's there was now a new partner, less bookish, more professional and not

Islay House, 1984.

averse from using telephone and typewriters – Sir Thomas Barlow, MP, a barrister by training. Tom Hodge introduced him to Howard Frank, thinking still of a full merger between the two firms. Frank seems to have envisaged an 'arrangement' with Sotheby's, a pooling of interests by which his firm would give chattel sales to Sotheby's in exchange for shares. Sotheby's, for their part, seem to have been attracted by the accommodation at 20 Hanover Square, and by the prospect of a long lease at a low rental, and a good West End address. But Barlow did not want to sell any shares in Sotheby's. The matter was ended sharply yet tactfully by Howard Frank, who wrote to Barlow in July: 'I am sorry to think we have spent so much time to no purpose, but I shall arrange *something* with you one of these days.' Barlow indeed became a client, and what Frank arranged for him eventually was new offices at 34 and 35 Bond Street which was becoming the new centre for book trade auctions. The building was shared with the Doré Gallery, a firm of bookbinders, and a basement wine cellar. Sotheby's moved there in 1917.

Howard Frank had other irons in the fire. A month later, Knight Frank & Rutley bought Walton & Lee, a well-known West End firm of estate agents specializing, like their purchasers, in large residential properties. They too advertised lavishly in *Country Life*, and it had been irritating Howard Frank for some years that Walton & Lee always had the front page by long-term exclusive arrangement. It was almost as

Supplement to "Country Life."

COUNTRY LIFE

THE JOURNAL FOR ALL INTERESTED IN COUNTRY LIFE AND COUNTRY PURSUITS.

VOL. XXXII.–No. 823. [REGISTERED AT THE G.P.O. AS A NEWSPAPER.] *SATURDAY, OCTOBER 12th, 1912.* Published Weekly, Price SIXPENCE. Subscription Price per annum, Post Free. Inland, 29s. 2d. Canadian, 35s. 10d. Foreign, 48s.

WALTON & LEE
Offices: 10, MOUNT ST., GROSVENOR SQUARE, LONDON, W.
TELEPHONES: 1505 MAYFAIR; 3645 GERRARD.
TELEGRAMS: "WALTONS, LONDON."

Incorporated with

KNIGHT, FRANK & RUTLEY
Offices: 20, HANOVER SQUARE, LONDON, W.
TELEPHONE: 1942 GERRARD.
TELEGRAMS: "GALLERIES, LONDON."
ALSO NEW YORK, WINNIPEG, VICTORIA (B.C.), SYDNEY, and BUENOS AYRES.

IN THE COUNTIES OF WILTS AND HANTS.

BORDERS OF NEW FOREST.

TO BE SOLD.

RESIDENTIAL AND SPORTING ESTATE of 1,084 ACRES. Noble Mansion containing:—

Grand hall, Billiard room, | Six reception, rooms, | Three bath-rooms, | 40 bed and dressing rooms.

Stabling for twelve, five lodges, cottages, three farms, etc.

GRANDLY TIMBERED PARK. EXTENSIVE VIEWS.

Plan, views and other details of WALTON & LEE, 10, Mount Street, W. (25,946.)

AMIDST LOVELY SCENERY IN THE NORTH OF ENGLAND.

3,000 ACRES FOR SALE

AT REDUCED PRICE.

FINE OLD HOUSE IN PARK.

Billiard, four reception, three bath, fifteen bedrooms.

GROUSE AND OTHER SHOOTING. TWO MILES OF FISHING.

Several farms. Stabling for seven.

All details of WALTON & LEE, 10, Mount Street, W. (17,598.)

BERKSHIRE.

ONE-AND-A-QUARTER HOURS FROM LONDON.

MANSION IN PARK OF 100 ACRES; billiard, four reception, four bath, 21 bed Stabling, farmery, cottages.

ELECTRIC LIGHT.

FOR SALE OR LETTING, FURNISHED.

For terms, etc., apply WALTON & LEE, 10, Mount Street, W. (24,863.)

PYTCHLEY COUNTRY.

VERY FINE MANSION, in large park, to be LET,

FURNISHED FOR A TERM OF YEARS.

Handsome suite of reception rooms, | Three bath-rooms, | 40 bed and dressing rooms.

Stabling for 30, accommodation for men, farmery.

SHOOTING OVER 7,500 ACRES.

FISHING AND GOLF.

All details of WALTON & LEE, 10, Mount Street, W. (20,036.)

(For continuation of Advertisements, see page v.)

The first full front-page advertisement in Country Life. *Howard Frank had to acquire the estate agents Walton and Lee to obtain this position: a position which the firm enjoys by exclusive arrangement to this day.*

if he had to buy the whole firm to get that front-page (which indeed Knight Frank & Rutley still enjoy today). So important was this medium that for many years the firm's letterheads carried at the top, in red, OUR ILLUSTRATED ADVERTISEMENTS APPEAR FROM WEEK TO WEEK IN 'COUNTRY LIFE'.

Walton & Lee had a top-class clientèle, and they had been established much longer than Knight Frank & Rutley. In August 1912, William Walton, the sole principal, was paid £4000 for the goodwill of the business; and he granted Knight Frank & Rutley a lease of the ground floor and basement of his elegant premises at 10 Mount Street for twenty-one years at a rent of £900 'free of all rates and taxes'.

The name 'Walton & Lee' continued to appear in the firm's advertising for several years. One of the most valuable acquisitions was Charles Phillips, a senior member of William Walton's staff and an auctioneer of great dignity, who remained with the firm for the rest of his life. Another was Reginald P. (Reg) Leslie, who specialized in the country house and estate market, managed the Country Department for many years and is remembered as 'an ace negotiator – a stickler for detail and system who . . . taught the tricks of the trade to many future partners'.

The first joint advertisement of the amalgamated firms appeared in *The Times* (a half-page) on 1 October; and there is evidence of fresh expansion – the last line, after giving the Hanover Square and Mount Street addresses, adds 'also at New York, Winnipeg, Sydney, N.S.W., Victoria, B.C., and Buenos Aires'. These were not exactly branch offices, but more probably loose 'arrangements' with local firms which Howard Frank generally preferred, unless he saw very long-term prospects or wanted something very badly (like the front-page advertisements in *Country Life*).

There was one more thrust of expansion to be made before the year ended. For some years now the firm had been successfully selling large properties – especially sporting properties – in Scotland. Walton & Lee too had had considerable experience north of the Border. There was also much business to be handled in the seasonal letting of Scottish grouse moors, fishing rights and deer forests. Since the 1910 sale of the 17,500-acre Faskally estate, which had received a good deal of publicity, Knight Frank & Rutley had had an increasing number of approaches to conduct auctions in Scotland. In this year, 1912, they were offering the most important property of all, the Menzies estate of 71,543 acres in Perthshire, 'by Direction of Lady Menzies of Menzies', to whose family it had belonged since the thirteenth century. Practically and diplomatically, future Scottish business needed to be handled on the spot.

So, on 7 December, it was announced: 'Messrs. Knight Frank & Rutley of 20 Hanover Square, W1, are opening offices for Scottish estates, shootings and fishings at 100 Princes Street, Edinburgh on January 2. Certain members of their London staff are proceeding to this branch to supplement the Scottish staff.' The manager was to be Cecil W. Ingram, who had joined the firm in 1911. He was a past master at producing 'particulars', and had prepared the enormous Crystal Palace brochure – a work of art in every sense. He was not a Scot, but nobody in Edinburgh ever held that against him. The estate business was in his blood. He was the son of a chartered

OPENING OF THE EDINBURGH OFFICE

JANUARY 1st, 1913.

Extract from the "Scottish Shout and Echo," Jan. 2nd, 1913 (Special Edition).

"Great excitement was observed yesterday in Princes Street when Messrs. Knight, Frank & Rutley's new branch office in Edinburgh was opened at 9.30 a.m. The first arrivals took up their places on the pavement at 11 p.m. the previous night so as to secure good positions in the morning, and when daylight appeared an enormous crowd was seen stretching from 100 Princes Street to Waverley Station, near which latter place most of the "nibs" were to be seen. The opening ceremony was performed by Mr. Provost Oats (of the well-known Quaker family), while a band performed on the pipes in the street (the road being up for repairs). Among the first to gain admittance to the offices and to entrust business to the firm were Mr. Harry Lauder (who refused to pay for any advertisements), Miss Annie Laurie, Mr. Roderick Dhu, Mr. Andrew Carnegie (who kindly brought a library each for Messrs. Ingram & Davis), Messrs. Deoch & Doris, Mr. Auld Langsyne, Mr. Robert Bruce with spider, Mr. John Walker, Mr. Dewar, Messrs. Black & White, and Mr. Redd Seel, the last four mentioned being in excellent spirits."

Extract from the programme for the Knight Frank & Rutley and Walton and Lee staff dinner held at the Trocadero Restaurant on 24 January 1913.

surveyor and land agent in Lewes and Eastbourne, and had been educated at Winchester and Uckfield Agricultural College. He had been a partner in a small estate firm, W. Brown & Co. of Tring, and Howard Frank was probably impressed by the fact that he had been assistant land agent on the Duke of Bedford's estates.

This took care of the estate business in Scotland; but what of the 'chattels', the *objets d'art*, the contents of mansions? The best-known Galleries in Edinburgh were Dowells Ltd, who ran auction rooms for pictures, books and antiques; and both Howard Frank and Cecil Ingram became directors of it. The firm needed younger blood: Alexander Dowell, the proprietor, was 90. Cecil Ingram managed the Edinburgh office for twenty years; and business in Scotland prospered so well that it was not long before a second office was opened in St Vincent Street, Glasgow.

Knight Frank & Rutley and Walton & Lee might have amalgamated, but the staffs did not yet know each other very well. So 'getting to know you' was the theme of the staff dinner at the Trocadero Restaurant on 24 January 1913. An elegant souvenir, dedicated to the branch office and designed and illustrated with cartoons by Bruce Ker, a man of all-round talents who was also a member of The Nuts concert party, has survived to tell us about it. We do not know who wrote the 'copy', which is largely in limericks:

No. 10 Mount Street

In aristocratic Mayfair
We've an Office that makes people stare,
Where the Staff sits sedately,
'Midst pillars so stately,
Selling houses in Grosvenor Square.

Winnipeg

Our Winnipeg agent's a 'nut'
And his office consists of a hut,
To his work he will go
Over ten feet of snow,
And the language he uses! Tut-tut!

The souvenir also contains a sketch of Frank Capon, the senior surveyor and valuer, whose chunky figure, still remembered by a few retired staff, with his flat cap, spats and toothbrush moustache, is thus captured for ever.

In Scotland the biggest property on Knight Frank & Rutley's list was proving difficult to sell. It certainly was not for lack of publicity. The 90,000 acres of the Menzies estate had already been advertised in 1912. Now, in September 1913, the firm's regular Thursday full-page in *The Times* announced that 'the particulars are in course of preparation' and that the estate would be offered by auction at Hanover Square in May 1914. It was the old problem: you try to sell an estate, including mansion, as a whole; if you cannot, you break it up into lots and try to sell them separately; and often you are left with the mansion (or castle) on your hands.

Castle Menzies, near the village of Weem, just north-west of Aberfeldy, is still today the official headquarters of the Clan Menzies. 'The historical castle is beautifully situate' (estate agents still lovingly use the eighteenth-century participle) 'about one mile from Aberfeldy Station, at the foot of the Rock of Weem, and bears the date 1571.' No need to add that a good deal of it was a new wing and porch built on in 1840. 'Scene of a hundred memories of romance and warfare!' enthused the *Estates Gazette*. 'The ancient turreted stronghold, with the original old iron-barred door defended by gun holes, is in a splendid state of preservation, and the outer walls are from six to seven feet thick.' Leading off the old banqueting hall is an apartment known as 'Queen Mary's sitting room'. (When you are selling a stately home in Scotland, as every estate agent knows, you are always grateful for any connection with Mary, Queen of Scots.)

To more practical matters: the first portion comprised the castle, Farlenger House (on the north bank of the Tay) and Foss House, some miles away. 'Castle Menzies shootings extend to over 11,000 acres of which some 6500 acres are grouse moor . . . the bag should be 1200 brace grouse and 2000 brace partridges . . . Six miles of salmon trout fishing in the rivers Lyon and Tay . . . the grouse moor at Foss extends to over 6500 acres . . .'

The Rannoch portion of the estate was 71,543 acres, including Rannoch Lodge and five other houses stretching along Loch Rannoch: 'On Talladh-a-Bheithe, Craganour and Corrievarkie 1800 brace of grouse and over 80 stags should be shot', and there are exclusive fishing rights on various streams and lochs . . .

The Menzies estate was eventually sold for £140,000, and Castle Menzies and the Foss estate went together for £30,000.

And what of John and Arthur Knight and the Galleries? ('Galleries, Wesdo, London' was still the firms's telegraphic address.) They were always in danger of being over-shadowed by spectacular property deals. From 1910 onwards Knight Frank & Rutley occasionally figure in *The Times* annual review of the highest-priced pictures at auctions, but they are generally swamped by Christie's. There is little evidence of the 'Old Masters Boom' which we find in the history of Christie's about this time, when enormous prices for pictures were being paid by American 'robber barons' like Frick, Widener and Pierpont Morgan. But John Knight was a furniture man; and the 'chattels' sales we find at this period seldom made front-page news. Chippendale, Sheraton and Hepplewhite were doing well, with unspecified 'pictures and porcelain'. A 'collection of paintings, engravings, coloured prints' is lumped together with 'books, carved ivories . . . snuff boxes and miscellaneous'. The contents of The Pleasaunce, Limpsfield Common, Surrey, offers a Broadwood grand piano, Turkish and Persian carpets, 'a small quantity of old wines, governess car, pony cart and other effects'. An 'Important Collection of Old English Porcelain, the Property of a Gentleman removed from Steventon, Berks' is announced with a little more panache: it comprises most of the English factories and some Continental services.

1914 opened with the spotlight full on Howard Frank – who was now *Sir* Howard. On Thursday, 1 January the New Year's Honours list in *The Times* singled him out:

Sir Howard Frank, whose knighthood was granted in the 1914 New Year's honours.

The world champion hackney horse, Lighthouse, with Miss Doreen Frank, in 1924. The horse was named after the old Beachy Head Lighthouse which Frank was to make his country home. Sir Howard Frank became President of the Hackney Horse Society in 1914.

KNIGHTS

> 'HOWARD FRANK, ESQ. A partner in the firm of Messrs Knight Frank & Rutley; a member of the Council of the Auctioneers' and Estate Agents' Institute, and also of the Royal Agricultural Society of England, and a director of the Norwich Union Fire Insurance Society. Mr. Frank sat on the Departmental Committee on the break-up of estates and many of the chief sales of landed property in recent years have been conducted by him.'

The *Estates Gazette*, unless it had advance news of the honour, must have had to re-jig that week's issue of the magazine with remarkable speed, for only two days later it came out with a special supplement containing a portrait photograph of the new Knight and a leading article of such warmth that it must have embarrassed even the subject. 'In offering our unqualified congratulations upon the occasion we feel sure this expression of Royal esteem will be regarded not only as a personal honour, but as the conferment of a rank of high favour upon the allied professions in which he occupies so distinguished a place.' His success had enabled him to combine business with public service. Thus he served on Lord Carrington's Departmental committee 'to consider the position of sitting tenants upon the sale of estates' (and in a few months' time would join yet another Government Committee 'for the prevention and relief of distress in agricultural districts').

A last glimpse of Sir Howard in peacetime before the storm breaks, as he hobnobs, on a blazing May afternoon, with Lord Leconfield at the Reigate and Redhill Horse and Hounds Society, where his chestnut mare, Terrington Modish, trots off with first prize; a glance at the 1914 sales, which totalled £1,968,000 for 268,500 acres (all but 50,000 of them in Scotland!) – including, unusually, two theatres in Shaftesbury Avenue, the Queen's and the Globe; and we leave the pre-war world.

VI
At War

Within six weeks of the outbreak of war on 4 August 1914, twenty-two of Knight Frank & Rutley's staff were in the forces. They had been about 100 strong in 1914; by the end of the war sixty-six of them were serving. Seven were killed, and they are commemorated on a plaque in the hall at 20 Hanover Square:

Robert H. Barclay
Charles R. Beasley
Frank Halstead King
John G. Overman
Sidney A. Ratcliff
Stewart W. Rumsey
George F. Thurley

Among the survivors were Cecil Ingram from the Edinburgh office who had been a Captain in the Royal Engineers; Bombardier E. Knight, RGA – who was known in the firm as Day, because John Knight once said to him 'I am the only Knight here'; Pte Charles J. Woosnam, RAMC, who eventually became Manager of the Galleries and a partner; Cpl A. Wetherill, East Yorkshire Regt, who became Foreman in the Galleries until his retirement in 1962; Trooper H. D. Kelleway, Surrey Yeomanry, survived to continue as a negotiator in the Country Department and eventually became a partner. Pte Sidney Mott, a surveyor, of the 12th London Regiment, had the worst experience of all trench warfare: badly wounded, he was caught in the barbed wire of No Man's Land and hung there for three days.

Many young men in the Army had reason to be thankful for their training as surveyors. It was possible, by fixing two dummy heads a known distance apart on the parapet of a trench, to draw the fire of a German sniper and so, by triangulation, to establish his position accurately and then call down fire on him from the artillery.

Henry Norman Harding, a junior surveyor of twenty, went to Egypt with the Westminster Dragoons Yeomanry in September 1914 to fight the Turks across the Suez Canal. A year later the unit, minus its horses, found itself at Gallipoli. The following year saw Harding in Palestine, where he rose to be Captain and was mentioned in dispatches; he was wounded at Beersheba and awarded the MC. 1918 found him back in Europe, in time to take part in the final push.

Two gallant officers who had not yet joined the firm, but whose lives were to be intertwined from 1914 onwards, were Will Gibson and Guy Coleridge. They met in September 1914 on Waterloo Station, on their way to Kempton Park Race-course where they were going to enlist in the Public Schools Battalion of the Middlesex Regiment. Both were eventually commissioned into the 8th South Staffordshire Regiment, and went to France in June 1915. They had arrived at Boulogne and were awaiting breakfast when Gibson was accidentally shot through the wrist by a brother-officer who had omitted to unload his pistol before cleaning it. Gibson was returned to England within twelve hours after leaving Dover, which is perhaps a record for a war casualty. However, he came back to France in three weeks.

The Battalion was in trench warfare in the Ypres Salient, was involved in the famous Hill 60 struggle, and took part in the big attack on the Somme in July 1916. On the night of 10 July both Gibson and Coleridge were wounded. Gibson received a bullet in the chest. His life was probably saved by a silver whisky flask in his breast pocket, a parting gift from his wife. Coleridge received injuries to his right leg which were to make him paralyzed for life. Both men won the Military Cross, to which Gibson added the DSO.

At home, the immediate effects of war, in the months after August 1914, had been predictable. Shortage of materials and labour meant no new civil building. Most firms found that estate business had declined by about half. There was a good deal of valuation work, especially of land taken by compulsory purchase for Army camps and airfields, and assessments and negotiation of compensation to clients either for land taken by Government departments, such as the War Office Lands Branch and the Ministry of Munitions, or for damage due to enemy action.

The whole of Europe and part of Asia were at war; but in the summer of 1915 a smaller battle was in progress, on Salisbury Plain. The preliminary announcement appeared in *The Times* in May: 'By direction of Sir Cosmo G. Antrobus, Bart. WILTSHIRE. The Historical Domain of AMESBURY ABBEY, including Stonehenge and comprising nearly the whole of the Parish of Amesbury.' The estate extended to 6400 acres.

Sir Howard Frank was well aware that there was going to be a row about Stonehenge, and that the press would be swamped with 'letters to the Editor', which in turn would beget leading articles.

'The sale,' said the *Estates Gazette*, 'recalls the famous lawsuit of 1904 concerning the safety of the stones. The owner's right to fence and enclose the ancient stone circle was strongly contested, and an action was brought against Sir Edmund Antrobus, the owner, for an order to remove the fencing and an injunction restraining him from enclosing the monument.' Judgment had been given for Sir Edmund.

But Sir Edmund had just died, and his elder son had been killed in the Dardanelles. Hence the sale of the estate. Knight Frank & Rutley, on 15 June, wrote to *The Times* on behalf of their client, Sir Cosmo, the younger son who had inherited the baronetcy: 'We write to explain that the property is under the protection of the Ancient Monuments Act, which ensures its preservation. Although Stonehenge is to be included in the sale of the Amesbury Abbey estate in September next, Sir Cosmo Antrobus, who is only tenant for life, proposes, if his powers permit him to do so, to impose conditions providing for the public having access thereto for all time. It is to be hoped, however, that Stonehenge may be bought either by the Government or by a learned society, and our instructions are that if any reasonable proposal be made

Stonehenge, part of the Amesbury Abbey estate, which was purchased by Mr Cecil Chubb for £6600 in 1915 as a present for his wife. Mr Chubb was shortly afterwards made a baronet: three years later Lady Chubb presented Stonehenge to the nation.

for its acquisition with the intention of preserving the monument in the public interest, we are to facilitate a sale by private treaty before the auction.'

Various archaeologists intervened. The Dean of Salisbury thought that 'there should be no public sale; but for (the nation) the market price of the few acres on which the great stones stand should be paid'. The Rev. E. H. Goddard, Hon. Sec. of the Wilts Antiquarian Society, wondered if the National Trust might give a lead; but

Stonehenge, after J. M. W. Turner, depicted in the Amesbury Abbey auction brochure.

'it is exceedingly difficult to raise money for any purpose unconnected with the War'.

Unknown to all the protesters, help was on the way, in the shape of Mr Cecil Chubb, a thirty-nine-year-old barrister, who lived nearby at Bapton Manor, Codford, Wilts. He had married an American girl, Mary Bella Fern, who, reading about the national monument at breakfast one morning, remarked to her husband: 'I sure would like to own Stonehenge.'

It was now certain that Mr Chubb would bid for Stonehenge. But how much? Knight Frank & Rutley had valued the stones at a minimum of £10,000, which was beyond Mr Chubb's means. The National Trust, with whom Sir Howard Frank corresponded, thought it far too high.

The auction was held at the crowded New Theatre, Salisbury, with Sir Howard on the rostrum. There was no bid for the Abbey and park, with 260 acres, which were withdrawn. The remaining lots were then offered, sixty-one of them selling for £61,490. For 'Lot 15' (Stonehenge) the auction particulars 'gave a detailed description supplied by the Archaeological Institute, as well as many historical notes written by Lady Antrobus . . . with a reproduction of Turner's well-known picture'. Sir Howard suggested an opening bid of £5000, which slowly rose to £6000. Would it stay there? Sir Howard pleaded with the crowd. He admitted that Stonehenge could not be valued, but surely £6000 was a poor price for such a property? Slowly the bidding crept up to £6600, at which Stonehenge was knocked down – to Mr Chubb, who shortly afterwards was made a Baronet, taking as his title 'Chubb of Stonehenge'. Three years later, Lady Chubb, true to her breakfast whim, presented it to the nation.

Sir Howard Frank, about this time, was at the centre of a movement by the Auctioneers' and Estate Agents' Institute to raise money to acquire a permanent home 'for paralyzed and totally disabled sailors and soldiers'. Every hospital train from France and Flanders contained men on stretchers – limbless, sightless, lungless – who would never work or walk again. The property Howard Frank had in mind was the Star & Garter Hotel, Richmond, whose freehold would cost £21,500. The *Estates Gazette* gave enthusiastic support, and Sir Howard's first appeal was to its readers, who were asked to send gifts, either in money or in goods which could be sold in auction sales being held all over the country by provincial branches of the Institute. The first auction would take place in London in November 1915.

In the third week of September Sir Howard Frank, as Chairman of the Executive Committee of the Institute, received the following letter from Buckingham Palace:

> 'Dear Sir Howard Frank,
>
> 'With reference to my letter of the 18th inst., I am commanded by the Queen to send you the accompanying Indian silver casket, which Her Majesty is graciously pleased to contribute towards your first sale in aid of the funds for the acquisition of the Star & Garter Hotel as a hospital and home for the paralysed and totally disabled soldiers and sailors.
>
> I am,
> Yours very faithfully
> E. W. WALLINGTON.'

In October Sir Howard Frank and George Head, President of the Institute, announced that it had been found that it would be more economical to rebuild than to adapt the old building.

Gifts were pouring in for the auctions. They included a house near the Crystal Palace, 'to be sold without reserve', a freehold ground rent of £6 per annum secured upon a residence at Sutton, Surrey, and 'a fine St Bernard dog'. One surveyor wrote, 'the scheme of identifying the profession with such a splendid movement appeals to me very forcibly. Surely our members will immediately rise to the occasion.' The London auction alone realized £3258.

Considering that the country was at war, progress was rapid. Fourteen months later, the Institute, represented by George Head, Sir Howard Frank, B. L'Anson Breach and J. H. Townsend Green, attended at Buckingham Palace to hand over the deeds of the Star & Garter Home to Queen Mary, together with the deeds of Ancaster House, opposite the Star & Garter, which was to be used as an annexe, and a further contribution of £13,705 towards the Endowment Fund.

The estate business was moving slowly but profitably. Hawkstone Park, 3546 acres near Shrewsbury, offered everything a country squire could wish for, even the unusual amenities of electric light and central heating. By way of contrast, the

Tehidy estate, on the north coast of Cornwall, contained tin mines and changed hands by private treaty in October 1915. It included 'a large portion of the town of Camborne', the famous Dolcoath tin mine, sunk 2250 ft below the surface, and 'Portreath, a bracing little seaside town'. The total area was about 7000 acres. The estate had been in the hands of the Basset family since the Norman Conquest.

The annual summary of property sales for 1915 (excluding Scotland) shows one or two estates which had been on offer, whole or in part, since the '1912 Brochure' (for example Red Rice and Membland Hall). In all, 37,883 acres had been offered, realizing £1,059,000.

It could not be pretended that the War was going well. There were shortages, inefficiencies, lack of central planning. Sir Howard Frank, together with other captains of industry, felt that war was too important to be left to generals and politicians. He was at the heart of a movement to bring in businessmen to advise the Government. Hence this letter to Sir Howard from Whitehall, dated 5 January 1916:

> 'Sir, – I am directed by the Minister of Munitions to inform you that he very highly appreciates your offer of your services to the Ministry, and is glad to take advantage of it. He has therefore much pleasure in appointing you to be Honorary Adviser on Land Valuation to the Ministry and hopes that you will be good enough to assist him in this capacity in connection with such matters as may be referred to you.'

Before the end of the year, the War Office and the Ministry of Munitions amalgamated their land-purchase organizations, and Sir Howard Frank found himself Honorary Chief Adviser to the combined Directorate of Lands at 6 St James's Square. In a month or two, his title was changed to Director-General. He was now dealing with the 200,000 acres already owned by the War Office, and also the additional 150,000 acres taken over since the beginning of the War, as well as buildings with a rental value of about £2,500,000.

At Hanover Square, where they had accommodation to spare, the remaining staff at Walton & Lee moved in from Mount Street, and the Royal Society of Literature, who had been given temporary house room, moved out.

During 1917, as if he had not enough to do, Sir Howard accepted the Vice-Chairmanship of the Committee for dealing with prisoner-of-war labour, a Vice-Presidency of the Auctioneers' and Estate Agents' Institute and membership of an Advisory Council to the newly-formed Ministry of Reconstruction, under the Chairmanship of Lord Salisbury. (We shall see that this was a preparation for a much larger post-war task which Sir Howard would be asked to carry out.) By the end of 1917, he had also been made Director-General of Lands for the Air Ministry. Somehow he still managed to put in an occasional appearance in his capacity as President of the Hackney Horse Society.

The sale of 1917 was undoubtedly that of the Earl of Shrewsbury's Cheshire estate. The Premier Earl of England was offering, at the Grosvenor Hotel, Chester, with Sir Howard on the rostrum, over 5000 acres with a rent-roll of more than £10,600 a year. Sir Howard explained that certain buildings on some of the

The famous pig Tirpitz which was auctioned in aid of Red Cross funds as part of the Earl of Shrewsbury's Cheshire estate and which eventually raised 400 guineas. Tirpitz had swum from the German cruiser Dresden, *sunk off Valpariso, and was rescued by HMS* Glasgow.

properties had been erected by the tenants, and the Earl, through his land agent Major Gardner, was anxious to treat them fairly. (So was Sir Howard – the welfare of sitting tenants had always been of special concern to him. There is a legend that, when some agricultural labourers had lost their cottages through an estate being sold over their heads, he had rushed out and bought them all £50 gold watches as some sort of consolation.) Major Gardner had agreed to settle with the tenants by purchase at valuation. All was concluded satisfactorily, and the total sum realized was £175,000. It was not the largest sale of the year (that was Lilleshall estate, near Newport, Shropshire, which went for £298,498) but it attracted a great deal of publicity.

1917, indeed, was a record year for estate sales: 109,000 acres were sold by private treaty, and only 45,000 by auction, bringing in £4,011,700.

One lighter note in the sale of the Shrewsbury estates was Sir Howard's auctioning, in aid of Red Cross funds, of the famous pig 'Tirpitz', which swam from the German cruiser *Dresden*, sunk off Valparaiso, and was rescued by HMS *Glasgow*. The Duke of Portland had sent a letter bidding 50 guineas: the bidding rose to 200 guineas, at which figure 'Tirpitz' was sold to Sir George Riddell, who put him up again, and the auctioneer added a further 200 guineas.

A long-awaited sale was that of the Duke of Sutherland's Scottish estates in Sutherland – 240,000 acres 'equal in size to more than one English county'. It was to have taken place in October 1914, but had been postponed on account of the war. In March 1918 preliminary announcements of an auction, to be held at Hanover Square on 30 October, began to appear. Meanwhile the Duke had presented Borgie Lodge and 12,223 acres to the nation to provide small holdings for ex-Servicemen. 330,698 acres were sold for £130,000.

The German cruiser Dresden.

HMS Glasgow.

The Birthday Honours List in June recorded that Sir Howard Frank had been made a Knight Commander of the Bath for his services to the Government. The *Estates Gazette* again presented its readers with a full-page portrait of him.

It was almost true to say that the more difficult an estate was to sell, the thicker were the auction particulars. The firm's compiler of historical notes pulled out all the

Gun dogs take to the water at Syre, Sutherland. In October 1918 over 330,000 acres of the Duke of Sutherland's Scottish estates were sold for £130,000.

stops for Bosworth Park (in April) and Motcombe, Dorset (in September). Bosworth, in Leicestershire, had a Queen Anne Palladian mansion, fourteen farms, excellent trout fishing, 3167 acres. The manor dated back to the reign of King John; but it was also only half a mile away from the reported site of the battle of Bosworth Field in 1485. Pieces of armour and weapons had been found. Here was a mound from which Henry, Earl of Richmond, had harangued his troops; there, among elms known as King Dick's Clump, had Richard Crookback raised his standard.

For the Motcombe estate (8134 acres, sold for £462,306) the particulars, 14½ by 10 ins., were 1 in. thick and lavishly illustrated. Lord Stalbridge, the vendor, lived at Stalbridge, where, in 1644, Charles I, on his way to defeat at the Battle of Newbury, had spent the night. Robert Boyle, chemist and philosopher, had written many of his books, and held first meetings of the Society for the Propagation of the Gospel there. But the *pièce de résistance* was a ghost story. A ghost is sometimes a selling-point, sometimes not. In this case it seems to have been an additional attraction. In the old mansion, demolished and replaced by the new one, lived a widowed mother with her eighteen-year-old son, who displeased her by marrying the gamekeeper's pretty daughter. One day, as he came home from hunting, his mother told him that his young bride was dead: she had been standing with her back to the fire, her dress had caught alight and she had been burnt to death. On her death-bed the mother confessed that she had pushed her daughter-in-law into the fire. At five in the afternoon, ever after, the mother's ghost (not the daughter-in-law's) appeared, her own ghostly garments on fire, crying 'I have done it, I have done it!' as she walked through walls and closed doors from one room to another and back again.

The Galleries were doing well enough: sales were fewer than they had been in peace-time, and prices were low: many wound-up estates yielded English pottery, silver, Japanese prints, antiquities from Greece, Rome, Persia, Egypt; prices were generally not high, and there was a universal fear that American middlemen and collectors were scooping the market to sell again when times were better.

As estates came on the market through the death of the owners, not only from natural causes but increasingly through officers being killed in action, estate agents were more and more involved in valuation for probate. In July 1918 came the appeal and judgment in the famous Ellesmere case, which set the pattern for probate valuations of large estates for the next fifty years, and resulted in even more subdivision of estates for sale.

The Earl of Ellesmere had petitioned by way of appeal against the decision of the Commissioners of Inland Revenue determining (under the Finance Act of 1910) the principal value of the Brackley estate in Northamptonshire. Death duty had arisen because of the death, in July 1914, of the Third Earl of Ellesmere. The petitioner appealed on the ground that the value of £82,316 was excessive, since this figure included certain rents and ground-rents which, the Commissioners had agreed, were worth £5316. Was not the principal value really only £77,000? Four years before the petitioner had consulted Messrs Knight Frank & Rutley about offering the property for sale, and it had in fact been sold in August 1915 for £68,000. The purchaser had since resold a large part of it in lots for £65,000.

The referee for the Inland Revenue gave it as his opinion that 'the price paid by a speculator for the whole of the various properties comprised in the estate in one lot is not the market price of the estate; but that the market price in such a case as this is the aggregate of the separate prices of the various parts'. The principal value was therefore £75,618. Mr Justice Sankey's judgment was based on the Finance Act of 1824, which defined 'principal value' as 'the price which, in the opinion of the Commissioners, such property would fetch if sold in the open market at the time of the death of the deceased'. The referee was wrong in ordering that all the costs of the appeal should be paid by the petitioner; nevertheless the appeal was dismissed – with costs.

The long-term result of this case was that executors of estates had to give serious consideration to the way in which properties were handled after death, not only to pay Estate duty, but to guard against any possible come-back later.

1918 ended with record sales figures – nearly £6,000,000, with the Motcombe estate and Meux's Brewery in London leading (£462,306 and £400,000 respectively), 431,000 acres being offered by auction and 211,000 acres by private treaty. All this, and the November Armistice too.

In 1977, Forsinard, forming part of the Duke of Sutherland's Scottish estates, was again sold by Knight Frank & Rutley.

But before we leave this last year of war, let us look at a man with a dream. Sir Howard Frank's friend William Hesketh Lever, recently created Lord Leverhulme, Chairman of Lever Bros, manufacturer of soap and founder of Port Sunlight, longed to help the poor crofters of the Outer Hebrides. In September 1918, therefore, he bought the whole of the Isle of Lewis, often called Harris-and-Lewis, described as 'an unique sporting domain of about 450,000 acres'.

But that was not what Lord Leverhulme wanted. His dream was to create a modern fishing industry, one that would ensure the prosperity of the islanders, based on a new port which would be called Leverburgh. We shall see, in a later chapter, how he got on.

VII
The Early Twenties

Peace, coming with such suddenness on 11 November 1918, ushered in a world needing reconstruction. Forests had been cut down ruthlessly to provide wood for army camps, railway sleepers, trenches and dug-outs in Flanders. Valuing timber was about to become a major task for surveyors, and standing timber found ready buyers; and in 1919 the Forestry Commission was founded to try to repair the ravages and provide for the future. As the great landed estates broke up and small-holdings became more numerous, ex-officers invested their gratuities in them; and not only their inexperience could be blamed for their failure, for, viewed nationally, farming was entering still deeper doldrums: scientific farming to feed the masses could only be done on large farms, it was felt by agricultural theorists. Britain now entered a period of land speculation – more to build than to farm.

We have seen that war supplies had been co-ordinated by committees of business men like those to which Sir Howard had been appointed. But now the supplies had to stop. All over the world were surplus stores, worth many millions of pounds, which would be wasted unless some use were found for them. Who could head such a vast enterprise? A man who had long experience of selling off miscellaneous goods, of valuation, of supply and demand? It did not take the Government long to think of Sir Howard Frank. He was already, in addition to all his other committee work, Deputy Chairman of the Ministry of Munitions Disposal Board; and in April 1919 he succeeded F. J. Kellaway, MP, as Chairman.

The property to be disposed of ranged from large areas of land to knives and forks, and it was scattered all over the world – in Europe, Egypt, Palestine, South and East Africa, Iraq and India. The Disposal Board's first report, issued as a white paper, appeared in July 1920. Sir Howard had worked on this, with Lord Inverforth the Minister of Munitions, since the end of 1918. In eighteen months more than £504,000,000 had been realized on sales of surplus war stores and raw materials, and further sales were expected to make another £130,000,000. The goods handled were 'lands, buildings and factories . . . materials, equipment, horses, mechanical transport, huts, furniture, watercraft, tools, machinery, motors and miscellaneous plant'. Over 700 firms of auctioneers were engaged in the sales: no wonder Sir Howard was praised for having done so much for his profession. The British taxpayer had much to thank him for.

There was a certain inevitability about the Birthday Honours of 1920, in which Sir Howard was made a Baronet. Apart from his services to the Government, he had been outstandingly generous to good causes, and it was about this time that he gave £5000 to the Disabled Officers' Fund.

Ex-servicemen returning to Hanover Square had found a staff reduced from about a hundred to barely forty. (We know this because they *all* signed a card of congratulations to Sir Howard on his baronetcy.) Arthur Knight had been made a partner, and in the spring of 1919 there was a very important appointment: Alfred J. Burrows, whose old-established family practice in Ashford was amalgamated with Knight Frank & Rutley. Mr Burrows, a member of the Council of the Auctioneers' and Estate Agents' Institution and one of the most respected and best-liked men in his profession, brought to Sir Howard something he very much needed – an immense knowledge of farms and land values. Those who knew him called him 'a first-class agriculturalist' and 'absolutely straight'. He also had, like Sir Howard himself, remarkable energy. Lucky the young surveyor who was trained by him – but, in those years long before Land Rovers, he would be walked off his feet!

At about the same time William Gibson, DSO, MC, made his first appearance, in the Town Department, for which he was well qualified. He was destined to become Senior Partner in the long term. To some rather forbidding, the martinet in him would cause him to be known to many as 'the Colonel'. Yet he had begun as a sailor, not a soldier. He had only joined the Army because the Navy would not take him: 'It is not the custom', they had the effrontery to tell him, 'to transfer from the Junior to the Senior Service.' The Junior Service was the Merchant Navy, which Gibson, then 15, had joined in 1902 as a cadet with HMS *Conway*. He had then gone to sea as an apprentice in the full-rigged ship *Forth*, taken his Second Mate's Certificate in 1907 and Chief Mate's Certificate in 1909 in both sail and steam. In 1910 he came ashore, took up articles with Chestertons the well-known London surveyors and in the following two years passed the Intermediate and Fellowship examinations of the Chartered Surveyors' Institution.

This was the man who, next to Sir Howard himself, probably exercised the strongest influence on the firm up to his retirement in 1956. He was made Town Manager in 1924. Always very close to Sir Howard, he became his executor.

In Edinburgh, Will Gibson's home city, the firm changed its address from 100 to 90 Princes Street; but they still needed galleries to dispose of chattels, and so they took over Dowells Rooms, famous in the North for the sale of landed property, jewellery and works of art. It was converted into a limited company of which Sir Howard became chairman and Cecil Ingram a director.

The first post-war tentacle towards the international market was the opening of an office at 20 Boulevard du Nord, Monte Carlo. Soon there was another office on La Croisette, Cannes, where a Colonel F. G. Aldous, DSO, had his own agency. There was a brisk trade in villas along the Corniche; generally for letting rather than selling. Correctly foreseeing a strong surge towards the Mediterranean sunshine, and the desire for pleasure and relaxation after wartime stress, Sir Howard added to this the fortunate circumstance that it was now actually cheaper to spend holidays in France than at home, the exchange rate of about 175 francs to the pound making it possible to get a complete meal, *vin compris*, for about six modern pence. The Roaring Twenties were beginning.

William Gibson, DSO, OBE, MC, joined the Merchant Navy as a cadet aged 15 in 1902 and qualified for his master's certificate under sail. He served with distinction in the First World War and was to become Senior Partner in 1939. He was also to command the 5th Bucks Batallion of the Home Guard during World War II.

Sir Howard was also involved with plans for the extension of the University of London, and acted on behalf of the Duke of Bedford and his trustees in negotiations with the Government for selling a suitable site in Bloomsbury. In May 1920 the Senate announced that a site of 11½ acres behind the British Museum had been provided in perpetuity for a new headquarters and colleges. The price paid was believed to be £55,000 an acre.

Two country sales of 1919 deserve mention – Ruthin Castle in Denbighshire and Sundon, Bedfordshire – the one Celtic-historical, the other full of modern problems. Ruthin dated back to Owain Glyndwr, and even, by local tradition, to King Arthur. At the auction £77,095 was the total of bids accepted, the castle and 478 acres being withdrawn and sold privately later.

The Sundon auction was an example of Sir Howard's concern for the sitting tenant. The estate of Mr F. A. Page Turner was auctioned at Luton Town Hall. The mansion, brick-and-tiled, was afterwards occupied by the Luton industrialist George Brightman; but for the present a middle-man had been organized, a Mr Albert Wilkinson. The 3140 acres of the estate included eight farms, smallholdings, woodlands, cottages and watercress beds. On the rostrum, Sir Howard offered the estate as a whole. Mr Wilkinson's opening bid was £75,000. The bids went up £1000 a time to £81,000, at which price it was knocked down to Mr Wilkinson. It was all over in five

The Citadel, Bloomsbury. In 1920 Sir Howard Frank acted on behalf of the Duke of Bedford and his trustees in selling an 11-acre site behind the British Museum, which was acquired by the Senate for a new headquarters and colleges for the University of London.

minutes. Sir Howard's friend Sir Trustram Eve, who was in the plot, afterwards revealed that Wilkinson and a Mr Cumberland had taken the risk on behalf of all the tenants, who would be given a chance to buy their own holdings at no profit to the buyer. If the property had been sold in lots, outside bidders might not have been so considerate and some tenants might have been homeless.

The international operations of the firm took an unexpected turn in the winter of 1920, when they were asked by the Government to value many square miles of forests in Poland for War Indemnity payments. This can be pleasant if tiring work in fine weather. But in Poland it was winter, which can mean a temperature of something like 40 degrees below zero. The chief surveyor was, of course, Frank Capon, who responded to almost every situation, whether of pleasure, anger or extreme cold, by beginning each sentence with the exclamation 'Ooh, my boy!' The survey area, a dense pine forest, was snowbound, and the team was transported in horse-drawn sleighs, accompanied by guards armed with rifles. They soon discovered what the rifles were for. First one grey shape appeared ahead, and vanished. All round, a distant howling drew nearer, more grey shapes appeared, racing alongside the sleighs. Wolves! The guards began to fire, some of the grey shapes fell back, and the rest of the pack turned upon their fallen comrades and ate them. 'Ooh my boy!' No doubt Frank Capon availed himself of an old surveyor's trick which he taught to so many young surveyors: to keep your hands warm, smother them with vaseline.

Among 1920 sales was that of the Wentworth estate, near Virginia Water in the heath and conifer district of affluent Surrey. It was, it seems, a difficult auction: what was described as a 'Tudor-Gothic' mansion with many bays, crenellated on top, was offered with 1796 acres. Eventually the mansion and 1125 acres were sold and its ideal purpose was realized – to be a country club with a golf course. 'Country clubs are not always a success, and sometimes the mansion comes on the market again,' comments a retired surveyor who remembers the sale; but Wentworth has survived to become a national institution.

In the hunting shire of Leicestershire, Quenby Hall, 'a perfect specimen of Jacobean architecture' with 2004 acres, 'including 15 of the best Stilton cheese-making farms and small-holdings in the country', were offered by Lady Henry Grosvenor. As a hunting centre it was 'unique, the Quorn, Cottesmore, Mr Fernie's and the Belvoir providing six days sport a week'. Knight Frank & Rutley's brochure, lavishly illustrated, carried five pages of historical background culled from Nichols's *History and Antiquities of Leicestershire*, tracing the history of the Ashby family from the thirteenth century. Yet the estate did not sell as a whole, and was offered again in lots two months later, realizing £47,773 less the mansion which was sold privately in 1922.

The Quenby auction particulars are believed to be the only Knight Frank & Rutley document containing a recipe – for making Quenby cheese, said to be Stilton in type.

In Scotland, the Marquis of Breadalbane was trying to sell his famous sporting and agricultural estates, 57,335 acres including part of Loch Tay and Taymouth Castle. Much was made, in the particulars, of the fact that 'Queen Victoria slept here', her bedroom and dressing-room being a special attraction. The whole description of the 'new' (1801) Castle suggested a total devotion to shooting – seven shoots yielding, in a good year, 13,435 grouse, 161 black game, 52 pheasants, 94 partridges, 30 stags, 10 ptarmigan, and so on, down to 559 rabbits. The names of the rooms are instructive: housekeeper's sitting room, still room larder, service room with service lift, men servants' smoking room, boot hall, butler's dressing room,

Quenby Hall, described in the brochures as 'a perfect speciment of Jacobean architecture which holds its own with any in the kingdom'. The particulars also contained the recipe for making Quenby cheese:

> *'Take the night's cream, and put it to the morning's new milk, with rennet; when the curd is come, it is not to be broke, as is done with other cheeses; but take it out with a soil-dish altogether, and place it in a sieve to drain gradually: and, as it drains, keep gradually pressing it until it becomes firm and dry; then place it in a wooden hoop; afterwards to be kept dry on boards, turned frequently, with cloth binders around it, which are to be tightened as occasion requires. N.B. the dairy maid must not be disheartened if she does not succeed perfectly in her first attempt.'*

ladies' maids' work room . . . The auction was not successful, and most of the estate was sold privately six months later.

The presence of Will Gibson was quickly felt in a succession of major deals in urban property in which he was a specialist. The first of these was Gunnersbury in West London; the philanthropic Lionel de Rothschild offered his residence and park to the Ealing and Chiswick Council as a public amenity. It was worth £250,000, and he was willing to let it go for £175,000. However, there was 'outlying parts' on which he did not scorn to make a handsome profit. These were sold privately to developers of housing estates; companies needing sports grounds; Kensington Borough Council, needing a new cemetery (at £4000–£6000 an acre, an enormous price for 1920); and the Ministry of Transport for a section of the new Great West Road (now the A4). Soon factories and houses would appear all along it, for ribbon development was not yet controlled. But Lionel de Rothschild was generous with the park, donating funds for its maintenance and pensioning the staff with free cottages for life. And once a year, when the park was open to the public, he strolled among them distributing pound notes to children.

During the past year, Sir Howard had sustained a blow by the death of his wife. His health temporarily declined, and there were vague reports of complications due to a 'local infection'. He had clearly been overworking for a number of years, and it seems likely that he was having the first symptoms of the heart trouble that was to recur for the rest of his life. He was, at this time, leaving more and more major projects to Will Gibson. But he still had time for horse shows, and his pride and joy was his new hackney horse, Lighthouse, which set out on its inevitably prize-winning career. Why 'Lighthouse'? Because Sir Howard had just bought the old Beachy Head lighthouse, converted to a fairly primitive week-end residence in 1901, and known as Belle Toute. From now on he had an obsession with lighthouses, and had a silver one above the windscreen of his Rolls-Royce: it lit up at night, so that he could easily pick out his car after a theatre or a party.

Will Gibson's next notable deal was the sale, by no means easy, of two landmarks in Leicester Square – the Empire Theatre, a music hall, and the Queen's Hotel, with a vacant corner site by Lisle Street. And in Scotland, Cecil Ingram contributed the sales of the Carlton Hotel, opposite Edinburgh's Waverley Station, and of Sir Harry Lauder's 10,000-acre estate at Glenbranter, Argyll. Glenbranter did not reach the reserve price at auction, but was eventually sold privately to the Forestry Commission.

In Reigate, Surrey, something was about to happen that most of the townspeople were hardly aware of: the whole town was to be sold over their heads, though it would make little difference to their daily lives.

'By direction of Somers Somerset Esq.' these were offered '400 properties, and comprising the greater part of the Town of Reigate, including the Principal Shops and Business Premises . . . mostly let at low rentals upon tenancies due to expire within the next few years'. There were also the Old Town Hall, Reigate Castle, the White Hart, the Swan and other inns, a large number of private houses, and the Priory Farm of about 115 acres 'with long road frontages available for development'. The annual rent-roll was £7829.

This was the first time the firm had disposed of a whole town, and the auction was planned to take three days in October 1921. There were 260 lots. The 'particulars' noted that the Manor of Reigate, whose origins went back to the De Warenne family

Large parts of the Marquis of Breadalbane's estates were sold in 1922. Kilchurn Castle, owned by the Marchioness of Breadalbane, was sold by Knight Frank & Rutley in 1985.

(one of whom, John de Warenne, became a Member of Parliament in 1297 at the age of 14), had been given to Lord Chancellor Somers in 1688 by William III of Orange soon after the flight of James II. Now, in 1921, the good people of Reigate were for the most part well pleased to be given the opportunity of buying houses and shops where they and their families had lived and traded for generations. These good relations were cemented by Knight Frank & Rutley who, during the sale, earned local merit by contributing to a big charity effort on behalf of the Red Cross – 'a mile of pennies' to be laid along the streets of the town. The firm 'adopted' a street and gave the required number of pennies to the Red Cross.

The auction, conducted by Will Gibson, realized £203,840. The sale, from survey to auction, had consumed so much of his time that he had spent scarcely an evening

Sir Howard Frank bought the old Beachy Head lighthouse in 1920 and used it as a country home for the rest of his life.

at home for months. A peace-offering for Mrs Gibson was indicated, and he bought her a crystal decanter and glasses which his daughter, Mrs Jean Heller, still has.

Towards the end of 1921 the *Estates Gazette* printed a sympathetic paragraph wishing Sir Howard Frank a speedy return to health: 'We have pleasure in stating, on the authority of his medical attendant, that . . . he is now convalescent and will probably be in a position to take an overdue holiday very soon.' The *Gazette* could not be expected to know that the 'overdue holiday' would be his second honeymoon. Some weeks before, Sir Howard had telephoned one of the partners and said: 'I think I feel fit enough to do a little work. Could you send a secretary to Cheyne Walk?' He paused. 'Not Spacky. Someone young and pretty like the girl who can occasionally be seen sitting outside Arthur Knight's door.'

The Empire Theatre, Leicester Square, which was sold by Knight Frank & Rutley in 1920.

'Spacky' was his regular secretary Miss Spackman: she was small, thin, mouse-grey and bird-like, with steel-rimmed glasses, and she gave Sir Howard a lifetime of devoted service. The pretty secretary who arrived at Cheyne Row was nineteen-year-old Nancy Muriel Brooks of Ealing, thirty-one years younger then Sir Howard. After what can only have been a whirlwind courtship, they were married at St Luke's, Chelsea. 'I think,' his widow (now Lady Coningham) says today, 'he thought I'd make a better wife than a secretary.' It was noticed that, in signing the register, Sir Howard gave his address as 'The Lighthouse, Beachy Head'. The honeymoon began in Switzerland, continued in Italy and the South of France, and ended in the United States where, near Niagara Falls, the couple lost all their luggage, which made it virtually impossible to stay in any hotel without being thought to have come there for an immoral purpose.

We saw, in the case of Breadalbane, how a great mansion was divided in specialised rooms, each yielding different kinds of furniture, decoration and ornaments. These were reflected in the 'Chattels' sales of the period: the contents of an Adam Room or a Chinese Room; 450- and 300-piece dinner services (Minton, Dresden, etc.); French and English antique furniture, carpets and tapestries. At the firm's sale of the contents of Cassiobury Park for Lady Essex in June 1922, a large panel of Brussels

Château Davachan, which was the scene of the 1920 peace conference. The Château, at St Remo on the Italian Riviera, was offered for sale in 1922.

tapestry, designed 'after Teniers', fetched 575 guineas, a Sèvres dessert service 100 guineas, a Chippendale mahogany chest 86 guineas, a Queen Anne silver cup and cover, 94*s* – all excellent prices at the time.

In April 1922 the famous Bath Assembly Rooms, where Jane Austen enjoyed the limited romance of her young life, came up for sale, 'renowned for its magnificent Suite of Entertainment Halls, which include a recently-equipped luxurious Cinema . . .' In June, instructed by Helen, Duchess of Albany, the firm handled the Claremont estate, near Esher, Surrey. The Palladian mansion, set in luxurious woodlands, had once belonged to Clive of India, and the whole estate of 503 acres realized £66,400. Parts were resold in 1926 and 1928, the prices rising as the surrounding area became more fashionable for building detached houses. Today there is a nine-hole golf course, and the house was long ago converted into a Christian Science girls' school whose most celebrated pupil was the late Joyce Grenfell, OBE.

On the Italian Riviera, Colonel Aldous was advertising, among other properties, the Château Davachan, San Remo, 'at which the Peace Conference was held in April 1920'.

Sir Howard Frank had spent part of his convalescence chairing a Committee to examine the advisability of concentrating in one department all Government purchases and sales of land and buildings and the management of the estates of the Crown and Government property. In the summer of 1922 it presented its report, recommending the creation of a Central Lands Department which should absorb the Office of Woods and Forests and concentrate all the professional surveying and valuation staffs of various departments except the Ministry of Agriculture and the Scottish Board of Agriculture – 'leaving the fighting services entirely unfettered'. All

Knight Frank & Rutley's first stand at the Royal Show held in Cambridge in 1922. At the entrance is A. T. Underwood, manager of the farms department. The Royal has always played a major part in the firm's activities: today Knight Frank & Rutley has a permanent site at the RASE Ground at Stoneleigh.

the Crown's agricultural properties should gradually be sold, and the proceeds invested in freehold town properties. And when the Central Lands Department came into existence, it should investigate all Government holdings to eliminate those that were unnecessary or could be displaced by alternative accommodation.

This summer, too, the firm made its first appearance at the Royal Show, held at Cambridge. Their pavilion at the Show was to become a permanent way of meeting clients and prospective buyers and supplying them with information – and refreshments.

What was office life like, in those post-war years, for young men of high spirits recently out of the Forces? There was, it seems, a good deal of practical joking when senior backs were turned. There were trouser-splitting leaps up the five steps to the Country Department – 3 ft 6 in. up and 4 ft forward – just to show that one could do it. These and many other things are remembered by Ronald Browne, an octogenarian retired surveyor. The filing room at the back of No. 20 Hanover Square looked out upon a back room of Busvines in Bond Street, where model girls could be seen changing. Busvines specialized in furs and riding habits 'by Royal Appointment'. If, on the other hand, one looked out into the Square, one might be lucky enough to see Worth's models posing for photographs in the Gardens. In those days 'the ground-floor corridors near the Galleries sales rooms used to be lined with pictures and furniture, and the rugs to be sold as well on Friday made the display colourful . . . Carriages drawn by tall bay horses or large cars would bring august clients to the porch of No. 20 . . . In the evening green open red-label Bentleys would be parked outside, with much deep drumming of exhausts . . . these glorious cars belonged to young Guards officers, come to collect models from Worth's.'

The most harassed member of the staff was probably Mr Coleman, the advertising manager, trying to pacify the printers while Sir Howard made endless alterations in red ink to the advertisement copy. Mr Coleman, a middle-aged bachelor, lived at Brighton and got up early enough to walk part of the way to London daily. Mr Alder, the tender-hearted cashier, used to lend money to typists who found themselves 'short' on the day before pay-day. Typists then earned 47*s* 6*d* (£2.37½) a week and were often heard to ask: 'How can a girl stay respectable in London and pay 10*s* 3*d* (51p) for her room and buy food and clothes?'

In a maturing profession, examinations were becoming more important, and young surveyors studying for them spent much time at the lecture rooms of Parry, Adkins & Parry, a firm of crammers near Victoria Station.

The chief negotiators at this time were Gordon Cannon, Norman Harding, Alec Siese and Herbert Kelleway. The first three had joined the firm immediately after the war: Kelleway (who married A. J. Burrows's daughter, a secretary in the firm) had been on the staff since 1907. Harding eventually took up a partnership in another firm; the other three became partners in Knight Frank & Rutley. Cannon is remembered as a brilliant tactician, pulling at the left side of his clipped moustache while planning an audacious deal. Siese, tall and athletic with wavy red hair, was 'terrifying' to some female staff, but apparently very popular with well-born lady clients. Harding was universally liked for his ruthless honesty and bluff kindliness and expected the same standards of conduct from other people.

The Knight Frank & Rutley Club still provided home-made concerts, whist-drives and debates; while most young men were expected to join the firm's Fire Brigade. All members got a day's Fire Holiday every year. The Captain was Reg Leslie, a senior surveyor. Sir Howard awarded an annual prize of a silver watch for the smartest boy on parade at fire practice. Only one alarm is recorded: smoke was seen pouring out of a basement room where stationery was kept. Hoses were unrolled into the Square to attack the blaze, and soon there was water everywhere, but not before the nozzle had smashed a window in Sir Howard's Rolls outside. The fire was actually put out by Reg Leslie with an ordinary extinguisher.

Christmas at Knight Frank & Rutley was kept with a lavishness that did much to make up for relatively low salaries. Sir Howard sent cards to all staff, friends and business associates, usually big reproductions of paintings of eighteenth-century sailing ships. The vestibule at No. 20 was piled high with braces of pheasants for sending to clients and senior staff. Senior surveyors received boxes of cigars; juniors got huge round boxes of Charbonnel & Walker hand-made chocolates. All staff received bonus cheques.

There was, in 1922, an unexpected piece of free publicity from Mr Somerset Maugham, who published a collection of oriental travel sketches called *On A Chinese Screen*. In Chapter XXVI, dismally entitled 'Rain', he tells how, drenched to the skin and sitting in 'the squalid discomfort of a Chinese inn', he has an attack of homesickness for England:

> 'You sit by the fire, your pipe in your mouth, and read *The Times* from cover to cover; not the leading article, of course, but the agony columns and the advertisements for country houses you will never be able to afford. ("On the Chiltern Hills, standing in its own park of 150 acres, with spacious garden, orchard, etc., a Georgian house in perfect condition, with original woodwork and chimney-pieces, six reception rooms, 14 bedrooms and usual offices, modern sanitation, stabling with rooms over and excellent garage. Three miles from first-rate golf-course.") . . . I know then that Messrs Knight Frank & Rutley are my favourite authors . . . Their style, as is that of Confucius, is glitteringly compact . . . Their mastery of words such as rood and perch . . . is amazing . . . They can play with technical terms with the ingenuity of Mr Rudyard Kipling and they can invest them with the Celtic glamour of Mr W. B. Yeats.'

Well, he hasn't quite got the style of Knight Frank & Rutley's auction particulars of those days, but he comes near enough to make one think that Sir Howard might have considered him as a possible copywriter. He certainly employed Miss Graham as a researcher for all the historical notes concerning the properties for sale and it was she who had to vet all auction particulars for their English. She spent many hours in the archives of the British Museum and was responsible for ensuring the British Museum received a copy of all auction particulars.

Sir Howard was accustomed to being consulted on all kinds of matters by the Government; and often he did not wait to be asked, dashing off letters to *The Times* and Cabinet Ministers. *The Times*, in the autumn of 1922, was looking for a buyer. It was in the last weeks of the Lloyd George government, and Sir Howard wrote to the Premier telling him of confidential talks he had had with Sir John Ellerman the shipping magnate, outlining the rival ambitions of Ellerman, Lord Rothermere and Lord Cowdray to own, and even edit, *The Times*; and how much money each would put up, indicating his own preference for Ellerman.

It is not easy to tell how warm was Sir Howard's support for Sir John Ellerman. Probably, knowing that Lloyd George was playing with the idea of editing the paper himself, Sir Howard wished to see it acquired by the Prime Minister's friends. As it turned out the paper was bought some weeks later by Col. J. J. Astor, afterwards Lord Astor of Hever.

For about a year Winston Churchill, then Colonial Secretary, had been looking for a country house – 'a country basket' as his wife called it. He was about to lose his seat at Dundee which he had held since 1908, and the 'wilderness' period was beginning. Knight Frank & Rutley, for their part, had been disposing of an estate near

On A Chinese Screen. *W. Somerset Maugham, in his collection of Oriental travel sketches, nostalgically reflected upon England, and in particular Knight Frank & Rutley advertisements in* The Times.

Westerham, in Kent, called Chartwell, since 1921. All of it had been sold except the house and park.

One morning in 1922 Sir Howard called his negotiators into his room and told them that Winston Churchill wanted a small residential estate in the Home Counties: who would care to tackle him? Norman Harding, then 28, volunteered, as if for a dangerous mission, and sent the prospective buyer a selection of particulars. Eventually Eddie Marsh, Churchill's private secretary, telephoned to say he could only view properties on Saturday afternoons – he was simply too busy at the Colonial Office on other days.

They travelled together in Churchill's official car. It was the darkest car Harding had ever been in, and he told Churchill so.

'Well, you see, it's armoured,' Churchill said. 'The windows are bullet-resisting and I have a loaded revolver—' he waved it at Harding. A man sitting in front by the chauffeur turned out to be Sergeant (afterwards Inspector) Thompson, CID. 'He also has a revolver,' Churchill said. He turned round and slid back a small shutter. 'You see that car behind us?' It appeared to have three men in it. 'That car will accompany us ten miles out of town, and on our return will pick us up again and escort us back to the Colonial Office or to my home – I have a number of threatening letters each week, some telling me the actual time and method of my death, and I don't like it.' At the time Churchill was deeply concerned with the 'Irish question'. The IRA was assassinating prominent people, among them Field-Marshal Sir Henry Wilson, killed on the steps of his own house in London by the order of Michael Collins, with whom Churchill was at that very moment negotiating.

Together Churchill and Harding inspected various properties. On the way, Harding said, they had 'interesting talks and discussions, the topics ranging all over the world. He was particularly interested in my Gallipoli experiences as he was the instigator of that campaign, and he told me . . . that in his opinion, if Gallipoli had succeeded, it would have shortened the war by at least two years. I told him that from what I had seen on the spot . . . the planning of the campaign was faulty, that the Generals concerned lacked determination, and that in spite of this, the campaign had been very nearly successful.'

One day Eddie Marsh telephoned to say that Churchill was at Trent Park, Barnet, one of the houses of Sir Philip Sassoon: would Harding meet him there that afternoon?

'I arrived, knocked at the door, a butler opened it and said he had a message for me . . . would I go down to the herbaceous border where Mr Churchill was painting? . . . There he was, in a smock and a large Panama hat, and as I approached him he looked round and said "What do you think of this, Harding?" and there was a half finished painting of the herbaceous border.'

Churchill was certainly jumpy about the IRA. 'One day when we were passing through Guildford a tyre burst with a loud report, and he quickly put his hand over his face and said, "Drive on, driver, drive on." We drove down the first side street and pulled up. The weight of the car had cut the tyre to ribbons.'

Winston Churchill's study, Chartwell Manor, which he purchased in 1922 when Colonial Secretary.

'The time was about three o'clock, and he said "Can we get a drink, Harding?" (it was out of hours). I said I thought it was possible. About twenty yards along the road was a small pub. I knocked on the door; the publican opened it and said: "We're closed." I said: "I have Mr Churchill outside and he wants a drink." The man said: "All right, come in" – and so in we went and had a drink while a fresh wheel was being fitted to the car.'

Harding was surprised that Mrs Churchill never accompanied her husband on these expeditions, and in a few weeks' time the reason became clear: his daughter Mary, now Lady Soames, was born.

Perhaps, after all, Chartwell, in its rather derelict condition, would suit Churchill? Alec Siese sent him the particulars, and Norman Harding, whom Churchill obviously liked, negotiated. 'The house was close to the road, but it had the great merit that the hundred acres surrounding it were not overlooked . . . I told him that of all the estates we had seen, this appeared to be the most favourable proposition at the price he was willing to pay.' Churchill then made an offer which was not acceptable, and there was more hanging about at the Colonial Office. 'He strode up and down, using every argument he could think of to lower the price, but I repeated that he could have it at the price my clients had named, but if not, he would have to go on searching. Eventually, with a very bad grace, he agreed to the figure named.'

'This was the only time,' Harding concludes, 'during my various meetings with him that he was anything but courteous, kind and considerate, obviously because he was not getting his own way.'

We know, from Lady Soames's biography of her mother, that the price for the house and 80 acres was £5000; and that Churchill had to spend nearly three times the original price in rebuilding it with the help of Philip Tilden, a fashionable architect who had worked for Sir Philip Sassoon at his 'folly' house at Port Lympne, Kent. Chartwell is a grey largely Victorian mansion commanding wide and beautiful views over the Weald of Kent. 'Before it to the southward a valley falls dramatically away, and in the bottom is a lake, fed by a spring – the Chart Well,' Lady Soames writes: 'This beautiful place . . . cast at once and forever its spell over Winston.'

VIII
Hope and Glory

The secret of Sir Howard Frank's extraordinary life, it was said, was that he never got bogged down in detail: details were what his staff were for. Such was his eminence that a client walked into his office one day and offered him 5000 guineas plus expenses to go to New York for one day to hold an arbitration. Above all, he loved the extravagant gesture. To a dissatisfied client whose house had been badly surveyed and was found to be full of dry rot he barked: 'How much did you pay for it?' 'Ten thousand pounds.' Sir Howard whipped out a cheque book and wrote out a cheque for ten thousand. A potential critic had been silenced.

In the mid-1920s Sir Howard took up yachting as well as horses, and soon became a well-known figure at Cowes and other regattas. His health had improved. That he should receive the GBE in the 1924 birthday honours seemed only natural. He was the man who had everything. Everything? By his first wife he had had a daughter but no son and heir. But in 1923 his new young wife had presented him with a son, Howard, and would bear him another, Robert, less than two years later.

He relied more and more on Will Gibson, who in 1924 became Town Manager. Gibson's experience and influence were seen in the new emphasis on commercial property, and the trend towards residential flats, such as Cecil Court in South Kensington and Abercorn Mansions in St John's Wood.

The firm was now helping to create New Devonshire House, in Piccadilly, over Green Park Station. Once the Duke of Devonshire's town house had stood here.

'A powerful group,' reported the *Estates Gazette*, planned to cover a large part of the site with 'the very latest type of modern buildings' aimed at forming 'a landmark in the architecture of London'. To achieve this, Berkeley Street would be widened by twenty feet and a new street would link it with Stratton Street to cope with the increased flow of traffic. The result, it was hoped, would be 'a new shopping street, more exclusive and certainly more harmonious in character than Bond Street', and 'the natural channel of communication between Mayfair and Clubland and Victoria'.

The top of the premises would be mansion flats. Knight Frank & Rutley had already sold 31,000 square feet to Thos. Cook & Son, and 50,000 square feet remained to be disposed of. This project marks the first recorded co-operation between Knight Frank & Rutley and the New York estate agents Douglas Elliman, who marketed Devonshire House in the States. The two firms, more than fifty years later, were to form a joint venture in New York.

The transformation of Park Lane, like Piccadilly, from a residential to a commercial street, was also well under way. In 1924 the Duke of Westminster, through Knight Frank & Rutley, disposed of Grosvenor House to – Lord Leverhulme! Grosvenor House stood on 'an island site of about 2¾ acres, with frontages also to Grosvenor

New Devonshire House, on the site of the Duke of Devonshire's former town house, was to be the very latest type of modern building aimed at forming a landmark in the architecture of London.

Street, Upper Grosvenor Street and Park Lane'. In 1826 a western wing had been added: it became the famous Grosvenor Gallery, a celebrated art collection mocked by W. S. Gilbert as 'greenery-yallery'. During the war, more prosaically, it had been the headquarters of the Ministry of Food. What would Leverhulme do with it? Live in it? No. Grosvenor House, with which Knight Frank & Rutley were to be much concerned over the years, was to be replaced by a modern hotel and a large block of luxury flats.

Lord Leverhulme was a disappointed man. In March 1924 he had put up for auction 'the greater portion of the Island of Lewis, in the County of Ross and Cromarty, extending to about 288,479 acres'. As we have seen, he had only bought it in 1918. It had the usual sporting facilities in profusion, but was difficult to sell, even in eight lots. A Mr Edward Valpy offered only £500 for 56,000 acres of shooting and fishing: incredibly the property was not withdrawn, and down came Sir Howard's shillelagh: Mr Valpy had got his land for a fraction over 2*d* (under 1p) an acre. The estate included the castle of Amhuinnsuidhe (pronounced Ah-min-sooey), 'Scottish baronial' in style with castellated gables and turrets, built by the Earl of Dunmore in the nineteenth century, which was eventually bought by a Mr Venables of Kent. The remainder of the estate was mostly disposed of in 1925, together with North and South Harris.

The great experiment to bring prosperity to these islands had failed. Leverhulme had not understood the crofters. There was a long legacy of bitterness among proud

Grosvenor House, with which the firm was to be much concerned over the years, was sold on behalf of the Duke of Westminster to Lord Leverhulme. It was replaced by a modern hotel and a large block of luxury flats.

people whose grandparents had known the Hungry Forties, when many Highlanders and Hebrideans had emigrated to the Colonies. The Crofters' War of 1882 against the evictions led to a Royal Commission, which begot an Act of Parliament, giving crofters security of tenure and the right to bequeath leases to their heirs and made landlords liable for improvements. Leverhulme had spent more than £1 million on industrializing agriculture; but the islanders resisted it. An Englishman – or even a Lowlander – could not hope to succeed.

Lord Leverhulme had tried to transform the village of Obbe into a major fishing port, which he named Leverburgh after himself. He built a pier, houses, kippering sheds, roads and lighthouses and blasted underwater rocks to clear the harbour. Here he did have a temporary success, but his death in 1925 removed the impulse: the plan was abandoned. Leverburgh was bought by his own company, MacFisheries, for £8000. His dream was preserved in his title – 'Leverhulme of the Western Isles'. But when he left Harris for the last time, he threw his shoes on the shore and walked barefoot to the boat: 'Never shall those shoes walk anywhere else.'

Leverhulme's London house, The Hill, Hampstead, came up for sale immediately after his death. It was bought by another friend of Sir Howard's, Lord Inverforth, who had been Minister of Munitions in the war and was now chairman of a steel company.

Sorting coal by hand at the pit head. This was still the state of the mining industry when, in 1925, the 17th Earl of Derby sold his Bury and Pilkington estates in south-east Lancashire.

Among many victims of taxation was the 17th Earl of Derby, who had been Postmaster-General, War Minister, Ambassador to France and was a friend of the Royal Family. His Bury and Pilkington estates in south-east Lancashire, date back to the Wars of the Roses and were sold by Knight Frank & Rutley to a firm of land speculators, S. H. and E. W. Green of Chesterfield. They included parts of Radcliffe, Whitefield, Manchester and Salford, and practically the whole of Bury, then a town of 60,000 people. The Stanleys had always been generous towards their tenants, most of whose leases ran to 999 years. Greens resold in lots and gave tenants the opportunity of buying their properties, which many of them were glad to do.

The team of young surveyors engaged in listing and lotting this huge estate (the greater part of which was eventually sold for over £900,000) saw for the first time how the other half lived. One of them remembers a world of clogs, cobbles and trams where people worked in unbelievable hardship down mines and in cotton mills. 'What amazed [us] was that anyone could be induced to work at the pit-head sorting the coal. This was sent along on waist-high conveyor belts and the pickers snatched

Auctioneer

By Direction of the Executors of the late F. L. LATHAM, Esq., Deceased.

Gadshill Place

Near Rochester

THE HOME OF CHARLES DICKENS

per

Solicitors:

MESSRS. ROSE, JOHNSON & HICKS,
9, Suffolk Street, Pall Mall, London, S.W. 1.

Auctioneers:

MESSRS. KNIGHT, FRANK & RUTLEY,
20, Hanover Square, London, W. 1.

Gad's Hill Place in Kent where Charles Dickens wrote Great Expectations, Our Mutual Friend *and* The Uncommercial Traveller.

lumps of the size it was their job to collect. The dust-cloud was so thick that the figures at the other belts could hardly be seen.'

The mills, by contrast, were 'wonderfully clean' but so noisy that many workers, by the time they reached pensionable age, were stone-deaf and could only communicate by lip-reading.

In Central London there have traditionally been nine great estates – Bedford, Cadogan, Church Commissioners, Crown Estate, Grosvenor, Howard de Walden, Portman, Ellerman and the City of London. We shall see that Knight Frank & Rutley have acted for most of them over the years. Lord Howard de Walden, in 1925, was selling parts of his estate which took in the domain of doctors and dentists around Harley and Wimpole Streets; and some of it was bought by Sir John Ellerman. De Walden had already sold part of his Regent's Park estate for £500,000 as long ago as 1911. In 1925 he sold 40 acres between Oxford Street and Euston, including Great Portland Street and Mortimer Street, to the Audley Trust. Perhaps the greatest transformation in this area, 'which could only have been effected by a single ground landlord', was that of Great Portland Street, which now consisted almost entirely of motor-car show-rooms.

In 1922 the architectural prize of the year for an office building had been awarded for Wolseley House, 160 Piccadilly (now one of Barclays' most beautiful banks), a vast, stone-pillared, space-wasting structure of 11,000 square feet, opposite the Ritz Hotel. It was on Knight Frank & Rutley's books in 1925, as was Winston Churchill's town house at 2 Sussex Square, Lancaster Gate, when he moved into 11 Downing Street as Chancellor of the Exchequer. There had been two 'historical' properties, close to one another in Kent: Gad's Hill Place, home of Charles Dickens from 1857 until his death, where *Great Expectations, Our Mutual Friend* and *The Uncommercial Traveller* were all written, whose owner wanted £6000 but had to be content with £4600 offered by a Mr John Burt of Cricklewood; and Cobham Hall, the novelist's favourite place to walk to from Gad's Hill. The building of 'the new Dover arterial road' (now the A2) meant cutting across the Earl of Darnley's agricultural acres, 2520 of them, with farms, three cement works beside the Medway, and a number of cottages. Cobham Hall was handled by the firm several times in the next forty years.

John Knight retired in 1925, and his work at the Galleries was taken over by his son Arthur. The year ended in triumph with record sales of £8,007,900. 'No record of any similar volume of real estate transactions by a single firm has ever been issued before,' commented *The Times*. 'It is equivalent to nearly one-fourth of the entire recorded dealings in landed property in Great Britain in the year.'

Sir Howard had also done well at various regattas with his yacht *June*, including a second prize in the Nore–Dover race. At Cowes *June*, a 56-tonner, raced successfully, winning, for the whole season, eight firsts, seven seconds and four challenge cups.

1924 is remembered for two main events: the first short-lived Labour Government, under Ramsay MacDonald, and 'Wembley', the British Empire Exhibition. 'Wembley' was an attempt to instil a little Imperial pride in British breasts amid the chaos after an appalling war. There was also a movement towards Empire Free Trade. Wembley, a rural area in Middlesex, seven miles from London, had just been connected to the Metropolitan Underground railway and was about to become a suburb. The Empire was coming to Britain, instead of the other way round

The Empire Exhibition held at Wembley in 1924 covered 132 acres including a stadium for 125,000 spectators. It was attended by 27 million visitors. In 1926 it was left to Howard Frank to dispose of the site; but it did not reach the reserve at auction and was sold privately. It was not a financial success.

(thousands of unemployed had been emigrating). 'Wembley' covered 132 acres and cost £4,500,000 to build. There was a stadium for 125,000 spectators. There were fifteen miles of streets with names like Drake's Way, Kipling's Way, Dominion Way. The Palace of Engineering was 'the largest concrete building in the world . . . six-and-a-half times the size of Trafalgar Square'. Next biggest was the Palace of Industry. There was a Palace of Arts, a reconstruction of Old London Bridge, a replica of Tutankhamun's Tomb which had recently been excavated in Egypt, real Indians and Maoris and Zulus you could talk to. The London & North Eastern Railway built a special new station near Wembley Hill to handle 16,000 passengers an hour, and an eight-platform bus station was built for 20,000 passengers an hour.

The opening of Wembley, on St George's Day, 23 April 1924, was a tremendous occasion. Sir Edward Elgar, Master of the King's Musick, conducted massed bands and choirs in *Land of Hope and Glory*. The Exhibition, whose President was the young Prince of Wales, was opened by King George V, whose speech was broadcast by the BBC to 7,000,000 people all over the Empire. Then he and Queen Mary did something no British monarch had ever done in public before: they rode, gingerly, for a short distance on the scenic railway. Altogether 27,000,000 people went to Wembley – which lost £1,500,000, one-third of its cost.

By the end of 1925 it was being found difficult to devise uses for the empty Exhibition. How could it, one paper asked, 'take advantage of the boom in trade which we all believe to be coming'? In *The Times* on Christmas Eve 1925 appeared a half-page advertisement by Knight Frank & Rutley who had been instructed by 'the Liquidators' to dispose of Wembley by private treaty, or if not so sold, by auction. The most hopeful part seemed to be the Stadium, 'subject to its lettings to the Football Association'. Surely some buildings could be converted to factories? There were besides the Civic Hall, theatre and concert halls, a club house, restaurants, administrative buildings, canteens, railway sidings and ready-built new houses for the employees of any industry that cared to establish itself there. Electricity, gas, telephone, drainage and fire stations were all laid on.

As with the Crystal Palace fifteen years before, the sale was conducted in an atmosphere of public debate. This time, however, it was not a question of 'saving Wembley' for the national heritage so much as overcoming financial problems.

One obstacle to the sale – undoubtedly the biggest of the year – was the Football Association. If the Stadium were used only once a year for the Cup Final and for events like the highly successful Military Tattoo in 1925, was it not being rather wasted? Could not the Football Association guarantee the liquidators against any loss due to the Cup Final? Were there not other important matches that could be played at Wembley?

There was no difficulty in auctioning the contents of the Exhibition, a task which Knight Frank & Rutley shared with Toplis & Harding in a two-day sale in January 1926, held in the Civic Hall. Over 400 lots were disposed of on the first day, leaving another 372 for the second.

By June 1926 it was known that Wembley's future was going to be decided 'under the hammer'. The buildings might still be difficult to sell, but there were 'vast areas of building land with good frontages' which attracted speculative builders.

In the rostrum at Hanover Square on 15 June 1926 Sir Howard rehearsed all the wonders of Wembley – to be sold as it stood. 'May I say half a million?' he began. The first offer was £200,000. The price advanced in a few minutes by ten thousands to £300,000, followed by other bids up to £315,000. 'Any advance?' None. Sir Howard said he could not sell at £315,000 which was less than the reserve: he had had a better offer privately. Wembley was withdrawn.

On 2 July the liquidators announced that Wembley would be sold to the Beecham Trust Ltd and Mr James White. A further call on the guarantors would still be necessary, however. The part played by Jimmy White, a gambling financier who used to sit at night in the Café de Paris with a telephone on his table dealing on the New York Stock Exchange, is not altogether clear. In the long term, much of the Exhibition area was acquired by Arthur Elvin, who made it a centre for international sport, especially the newly-fashionable greyhound racing.

IX
Changing the Face of London

Debutantes running canteens, Lady Diana Cooper folding copies of *The Times* (four pages) because there was no machinery to do it, Lady Louis Mountbatten carrying buckets about the emergency food centre in Hyde Park, Winston Churchill editing an emergency *British Gazette*, undergraduates driving buses and Tube trains – this was the General Strike, the great event of 1926. It lasted only nine days in May, but everyone was made to feel that Britain was on the very brink of bloody revolution.

Knight Frank & Rutley responded gallantly to the crisis. One young surveyor drove a London bus, others were conductors on the uncomfortable vehicles of those days (solid tyres and open tops with slatted wooden seats). Another surveyor got a much-envied job as fireman on a steam locomotive. Several staff (including Will Gibson) became special constables: Will Gibson proudly displayed his truncheon in his home for years afterwards. Sir Howard toured the streets of London in his Rolls offering lifts to everyone: he would see a pedestrian, get his faithful chauffeur Shaddock to stop, and ask him where he wanted to go. Once he saw two girls standing on the pavement and sent Shaddock to ask their destination. It seems that they were loitering there for quite another purpose.

The face of the West End was changing, as Piccadilly and Park Lane became less residential and more commercial, soon to be followed by Mayfair and Berkeley Square. Lord Leverhulme's desire to restore Grosvenor House to its old rôle of an art gallery had been frustrated by his death, and the firm now sold it to a syndicate who would soon pull it down and build upon its site what we now know as the Grosvenor House Hotel. The firm also sold Leverhulme's pictures at his Rivington Hall, Cheshire, residence – a three-day sale of paintings, drawings and engravings by Crome, Constable, Cuyp, Romney and others.

On the Riviera, where Alec Siese was specializing in villas and spending three months a year liaising with the firm's on-the-spot representatives in Monte Carlo, Cannes and Nice, new villas were being built for the holiday public: developments such as The Domaine Rothschild, Grasse, where a 337-acre building estate was being created amid the pine trees and olive groves – perhaps a little far inland to be described as 'Cote d'Azur' but nonetheless desirable. In Newcastle-upon-Tyne the firm's growing interest in urban commercial property was to be seen in their offer of an important central site containing the Assembly Rooms, in a site of 2877 square yards and a further 3426 square yards occupied by an office block known as Westgate House.

Sir Howard, ever restless, had moved from No. 19 to No. 5 Cheyne Walk. Folklore says that, about this time, he kept a motor-launch on the Thames opposite his house

During the General Strike in 1926, surveyors could turn their hand to anything. One drove a London bus, others were conductors: one even was a fireman on a steam locomotive.

to take him to the office. It is difficult to imagine how he did this, unless he was met by his chauffeur at Westminster Pier.

There was a plan, in 1927, to move Covent Garden Market to the site of the Foundling Hospital in Bloomsbury. It came to nothing. There were a number of such plans over the years, and Knight Frank & Rutley were to be deeply involved in the one by which, nearly fifty years later, the Market actually emigrated to Nine Elms.

Alfred J. Burrows, who still commuted between his family business in Ashford and 20 Hanover Square, was this year elected President of the Auctioneers' and Estate Agents' Institute. Within the firm, Charles Phillips was made a partner. He was a brilliant auctioneer (some of those who knew him have placed him higher than either Alfred Burrows or Sir Howard) and an all-round surveyor and valuer; and it seems hard that he should have had to wait until his sixty-eighth year for this promotion; harder still that he should have died less than two years later. He always wore a frock-coat at auctions, and had a horror of any bidder he suspected of being a speculator. Nothing seemed to ruffle his dignity, not even being stuck in the office lift: he just went on dictating letters and instructions to his secretary. When you returned from a holiday, you knew he would greet you gravely, 'I trust you have had a tolerable vacation.' After his introductory remarks at an auction, he invariably concluded with: 'And that, in a brief, bald and imperfect fashion, is the property I am offering you today.' And he closed every auction with a polite: 'Thank you for your attention.'

Will Gibson was made a partner in January 1928. He had been with the firm for nine years, had managed the Town Department for four years, and was already Sir Howard's friend and closest colleague. Sir Howard must have seen him as a future senior partner, even though A. J. Burrows was, by seniority, the obvious successor.

Mr Burrows, during his Presidency of the Institute, was a tireless advocate, in speeches and articles, of more professionalism; and in all he said and wrote there was a strong emphasis on agriculture, now languishing: it was the world of Kent he knew so well. The Institute at this time had 6000 members, and 1928 was seeing a record number of students (about 1000) up for examination.

A very typical Burrows sale was that of Surrenden Dering estate, near his home town of Ashford, Kent – land of which he knew every square foot – for Sir H. E. Dering, Bt, in July 1928. A mansion and 3284 acres was bought as a whole and re-sold in lots. The buyer was a timber merchant, with whom Mr Burrows negotiated to preserve a magnificant avenue of elms three quarters of a mile long, and raised a fund to save them for public enjoyment.

In the same month a young man with unusual qualifications joined the firm. William Cunningham (a future partner) was by training a naval architect, which had an immediate appeal for Sir Howard Frank. He had been working as a draughtsman for William Doxford & Son of Sunderland, designers and builders of cargo boats. There was a slump on Wearside in 1928: should he try London? Somehow estate agency attracted him. Could his experience be used there? He had heard that Knight Frank & Rutley were 'the best estate agents in Town'. He applied for a job and got it – at £4 a week. He joined what was then known as the Structural Surveying Department, which surveyed large properties – factories, hotels, farms, anything – for all other departments. It was managed by Frank Handover, whose staff consisted of a typist, an office boy and now Willie Cunningham. Mr Handover's duties included looking after Sir Howard's own properties, among which were his yachts, especially the *Lamorna*, which he had raced against Sir Thomas Lipton's *Shamrock*.

Soon after young Cunningham arrived, Mr Handover went on holiday. His first job each morning at 9.30 was to check and produce an up-to-date list of Sir Howard's stocks and shares. He had also to check and pay all his personal accounts including the crews of his yachts (then costing him £200 a week). This was when Willie Cunningham really got to know Sir Howard, who showed him a bill for some new sails for one of the yachts: 'What d'you thing of that, Cunningham'? Willie measured the sail on the plans. 'I think it's far too high, Sir.' 'Really?' Sir Howard stared. 'And what the devil do *you* know about it?' Willie explained about his previous job, in which he had got to know the whole shipbuilding market. Sir Howard wrote to the sailmaker: 'My structural surveyor tells me that your account is far too high' – and got a 30 per cent reduction. Willie had made his mark.

Looking after Sir Howard's own properties brought its own rewards: he would say to Willie Cunningham, or anyone else who had helped him: 'Make out a cheque to yourself.' The first time this happened, Willie was so taken aback that he forgot to ask how much. The cashier told him: 'Well, it's usually £20.' This, for Willie, was five weeks' salary. 'But I can't take all that!' In the end he made out a cheque for £15. Two years later Handover retired and Cunningham succeeded him as manager of the Structural Department and was given an assistant.

In August 1928 Sir Howard was asked to join yet another Royal commission – on Police Powers. Britain had, at this time, the most unpopular Home Secretary in her history, Sir William Joynson-Hicks, known as Jix, whose self-appointed mission was to stamp out vice – vice being anything that gave people pleasure. He had used the police as a kind of private army to stamp out night-clubs, especially those run by the notorious Mrs Meyrick. The police, goaded by Jix, were apt to pounce on innocent people in public places and accuse them of loitering and soliciting. They did this to a Miss Savidge, a respectable girl who had spoken to Sir Leo Money on a bench in Hyde Park. The police had grilled her with excessive severity . . . Hence the Royal Commission.

The twenties were the age of radio, a miracle that transformed people's lives. The BBC was outgrowing its first home in Savoy Hill, and John Reith was planning a mighty palace of radio to be known as Broadcasting House. But where should it be? To build a vast stone battle ship such as the BBC wanted, you must first 'amass' a site of the right size and in a city this usually means a certain amount of demolition. The BBC's civil engineer, whose name was Marmaduke Tudsbery Tudsbery, had been searching for a site since the middle of 1926.

Towards the end of 1927 a developer named Jackie Phillips came into the picture. He was a flamboyant 'fixer' with an ear trumpet who speculated in property. Not the sort of man you would expect to get on with the upright, military Will Gibson; yet they hatched a big deal together. One evening as Gibson was signing letters Phillips came to see him without an appointment. He was interested in Lord Waring's house in Portland Place – could he look at it this very evening? Gibson, who knew perfectly well why Phillips wanted it, asked, 'What's the hurry?' And then, 'If I tell you what my client's house is worth, and what to do with it, will you pay my firm's commission?' The result was a lease at £42,000 a year. Working with Knight Frank & Rutley, Phillips collected other sites around Portland Place; so that in December 1928 it was possible to announce that 'the British Broadcasting Corporation have just taken on a long lease at a rack rent, with an option to purchase, what will be the finest building of its kind in the world'. It would contain three acres of floor space, a concert hall with seats for an audience of 1000, nine soundproof studios, band rooms, waiting rooms, engineers' rooms, announcers' rooms, rehearsal rooms, buffets and kitchens. The architect was Lt-Col G. Val Myer.

Two more Kentish estate sales, in which one detects the hand of A. J. Burrows, came along in the summer of 1929: Broome Park, near Canterbury, and Hothfield, adjoining Ashford.

Britain was now experiencing its second Labour Government. It had come to power in an atmosphere of slump and the approaching Wall Street Crash, which had its repercussions on the City of London. Sir Howard was one of many businessmen

Broadcasting House. In 1928 the BBC moved from its first home in Savoy Hill. Will Gibson was heavily involved in acquiring a number of sites around Portland Place, upon which Broadcasting House now stands.

who were wondering whether business could get along with a Government that so far did not appear too doctrinaire. Indeed, it was probably going to need help. When Ramsay MacDonald became Prime Minister again in 1929, Sir Howard wrote to him, congratulating him and urging him, in picking his cabinet, to give 'younger men with a knowledge of business' a chance. The Prime Minister does not seem to have heeded his advice. On 24 October 1929 Sir Howard wrote to *The Times* supporting Lloyd George's suggestion of a 'committee of businessmen'. 'How many times have we been told by the leaders of the respective parties that the first item on their programme is economy in national expenditure, but it is never carried out. Agriculture is in a bad way. In trade we are drifting along as we have drifted before, and there is danger in believing that because the country has weathered periods of severe depression in the past, it will necessarily recover from the present crisis without a more active policy.' A committee of businessmen might well be the solution, 'provided that the Government would undertake to act, so far as was possible, upon the recommendations of that committee. Given that assurance, the right type of men would be willing to serve, but not otherwise'.

24 October was the day on which the skyscraper suicides began on Wall Street, and little more was heard of the businessmen's committee.

Sir Howard also contributed to a discussion, in *The Times* correspondence columns, on the proposed new Charing Cross Bridge. Again, it is a plea for a committee of 'practical men' to cut through all the bureaucracy and hesitation and limited local thinking.

There was a new office boy at 20 Hanover Square. He had arrived in November 1929, and his name was Geoffrey Gay. He was fifteen, and he had left St Paul's School early because his father had had a severe reverse in business. He was the grandson of Sir Henry Lytton, and had inherited some of the great Savoyard's theatrical talent, especially as a raconteur. Because he could not afford to be articled, he was glad to begin in the post room, where all unarticled beginners started. There was no doubt about his keeness to get on. The high point of his day was about six o'clock in the evening, when he rushed round all the offices, collecting letters for signature, and then dashed – somewhat noisily – down the main stairs, four at a time, to the post.

This brought about his first, rather violent, meeting with Sir Howard, who was just coming out of the Senior Partner's Room. 'Boy!' roared Sir Howard. (It was the custom, especially with Sir Howard and Will Gibson, to shout for an office boy as prefects shout 'Fag!') Sir Howard, 6 ft 3 in., towered over young Gay: 'Boy! You'll break your bloody neck if you do that. I'm the only person here who's allowed to come downstairs at that speed.' He examined the boy closely: 'Here, we don't know each other, do we? Come into my room.' Young Gay told the Senior Partner his name. Sir Howard was quick to size people up, and was never dismayed by ambition. 'What do you want to *do* here?' he asked. 'Sit at your desk, Sir!' Geoffrey Gay replied. Forty-three years later, as Senior Partner, he did.

'I stayed for about a year in Post Room,' Geoffrey Gay remembers. 'Then I went on to Country Registers. Then into the Galleries . . . although they interested me very much my mind was made up that the future for the firm was on the commercial side.' Geoffrey Gay therefore asked William Gibson, partner in charge of the Town Department, if he could transfer to it, and so became assistant to various negotiators and ultimately to the Town Manager, Sidney Towersey, who allowed him to specialize in shops, gradually becoming more and more involved with vacant possession shops and offices.

His memory is very nearly 'total recall': 'My first "let" was to a woman bookie in Avery Row, off Bond Street. The rent was £115 per annum, on which the firm made £11 10*s* 0*d* commission.'

Sir Howard had chaired the Committee on Crown and Government Lands in 1921, and had sat on every similar committee since. It seemed inevitable, therefore, that the hard-pressed Government in 1930 should ask him to chair a committee on government properties. This involved considering more than 3600 properties of varying sizes the more important of which had to be visited, concentrating on those in areas whose commercial value had substantially increased with time. War Office properties such as Hyde Park and Regent's Park Barracks; and the Royal Army Clothing Depot in Pimlico – was not Pimlico coming up fast as a residential district?

The Duke of York's Headquarters, with its valuable frontage on King's Road, Chelsea, should perhaps stay where it was, as there was room for anti-aircraft artillery which might be vital to the aerial defence of London. Admiralty dockyards such as Sheerness and Rosyth; Air Ministry properties such as Hendon Aerodrome, in a suburb ripe for development – could alternative accommodation be provided so as to ensure a profit for the Exchequer? Office of Works properties – the Civil Service Commission, the Stationery Office, and the Geological Museum in Piccadilly – tended to be situated in very valuable thoroughfares . . . The Committee, with admirable speed and brevity, reported within one year.

Early in 1930, Knight Frank & Rutley, 'by direction of H. Gordon Selfridge', announced that the 700-acre Hengistbury estate, near Christchurch, Hampshire, with 'sea frontage extending to Hengistbury Head', was to be sold. For Mr Selfridge, founder of Selfridges in Oxford Street, this sale was the collapse of a dream. He had wanted to build a monument to himself that would never be forgotten: a Palace of Nations, a mixture of Gothic and Romanesque, with cloisters and gardens, a theatre, several banqueting halls, 250 four-room apartments for guests, a world cultural centre with 'studios, laboratories, observatories', to be built here at Hengistbury. He, an American, would make this part of England's heritage. It would cost £3 million . . . But the Midland Bank Ltd, already tired of his mounting overdraft, foreclosed.

Hengistbury was 'saved for the nation' by a private sale in which 400 acres of it were acquired by Bournemouth Town Council for £25,250. Mr Selfridge, we are told, let it go for that price 'on condition that the historic headland, which overlooks the Solent and the Needles, should be preserved as an open space'.

In June 1930 Sir Howard gave a memorable dinner at Claridges in honour of Mr Edward W. Beatty, KC, President of the Canadian Pacific Railway. In speeches and letters to the press Sir Howard had hammered away at the need for more trade between Britain and her Dominions. CPR were known to be looking for a site on which to build a first-class West End hotel, in a block which would also house their own London Offices. Knight Frank & Rutley had been buying up the east side of Berkeley Square as far as Bruton Street.

What is remarkable about this occasion was the position in national life which Sir Howard now held. Among more than sixty guests who accepted invitations were the Prime Minister (Ramsay MacDonald), two Marquesses (Salisbury and Londonderry), three Earls (Derby, Inchcape and Cromer), two Viscounts (Hailsham and Brentford), nine assorted Barons, the Lord Mayor of London, the mayor of Westminster, seventeen Knights, one Air Chief-Marshal and two Brigadier-Generals.

Among seven MPs were Winston Churchill and Neville Chamberlain, and among other guests were Lord Dawson of Penn, the King's doctor, and two press magnates (Lord Riddell and Sir Edward Iliffe). Many of these men were Sir Howard's clients or friends or ex-colleagues on various committees. A bomb on Claridges that evening could have removed half the Establishment. We do not know whether Mr Beatty was impressed: he certainly ought to have been. In his speech of thanks to Sir Howard, he echoed the theme of more trade between Britain and Canada – Canada would fall into the arms of the United States if that trade did not materialize . . .

The CPR hotel was never built. Minds were changed as the Depression settled upon the world. Was the Claridges dinner wasted? Possibly; but the Berkeley Square site was certainly not wasted. The CPR did buy the site, but soon disposed of it. It was eventually leased to a development company and the building was constructed by Sir Robert MacAlpine's construction company: we shall follow its progress later. Meanwhile 'the finest available site in the West End of London' (54,460 sq. ft) was advertised as being 'immediately available for the erection of the most important hotel, flat or business buildings in London, with shops on the ground floor'.

If Mr Edward Beatty of the CPR had wanted to buy an hotel as it stood, he might well have considered the Hotel Cecil, between the Strand and the river Thames, but Shell-Mex Ltd were there before him. Since January 1930 it had been known that the affairs of the famous old hotel, owned by the United Realization Company, were in liquidation. Completion of the sale to the oil company on 30 June (for a reported price of £1,520,000) would be followed by the sale by auction, in May, of the entire contents of the hotel. *The Times* reported: 'The auction will dispose of the furnishings of nearly 600 bedrooms, a quarter of a million pieces of plated ware, china, glass and linen, the equipment of four Masonic Temples, the contents of the grill rooms and restaurant, the ballroom, ten banqueting halls and Palm Court.'

It was reckoned that the sale of contents would take twenty days; this was soon changed to thirty days, the wine five days and the trade plant another five days beginning on 5 May. In fact, the trade equipment was still being auctioned in mid-July.

There were 11,835 lots. 'Some articles, such as a grandfather clock bought by a Canadian, have been sold privately to regular clients of the hotel who wished to have souvenirs of the place, but these have very slightly reduced the items in the bulky catalogue' – a catalogue (price one shilling), piles of which were carried about by the new office boy, Geoffrey Gay. 'Hundreds of carpets' were listed, 'thousands of chairs of many kinds, innumerable bedsteads and bathroom suites, and a large variety of writing tables'. Miscellaneous lots included a model of the airship R.101 (that triumph of British engineering which would crash in flames in a few months' time), two microphones, 'a gold-plated, seven-day shaving set, flags of various nations, palms in oak tubs, pianos, an organ, cash registers and paintings'. The management was disappointed that a treasured curiosity, a bust of the ex-Kaiser, had vanished, presumed stolen.

What sort of hotel it had been can be judged perhaps from the quality of the

Arthur Knight auctioning the contents of Hotel Cecil. The sale disposed of the furnishings of nearly 600 bedrooms, a quarter of a million pieces of plated ware, china, glass and linen, the equipment of four Masonic Temples, the contents of the grill room and the restaurant, the ballroom, 10 banqueting halls and the palm court.

Stanley Baldwin and Winston Churchill leave the Hotel Cecil.

furniture in the banqueting rooms, private dining rooms, drawing room, reading room and lounges: 'Georgian and French pattern mahogany, walnut and kingwood writing and occasional tables; 120 Louis XV and XVI pattern painted-frame bergeres with coffee-tables and screens to match; 190 carved mahogany and walnut settees and easy chairs; 1050 mahogany, oak-and-walnut-frame dining-chairs, upholstered in leather; 250 mahogany dining-chairs with seats in blue cloth; . . . cabinets, bookcases and tables with gilt claw feet.'

The spacious Upper Palm Court was used for the sale, which on the first day, 'from 10 a.m. till 6 p.m., an hour later than the advertised time of closing', was crowded with more than 1500 buyers. Catalogues were in such demand that more had to be printed at very short notice. Arthur Knight was on the rostrum, and announced on the opening day that everything would be sold without reserve. The first lot offered was a large Axminster carpet, which fetched seven guineas, followed by a mahogany bedroom suite knocked down for ten guineas. The buyers included a number of dealers, but most were private buyers.

The sale of the Cecil's cellar of over 72,000 bottles of choice wines began on Tuesday, 10 June in the Princes Hall, Thames Embankment, at the rate of 600 lots a day for five days, including 'champagnes, sherries, ports, choice old brandies and liqueurs, and British Empire, French, Italian and Spanish wines'.

The serious newspapers followed the sale as if it were a sporting event, chalking up the weekly score. By the 30 May the total had reached £50,000. It was now felt that the sale of the hotel's 'trade fixtures, plant and machinery' would probably take ten days, not five. (In fact it took only five days.)

Among the last items sold were 500 white glazed lavatory basins and WC pedestal latrines . . . (was nothing to be left for the incoming Shell-Mex staff?)

The sale of the contents of the Hotel Cecil realized a gross amount of £1,622,705. Nobody liked the passing of the old hotel, least of all Arthur Knight, an auctioneer who sometimes regretted his rôle. The Hotel Cecil, however, unlike Stonehenge or the Crystal Palace or even Wembley, could not be 'saved for the nation'. The nation would need petroleum more urgently in the years to come.

X
Town, Country – and Tyneside

At Cowes, in the special races for the testing of Sir Thomas Lipton's new America's Cup challenger, *Shamrock V*, in June 1930, Sir Howard Frank entered his new J class yacht *Astra*, a 24-metre Bermudian.

In August the Franks were at Brixham Royal Torbay Regatta, competing with HM the King's *Britannia*, Lord Camrose's *Cambria* and Lord Waring's *White Heather*. *Astra* came third. But the news event of the Regatta was made by Lady Frank, who dived fully dressed into the harbour by Brixham fish market to rescue a drowning child. She was awarded the Royal Humane Society's medal.

This was Sir Howard's last complete yachting season. His health was now uncertain; there were rumours of a 'serious operation' pending; and in the following year, while retaining his membership of all three of his yacht clubs, the Royal Southern, Royal Thames and Clyde Corinthian, he decided to give up racing. Symbolically, his next vessel, a 115-ton ketch, was called *Easy Going* – but he changed her name to *Cynara*. And he sold *Astra*.

He was still tirelessly writing letters to *The Times* about the state of the nation – lack of leadership, the ill-conceived dole system for the unemployed, the need for 'a strong Government determined to reduce national expenditure, but at the same time to maintain a Navy, Army and Air Force sufficient to protect ourselves and our Colonies'.

Truth to tell, the firm itself was not doing too well. A profit-and-loss table for 1916–35 shows a record profit of £94,923 for 1919, the peak of the immediate post-war boom, plunging to £18,780 in the 1922 slump, bobbing up and down between £53,000 and £30,000 during the next few years, plunging again in 1931 to just under £16,000 and in 1932 to £13,418. Certainly it was not easy to sell country properties such as the Earl of Verulam's Gorhambury at St Albans, built in 1778 to the designs of Sir Robert Taylor, with 'the historic ruins of Sir Francis Bacon's house', '22 capital farms' and 'nearly 14 miles of frontage to main roads' including the 'proposed St Albans by-pass'.

In September 1930 the firm took space in *The Times* and *Daily Telegraph* to advertise Thames House, Westminster – 'Europe's Best Office Building is growing week by week . . . now being roofed.' The firm had a letting office in Imperial Chemical House nearby, and would soon have one in Thames House itself. Sir Harry (afterwards Lord) McGowan, Chairman of ICI, had built Imperial Chemical House near Lambeth Bridge, and it had made a deep impression as an ultra-modern office block. Its architect, Sir Frank Baines, then interested Lord Melchett, McGowan and Clarence Graff of ICI in forming a company to build a similar building on the other side of Horseferry Road – a 725,000 sq. ft site – in two blocks. There was a feeling

Sir Howard Frank's 24-metre Bermudian, Astra, *in competition at Cowes in June 1930.* Astra *took part in special races to test Sir Thomas Lipton's America's Cup challenger,* Shamrock V.

that Britain was well behind America in designing office blocks (almost no research was done to find out what tenants wanted), and so McGowan asked the Chase National Bank to 'headhunt' in New York and find an American property man who was 'not too aggressive or hustling' and who could get on with the British. Chase National found, at Cross & Brown, the real estate firm, a large man named Malcolm Mackenzie. He was destined to have a profound influence on Knight Frank & Rutley.

'Unfortunately,' Geoffrey Gay remembers, 'he could not arrive early enough to have a part in the design of the building, but he "fronted" the letting arrangements . . . He was a man of great personality and had a brilliant brain. It was an analytical brain, and he was one of the fastest people I ever met who could do mental arithmethic. His mind was like a computer.' He could watch his assistant's calculations on paper upside down, Ronald Browne remembers, and tell him where he was going wrong. 'In a taxi we were talking about a collision at sea and I asked him how long he thought it would take a liner to stop. He didn't reply for some minutes, and then gave me the answer – about three miles. He had worked out the tonnage, submerged displacement, speed and water-resistance – all in his head.'

Sir Harry McGowan paid him £5000 a year, an enormous salary for those days. Quite unable to cope with duo-decimal pounds, shillings and pence, Mackenzie invented a metric-sterling system of his own for calculations. His training as an engineer stood him in good stead when surveying or valuing commercial buildings.

Dour to the point of brutality, he seldom wasted words on breaking bad news gently: Willie Cunningham remembers him picking up the telephone to tell Robin MacAlpine that a long-matured plan for Berkeley Square House had fallen through: 'Robin? That deal's cold turkey. Goodbye.' As for getting along with the British, he was perhaps a little short on respect for tradition. Being shown round a stately home, he would ask in exasperation: 'How did they *heat* these damn places?' To a young surveyor who tried to impress him with the traditions of the British Army, saying – '*your* Army doesn't have them to the same extent, does it?' – he barked: 'Well, it was good enough to beat you guys at Yorktown!'

Mackenzie had a luxury service flat in St James's, and enjoyed a very full life. He weighed 17 stone and got through six Churchillian cigars a day. Gradually his transatlantic idioms became part of the Hanover Square vocabulary. His favourite expression, 'a considered guess', anticipated the modern 'guesstimate' by about thirty years. He was expert at planning office space for clients – getting quarts into pint pots – and persuaded many of them to adopt the long-resisted 'open plan' system, which he called 'a grand parade of staff', but which of course could only be done in a modern building. Somehow Mackenzie learnt Britain's various Building Acts with their provisions about 'plot ratio' and 'coverage', and the restrictions which still made skyscrapers impossible; one of them being that London buildings in those days had to be 'no higher than the fire-hoses could reach'.

The crisis year of 1931 came, and Sir Howard's letters to the press and to men in authority echoed the same themes – strong government, better leadership, better organization of agriculture. In February he wrote to Lord Derby about the state of the Conservative Party and its indolent leadership: could he not persuade Stanley Baldwin to resign? Another General Election with Mr Baldwin as our leader would see the defeat of the Conservative Party!

We do not know how, or whether, Lord Derby replied to this letter; there was anyway a completely different solution in store. Meanwhile Lord Derby was putting his own Derby House, in Stratford Place, on the market: it would eventually become the Oriental Club. The firm had difficulty in selling Sir Austen Chamberlain's sixteenth-century house Twitty Ghyll, near Mayfield, Sussex, which was withdrawn from auction at £4400 (less than its value), but managed to let Goldsborough Hall, the Lascelles family home in Yorkshire, for the Earl of Harewood.

In February 1931 John Knight died at the age of 72 at his Tulse Hill home, Clarendon Lodge. His obituaries praised his 'geniality' and 'unassuming nature'. 'He possessed considerable knowledge of old furniture, pictures and works of art generally,' said the *Morning Post*, 'and was associated with the dispersal of several well-known collections. He was noted for his benevolence, and lived to see the opening of the new entrance to Brockwell Park, for which he had given the land'. Those 'well-known collections' included, said *The Times*, 'the Leverhulme treasures, the collection of Lady Henry Grosvenor at Quenby Hall, Leicestershire, the Earl Sydney collection at Frognal, Sidcup, the contents of Stafford House for the executors of the Duke of Sutherland, the collection at Craig-y-Nos Castle, the

In 1931 Knight Frank & Rutley offered for sale a national newspaper, the Sunday Referee, *together with the machinery and plant of the Rotary Presses Ltd.*

furniture of the late Duchess of Albany at Esher (Claremont), and the Isaac Lewis collection'. John Knight left £94,766.

It fell to the firm, about this time, to auction a newspaper, the *Sunday Referee* 'together with the goodwill, printing plant and machinery, and the lease – offered by Sir Oswald Stoll, the Australian theatre and cinema magnate, joint owner with Sir Robert Donald, chairman of Anglo Foreign Newspapers. It was the worst possible time to try to dispose of the fifty-four-year-old newspaper, which had only been a Sunday paper since 1928, but the owners were sure they could get £30,000. At the auction on 20 February no bidder reached the reserve. The paper, printing works, plant and premises were first offered together; the starting price was £12,000, and the properties were withdrawn at £21,000. The goodwill was then offered separately: bidding started at £7000, and the property was withdrawn at £9500. For the plant and premises together, in a separate lot, bidding opened at £12,000, and advanced to £16,750, at which figure it was withdrawn.

So the *Sunday Referee* staggered on until June 1939, when it was incorporated with *Sunday Chronicle*.

The commercialization of Park Lane proceeded apace: in April 1931 the new Dorchester Hotel opened its doors, and Knight Frank & Rutley were instructed to let the shops which were part of its structure and had entrances both from the street and from within the hotel.

Country properties were still difficult to sell, especially in Scotland, where one problem was the sheer difficulty of access to inspect them. Sir Howard, so far from the nationally recommended policy of retrenchment, actually increased his advertising, and in a new direction. In June and July the firm took space in *The Times* and *Daily Telegraph* across two columns for an advertisement in large type headed

FLYING SERVICE, with a photograph of an aeroplane: 'Messrs. Knight Frank & Rutley have made arrangements for a Flying Service to be available on special terms for viewing properties. Motor-cars will call for applicants to take them to the Aerodrome. Particulars of the nearest landing-place to the property can be seen at Hanover Square.'

September was crisis month: the worst crisis since the General Strike, with the same feeling of imminent national collapse, and panic measures to save the pound, such as cutting the dole and benefits of all kinds, even cutting the King's salary by ten per cent. Prayers were said in churches for national recovery ('God save our gracious pound,' said Malcolm Muggeridge). In the middle of all this there was a naval mutiny at Invergordon in protest at pay cuts. The King asked Ramsay MacDonald to form a National Government, which was confirmed by a General Election in October. Sir Howard need not have worried about Stanley Baldwin. Seeing which way the country was moving, the day after the election results began to come in, he devoted the whole of the firm's regular Thursday back page in *The Times* to a map of Britain showing the state of the polls at 9 p.m. the previous evening. At the top and bottom were a few lines of copy: 'A National Government, with a big majority, restores confidence in the Country, and the financial stability of the Nation is assured . . . Investments in real property judiciously bought afford even greater security than before, and purchasers may look for a gradual increase in value. At any time you can *see* your property.' Followed by the firm's name and address.

Sir Howard had correctly sensed a wave of relief and patriotism sweeping over the country. But an immediate result of the 1931 crisis in the property market was a rush for *urban* investments, an almost hysterical yearning for bricks and mortar, the other end of which was flight from the land for the next few years.

On Sunday evening, 10 January 1932, Sir Howard and Lady Frank returned to 5 Cheyne Walk, with their two young sons, from their country cottage in Kent. After dinner, sitting quietly in an armchair, he had a heart attack and died in a few minutes. He had had 'heart trouble', never very clearly defined, for some years, but was unable to control his own energy and, only two days before his death, had played a round of golf at Walton Heath. He was 60.

The press obituaries were those normally accorded to an elder statesman. The headlines stressed his 'service to his country'; the '£630,000,000 deals' of his War Disposal Board, the numerous benevolent institutions he was interested in, including his vice-chairmanship of the Cheyne Hospital for Children in Chelsea. The London *Evening News*, under a banner headline: 'The Man who Sold Million-Pound Slices of London' showed how he had 'saved the face of London' – by selling Devonshire House, Piccadilly, the first of the noble London mansions to give place to luxury flats; Grosvenor House, Park Lane – more flats; the Hotel Cecil, replaced by Shell-Mex House: the Golden Cross site by Trafalgar Square, where South Africa House was now rising; the disappearance of Meux's Brewery in Tottenham Court Road, where the new Dominion Theatre now stood; the completion of Broadcasting

House in Portland Place; that mysterious site in Berkeley Square, said to have been 'bought by Canadian Pacific Railways for a palatial £3 million hotel' on land said to be worth £1 million . . .

Then came more personal reminiscences. Of Howard Frank as a golfer it was said that his 'swing was very nearly a perfect 8'. He had played for love, occasionally for money, never to win. At 20 Hanover Square, the cashier remembered Sir Howard breezing in after a game at Walton Heath and saying: 'Send Lord Riddell a cheque for one-and-sixpence. I bet him a penny a hole, and lost every one, including the nineteenth!'

Lord Riddell wrote a long piece in *The Times* about him: he was the 'prince of negotiators, his skill in reconciling vendors and purchasers was phenomenal . . . This was largely due to an ingratiating manner, relentless perseverance, simple, direct methods free from mystification or finesse – he knew what each party would be prepared to concede in the final issue.' He had always remained completely professional, in that he declined to *deal* in property. As an auctioneer he had begun a new era, with his brevity and his blackthorn. His 'particulars' were works of art. Above all, Lord Riddell had enjoyed Sir Howard's 'boyish pranks and quips' and his 'steadfast, warm-hearted friendship'. He was perhaps a man who had 'worn himself out'.

The *Yachtsman* mourned his death as 'a shattering blow: especially as it had come so soon after Sir Thomas Lipton's. Nature intended him for a mariner. The Fates made him a merchant prince.'

The funeral at Tunbridge Wells, attended by family and close friends only, was held on the same afternoon as the memorial service at St George's, Hanover Square. It seemed that all London had stopped, for everybody was at St George's while 20 Hanover Square was empty, with blinds down: Lord and Lady Riddell, Lord Ebbisham, Sir Frank and Lady Newnes, Lord Inverforth, Lord and Lady Waring, Sir James Dunn, Gordon Selfridge, Sir Lawrence Chubb, Sir George Berry, Lords Cavan, Camrose, Cromer . . . and the entire staff of Knight Frank & Rutley.

Among hundreds of letters to Lady Frank was one from Sandringham: 'The Queen heard with much regret the sad news of the death of your husband. Her Majesty became acquainted with him last year when he so kindly assisted her to find a suitable Grace and Favour Residence and appreciated so much the tactful but firm manner in which he carried out all the negotiations. The Queen knows that at such a time words can do little to bring any real comfort but Her Majesty desires me to assure you of her sincere sympathy with you in your sorrow.'

Sir Howard had left over £100,000 and there were legacies to many employees of the firm. His house in Cheyne Walk was sold to the Marquess of Queensberry.

The natural successor, as senior partner, was Alfred Burrows, perhaps the best-known name in the profession, after Sir Howard. With the sole exception of Sir Howard, 'it is correct to say,' commented *The Times*, 'that Mr Burrows has sold a larger area of agricultural land than any other auctioneer in England.' A. J. Burrows had been in practice since 1891; his was the Kentish voice of solid sense, over-

THE FIELD

THE COUNTRY NEWSPAPER

WITH WHICH IS INCORPORATED "LAND AND WATER"

VOL. CLIX. NO. 4125. SATURDAY, JANUARY 16, 1932 REGISTERED. PRICE 1s. POSTAGE { INLAND, 1½D.; CANADA AND NEW-FOUNDLAND, 1½D.; FOREIGN, 3D.

Sir Howard Frank's obituary picture which appeared on the front page of The Field *on 16 January 1932.*

shadowed by the glamour of Sir Howard; he had his roots in the land, and to the land he would ultimately return. And he had done much for the staff at Hanover Square, including an annual summer outing by motor-coach to his house with its beautiful gardens at Kennington, near Ashford. Here they would have treasure-hunts, competitions and games, including the annual inter-office tennis tournament, London versus Ashford, for the Burrows Challenge Cup.

The partnership now invited Cecil Ingram, at the Edinburgh office, to join them, while however remaining in charge of the Scottish branches. A fellow of the Chartered Surveyors' Institution, he had managed the firm's Scottish business for eighteen years, having previously been the Duke of Bedford's agent on the Woburn estate, worked for his father's firm at Lewes, Sussex, and then spent some time in charge of the Land Agency Department of W. Brown & Co. of Tring, Herts.

Sir Howard's death seemed to have a temporarily paralyzing effect on the firm. It was difficult to imagine life without him. Yet, whether intentionally or not, he had made some provision for the distant future. He had met a young man of twenty-one named Peter Oldfield, who was still at Oxford, where he was reading Rural Economy, and been impressed by him. Oldfield had been born at Harewood, Yorkshire, where his father, a surgeon, was a tenant of the Earl of Harewood. He had been to school at Repton, where his headmaster was the great Geoffrey Fisher, the future archbishop of Canterbury. So far his life had been entirely devoted to sport, above all cricket. He hunted, steeplechased, kept wicket for Oxford University, was Master of Oxford University Draghounds, played polo. He had just played cricket for the England XI against the Australians and was about to go to the West Indies with the MCC. He had also played for the Gentlemen against the Players at Lords.

'It was pretty clear that I had no vocation for medicine,' Peter Oldfield says today. 'My father suggested that I try dentistry or a job with Montague Burton the multiple tailors. Then I had an interview with Jackson-Stops in Leeds; but I wanted to work in London, so I went to see Sir Howard, and Hollis & Webb, the Leeds surveyors gave him my family background.'

It seems probable that Sir Howard was impressed as much by the young man's social contacts as by his brilliant sports record. Young Oldfield knew the son of Lord Rosebery at Oxford, and Lord Rosebery had put him up for White's Club. 'Can you bring in new business?' Sir Howard asked. 'I'll pay you 5 per cent of our net commission.' Peter Oldfield was confident that he could (he soon justified this by earning £6000 in commission in his first year).

Sir Howard interviewed him only twice, and at the second meeting the crunch came. It so happened that the day before Oldfield had played both cricket and polo for Oxford on the same day. 'Look,' said Sir Howard, 'you have got to choose between sport and earning a living!' Young Oldfield joined as an articled pupil.

Sir Howard probably saw him as a personal assistant who could be trained for partnership, but Sir Howard's death intervened. With respect, Peter Oldfield is eternally grateful that it fell to Alfred Burrows to take him on as a pupil, and his articles were served mainly at the London office, on the agricultural side, which was to be his speciality. A few years later he distinguished himself, in the Second World War, in quite another capacity, his pockets full of bombs. In the fullness of time he became Senior Partner.

Knight Frank & Rutley have always dealt in islands. Islands should be sold in the summer, when the sea is calm. The great drawback is that in rough weather you may have some difficulty in getting to and from your seagirt paradise. Jethou, where novelist Compton Mackenzie had thirteen unexpired years of his Crown lease to dispose of, is one of the smaller Channel Islands (44 acres, half a mile across). It had brought Mackenzie much happiness. He was a lifelong nesophile, buying, living on and selling several islands in the Channel and the Hebrides. He inspired D. H. Lawrence's story *The Man Who Loved Islands*. He had first seen Jethou in 1923, when he had visited it from Herm. There were, he thought, 'far too many rabbits', and the only sanitation was an earth closet. However, there was no income tax and the lease of the house was 'for life and a year after' (as distinct from the Crown Lease of £100 per annum). To Jethou he had brought his 10,000 books and 1000 gramophone records; and from here he managed to edit a monthly magazine, *The Gramophone*. Yet few people seem to want to live on a small island for ever, and as Knight Frank & Rutley say, 'Jethou comes on the market every ten years or so.'

In January 1933 three new partners were elected – Gordon M. Cannon, Herbert D. Kelleway and Charles J. Woosnam. Herbert Kelleway had been with the firm for over a quarter of a century, and for the last thirteen years had been managing the Country Department. Charles Woosnam had joined the firm in 1907, becoming an auctioneer three years later, and since 1926 had been manager of the Furniture Auction and Valuation Department. Gordon Cannon had joined in 1920 as one of the principal negotiators, and had specialized in private treaty transactions. He was far more a 'character' than the other two. He is recalled by a retired member of the staff as a salesman for whom *one* sale was never enough: he liked to find a speculator who would buy a whole property and either instruct the firm to resell it by auction in lots, or give Cannon a free hand to break it up. When planning a deal like this, he was observed to be pulling at the right side of his small clipped moustache.

One of the things that made Malcolm Mackenzie despair of ever understanding British business methods was overhearing Cannon telephoning a client thus: 'My Lord, *you* know the place is not worth £75,000 and I know it is not worth £75,000; but Her Ladyship likes it, and what is £75,000 to you?'

So the firm, for the first time in its life, had as many as seven partners – or eight, if we include Sydney Clements, whom A. J. Burrows had made a partner at Ashford: he was an agricultural specialist who operated only in Kent.

The face of London was still changing. (It always is.) Will Gibson's Town Department was very active in 1933. Hailed by the *Estates Gazette* as 'a sale without parallel in the London area', 78 acres of Kensington, centred on Earl's Court Station, were bought for a rumoured £1 million. 'The estate has all been developed within the last sixty or seventy years. Where before stretched fields and market gardens . . . are now serried ranks of houses and shops, producing ground rents of many thousands of pounds per annum.'

The firm had had, and were to have, sundry dealings with the Foundling Hospital Estate. When the Hospital had removed to the country in 1924, the old buildings and the 55-acre estate in Bloomsbury had realized £1,650,000. The controlling interest in Foundling Estates Ltd, which covered 'many of the best known streets and squares in the district', was now sold to Sir Harry Mallaby-Deeley, MP, a lawyer who described himself in *Who's Who* as 'Lord of the Manors of Ravensburg, Biggin and Tamworth', but who lived in Surrey.

A valuable unexpired lease of thirty-seven years at the Grafton Galleries, in the sensitive Berkeley Square area (they would soon become the Building Centre); Maida Vale Skating Rink bought for the BBC for conversion into extra studios; and Hanger Hill Garden estate, adjoining West Acton Station on the Central London Railway. Hanger Hill was typical of the suburban tentacles following the lines of extended tube railways, which was happening during the 1920s and 1930s. This was the decade in which you could buy a house on a housing estate for as little as £450 – £25 down and the rest on easy payments over twenty-five years. Hanger Hill comprised 365 houses with a rent roll of over £40,000 a year, all built since 1925. What was different was the five-year lease system, under which the landlord carried out external repairs, each tenant paying a 'garden rate' for maintaining gardens and shrubberies, and a communal sports ground and clubhouse, with provision for dancing, tennis, bowls and billiards. It is very nearly what has come to be known as the 'condominium' system. Will Gibson sold it for £400,000.

Not much doing in Scotland; still less in agricultural property. In depressed farming conditions, prices for agricultural land were the lowest for forty years. 'Single farms can be bought for almost one-third of the price they realized in the 1870s,' A. J. Burrows noted.

The galleries were jogging along, with no very outstanding sales; but there was one small triumph – a sale that would perhaps normally have gone to Sotheby's – two autographed letters of Charles Dickens were auctioned for 39 guineas. Both of them were to Daniel Maclise, RA, written from Genoa; and one of them contained a humorous description of his cook falling in love with, and marrying, an Italian.

In January 1934 it was announced that Cecil Ingram had 'taken over the firm's Scottish business under his own name . . . Although the firms will be distinct, they will continue to work in close association'.

The new branch of Knight Frank & Rutley was much nearer home – at Welwyn Garden City, to serve Welwyn, its sister-town Letchworth and the surrounding district, towards which suburban London was pointing. Welwyn, believed to be the hot-bed of militant vegetarianism, was the great housing and design-for-living experiment of the 1920s, with houses by architects like Louis de Soissons, full of loggias, roof-gardens and pergolas.

The outstanding transaction of the new office's first year was the sale of the whole of the Letchworth Properties belonging to Garden City Tenants Ltd, comprising 278 modern dwelling houses at a price 'in the neighbourhood of six figures'.

In Kent, Lord Darnley, a client for whom the firm had acted before, and would act several times again, was developing part of his Cobham Hall estate on high ground overlooking a golf course and a deer park: houses could be designed to suit individual requirements.

Two future partners joined the firm in 1934, both straight from school: Stanley G. Baker (always known as George) and Jack Guy. George Baker started traditionally in the post room, licking stamps; qualified as a surveyor and became a negotiator with an enviable reputation for 'getting on well with farmers'. Jack Guy specialized in 'chattels' and was the partner in charge of the Galleries up to their closure in 1970. George Baker counts himself fortunate in having been taught his job by Reg Leslie, a great negotiator. 'He was a real martinet,' George Baker recalls, 'unqualified by examination – but he could sell anything. He could sell an estate without seeing it!'

Hardly anybody seemed to want to buy a castle, and Gwydyr Castle, 'the ancient Royal residence of Wales', a Tudor mansion near Llanwrst, Denbighshire, was a long time selling. It had been burnt out in the 1920s and restored, and the particulars managed to find links with Queen Elizabeth, Charles II and Mary, Queen of Scots, a 600-year-old 'lovers' tree' and trees planted by George V and Queen Mary.

Alfred Burrows was clearly a very hard-working Senior Partner. Indeed, he spent a great deal of time in the train, commuting between Ashford and London, working on various files as he travelled. He had a flat on the opposite side of Hanover Square to No. 20, in a Victorian block on the site of what is now Esso Europe House, so that if he was working late he need not go home to Ashford. He had sometimes been known to make the London–Ashford journey twice in one day, so as to be able to sign letters in both offices.

Always an active propagandist in the movement to restore faith in the land, he gave evidence to the Royal Commission on Tithe Rent Charge, a burden that was crippling many small farmers. He also gave his support to the idea, recently supported, of a Land Investment Corporation.

In their annual report for 1934, Knight Frank & Rutley claimed that a revival in agricultural land had already started: there was a 'sustained demand, purely as an investment, for agricultural estates, free if possible from the burden of too large a house'.

Two more partners were announced at the beginning of 1935. Alfred J. Baker (no relation to George), who came straight from Curtis & Henson, had been in the property and estate business in the West End for over thirty years and had held an auctioneer's licence for seventeen years. He was both a property and a 'chattels' man, and had 'dispersed' the contents of many large houses in London and the country. He was an amateur actor, and looked the part, in bow-tie and wing collar. He specialized in Dickens rôles, which he delivered in monologue after the manner of Bransby Williams.

The other new partner was Malcolm Mackenzie. He had taken some persuasion, saying that he was not sure he wanted to stay on in London: he would only join the firm if he pulled off a really big deal. The big deal turned out to be the long-postponed development on the Berkeley Square/Bruton Street site. It was understood that Malcolm Mackenzie, who had been associated with the Thames project since 1930, would specialize in the letting and administration of office premises.

Lord Forres wished to sell his 165-acre estate, the Fishery, at Denham, Buckinghamshire. It was snapped up by London Film Productions, whose chief, Alexander Korda, intended to build 'the largest and most up-to-date film studios in the country'. It had taken a Hungarian to charm enough money out of the City to save British films from mediocrity. Never mind the 'excellent trout fishing' in the River Colne which ran right through the estate: what attracted Korda was the fact that 'without leaving the estate it will be possible to film almost any required exterior provided the setting is English in type'. The studios would cost between £250,000 and £300,000 to build, and the Great Western Railway would be asked to run a special studio train to Denham at nine o'clock in the morning.

1935 was Jubilee Year, in which a modest monarch was bewildered by his own popularity. George V, in poor health, had less than a year to live. Knight Frank & Rutley, always rising to a patriotic occasion, devoted part of their regular full-page advertisement in *The Times* to publicity for King George's Jubilee Trust, inaugurated by the Prince of Wales to help 'youths and girls just entering the age of semi-independence' – that is, the transition from school to job – or, more commonly, to unemployment. The firm took the opportunity of expressing its 'gratitude for the wise rulership that has brought our country intact through the troubled waters of the last twenty-five years'.

A variety of urban properties were being handled by the active (but not really expanding) Town Department. In Knightsbridge, London, at the junction of Sloane Street, a 70,000 sq. ft site with a back view of Hyde Park was offered jointly by Knight Frank & Rutley and Henry Chapman & Co. (Today it is Bowater House.) In Essex, almost the whole west end of Clacton-on-Sea was offered at an auction conducted by A. J. Baker.

The country residential estate market was improving slightly, as the general stability of the country increased: this was the period between the rise of Hitler and the drift towards war, when the implications of what was actually happening in Germany were still not generally understood. There was a revival in the Scottish sporting estate, such as Assynt, in the north-west Highlands, 118,000 acres – '5½ miles of first-class salmon fishing in the river Inver, excellent stalking on Glencanisp and Loch Assynt Forests, capital grouse bag' – this was the old Knight Frank & Rutley style.

On the borders of Northamptonshire and Buckinghamshire, the Horton Hall estate of 3628 acres, with a Georgian house, 'twelve important farms', small holding, cottages and 200 acres of woodlands – and 'three hunts in the district'; on the borders of Gloucestershire and Worcestershire, the 4475-acre Toddington estate, with its 'Gothic-style' mansion, stables, stud-farm, dairy and sheep farms, orchards and sporting facilities, and even some historic ruins, those of Hailes Abbey, a shrine for medieval pilgrims; and two estates as interesting for their contents, auctioned by Arthur Knight, as for the houses themselves – Burford Priory, 'one of the architectural gems of the Cotswolds', and Hatley Park, Cambridgeshire, a many-bayed brick house built for Sir Robert Cotton at the end of the seventeenth century.

Burford Priory 'chattels' were rich in old furniture – Queen Anne walnut chests, bureaux and bookcases, William and Mary carved walnut chairs, carved oak Elizabethan dower chests, Spanish painted leather chairs, and a brass studded chest 'formerly the property of Princess Katherine of Aragon'.

Three historic houses came up for sale: Thomas Marlowe, sometime editor of the *Daily Mail*, was disposing of Osborne Cottage in the Isle of Wight – it had been built by Queen Victoria for her mother the Duchess of Kent. The Old Palace at Bekesbourne, Kent, a fragment, remodelled in the eighteenth century, of a former country palace of the archbishops of Canterbury, was auctioned by (who else?) A. J. Burrows himself; and Minster Abbey, Thanet, dating back to the eighth century, was described as 'the oldest dwelling house in England'.

But the outstanding sale of 1935 was something so extraordinary (if only because it was such a poignant symbol of the social distress of the 1930s) that it is worth examining in detail. It stands beside the Crystal Palace, Stonehenge, Wembley and the Hotel Cecil in the annals of Knight Frank & Rutley.

The 46,000-ton, triple-screw, oil-burning transatlantic liner *Olympic* was laid up at Southampton in April, and for some months no one knew what was to become of her. She now belonged to Cunard, but had originally been a White Star vessel until the merger, forced by the Government in 1930, that ended the fierce competition between the two lines. She had shared the Atlantic express service with the *Majestic*, *Berengaria* and *Aquitania* during the 1920s, and had since 1934 been outclassed by the new *Queen Mary*, launched by the Queen herself with a bottle of Australian wine.

Her past had been chequered. Built in 1911 as a sister to the *Titanic*, she was at that time 'the largest ship in the world'. *Olympic* and *Titanic* were White Star's reply to Cunard's *Lusitania* and *Mauretania*. *Olympic* accommodated 105 passengers first class, 520 second and 1020 third.

On her very first visit to Southampton in 1911 she had rammed the cruiser *Hawke* in Spithead. Her war record as a troopship, however, was magnificent. In October 1914 she had tried to tow a mined battleship, the *Audacious*, to safety off the Irish coast, but the battleship sank: *Olympic* managed to rescue the complement. In 1918 she was torpedoed by U-boat U103, but the torpedo missed and she sank the U-boat by ramming. In 1934, just a year ago, she had disgraced herself again by sinking the Nantucket lightship with all hands.

Just about this time, Sir John Jarvis, High Sheriff of Surrey, had persuaded his county to 'adopt' the distressed town of Jarrow, on Tyneside. In September 1935 he announced that he had bought the *Olympic* for over £100,000. He wished to make it clear that he had no interest in any firm of shipbrokers: he wanted to establish

The 46,000-ton Cunard liner Olympic. *A sister ship of the* Titanic, *she had sunk U-boat U103 by ramming in 1918: less famously, in 1934 she had sunk the Nantucket lightship with all hands. A floating 'Hotel Cecil', Arthur Knight's sale of the contents was a highlight of 1934.*

shipbreaking as a new industry for Jarrow. Breaking up the *Olympic* would provide about eighteen months' work for the town, and the wages bill would be about £100,000. The Surrey fund would also pay part of the cost of dredging the Tyne to enable the ship to get far enough up river (about £2600). He had provided the £100,000 himself, to avoid the risk of the *Olympic* being bought for demolition by any other country, but had arranged for her to be re-sold at the same price to Thomas W. Ward, the Sheffield steel company. They would break the ship up at Palmer's Works, Jarrow.

By the end of September it was known that Wards had instructed Knight Frank & Rutley to auction the entire contents and equipment of *Olympic*, and that the sale would probably take two weeks. From now on all was drama and emotion. For the *Olympic* would have to make her last voyage from Southampton to Tyneside, and there would not be a dry eye at either end *or* in the middle. Knight Frank & Rutley's preliminary advertisement in *The Times* on 10 October gave some idea of what a floating Hotel Cecil contained: the furnishings of 530 staterooms and cabins, panelling in carved mahogany inlaid with mother-of-pearl; satin-wood, walnut and sycamore; the equipment of the Turkish bath and swimming pools, the fittings of more than 500 bathrooms; four passenger lifts; the contents of all the kitchens. The auction, conducted mainly by Arthur Knight, would begin on 5 November.

On Friday, 11 October the *Olympic* left Southampton for Jarrow, to a salute of sirens. She was due to reach Jarrow on Sunday, 13 October, sailing into Palmer's shipyard on the high tide at 3.50 p.m. A whole day before this, thousands of people were swarming on to piers at South Shields and Tynemouth and along the river banks, hoping to see something. Newsreel cameras in aeroplanes followed the ship all the way. She arrived punctually, escorted up-river by six tugs to a greeting of sirens.

On Monday a civic reception was held on board for 200 guests who included representatives from all Tyneside boroughs. Sir John and Lady Jarvis were received by the mayor of Jarrow. Suitable emotional speeches were made.

On 22 October the *Olympic* catalogue was ready: a gorgeous affair, quarto size, of 365 pages listing 4456 lots. A private view was held on 31 October, and public views on 1, 2 and 4 November. The catalogue price was reduced to 2*s* 6*d* (12½p) for public views and the auction itself.

The opening day of the sale began with a moving little speech, widely quoted in the press, by Arthur Knight: 'I have, in my time, broken up many a noble and historic home; and today I have the unhappy task of performing the last rites for this magnificent ship which has been for many years the home of the gallant crews sailing in her. It is impossible to be unmoved by helping to destroy such a monument to man's achievement, and I feel I owe the *Olympic* my apologies before starting my undignified labours.' He proceeded to Lot No. 1 – two settees from the engineers' smoking room, knocked down for £7.

The newsmaking lot was the furniture of staterooms which had once been occupied by the Prince of Wales: the first was in ormolu-mounted mahogany, the second in carved satinwood; the suites realized £87 and £42 respectively. They were bought by a Mr H. Hutton, of the Marquis of Granby Hotel, Bamford, near Sheffield.

Panelling from the public rooms and staircases remained mostly unsold when it was offered on the last day (15 November). Three of the first-class electric passenger lifts went for £30 each . . . and suddenly the sale seemed to peter out, a number of lots still unsold. It had been *diminuendo* for most of the second week. The biggest buyer (of 394 lots) was Mr C. T. Hawtree, of the Majestic Lido Hotel, Douglas, Isle of Man. The ship's bell was bought (for 26 guineas) by J. Hogg & Sons, brass-founders and ship-fitters, of North Shields.

The total realized was not published. Perhaps the drama and the emotion had been overdone. The general feeling was that better prices might have been obtained if the sale had been held in Southampton after all.

XI
End of the Thirties

Economically the country seemed to be recovering, always excepting the 'distressed areas', but these too would show a marginal improvement as the nation began to re-arm. For Knight Frank & Rutley 1935 had been reassuring. Sales and purchases of country and town properties had amounted to £3,757,225 with a total area of 51,795 acres in England and Wales, and 123,030 acres in Scotland. Valuations in a total of £7,785,737 had been made for estate duty, mortgage and other purposes and for the re-evaluation of business assets. In the auction galleries at Hanover Square and on owners' premises all over the country, sales of 'chattels' had resulted in the dispersal of 36,594 lots.

The firm was optimistic about the future of agricultural estates. There was a big demand for land 'ripe for development; the extended electrification of railways, the vast programmes for road improvements, and the cheapening of motor cars and transport facilities have all contributed to this'. There was a boom in mansion flats, especially in London. The restrictions of the new Town and Country Planning Act (and the Ribbon Development Act and the Green Belt Scheme) were making it far less easy to acquire sites for building: preparation and submission of plans to local authorities were being delayed, and 'rarely is a negotiation for the sale or purchase of an important site in London now consummated in under six months'.

Very large blocks of flats such as Park West, Edgware Road, and The High, Streatham, were being built by developers who usually put up a quarter of the capital themselves, borrowed the rest at 5 per cent and aimed to make 7–9 per cent on their investment. Property was not yet regarded as a sound investment for, say, a pension fund, and only rarely would an insurance company produce long-term finance for a block of flats or offices. Knight Frank & Rutley had for some years had their eyes on Park Lane where, since 1930, the new Grosvenor House development had been going up: in two years' time the firm would be advertising it as 'Mayfair's premier position . . . Unsurpassed prospect over Hyde Park', with rents from £350 per annum.

Two stately West End hotels came under the hammer in 1936: neither had been able to cope with the recession. The Metropole, in Northumberland Avenue, had only ten years before been famous for its Midnight Follies, said to cost £1000 a week. The Belgravia was less glamorous, but conveniently near Victoria Station. Both were offered with contents. Gordon Hotels, through the Guaranty Property Co., leased the Metropole to the Government as temporary offices.

The auction of contents, not quite on the scale of the Hotel Cecil, took twelve days, and was held in the Metropole's Great Banqueting Hall. The Belgravia auction, of much the same kind of contents, took only seven days. Arthur Knight officiated at both of them.

MR. PICKWICK OUTSIDE THE GOLDEN CROSS.

By courtesy of Messrs. Chapman & Hall, from the "Pickwick Papers."

FROM 1643

The Golden Cross

has been a symbol of hospitality and progress. Originally the Inn of the Village of Charing, it became a famous coaching hostelry and a hub of life and activity, and was associated with the adventures of Mr. Pickwick.

NOW IN 1936

GOLDEN CROSS HOUSE

is still at the Centre of one of the busiest areas in the Metropolis and embodies all that is progressive in modern office construction.

THE NEWLY ERECTED BUILDING

BEARS THE HALL-MARKS OF COMPLETE EFFICIENCY,

abundant light, air, labour-saving planning and a

COMMANDING CORNER POSITION

Facing Charing Cross Station.

THERE ARE TWO EXCELLENT SHOPS WITH LARGE BASEMENTS

To be Let with or without mezzanine floors over.

THE ONLY REMAINING OFFICE SPACE AVAILABLE

is the First Floor, about 8,635 sq. ft., a Corner Suite on the Second Floor, and two small Suites on the Fourth Floor.

Sole Agents:—MESSRS. KNIGHT, FRANK AND RUTLEY,

20, Hanover Square, London, W.1.

Golden Cross House, Charing Cross. The advertisement was illustrated by the Phiz cartoon of Mr Pickwick outside the original hostelry being threatened by the 'pugnatious cabman'.

No longer an hotel, only the site of one, Golden Cross House ('commanding corner position facing Charing Cross Station') was a new ultra-modern office block with shops on the ground floor, for which the firm were letting agents. As so often, they tried to invest it with an air of tradition by showing with it a Phiz illustration of Mr Pickwick outside the original hostelry being threatened by 'the pugnacious cabman'. It worked: there were paragraphs in the papers about it. But the big selling points of Golden Cross House were 'light and air': these, together with 'the hallmarks of complete efficiency', were selling offices. 'It is the *upper* floors of office

The Phiz cartoon.

buildings which now invariably let first,' Knight Frank & Rutley reported at the time; and they attributed this to a desire for 'abundant light and air' and 'freedom from noise'.

The 1930s saw the beginning of the 'industrial estate' – such as the Rylandes estate at Dagenham, already developing as a car manufacturing centre with firms like Fords, Briggs Bodies, Texas Oil and British Ropes nearby.

In the country Knight Frank & Rutley at this time were handling the Wittington and Medmenham estates on the Thames for the executors of the late Lord

Devonport (about 1906 acres along 2½ miles of river bank); Crewe Hall, Cheshire, 4380 acres, sold by the Marquess of Crewe to the Duchy of Lancaster as an investment; and Sunninghill Park, Ascot, acquired by the firm for Philip Hill the merchant banker. Sunninghill changed hands frequently: famous as a place for race-week parties, it had been occupied by the Guinnesses, Sir Henri Deterding and the Drexels from America.

Worth Park, near Crawley, Sussex, was a very different proposition. There was no Crawley New Town as yet, and very little development round about. Worth Park had been the seat of Sir Francis Montefiore, for whom the Public Trustee acted as vendor. The sale, conducted by Alfred Burrows at the Montefiore Institute, Three Bridges, was exciting. Somehow more than 400 people managed to crowd into the sale room, but many more failed to gain admission. The estate of 584 acres, included Farmleigh, the residence of the late Sir Francis; Worth Cottage; the Manor House, Crawley, twenty-two cottages, good farmland and 200 acres of woodlands. But what attracted urban bidders was (as noted by an observer) the 'considerable latent development value, as the property was bounded on all sides by important roads'.

There was also a 'mystery buyer'. Bidding for the bulk of the estate began at £40,000 and rose to £57,750 and there was a rustle of excitement when Mr R. Toms who was standing at the back, made a bid of £60,000 . . . the property was eventually knocked down to him for £61,750. This was presumably Reginald Toms, one of the new developers who had pioneered some of the great blocks of flats around London, and turned his World War I gratuity into a fortune.

With the spread of London's suburbs went another trend: new shopping centres. They were to be found in places like Neasden, Southgate, Pinner, Rickmansworth, often following the extended Underground lines which tended to come to the surface once they had left the metropolis behind. Edward Lotery was the developer who specialized in shops: his trademark was a certain herringbone pattern in the brickwork above them. The new shopping centres were often financed by banks, insurance companies and other institutions; and Lotery sometimes lent shopkeepers capital (this, it is said, is how Tesco began).

The trick in letting shops was to interest a big multiple first: Woolworths, Home & Colonial, Timothy White, Marks & Spencer, Boots. Other shops of all kinds would then follow. Besides Knight Frank & Rutley, Hillier Parker and Healey & Baker were doing a lot of this; and Knight Frank & Rutley's specialist was Ted Fisher. He had joined the firm in 1913 at the age of sixteen and had been Town Manager for the last few years, specializing in investments and business premises. He was a leading valuer of all property all over the country, travelling long distances with rolls of plans, often in a great hurry for a company prospectus. He looked astonishingly like J. Arthur Rank, and was plagued, in restaurants, by girls asking to be auditioned for his next film. Be this as it may, there was no one to touch him as a valuer of shops.

In November of 1936 Charles Woosnam died at the early age of fifty-two. He had been a partner for only four years, specializing in antique furniture sales; and it seems a pity that he should have left the scene just as London had become the centre of the world art and antique market, aided by the new stability of sterling, leaving Paris in second place. These were times when Old Masters suddenly appeared in country house sales, and 450-piece dinner services were offered.

The world Charles Woosnam knew has been remembered for us by Ronald Browne. You noticed the Galleries as soon as you entered the door of 20 Hanover Square, for they began in the hall with a corridor full of oil paintings, rich carpets, old furniture, statuary – and led off into other rooms now used as offices. It was 'a pleasant jumble . . . delicate cut glass or finely glazed porcelain gains effect from having as its neighbour a suit of armour; a polished table appears to have emerged from a country mansion, when used to display a crested dinner service, and a fragile cabinet seems more dainty when it happens to be placed next to an elephant's foot converted at much cost for the mundane task of holding sticks and umbrellas'. The most dangerous items were hanging cut-glass chandeliers, difficult to suspend, fatally easy to let fall. It was wise to make certain that each was adequately insured.

In December, H. D. Kelleway (he was A. J. Burrow's son-in-law), retired, or rather 'relinquished his partnership', as he was a comparatively young man and seems to have had other business plans. He had been with the firm since 1908, specializing mainly in country properties.

The year ended in gloom. Not only had the Crystal Palace been burnt down, but Edward VIII, who had been King for less than a year, abdicated. And this latter event was later to lead to the sale of the contents of Fort Belvedere, a Royal task for which there is no documentary evidence, so discreetly was it carried out.

In February 1937 the *Auctioneers' Journal* and other professional magazines carried an announcement (a surprise to some) that A. J. Burrows was splitting off his Ashford practice and amalgamating it with the old-established Kentish firm of Winch & Sons, Cranbrook. He had never lost his independence or abandoned his Kentish roots, and the move was obviously a preparation for semi-retirement. The partners of Knight Frank & Rutley were now Arthur Knight, William Gibson (the obvious heir apparent as Senior Partner), Gordon Cannon, Malcolm Mackenzie and Alfred J. Baker, with Edward Fisher as the latest recruit.

The emphasis was now on building land. Around High Wycombe and neighbouring Stokenchurch, houses were going up at a density of ten or twelve to the acre. At Berkhamsted, shops, factory sites and houses were being 'infilled' with new houses. At the Buchan Hill estate, Sussex, land on the Crawley–Horsham and London–Brighton roads was fetching £100–£200 an acre. Along and behind the Kingston by-pass, the Surbiton (or Lovelace) estate, 700 acres, including Surbiton Golf Course, was 'ripe for development' within the new restrictions; and, said the particulars, 'when the Chessington line of the Southern Railway is opened the estate will be served by four first-class stations'.

In Lytham St Anne's, the Lancashire seaside resort next door to Blackpool, Knight Frank & Rutley almost repeated their Reigate experience by selling the greater part of the whole town. The deal had dominated the life of Will Gibson and the Investment Department for months: it involved nothing less than 5½ miles of

The Coronation of King George VI, May 1937. Knight Frank & Rutley were retained to acquire sites for seats along the processional route – lettings of about £20,000 were arranged in this way.

A view of the Rialto Bridge over the Grand Canal by Canaletto. Part of the Margrave Pallavicini Collection, one of the many great treasure houses sold by Arthur Knight, who died in June 1937.

coastline, 6000 houses, 500 shops, 25 churches, 19 banks, and the Royal Lytham St Anne's Golf Club. The freehold ground-rents were sold for £25,000 by H. T. de Vere Clifton, whose family had held the land for many centuries.

1937 was Coronation Year. It had been prepared for Edward VIII; the same arrangements would do for George VI. For Knight Frank & Rutley this meant an unusual assignment: they were retained by a well-known theatre seat company to acquire sites for seats along the processional route. Lettings of about £20,000 were arranged in this way.

Will Gibson had his own Royal assignment in this year: he was commanded by the King to value certain properties at Sandringham: a few years before he had explored the house itself, and his enduring memory was George V's bedroom, and the extreme hardness of the mattress: the monarch did not pamper himself.

In June, Arthur Knight died suddenly at his seaside home in Bournemouth: he was only fifty-seven. He had been with the firm for over forty years, and like his father was an authority on furniture and pictures. He had auctioned the furniture and pictures at Hornby Castle for the Duke of Leeds; the duchess of Albany's furniture at Claremont; Lord William Cecil's Italian majolica and Limoges enamels; the

The development of Berkeley Square House as commercial office space was another major change in the face of Mayfair.

contents of Stafford House, for the executors of the Duke of Sutherland; and the Gobelins tapestries of Lord Addington. Some of his sales – the Hotel Cecil and the *Olympic*, for example – 'had no precedent in the annals of the hammer'.

Berkeley Square House, the long-term creation of Malcolm Mackenzie, was at last a-building, and even while the foundations were still being laid more than 12 per cent of the space had been let. The promoter, to whom Knight Frank & Rutley had sold the site, was Sidney Bloom, one of the pre-war 'whizz-kids' of property. The freehold of the land had been amassed over many years by Maitland Kisch. The layout and amenities had been planned by Bloom on the advice of Malcolm Mackenzie, assisted by Geoffrey Gay, and the block had been designed by Gordon

THE EVICTED GHOSTS.

Low's cartoon which appeared in the Evening Standard *on 28 July 1930 depicted stubborn resistance to change by local residents.*

Jeeves with Hector Hamilton as consulting architect. It was built by Sir Robert MacAlpine & Sons who then bought it, and Knight Frank & Rutley, having nursed the project from the beginning, became letting agents.

Flats were no longer booming, but there was a good market at the top for those providing quite unusual amenities, such as the 7-acre Dolphin Square, which was going up on the Thames Embankment between Chelsea and Vauxhall bridges: promoted by Richard Costain, it was at the time 'the largest block of flats in Europe'. Here the blocks 'surround an internal garden greater in extent than that of Berkeley Square and where the layout includes English, Mexican and Spanish gardens', also a swimming bath, restaurant, gymnasium and squash courts. 'The demand for accommodation has been phenomenal,' Knight Frank & Rutley reported. 'In the South block, which comprises half the development, 98 per cent of the flats have already been let, while lettings are proceeding rapidly in the North block, which is not yet completed.' The firm were also sole agents for two important blocks of flats in Mayfair: Grosvenor House and Hereford House; and for a new block of duplex flats on the corner of Park Street and South Street, where 'every flat is arranged on two floors with its own private and internal staircase . . . and each principal bedroom has its own bathroom' (a new idea imported from America).

1938, the year of fear and the Munich Crisis, saw a sudden interest in small islands off the Scottish coast. Were their purchasers seeking retreats from bombing if war should come? Four tiny islands in Invernessshire came up for sale in April – Canna, Sanday, Hyskeir and Humla, about 3000 acres all told. Canna, about five miles long, had two residences and was reached by six hours sailing from Mallaig. Its industries were crofting and lobster-fishing, there were wild goats and grey Atlantic seals, Vikings' graves and a cross to mark the site of St Columba's chapel. The four islands were bought privately by Mr John Lorne Campbell.

The country estate sale of the year was Rufford Abbey in the Dukeries. Its 18,700 acres comprised the Abbey itself, founded in the twelfth century and partly rebuilt in the sixteenth and seventeenth centuries, standing in a 500-acre deer park; and the greater part of the villages and parishes of Old Ollerton, Eakring, Wellow, Bilsthorpe and Ompton, as well as parts of Walesby, Egmanton, Edwinstowe, Farnsfield, Kirton, Blidworth and Tuxford. There were some seventy farms, thirty-eight small holdings, four inns (including the famous Hop Pole at Ollerton), houses, shops, hundreds of cottages and 2000 acres of woodlands. The estate had been acquired from the Savile Nottingham Estate Trustees by a syndicate of North Country businessmen led by Sir Albert Ball, JP, three times Lord Mayor of Nottingham. Sir Albert was the vendor.

Straight away some 1700 acres were sold to three collieries in the district. A number of farms, inns, shops and houses were bought by their tenants. The Rufford 'collection' was dispersed early in the summer jointly by Christie, Manson & Woods and Knight Frank & Rutley. It was thought that there would be 500 lots which would take 'several days' to sell. The 'particulars' ran to over 100 pages.

The auction was A. J. Burrow's last great performance on the rostrum, which he shared with A. J. Baker. It began on 22 November and was reported dramatically by the North Country press, led by the *Sheffield Telegraph* which recorded much of it in photographs. 'Going, going, gone! Little old ladies buying their own cottages. Tenants look back on their memories.'

The house carpenter took reporters to see 'Sir George's Room', said to be haunted. Many of the Abbey staff could remember Edward VIII speaking to them when he came here to shoot.

On the third day of the sale, A. J. Baker sprang a surprise: certain plots of land in the village of Eakring – about sixty acres in all – would be withdrawn, because it was believed that oil in considerable quantities lay beneath the surface. The tenant of Pond Farm, Eakring, confirmed that oil had been found in all five of his fields less than 3000 feet below the surface. 'Village May Be Oil Town – Eakring Prepares to Welcome Prosperity. Old-World Eakring . . . Quiet Scene May Disappear,' lamented the *Sheffield Telegraph*; 'never since the famous Rev. William Mompesson came to Eakring from plague-stricken Eyam, and was forced to preach in the field because the villagers were frightened of infection, has the village known such a stir.' The villagers, many of them farm labourers keeping families on 36*s* (£1.80) a week, were not wedded to 'old-world Eakring' and welcomed the prospect of higher wages

A. J. Baker auctions Rufford Abbey. With 18,700 acres, it was the country estate sale of 1938.

which the oil industry must bring.

But the oil industry never came. The total sales of the freehold estates amounted to £250,446, including timber. As for the Abbey, it remained unsold until the Government found a use for it during the war. It now belongs to the Nottinghamshire County Council.

In London, the long-term work of Malcolm Mackenzie and his colleagues was crowned by the letting of almost the whole of Berkeley Square House, except the shops, to HM Office of Works on behalf of the Air Ministry to use as headquarters offices. The space occupied was 330,000 sq. ft. Nearly seven miles of partitioning had been used to divide it into offices. The owners were now Berkeley Square House Ltd, a subsidiary of the United Investor's Cooperative Society. The development of the site had involved the diversion of South Bruton Mews, and the demolition of the house in Bruton Street where the little Princess Elizabeth, one day to be Elizabeth II, had been born.

The finished product was a justification of the new ways of looking at property which Mackenzie was teaching the younger surveyors and negotiators; the use of amortization and sinking funds to redeem capital, new methods of valuation as well as financing; above all, the importance of admitting the letting agents into the birth of a scheme, so that they could advise on the planning and design, using their experience of the market. There was much that architects did not know. It was not the architect who was going to have to let the building.

By the end of the year, the ground floor and basement of Berkeley Square House were already being converted into air-raid shelters. On 30 September, after a month of such international tension as had not been known since 1914, Neville Chamberlain flew back from Munich and waved a piece of paper at the newsreel cameras: 'It is peace for our time.' A wave of relief swept over the country, followed by a guilty sinking of the heart. Will Gibson had just come back, with others who had survived or lost relatives in the battles of the Somme in the Great War, from a pilgrimage to France to attend the unveiling of a memorial to the 17th (Northern) Division at Fricourt. Old soldier – and old sailor – that he was, he had no illusions about 'peace for our time'. Everybody expected, in the event of war, immediate mass bombing. Will Gibson therefore began making a list of suitable country properties for the war-time evacuation of offices, including two film studios, Denham (the site of which he had sold in 1935) and Pinewood. Since all fit young men (and many women too) would join the Forces or be conscripted, firms would need to operate in the country with shrunken staffs. Rent would not be payable until war was actually declared.

These were not easy ideas to sell. The Munich Crisis had different effects on different clients – almost a kind of 'double-think'. On the one hand there was a new sharp interest in 'safe' country properties; on the other, there was often a flat disbelief in the possibility of war: 'D'you mean to sit there and tell me that (a) there may be a war, and (b) if there is, any hostile plane will be able to get through our defences and drop bombs on London?' Field-Marshal Goering could have told such optimists that at the time of Munich there were only eleven anti-aircraft guns to defend the whole of the metropolis.

One feature of the estate market since Munich, the firm said in its annual property review, was 'a continuous inquiry from people who do not intend to be caught again in a similar predicament and feel the necessity of having, or building, a place, however small, in the country which can be used not only as a *pied-à-terre* but also in emergency'.

In January 1939 it was announced that A. J. Burrows had severed his connection with the firm and retired to Ashford; and that Will Gibson was now Senior Partner. In the early spring Malcolm Mackenzie went to the United States, taking Willie Cunningham with him: they were studying the up-to-date methods of property development; in particular, country and sporting clubs as part of what would one day be called the Leisure Industry. Whatever they learned would have to be put into cold storage as the war clouds drew nearer.

In London a Royal residence was sold: 41 Belgrave Square, once the home of the

Inch Kenneth on the island of Mull in the Inner Hebrides – 'I was very much taken with Inch Kenneth' wrote James Boswell in his journal of a tour of the Hebrides. 'I said I was resolved to have it for an elegant retreat for our family for a month or two in summer. I really indulged serious thoughts of buying it.' In 1939 it was sold to Lord and Lady Redesdale whose daughters were the Mitford sisters. It was to be Unity Mitford's last home.

Duke of Kent, was in a square still inhabited by three Dukes and two or three Earls, for in the last twenty years Belgravia had supplanted Mayfair as a fashionable/expensive residential quarter. This was part of 'the westward trend of commerce'.

In Kent, two ancient properties: the village of Chiddingstone was sold by the firm to the National Trust on behalf of Col Henry Streatfield, whose family had occupied the castle as far back as 1600: the castle, a mock-Gothic affair added to a seventeenth-century house, had become a girls' school. And Chilham Castle, near

Canterbury (it is really a Jacobean house) was put up for sale by Sir Edmund Davis, who had modernized everything – ten bathrooms, an indoor swimming-pool and 'model domestic quarters'. With it went an estate of 2100 acres. The whole was eventually acquired by Viscount Massereene and Ferrard, whose seat it now is.

In Somerset, the Earl Poulett instructed Knight Frank & Rutley to dispose of the agricultural portions of the Hinton St George estate, 3200 acres between Yeovil and Taunton, famous for dairy produce. It was bought by the Oxford University Chest, which we shall meet again in 1958.

Our last view of the pre-war world will be an island off Mull in the Inner Hebrides, Inch Kenneth. It had been visited in 1773 by Dr Samuel Johnson and James Boswell. They were guests of Sir Allan Maclean, and Boswell went overboard for it – it was after all replete with Scottish history: St Kenneth, one of the bretheren of St Columba, had re-built the chapel whose ruins were still there; and Staffa, with Fingal's Cave, could be seen across the sea. 'I was very much taken with Inch Kenneth,' wrote Boswell in his *Journal of a Tour of the Hebrides*. 'I said I was resolved to have it for an elegant retreat for our family for a month or two in summer. I really indulged serious thoughts of buying it.'

By 1939 it had left the Maclean family and was owned by Sir Harold Boulton, a composer remembered today by only one work, the 'Skye Boat Song'. In the summer of 1939 he offered it for sale by private treaty and it was not long in finding a buyer. Peter Oldfield was the negotiator, and the buyers were none other than Lord and Lady Redesdale, 'Farv and Muv' to the spectacular Mitford sisters. The price was £8000. It would soon be the home – indeed the last home – of Unity Mitford, who died in 1948, never having completely recovered from her suicide attempt.

Offshore islands are seldom easy of access, but Inch Kenneth was better than some. Here, in a white, bow-fronted small mansion, built by Sir Harold Boulton in what has been described as a 'Home Counties' style, Lady Redesdale lived and kept sheep, a few cattle, Shetland ponies, a goat and some hens; and while in residence made her own butter, cheese and bread. Years later it became her permanent home until her death in 1963.

XII
At War Again

On a sunny Sunday morning in September 1939 the ragged voice of Prime Minister Neville Chamberlain broadcast to the nation. We were at war.

At Hanover Square offices were depleted as young men either volunteered or joined their Territorial units. On 8 September Will Gibson sent a memorandum to all staff: 'During the state of war the earnings of the firm are likely to be seriously reduced . . .' Everybody earning more than £165 per annum (and this was a respectable salary for a young man in his twenties) would have to take a pay cut, and this would be calculated on a scrupulously fair sliding scale so that the partners would be making the greatest sacrifice. The great aim was to preserve the business so that everyone should have a job to come back to after the war.

Will Gibson had considered the possibility of evacuating some or all of the staff to Denham or Pinewood film studios, under a plan formulated by the City some three years before. However film production continued well into 1941, and the movement *en masse* into the country was found to be unnecessary.

Will Gibson compromised, and acted quickly. The day after war was declared, because no one knew when the bombing was going to begin, he moved the Accounts Department to his own home, Braid House, Gerrards Cross, and installed it in the largest ground-floor room, putting up Arnold James, the chief accountant, as 'house guest' until the department was able to return to Hanover Square. Two assistants were found billets nearby. Those staff who remained at No. 20 saw the iron railings of the square taken away for scrap metal, and large air-raid shelters built all over the Gardens.

The surveyors were temporarily accommodated in a house at Bushey, Hertfordshire, and one of them, Ted Osborne, alternated between Bushey and Hanover Square. Another, Alwyne Daborn, with one or two assistants, went to Shrewsbury, partly because his wife came from there, and also because it was convenient to have a branch office on the way to the north. Some of the Country Department were billeted at Gordon Cannon's house at Weybridge, where they turned farm buildings into offices.

At Gerrards Cross, all was friendly chaos, and Gibson the martinet found that military discipline no longer worked. His two daughters, Jean and Nancy, had been pressed into service – Nancy because she was a good secretary and Jean because she had a head for figures.

The Blitz started in earnest with the Battle of Britain in the autumn of 1940, and the Accounts Department sat tight at Gerrards Cross. In the following spring there seemed to be a let-up in bombing, and everybody returned to Hanover Square, the Accounts Department resuming its normal place over the porch at No. 20. There was always Gerrards Cross to fall back on, and, at the height of the bombing, Will Gibson was generous in offering all the staff in turn a quiet night's sleep in the country. For this was a time when town personnel often had no sleep at all: they worked all day, interrupted by raids, and were generally on air-raid precautions and fire watching at night.

When France collapsed in 1940, Anthony Eden (afterwards Lord Avon) made a famous radio appeal for what were called 'Local Defence Volunteers' to repel the German invasion which everyone expected. Will Gibson responded at once, and quickly rose to command, as befitted a man with a distinguished record of service from the First World War. Local Defence Volunteers, who had begun drilling in civilian clothes with broomsticks, were eventually renamed the Home Guard, given uniforms and weapons and placed under army administration. Will Gibson was made commander of the 5th Bucks Battalion.

He had begun by attending a Home Guard course in 'irregular warfare' at Osterley Park. In 1940 morale was very low, and the most shattered man under his command was Private Sir Nevile Henderson, whose diplomatic failure as Ambassador to Berlin had left him with a burden of defeat. He responded, however, to Will's leadership.

Gibson devoted all his spare time, evenings and week-ends, to training his men and running his battalion. Martinet he might be, but in the country he could relax. Yet he could be fierce on expenses: 'Why have you charged fourpence for this bus fare? It's only threepence!' The only staff member who never relaxed was Arnold (Jimmy) James, who walked about the village in bowler hat and umbrella as if in the West End, and as part of his duties walked the Gibsons' dogs when he took the mail to the post-office. Only in his retirement, many years later, did he relax sufficiently to wear a deerstalker.

He had taught Jean Gibson bookkeeping; but Jean was no longer at Gerrards Cross: she had volunteered for a mysterious organization, then unknown to the general public, called SOE. She was to be sent abroad, for she was now engaged to a young officer in the Oxfordshire and Buckinghamshire Light Infantry whose unit was in Italy. His name was Pat Heller, and one day he would be Senior Partner of Knight Frank & Rutley. But this was in the remote future: for the moment, as he walked down a street in Bari, he was the most surprised young man on earth to see his fiancée. They were married next morning by an Army chaplain.

At home, business was not quite as usual: the miracle was that there was any at all. In war only very well-heeled, long-term risk-takers want property, especially as long as there is any doubt about victory. The government requisitions what it wants, and if what it wants is country mansions which are almost impossible to sell, there is some business for the property agent. (Thus Lord Iveagh's Norfolk estate was taken over by the RAF, and Lord Melchett's Melchett Court by the Army.)

At 20 Hanover Square there were daily telephone calls from clients saying: 'Our building has been half-flattened. Come and look at it.' The staff at No. 20 (some of them temporary) were running around after raids, inspecting a factory in the East

A new form of business developed during World War II. Clients whose property had been bombed were quick to call for a valuation, be it for a factory which had been blitzed in the East End or a shipload of timber which had been reduced to charcoal in a Thames-side wharf.

End, or a shipload of beautiful timber reduced to charcoal in a Thames-side wharf. There was no lack of valuation work – and (especially in war conditions, with slow transport and bombing-alerts) a survey or valuation could take anything up to three weeks. The result was often contained in what was called a 'schedule of Plight and Condition'.

The firm were also responsible for looking after certain clients' properties, either because their owners were in the Forces or because the government or the Forces were occupying them or might reasonably be expected to damage them, incurring post-war compensation.

Urban property damaged by bombing was either shored up for the duration of the 'emergency' (this being longer than the duration of the war) or pulled down if it were dangerous. The Compensation (Defence) Act 1939 based compensation on the annual rental value under lease, the lessee paying rates, taxes and maintenance.

For the first two years of the war, there was a steady demand for agricultural land as Britain learned to 'dig for victory'. The country estate market was not entirely dead: Tennyson's Farringford estate at Freshwater, Isle of Wight, came on the market. In March 1940 the firm was still hopefully advertising the Isle of Jethou ('to let, for the duration of the war'): three months later it was full of German troops. At the end of 1940 the firm listed twenty-four properties in the country to which

In March 1940 the firm was still advertising the Isle of Jethou ('to let, for duration of the war'): three months later it was full of German troops.

companies, institutions, corporations and private buyers had 'evacuated' themselves to escape the bombs. There was also a big demand for timber.

Knight Frank & Rutley now had twenty-one people in the Forces. Malcolm Mackenzie, a reservist in the US Navy, had been called up and by the end of 1941 was Naval Attaché in Melbourne, Australia. George Baker, one of the many who had their professional studies cut short, had joined the army a few weeks after the outbreak of hostilities: he spent nearly seven years in the army, ending as second-in-command of a 'forward airfield' unit of the Indian Army Engineers. Kenneth Maycock, a negotiator in the Country Department, had six-and-a-half years in the army, beginning as a machine-gunner in the Middlesex Regiment, serving in Northern Ireland, Egypt, Sicily and Italy; transferred to mule transport (he had learnt to ride, unconventionally, in Argentina), he joined the Lovat Scouts in Greece where his mountain warfare experience came in useful, and was demobilized as a major.

Jack Guy, a future partner in charge of the Galleries, having been told he was unfit for military service, reported to 88th City of London Heavy Anti-Aircraft Regiment, became an expert on radar, then top-secret, and eventually served in the Middle East, Sicily and Italy. Ronald Browne, surveyor and all-round property man, was in the Royal Navy, and, among many adventures, found himself helping to put out a fire on board the troopship *Georgic* at Port Tewfik on the Suez Canal: a mine had exploded, and passengers were rescued by sliding down ropes.

Peter Oldfield, a founder member of the SAS, who narrowly escaped execution by a German firing squad.

Geoffrey Gay was one of several staff who had joined the Honourable Artillery Company in peacetime. He had been at Dunkirk as a subaltern with the Durham Light Infantry. He was then sent to Iceland, and is thus able to confirm a story which all soldiers in other theatres of war had heard but did not quite believe: that the War Office, totally ignorant of the country, supplied the occupying army with an Eskimo interpreter and a Railway Transport officer, also a locomotive. A glance at any school atlas could have shown that there are no railways in Iceland. There are no Eskimos either. After hard training in snow and ice warfare, Geoffrey Gay was suddenly sent to Rawalpindi, and then became Lt-Col Chief of Staff, Sind District. Here he carried out a memorable combined operation by air, land and sea against smugglers who were carrying arms and ammunition to the North West Frontier in dhows.

To Peter Oldfield fell the glamour – and the hardship – of helping to start the Special Air Service. He had been made a partner in 1940, with Alec Siese, while away on active service, an unusual distinction. He had joined the Warwickshire Yeomanry, then still a cavalry regiment, and gone to Palestine. In Cairo he had pioneered the Air Photographic Reconnaissance Unit at GHQ, which often helped the SAS. Oldfield saw at once that the SAS, raised by David Stirling with the help of Fitzroy Maclean and others, combined brilliant leadership with surprisingly low casualties. David Stirling had destroyed 250 enemy aircraft on the ground, which was more than any RAF squadron could claim. The fact that GHQ regarded this sort of thing with suspicion made it all the more attractive. Peter Oldfield was a founder member of SAS and became second-in-command to Stirling.

The enemy were dug in at El Agheila. Stirling planned to have 220 men attack and mine 400 miles of road between Agheila and Tripoli, so that the Germans could not use the coast road at night. This would force them to bring up supplies in daylight, and thus become an easy target for the RAF. On 13 December 1942, the SAS arranged themselves along the coast road: Peter Oldfield had a roving assignment in the Tuorga area. He was taken prisoner, but not before he had done a great deal of damage. The story is told in Virginia Cowles's *The Phantom Major*: 'He had mined the road in several places, set fire to a number of lorries, shot up a German HQ, and destroyed several fighter aircraft on Tuorga airfield' (twenty-two, to be precise). He had then attacked a convoy, been seriously wounded (a shot through the neck among other injuries) and been captured with his driver.

The Germans were so unnerved that there was talk of shooting the two prisoners out of hand. Oldfield's life was saved by a German, a surgeon, who thought it wrong of his superiors to execute badly wounded men. So in the middle of the night he smuggled Peter into a lorry and sent him to a hospital in Tripoli. Peter was now a German prisoner, and very ill indeed: for nine months he was paralyzed and had to be fed with a fountain-pen filler. After further escapes from prison camps in Italy, he made his way over the frontier to neutral Switzerland. He weighed only seven stone. When, after the war ended, he reported back for duty at Hanover Square, Will Gibson made him take six months off to recover.

Three of Knight Frank & Rutley's staff were killed: Ian R. Banting, Robert R. Brackenridge, and Walter R. Gwillim – Banting and Gwillim had been articled pupils. They are commemorated by a plaque in the hall at 20 Hanover Square.

The offices at Hanover Square were run by Nelson Lovett, head of the Management Department, supervised by Willie Cunningham. One day's memoranda from Lovett to Cunningham tells us something of the daily problems of war-time London: a claim for shop windows blown out in Camberwell, SE; broken glass and a lift out of action in Dartmouth Street, SW1; a shop front blasted out in the same district; an incendiary bomb in King Street, SW1. And often the most dreaded telephone call of all – from a client whose entire building has been reduced to rubble.

The firm had its civilian casualties too. Towards the end of 1941 it lost two partners, A. J. Baker and Gordon Cannon. Overwork in wartime conditions undoubtedly hastened their deaths.

Just before his death, at the age of fifty-seven, A. J. Baker had engaged a secretary, fresh out of school, at 23*s* 6*d* (£1.17½) a week with the promise of another half-crown (12½p) after six months. Her name was Doris Russell, and today, more than forty-five years on, she is Mrs Doris White. When she left the firm in 1983, she was the longest-serving woman member of staff. In 1941 she was assigned to the Galleries, where her first impression was 'a strong smell of mothballs from carpets just being unrolled'. With the shortage of manpower, at the age of seventeen, Doris frequently took over the job of 'clerking' auctions. There were then three Galleries at Hanover Square, she remembers – 'one on the ground floor, a huge area now reconstructed and occupied by the whole of Advertising and Country Surveyors. On the first floor, under the domed roof, was another gallery, now occupied by building surveyors and a further huge room at the rear of No. 19 Hanover Square'. In the hall, for some years, was a sedan chair which had been converted into a telephone booth.

In December 1941 came news of the death of Frank Capon at the age of seventy-three. A character, immensely well liked in the profession, he had been valuing estates for forty years, both at home and abroad, and had given evidence in important arbitrations, one of which had recently concerned the acquisition by the Air Ministry of a large area in Southern England. He owned an ancient measuring wheel, fitted with a dial, which he had had for fifty years. Sometimes known as a perambulator, it had handlebars like a bicycle, a circumference of two yards, and a trocheameter or revolution-counter. It was used to record approximate distances when surveying. Frank Capon left his wheel to the Auctioneers' Institute.

Looking back over the year, Will Gibson reported that the firm had sold or bought for clients over 46,000 acres of freehold land, by both public auction and private treaty. 'The demand for farms has far exceeded the supply.' This was emphasized at the Shrubland estate, near Ipswich: Baylham Hall, a moated Elizabethan house, was attractive enough, but it was the eight farms which drew the liveliest bidding. Two Hampshire estates, West Park, near Fordingbridge, and Cowesfield, near Romsey, showed similar trends. West Park, once the home of Sir Eyre Coote, with 5500 acres, was acquired by the Pall Mall Trust as an investment, who retained the agricultural portion of the estate and sold off the rest. Cowesfield's main attraction was 50 acres of woodlands – '30,000 cubic feet of ash and oak'. Prices were rising.

In London, no one was buying residential property, though there was a demand for small flats. Lettings of office premises were doing well – air raids were decimating the supply, as was Government requisitioning. Flats were being used as offices, making flats even scarcer. The Galleries were selling off the contents of many houses, getting higher prices for silver and jewellery. 'Prices have risen for all types of furniture, except very large old-fashioned pieces of the Victorian era.' Even at the lowest point of a war – and the military situation in February 1942 gave no reason for optimism – there is always somebody who can afford to buy a sporting estate in Scotland; such as Shinness, in Sutherland, 12,500 acres, offered by the executors of 'the late G. W. Beldam, the well-known Middlesex Cricketer'. 10,000 of those acres were grouse-moor. On Southampton Water the 1200-acre Hook and Warsash estate, including a golf course and several farms, was regarded as full of possibilities for post-war residential development.

Two new partners were created in 1942. Taken together, they demonstrated that there are more ways than one of being 'taken into partnership'. Relations with the 12th Duke of Bedford had never been easy; it was unwise, for example, to get into an argument with him about the war, for he was a militant pacifist. Passionately interested in the Oxford Group and Major Douglas's theory of Social Credit, singularly incompetent at business and at running his estate while turning a deaf ear to advice, he had by 1942 placed most administration in the hands of a formidable lady named Mrs Osborne Samuel.

There was the question of whether, and if it happened, on what terms, Woburn Abbey should be taken over by the War Office for a purpose so hush-hush that neither Mrs Samuel nor anyone else knew what it was. It had already been used by the Royal Navy as a centre for the WRNS and priceless pictures and antique furniture were stored higgledy-piggledy in one wing. It was not difficult to foresee substantial post-war dilapidations. What should the War Office be charged? Willie Cunningham apparently advised to the Duke's satisfaction, for on his next visit Mrs Samuel said: 'The Duke wants you to take over the whole estate. Your salary would be £2500 a year, and you would have a car, a chauffeur and a free house!' Willie asked if he could think it over and hurried back to tell Will Gibson.

'Well?' asked Gibson, 'What are you going to do?'

Risking all, Willie said: 'I think my prospects at Knight Frank & Rutley are better than that.'

'They certainly are,' Gibson said. 'Actually, we were thinking of making you a partner . . .'

Guy Coleridge, MC, Will Gibson's brother officer in World War I, had travelled far and wide in the 1920s and 1930s, but had always kept in touch with his old friend. He had spent many years in India as a cotton broker with Gill & Co. of Bombay, returning to England in 1936 to join Hanneys, a Liverpool cotton firm. On the outbreak of war, being disabled (he still wore a surgical boot on his right leg and needed two walking sticks), he could not hope to rejoin his regiment, but managed to secure an administrative job as Chief Postal Censor. He did not much enjoy the work; at the same time he saw little future in cotton and he had some capital to invest. So Will Gibson offered him what was originally intended to be a sleeping partnership; but auctioneers, too, were in short supply, and Guy Coleridge soon found himself limping on to the rostrum. In another year or two he was running the Galleries.

He is remembered as 'much respected, decisive, energetic, enthusiastic', and his very tall but stooping figure as he got out of his Rolls-Royce (always driven by his wife Cecily) was a familiar sight about the West End. Once the war was over, he would build up the Galleries, now only just keeping their heads above water, into profitability again.

The victory at El Alamein in October 1942 had a sharp effect on business confidence. Reporting progress for the year in the *Estates Gazette*, the firm stated: 'The volume of (country) business transacted had been restricted only by the number of suitable properties available.' A new Defence Regulation, restricting a farm purchaser's power to give notice to quit, had raised the prices of farms offered with vacant possession. In urban areas, especially in London, 'business concerns are looking ahead and buying for occupation after the war'. Moreover, the United States Army was now here, creating a lot of requisition work, including the two principal USA Service Clubs, 45 Park Lane (for senior officers) and the Washington Hotel in Curzon Street.

Wealthy men were again beginning to invest in horseflesh. A former part of the Lavington estate in Sussex, only four miles from Goodwood, when it had belonged to Lord Woolavington had been the Westerland Stud Farm, sold in the spring of 1943. With the 1300-acre Ifield estate, near Crawley, offered by the executors of Sir John Drughorn, Bart, shipowner, the emphasis was on beef and dairy cattle. This was a rare case of an estate being sold three times in one day – first as a whole, the bidding having risen from £30,000 to £128,000; then by the purchaser, representing Pedigree Stock Farms Ltd, who in the interval exchanged contracts with two directors of a Sheffield firm; who in turn re-offered the major part of the estate in lots.

In June, when the Home Guard was stood down, there being no more fear of invasion, the name of Lt-Col W. Gibson appeared in the Birthday Honours List – an OBE to add to his DSO and MC.

On 6 June 1944, 'the greatest and most scientific invasion of all time', involving the Mulberry Harbours, the PLUTO undersea oil pipeline, over 700 ships and 4000 landing craft, took place across the Channel. It came to be known as D-Day, and the new confidence it begot in the near-certainty of victory had a remarkable effect on property values. Oliver Marriott, in *The Property Boom*, traces the beginning of that boom (which was to last about twenty years) to this period, in which the first activities of a new kind of property developer were to be seen. Some of them, like Cotton, Gold, the Levys and Walter Flack, were thought of as whizz-kids; others, like Clore and Colman, would build up mighty businesses; and one of the few qualified developers, Harold (now Lord) Samuel, laid the foundations of what has been called 'the City's most respected property company', Land Securities.

Just after D-Day, a Wiltshire estate of 1136 acres, Crowood, near Ramsbury, came on the market. It was essentially a farming estate, and the buyer it attracted had recently come out of jail where he had been interned, under Defence Regulation 18.b, since June 1940. Sir Oswald and Lady Mosley had been living on a small agricultural holding at Crux Easton, Hampshire, while looking for a larger estate so that the Fascist leader could resume one of the enthusiasms of his youth, farming, which he had observed on his family's hereditary farm in Staffordshire. He enjoyed his years at Crowood, but eventually gave it up: 'I was a novice to arable farming, and, as always, I was in too much of a hurry.'

D-Day had been followed by the German 'revenge weapons' V1 (a pilotless plane

Sir Malcolm Campbell with Bluebird, *whose 87-acre estate with its Georgian house was sold in 1944 to the Maharajah of Baroda.*

filled with high explosive) and V2 (a rocket capable of reaching a height of 70 miles before falling and causing destruction on an unprecedented scale). Yet this did not deter the new appetite for urban property. 'There are more investors than there are vendors,' Knight Frank & Rutley reported. 'Considerable funds are available for mortgage purposes at low rates of interest . . .'

A new partner was appointed in January 1945: Edward Osborne, who had been with the firm for thirty years, having served his articles under Sir Howard Frank and gained much of his practical knowledge from Frank Capon. He had specialized in country estates and was an expert valuer.

In May, Germany surrendered unconditionally; and in August, after the fearful demonstration of atomic power at Hiroshima and Nagasaki, Japan did the same. A tired coalition Government, which retained Churchill as a 'caretaker' prime minister until the General Election in October, was thrown out by the electorate which voted in a Socialist government under Clement Attlee.

What would the Government's post-war plans be? How soon could the country expect de-requisitioning, the relaxation of war-time controls which optimists looked forward to as a 'bonfire of restrictions'?

Meanwhile, there was much for the firm to do. Sir Malcolm Campbell, the speed king, sold Headley Grove, Surrey, his 87-acre estate with its Georgian residence, to the Maharajah of Baroda. Port Lympne, near Hythe, Kent, whose eccentric owner,

Sir Philip Sassoon, recently dead, had built it in 1913 to the design of Sir Herbert Baker with additions by Philip Tilden, was looking for a buyer. It was not going to be easy to sell: Chips Channon, in his famous diaries, described it as 'a triumph of beautiful bad taste and Babylonian luxury, with terraces and flowery gardens and jade-green pools and rooms done up in silver and blue and orange'.

In Cornwall, 4200 acres between Bodmin and Wadebridge, sold for Sir John Molesworth St Aubyn, Bt. (with the assistance of Button, Menhenitt and Mutton) to the Duchy of Cornwall; in Radnorshire, Lord Ormathwaite's Welsh estates, of which 8874 acres were sold for a total of £115,000; and two notable estates in Hampshire, Oakley Hall (3590 acres), and the resale of 2000 acres of it as a separate estate: category – 'agricultural and sporting'.

The General Election was by no means the only excitement of the autumn of 1945. The Ministry of Works instructed Knight Frank & Rutley to sell by auction the entire contents of the German Embassy in Carlton House Terrace (Nos. 7, 8 and 9). Described as a sale of 'modern furnishings and collections of seventeenth-century pictures', the greater part of it took place in the Brasserie Restaurant at Earl's Court Exhibition. It was expected to last eight days (in fact, since a number of items were withdrawn, it took only six).

The auctioneer was Guy Coleridge, who told those who attended the press preview on 19 November that there would be 1900 lots from which he hoped to raise between £50,000 and £75,000, the proceeds to go towards German debt reparations to Britain. Silver plate and pictures would be auctioned separately at Hanover Square Galleries on 10 December. Surveying the collection, ranging from a vast mahogany conference-table to vacuum cleaners, a *Times* correspondent observed: 'There is enough furniture for several blocks of flats, but much of it is too big for the private home. Ribbentrop's dining-table, for instance, is 25 ft 6 in. long, and with it go 42 dining-chairs.' And who would want to give houseroom to a huge globe 'on which are marked in blue ink some of the Nazi conquests dreamed of in 1936'? (Answer: plenty of curio-hunters.) 'The 980-piece Dresden china dinner-service is to be sold in five lots.'

The sale began on 26 November, and was so crowded that many people had to stand. Admission was by catalogue, which cost 10*s*; even so, there were one or two demonstrators protesting at the whole affair, which was thought by some to be glorifying the Nazi regime.

The first day's proceedings were broadcast direct to the United States (this was not quite without precedent: the sale by Sotheby's in 1937 of Victor Rothschild's pictures from 148 Piccadilly, was covered by the BBC). 300 lots were disposed of, realizing £19,800, of which carpets accounted for more than £7000 – one being knocked down for £480.

On the second day a bust of Hitler went for £500: it was bought by the owner of Blackpool Pier. Eleven German flags, four of them designed to fly over conquered London, made £313. On the third day, Ribbentrop's semi-circular dining-table went for £1000 to Mr Billy Butlin: it would be used 'for the deliberation of the campers'

Joachim von Ribbentrop, Hitler's ambassador to the United Kingdom 1936–38, outside the German embassy, 7–9 Carlton House Terrace. After the war Guy Coleridge auctioned the contents of the embassy in a six-day sale: anything bearing the Nazi swastika was withdrawn on instructions from the Government.

committee at Skegness holiday camp'. A Sheffield dealer bought thirty-six mahogany armchairs, upholstered in green and silver brocade, for £1000 and immediately resold them to Mr Butlin's representative for £1200. Proceeds for the day: £14,500. The fourth day realized £9000. The remaining two days at Earl's Court made it clear that the target sum of £75,000 was a possibility.

On 10 December came the sale of silver and pictures at Hanover Square – and a surprise. Guy Coleridge announced that he had received instructions from the Government that everything bearing the Nazi swastika was to be withdrawn; so were three oil paintings of Berchtesgaden, Hitler's Alpine retreat (it was not clear whether they were Hitler's own work). It *was* clear that many of the high prices were being paid by souvenir hunters, whose motives were regarded by the new Government as suspect. A letter to *The Times* on 1 December concentrated on the bust of Hitler: 'The price paid (£500) can be justified neither by artistic merit nor by the normal healthy enthusiasm of the souvenir hunter. It does not, however, require a great effort of imagination to realize that such articles, though ridiculed now, might one day be

After the May 1945 General Election, Winston Churchill was in sudden need of a London house. Will Gibson acquired 27 Hyde Park Gate on his behalf.

triumphantly produced to serve as "holy" relics in some attempted revival of Nazism. In Germany, no chances are being taken, and a determined effort has been made to destroy all vestiges of the Nazi regime.'

Winston Churchill, putting a brave face on the country's rejection of him in time of peace, was seeking a new home. Clementine, his wife, early in 1945 had seen a house at 28 Hyde Park Gate which she found charming, and wrote to her daughter Mary: 'I must be careful not to run Papa into something which is more than he can afford.' Could he afford both his beloved Chartwell and a town house? Was 28 Hyde Park Gate big enough? What probably decided the issue was the fact that the house next door came on the market at the same time. The expense was partly justified by the fact that the top two floors could be converted into a maisonette which was lettable.

Churchill was an old client of Knight Frank & Rutley, who had found Chartwell for him. Will Gibson and Willie Cunningham went to see him and were received by him with his usual informality – in his bedroom, where he made his entrance naked but for a towel, flopping round the room in slippers and looking (Willie Cunningham remembers) 'like a large pink baby'. Though it was five o'clock in the afternoon he had just got out of his bath. No. 27 had been empty for some time, and Churchill had asked the firm to survey and value it. There was a good deal of dry rot and the price was too high, Will Gibson reported. Then he asked, 'Why do you want the house next door, Sir?' thinking perhaps that Churchill ought to retire, his work done.

'Oh, for staff, you know – my secretary Miss Hamblin, a couple of detectives, perhaps – about six people.'

Gibson did a little mental arithmetic and thought that No. 27 would take £1400–£1500 a year to run. Could Churchill afford it? he wondered. No decision was arrived at that afternoon, and Gibson thought the deal was going to fall through. Churchill went to America and made his 'Iron Curtain' speech; then suddenly cabled back from Fulton: '*Buy No. 27.*'

When the time came to send Churchill a bill, Will Gibson said to his partners: 'He's such a great man. Let's not charge him.' And he wrote to Churchill saying that the firm would like to make him a present of its services.

It was Clementine Churchill who replied: 'We are both touched that you and your partners should want to refrain from sending in an account for the work you have recently carried out for us, and we thank you all most warmly for your thoughts. We feel, however, that this would preclude our asking you to undertake further transactions on our behalf: and as we hope you may continue to do so in the future, we feel that we cannot accept your generous offer.'

XIII
Reconstruction

Post-war Britain was hedged about by Government restrictions of every kind. The hopeful phrase 'ripe for post-war development' which had appeared in so many 'particulars' was frustrated by building controls, slow de-requisitioning and restrictive planning legislation (in which, however, some of the new rising property tycoons found a few useful loopholes).

It has been argued by some that Knight Frank & Rutley lost opportunities during these post-war years by being too rigidly 'professional'. It can equally well be argued that 'professionalism' was far better for their long-term reputation. The partnership now seemed to divide into debating camps: consolidation *versus* expansion. 'I knew,' Peter Oldfield remembers, 'that my task, if ever I got the chance, was to rejuvenate the firm.'

By June 1946 most men had been demobilized, and Will Gibson called a staff meeting. He wished to honour his promise to review salaries within six months after the end of the war. In the past, participation in the staff bonus scheme had been limited to those earning £300 per annum or more, and secretaries, typists and juniors were given Christmas boxes. In future the entire staff would share in the bonus scheme.

If there were no major projects yet, there was no lack of 'professional' bread-and-butter. Estates were coming on the market because officers had been killed, or their owners, unable to endure the greyness of a post-war world committed, for the foreseeable future, to a Labour Government, were emigrating to what were still called the Colonies. There was a great deal of valuation work for compensation claims – country properties damaged by the Forces' occupation, town properties destroyed by enemy action.

The market was changing. Country houses now wanted were those with labour-saving equipment which needed far fewer servants. Some properties could not be sold (such as a highly attractive old mill by the river Wey) because they needed rehabilitation and the necessary permits and licences could not be obtained. Office accommodation in shattered London was desperately hard to find. Not much chance of expansion overseas – not, at least, in traditional directions. Currency restrictions made it difficult for most people to buy or rent property abroad.

Lord Astor of Hever, in 1946, wanted a South of France property, and this suggested fresh possibilities. So the firm took on a war hero, Peter Churchill, who had met his wife Odette when they were both in Special Operations Executive in occupied Europe, to try to develop the market which, before 1939, had justified three agency offices in Cannes, Nice and Monte Carlo, under the direction of Alec Siese. Most of the work was letting furnished villas 'for the season'. It was nobody's fault that, after the war, this ceased to be worthwhile: the market, for about fifteen years, simply was not there.

At home there was a 'seller's market' for small (preferably eighteenth century) country houses with not more than 150 acres; and owners of estates in the hunting shires were tending to change to those districts offering shooting and fishing (a mile of the Test fetched £8000) – sports which cost less and could be enjoyed when they were older. 'Those with a high rate of surtax are taking advantage of Section 33 of the Income Tax Act, 1945, which allows the landowner to claim one-tenth of the cost of improvements each year for a period of ten years.'

The Galleries were doing well. There were goods for sale, and Guy Coleridge was building the 'chattels' business up into real profitability, as owners moved from mansions into flats. In 1946 there were sales of 45,000 lots in 103 auctions. It was not a good time to sell Old Masters, for which prices were no higher than they had been in the 1920s; though a world-wide market in Impressionists and modern paintings was on its way. No, the 1946 market was for basic necessities such as furniture and bed-linen because everything was 'in short supply'. There were also highly successful sales of guns and furs, started by Coleridge. (One of the anomalies of post-war Britain was that, even for furs bought in an auction, one had to surrender the requisite number of clothing coupons.)

Knight Frank & Rutley already had responsibility, as we have seen, for Woburn Abbey, looked after by Willie Cunningham. Now the 12th Duke of Bedford asked William Gibson personally to look after the Bedford London estate; and to do this he was to join the Board of London & Devon Estates Co., the company which administered all the Bedford properties everywhere. It was an honour which he accepted with some misgiving.

There was not much good industrial property about; however, in September 1947, the firm renewed its old acquaintance with Wembley Exhibition by purchasing, for British European Airways, two freehold factories. One of them was the old India Pavilion, and the two together provided 140,600 sq. ft which went for under £2 per square foot.

Among many country estates were Headley Court, Surrey (not to be confused with Headley Grove): this was the Dowager Lady Cunliffe's house, bought, after a long search for suitable premises, for the RAF as a rehabilitation centre for flying personnel (which it still is).

The young Princess Elizabeth had just got engaged to Lieut. Philip Mountbatten. They would of course, need somewhere to live, and Knight Frank & Rutley, with other estate agents, were searching for a suitable residence. It was assumed for some time that the Royal couple would occupy Sunninghill Park, near Ascot, which had been bought by the Commissioner of Crown Lands in 1944, a twenty-five-room mansion with 300 acres of Royal farmland found for them by Knight Frank & Rutley. But it had been used, during the war, by both the British and United States Air Forces: could it be refurbished in time? For the sake of social justice, the answer was No – 'only a few rooms will be repaired'. The matter was resolved by a fire – due, the CID said, to a 'carelessly dropped cigarette-end in the newly timbered library'. Arson was ruled out. So the Princess and her husband had to make do with Clarence House, after a honeymoon at Windlesham Moor (a property which has been several times on the firm's books).

In October the firm again had the experience of offering a whole village. Castle Combe, in Wiltshire, once voted 'the prettiest village in England', probably is. The sale caused 'nation-wide interest' and the firm went to town with (for those days) luxuriously-illustrated 'particulars', showing the seventeenth-century Cotswold manor house, smaller houses and cottages dating back to the fifteenth century, and two picturesque pubs, the White Hart and the Castle. At the auction at Chippenham, bidding began at £40,000, but the village as a whole was withdrawn at £48,000 to the disappointment of the vendor, Mrs K. R. Maurice, who had hoped that it might pass to the nation.

It did not exactly do this, but in 1966 it became the temporary property of 20th Century Fox, who re-christened it Puddleby-on-the-Marsh and used it as a setting for *Doctor Doolittle*, starring Rex Harrison. This could hardly have been foreseen in 1947, and the great source of satisfaction, when the village was offered again in lots, was that the Castle Inn fetched £4250, and other houses were bought by their tenants at prices they could afford. Mr Hammond bought his bakery for £1700, Mrs Eels bought her general store for £600, and a row of three cottages went for £510.

Four years after the end of the war, urban re-development was still very difficult. In Haymarket long and involved negotiations by the firm, representing the New Zealand Government, resulted in the acquisition of 'the unexpired term of the Crown Lease of the Carlton Hotel, His Majesty's Theatre and the Royal Opera Arcade'. It was understood that 'when rebuilding is permitted, it is the intention of the New Zealand Government to erect a new building on the hotel site. In the meantime (and this is a very 1949 touch) the hotel will continue to house the Food Ministry'.

Since mid-1948 the BBC had been aware that it ought to be expanding its television service. Their lease at Alexandra Palace was due to run out in 1956. In a few years' time commercial TV would arrive (as it had long ago arrived in America) and the BBC would no longer have a monopoly. The Director-General, Sir William Haley, thought priority should be given to building two new studios and ancillary offices, and the new accommodation should be ready in about three and a half years' time, i.e. by the beginning of 1952. 'In parallel,' says Lord Briggs in his *History of Broadcasting in the United Kingdom*, 'if the Government approved, new regional transmitters could be opened at the rate of two in three years, thus giving nationwide coverage by 1955/56. The government did approve . . .'

In March 1949 the BBC decided upon a 13½-acre site at White City which had housed the Franco-British Exhibition of 1908, and obtained the London County Council's permission to develop it. So it was possible for Norman Collins to announce, at the Television Society's annual dinner on 1 April, that the new TV Centre at White City would be the largest in the world, occupying over 6 acres out of the 13½; and towards the end of the year Graham Dawbarn was appointed architect for the first stage, in association with Will Gibson's old acquaintance from Broadcasting House days twenty years before, Marmaduke Tudsbery Tudsbery, the Corporation's civil engineer.

The new White City television centre would not be ready until 1960; but meanwhile, through Knight Frank & Rutley, the BBC acquired the old Rank Film Studios with 3½ acres of floor space at nearby Lime Grove. This was arranged with the utmost urgency by Geoffrey Gay, whose task was not made easier by the fact that, earlier in the year, the BBC had rejected them. Other West London acquisitions for the BBC were to follow: Ealing Studios, King's Theatre, Hammersmith, the Shepherd's Bush Empire, Riverside Studios, the Playhouse Theatre and a lease on the Golders Green Hippodrome.

For the Galleries, the outstanding sale of 1949 was Kimbolton, seat of the Duke of Manchester, who was now farming in Kenya. Kimbolton Castle, 'once the home of Queen Katharine of Aragon, and now with its Vanbrugh front and Pellegrini murals a building of considerable beauty and architectural importance', is in what used to be Huntingdonshire. It was about to become a public school. But the contents attracted even more attention than the building.

Guy Coleridge was on the rostrum. The highest price was £3045 for 'Prometheus, chained to a Rock attacked by an Eagle' (Rubens and Snyders). A Canaletto of 'The landing of Charles, Earl of Manchester, at Grand Square, Venice' went for 200 guineas, and Sir Joshua Reynolds's portrait of Elizabeth, Duchess of Manchester, and her son, as Diana and Cupid, for 100 guineas. By the second day of the sale, prices were still lower: 30 guineas for a Veronese 'Marriage at Cana', a Tintoretto for only 30 guineas, and several Van Dycks fetching between 21 and 32 guineas each! The third day was devoted to furniture, which did a little better. Rupert Richardson-Gardner, a future partner who was present, remembers 'an octagonal English cabinet with a beehive front' as the star piece. A Spanish coffer which had belonged to Katharine of Aragon with her initials on it, realized £750; a Chippendale dressing table £600; and an early nineteenth-century nobleman's coach £100. At the end of the fourth day the entire ducal collection had been knocked down for £19,000.

A new partner was appointed in January, 1950. Charles A. H. Stenholm had joined the firm in 1945 from Daniel Watney & Sons, chartered surveyors, where he had specialized in valuation. He became business premises manager at Knight Frank & Rutley and had got his Fellowship of the RICS in 1947. Among many important property transactions and valuations, he had recently valued and sold Hugh Town in the Scilly Islands for the Duchy of Cornwall. 'He had a flair,' a colleague says of him, 'for dissecting complicated Acts of Parliament, in fact all legal documents' – and he was an occasional auctioneer. He was a leading light in the fencing world, and had represented Britain at both epée and sabre.

Simultaneously came the news that A. J. Burrows, by now the Grand Old Man of the profession, had at last retired at the age of eighty-five. He had been an auctioneer

The Shepherd's Bush Empire was sold to the BBC for use as a television theatre, for shows with audience participation such as 'What's My Line?'

and estate agent for over sixty years and had held almost every possible honour and appointment in the property world, and many offices in the public life of his native Kent.

The islands of Skomer, Midland and Gateholme, off the Pembrokeshire coast, 763 acres of igneous rock, were up for sale in the spring. Skomer is particularly famous, among ornithologists, for being a habitat of the Manx shearwater, to say nothing of puffins, razorbills and guillemots. It has the disadvantage of all offshore islands – you cannot get to and from it in an outboard motor-boat when there is a gale blowing. George Baker, in charge of negotiations, had to complete his survey for the 'particulars' in record time, his host looking nervously at the sky and saying 'you'd better be getting back now, I don't like the look of it . . .' Skomer was bought by Mr E. P. Lee, Chairman of Coventry Climax Engines Ltd.

Queen Marie of Yugoslavia sold her country estate, Great Swifts, at Cranbrook, Kent. Mrs Warwick Bryant offered Windlesham Moor, back on the market now that it was no longer needed by Princess Elizabeth and the Duke of Edinburgh. Headley Grove was for sale again by order of the Maharanee of Baroda, her marriage to the Maharajah having been dissolved. A large sporting estate in Scotland, Rhifail, 14,720 acres, once part of the Duke of Sutherland's estates . . . Standard Country Department transactions, you would say, but still no new developments.

Will Gibson was not well. He had been operated on for simple hernia, his daughter Jean says, in 1948, but while he was in hospital 'trouble flared up, later traced back to the dysentery he had suffered as a young man, and he underwent three major operations. He nearly died . . .' At Hanover Square few people knew this. He was sixty-three and he would soldier on until 1956 before retiring.

The two new partners who were announced in January 1951 could hardly have presented a more striking contrast to one another. Geoffrey Gay had been with the firm from his boyhood. Rupert Richardson-Gardner came in from the outside world to take charge of the Galleries.

Geoffrey Gay had become assistant to the then Town Manager, Sidney Towersey, eventually specializing in shops and offices. (At that time, in the 1930s there was only one partner and five negotiators on the Commercial side.) After the war he had expanded the office business and, with a certain amount of valuation, helped to set up a separate department for Licensed Property, eventually becoming Manager of the Commercial Department. He was currently engaged in a number of very large long-term projects such as the amassing of buildings on the west side of Grosvenor Square (which had been going on since 1947) to form a site for a new United States Embassy, completion of the negotiations for the New Zealand House, and further acquisitions for the BBC.

Rupert Richardson-Gardner joined Knight Frank & Rutley (in his own words) 'by accident'. Guy Coleridge had been ordered by his doctor to rest his injured leg for six months. Who was to replace him temporarily? Richardson-Gardner had been an officer in the Coldstream Guards; then a merchant banker; then fifteen years in Bombay, where he met Guy Coleridge whom he had also known as a cotton-

It took Geoffrey Gay more than four years to amass the buildings on the west side of Grosvenor Square to form a site for the new United States Embassy.

broker in Liverpool. After 1945 he had become a stockbroker on half-commission. But – 'I was sick of the Stock Exchange,' he says; 'fed up with explaining to old ladies why their portfolios weren't making any money under Chancellors like Dalton and Cripps.'

Richardson-Gardner was a man of taste, with a love of *objets d'art*, but he wasn't a specialist in anything. So Coleridge sent him to Perez the carpet people for a six months' crash course in carpets. At this time, furniture sales were held in the West Gallery on Wednesdays at 1 p.m. (for run of the mill goods) and Fridays (for the best stuff). Richardson-Gardner soon developed his own auctioneering style. 'All auctions are really battles between two people at a time,' he believes. 'Never exclude anyone who has already bid – look at them and ask: "And you, Sir?" – "And you, Madam?"

1951 was the year in which the Royal Institution of Chartered Surveyors brought in stricter regulations about advertising. Knight Frank & Rutley had always led the field in publicity, but could hardly have been accused of excessive claims beyond the usual estate-agent-ese. However, they had often taken whole pages of *The Times* and *Telegraph* to announce their total turnover and acreage at the end of the year, and this was now frowned upon. At the end of 1951 they took a page in *Country Life* to show a single photograph – of their name-plate outside 20 Hanover Square, without a line of copy. This was condemned as sensational.

The Country Department continued its serene course. Glandyfi Castle, Cardiganshire, sold to a private buyer within six weeks of advertising; the Peterwell estate, near Lampeter, 1495 acres; Clifford Manor, Warwickshire, near Stratford-on-Avon,

1072 acres: and a preliminary announcement, in October, of a spectacular sale which took place in the following year; historic Hengrave Hall, near Bury St Edmunds, whose owner, Sir John Wood, had recently died. The 5200-acre estate had everything – good agricultural land, sporting facilities, thatched cottages, and a sixteenth-century mansion built for Sir Thomas Kytson, a wealthy London merchant who incurred Royal displeasure and lost his head. One of his descendants, Penelope, married the Sir John Gage who, it is claimed, first brought greengages to Britain, and the original tree was said to be still alive in the gardens of Hengrave Hall.

Malcolm Mackenzie was due to retire at the end of 1951, and he had just completed a world tour in search of business opportunities. He was known to favour expansion abroad, and in this he was supported by Geoffrey Gay. He had visited Canada, the United States, Australia, the Bahamas (where Alec Siese had joined him for part of the time, to study the development of Lyford Cay), New Zealand, South Africa, Ceylon and East Africa, and had written a long report on how he thought the firm should tackle overseas markets, in particular Australia.

The Mackenzie report was not implemented – yet. The partnership was divided about 'abroad'. Will Gibson had never much liked it. The large gourmet American was thanked for his advice. The firm had other reasons to thank him, too – for teaching them many things: how to estimate development costs, new ways of acquiring sites for clients, how to enlarge small opportunities . . . His aptest pupil was Geoffrey Gay.

Mackenzie's other firm friend was Willie Cunningham, whom he entrusted with a dream – the dream that even the toughest Yank keeps close to his heart – to see Ireland. Would Willie and his wife Edith please show him around the Emerald Isle? They did, and it must be assumed that he went back to New York a happy man. He remained 'overseas consultant' to the firm, and was instrumental in bringing in new business from the New World. His monument in London is still Berkeley Square House.

XIV
Ex Africa . . .

Malcolm Mackenzie, on his world tour, had visited East and South Africa, but not West Africa. He had recommended Australia, but this was not the new direction in which capital was to be risked. It came out of the blue. One morning in 1951 there had been a telephone call from a Mr Read, manager of the Bank of West Africa in London. Would Knight Frank & Rutley care to undertake a very large valuation in West Africa? The firm concerned was Paterson Zochonis, the third largest British firm in West Africa. They did everything – import-export, of palm oil, ground nuts, beer; they had soap factories and they owned offices, warehouses, harbours, river-boats. Based mainly in Nigeria, they had interests in all West African countries. The valuation was for probate, Mr Zochonis having died recently, and it would include assets in Paris and Manchester, where the firm's head office was.

To Malcolm Mackenzie it was the kind of opportunity he had dreamed about. He was enthusiastically supported by Geoffrey Gay. How on earth did one assess a fee for such a task? Geoffrey Gay got the partnership to agree on one thing: he would go to Manchester to talk to Paterson Zochonis, forever afterwards known as 'PZ'. In Manchester he was asked what Knight Frank & Rutley would charge. 'We can't tell you till we've seen all the properties,' Gay replied. This did not seem to upset the prospective client as much as had been feared. Gay said boldly that the job would need six months in the field, inspecting the enormous number of assets, consulting title deeds, etc; he would need two, perhaps three, assistant surveyors; and it might be another year before completion was possible. In addition to all full expenses being paid, the fee which Knight Frank & Rutley received was the highest valuation fee ever known at that time. One of the surveyors he wanted to take with him was Richard Davis, a valuation expert who afterwards became a partner.

The partnership's caution was understandable. Nigeria, not yet independent, looked politically unstable. The oil boom had not yet begun. Yet other firms were working successfully there, and over the next few years Knight Frank & Rutley would get to know them well and do business with them – the United Africa Company, Taylor Woodrow, Elder Dempster, Mandilas & Karaberis, agents for Carrier Engineering and Volkswagen. Carrier Engineering were trying to introduce refrigeration and air-conditioning into a country which, looked at from Britain, still bore the popular stigma of the phrase 'white man's grave'.

Geoffrey Gay got his way. The surveying team covered 20,000 miles by car (often carrying their own petrol supplies because there are few garages in the bush) by lorry, canoe and mammy-wagon, a form of transport peculiar to West Africa – a primitive truck full of travellers hitching a ride wherever the wagon happens to be going. The result was the biggest document ever prepared for a client: about 170,000 words, 660 pages and three columns – part of it in French because it covered PZ's assets in French African colonies as well. The countries visited, for commercial, residential and rented properties, furniture, equipment, plant, machinery, road, river and marine transport, were Nigeria, Gold Coast, Sierra Leone, French Cameroons, French Guinea and Liberia. Through this undertaking, Knight Frank & Rutley gained a firm foothold in Africa which they were to develop to the full.

In 1952 a young man of twenty-two joined the firm as an articled pupil. Nine years' later he would be a partner, and twenty-six years' later Senior Partner. Samuel Goodenough had been an Eton College Scholar (in mathematics) and at Oxford had taken an honours degree in Litterae Humaniores. His decision to enter the property business was the result of a lot of soul searching. He had considered banking and the church: for both, there were ample precedents in the family. His grandfather had been chairman of Barclays Bank and founder and Chairman of Barclays DCO; his father was also chairman of DCO and later of Barclays Bank and his mother was a member of the Gibbs family of Antony Gibbs the merchant bankers. He was also a great-great-great grandson of Samuel Goodenough, bishop of Carlisle, classical scholar and botanist, who was the son of the Rev. William Goodenough, Rector of Broughton Poggs, Oxfordshire, where Sam Goodenough lived in the area where his family have been since the Reformation. He was the organist at Broughton Poggs (early Norman) church from the age of fourteen.

His father, Sir William Macnamara Goodenough, Bart, had acquired the whole of the Foundling estate in Bloomsbury for the Dominion Students' Hall Trust which was started by Sam's grandfather F. C. Goodenough. The original building in Mecklenburgh Square, known as London House, was founded in 1930, the year of Sam's birth, as a hall of residence for male post-graduate Dominion Students in London. Subsequently the activities of the trust were greatly expanded by the building of William Goodenough House – for girl students – named in memory of Sir William, and later still by Julian Crossley Court with flats for married students, and named after Sir William's brother-in-law Sir Julian Crossley, also a Chairman of Barclays DCO.

London House was administered by Knight Frank & Rutley, who had a Foundling Estate office at 11 Grenville Street, WC1, supervised by Will Gibson, but run largely by Pat Heller since 1948. Pat Heller was responsible for the management of 26 acres in Bloomsbury, comprising residential property, hostels, hotels, shops, offices and industrial premises with a rent-roll of about £100,000 per annum, an office staff of seven and a building maintenance staff of seventeen men. In 1950 Pat Heller had been transferred to head office in Hanover Square to become negotiator and first assistant to the manager of the Investment Department.

Sam Goodenough was the last Knight Frank & Rutley pupil to complete his articles, for which he paid 500 guineas and received, in addition to tuition, £1-a-week pocket money, which was enough to cover the cost of his lunch. During the next few years he was closely involved in farm sales and estate management, coordinating modernization schemes, forestry, house and cottage improvements, rent reviews and valuations for sale and purchase. He was also responsible for handling many substantial sales of land for residential development during the house-building boom in the fifties. As time went on, he showed an outstanding talent for selling Scottish properties, and especially for writing romantic (but accurate) 'historical notes'. His particular memory is of the guest-house at Dundrennan Abbey on the Solway Firth where Mary Queen of Scots is believed to have spent her last night in Scotland, leaving in the morning from the jetty. Sam Goodenough wrote a press release about it, describing the 'wild white violets' around the jetty, which made headlines in America. He had no difficulty at all in selling it to a lady who was overcome by the romance of it all. And even the Scots themselves are sometimes bewitched by a phrase like 'halfway between London and Reykjavik'.

The sale of 1952 was Hengrave Hall, already announced in 1951. The house and most of the estate were sold before auction for £165,901 to a convent school. There was an auction of chattels at the Athenaeum, Bury St Edmunds, and it took eight days. It was, Anthony Coleridge (son of Guy and at the time a pupil at Knight Frank & Rutley) remembers, 'an auctioneer's dream', with a husband and wife bidding against each other. The auctioneers were Rupert Richardson-Gardner and Peter Harrison, a young auctioneer and valuer of *objects d'art* who had joined the Galleries staff in 1949; the sale was conducted in conjunction with Arthur Rutter Sons & Co.

The first day realized £4300 – all books and silver, including a fifteenth-century French illuminated MS, a 'Book of Hours', which went for £135. The second day made £4250, the largest item being a Steinway grand piano. Early English and Continental porcelain dominated the third day, realizing £6000. The remaining five days disposed of furniture, pictures and 'miscellaneous'. Grand total for the whole collection was £40,000. There had been only one untoward incident: a rare tea pot 'went missing' and was found being used by the porters who were enjoying a cuppa behind the scenes. It was later sold for £800.

1953 was a mixture of glory and disaster. Glory, in that it was the Coronation Year of HM Queen Elizabeth II and the firm, as always, rose to the occasion by having its 'particulars' done up in plush red fabric covers with gilt lettering, and devoting an entire advertisement to wishing the new Queen well. Disaster, in that there were appalling storms and floods that winter and serious trouble with a client, the 12th Duke of Bedford.

Will Gibson had resigned from his stewardship of the Bedford London Estate Office, after more than three years, in 1951: a large part of the estate had been acquired by the University of London. But Willie Cunningham was still consultant to Woburn Abbey which was (in the present Duke's words) 'a shambles' after wartime occupation by the forces. Owing to strict Government regulations about rebuilding, no repairs could be carried out without a licence; and the regulations themselves were not always clear. It was thus that in March 1953 Willie Cunningham and the Duke's resident, Mrs Osborne Samuel, having been prosecuted by the Fraud Squad, were sent for trial for overspending and building without a licence.

Woburn Abbey: In March 1953 Willie Cunningham was prosecuted by the Fraud Squad for overspending on building. Owing to strict post-war government regulations about rebuilding, no repairs could be carried out without a licence.

The case went to Assizes. It was alleged that Mrs Samuel had carried out £9500 of work at Woburn in excess of the £70,000 allowed, and that Willie Cunningham had carried out unauthorized work in eradicating dry rot in the Chinese dairy adjoining the main Abbey building.

The dreaded Mervyn Griffith-Jones prosecuted: the subtle Christmas Humphreys defended. There was evidence that Willie Cunningham's part in the whole business had ended in the 1950, and the Duke's solicitors testified that the building allowance was £10,000 a quarter which had actually been *under*spent. The repairs were urgently needed so that the Abbey could be opened to the public. The climax of the trial was Humphrey's demolition of a prosecution witness, a surveyor who had acknowledged receipt of a letter from Knight Frank & Rutley making it clear that they had agreed on the site that the work on the Chinese dairy was within the budget: 'My lord, a man who ignores that must be either a fool or a liar!'

Willie Cunningham, now described as 'former surveyor to the estate', pleaded guilty (through ignorance) to one charge, and was given a complete discharge but ordered to pay £100 costs. Mrs Samuel pleaded guilty on seven counts and was fined £50: and London & Devon Estates, the Duke's company, were fined £5000. An extremely bored judge, summing up, said: 'Everybody concerned was most anxious to comply with the regulations, but the great misfortune was that nobody did, and each person concerned thought somebody else was doing it.'

The storms and floods of January 1953 made history by their violence. All round the coast there was destruction of property, and the Lord Mayor of London, Sir Rupert de la Bere, organized a national Flood and Tempest Distress Fund, creating a special panel of surveyors to assess the damage. The member for Knight Frank & Rutley was George Baker, assisted by a young valuer named Moon. They were concerned with house property along the coast, especially the Docking area of North Norfolk. 'Some properties had been washed away altogether,' George Baker remembers. 'Claimants provided such evidence as they could (snapshots, etc) of what the property had comprised, together with the sum of money they claimed the place was worth including, in many cases, the furnishings. We had to inspect the site or what was left of it and estimate if the claim was a fair one. We then swapped cases with other valuers so that a second opinion was obtained.' When it was all over, Monty Evans, Chairman of the panel of surveyors, wrote a warm letter of thanks to Will Gibson: '(Mr Baker and Mr Moon) tackled this difficult job not only most efficiently but very cheerfully. I really cannot speak too highly of them . . .'

Since 1951 there had been a Conservative Government, one of whose consequences was the 1953 Town and Country Planning Act, which amended the 1947 Act by removing development charges. This was bound to release a lot of building activity and boost the market in urban property, especially in offices and shops, and above all in the City which, in the late 1950s and early 1960s, became a forest of tower-cranes erecting small skyscrapers. This coincided with London's regained rôle as an international financial centre. With shops went hotels and licensed premises, which became a separate department of Knight Frank & Rutley under Robert Rutty, who had joined the firm as Manager in 1952.

In September the firm again helped BBC Television to move westwards by negotiating the sale to them by Stoll Theatres Corporation of a famous old music-hall, the Shepherds Bush Empire, to use as a TV theatre (it seated 1650) for shows with audience participation such as *What's my Line?*

The demand for good farms was now keen, but there was still a reluctance, especially on the part of newly-rich capitalists, to invest in land for long-term appreciation. In 1954 the firm produced and circulated two leaflets to outline the wisdom they had been preaching for many years. One explained the taxation benefits and death duty savings by investing in landed estates; the other, the little-understood problem of owning woodlands. Only one-eighth of the timber used in Britain was home-produced. If only owners would expand their woodlands, forestry could again become a major industry. There was tax relief and financial help from the Forestry Commission. A Scots pine took sixty years to grow, but a Douglas Fir only thirty years and it had a higher rate of return.

A number of Scottish estates were sold in 1955, and the biggest sale was undoubtedly that of the Duke of Argyll's Kintyre, 28,857 acres of 'the finest farmland', to defray the late 10th Duke's death duties. The auction, at Cambeltown, was conducted by Peter Oldfield. The estate was eventually disposed of in individual lots, after the top bid of £174,000 for the estate as a whole had been rejected as inadequate. The estate ('part of the ancient Celtic Kingdom of Dalriada') straddled

In 1956 Knight Frank & Rutley were appointed Surveyors to The All England Lawn Tennis Club. A major task at Wimbledon would be to raise the whole roof in a single operation, thus admitting 1900 more seats at the Centre Court.

the Kintyre peninsula, contained seventy-eight farms, extensive sporting rights, cottages, village and town properties, and an eighteen-hole golf course, and had been valued at £250,000.

Prices were 'slightly higher than expected', and reasonable 'upset prices' had been agreed to enable tenants to buy property which in many cases had been rented by their families for many generations. Some properties had not changed hands for 300 years. At the end of the sale 34 of the 145 lots offered remained unsold, and £167,405 had been realized. Another notable Scottish property this year was the 6450-acre

Dalmunzie estate at Spital of Glenshee, Perthshire.

Less glamorously, but with an eye to the future, the firm in this year started a separate Factory and Industrial Department, bringing in Rowland T. Entwistle from another firm to arrange it. There was a steady demand for offices, and it was becoming more possible to satisfy it – with, for example, a large (over 20,000 sq. ft) block in Curzon Street called Sunderland House.

From the staff's viewpoint, 1953 was a landmark in that the first staff pension fund was begun, with the ultimate target of retirement on two-thirds of final salary.

Farmland prices were rising, and farms were being bought often by men who were not necessarily farmers themselves. They needed professional advice, if not actual management. Knight Frank & Rutley had a good deal of this kind of responsibility in the neighbourhood of Hereford, which is not the easiest place to get to from London and was consuming a lot of staff time and travel expense. The firm's largest property for management was the 16,000-acre Guy's Hospital estate, enthusiastically described by one of the firm's present partners as 'the best land in England – the most valuable estate we've ever handled'. The time seemed ripe, and the local opportunities for expansion looked promising; and so, in November 1955, an office was opened at 22 Hightown, Hereford.

The nucleus of the new branch, which was supervised by Peter Oldfield, was Alan Hutchison, a local estate agent who had been operating for the firm at Callow Farm, his home. For a year or two he carried on with a secretary and a receptionist; they were eventually joined by John Inge (now at head office, and a partner) and E. R. Ames Hutchings, who, to avoid confusion of his name with Alan Hutchison's, was always called 'Mr Ames' until he could stand it no longer and pleaded to be allowed to use his own name.

Another stage in the westward trek of BBC Television was achieved when the BBC acquired the four acres of the Ealing film studios where the great Ealing comedies had been made, from Robert Hamer's *Kind Hearts and Coronets* to *Passport to Pimlico*.

By way of contrast, the St Tudwal Islands, off the Caernarvonshire peninsula, owned by Clough Williams-Ellis, the creator of Portmeirion, were inhabited by grazing sheep, sea-birds and seals. Even the light tower was automatic and untouched by human hand. The new owner, in 1956, was the Hon. Giles St Aubyn, son of Lord St Levan and a housemaster at Eton.

Mr Evelyn Waugh, an old client of the firm, was not easy to please, but when his mind was made up his enthusiasm was infectious. In 1956 he was looking everywhere for a house – Radnor, Montgomery, North Devon; then on 9 July, 'Laura, Teresa and I drove to see the house at Combe Florey that is for sale – cosy and sequestered, with great possibilities.' Anxiously he awaited news of the survey. Then, on 10 October, Kenneth Maycock sold it to him.

The Galleries were suffering (but not very much) from a scarcity of quality goods. Some of the best stuff had gone overseas and was not coming back. Yet London was becoming, once again, the art centre of the world; some of those goods would return.

The exchange rate was in favour of American, French and Italian buyers, and in 1959 the Treasury allowed vendors to take out money in any currency. Old Masters were doing poorly; post-Impressionists much better. There was the occasional craze, such as Japanese netsukes – little carved button ornaments in wood or ivory fetching up to £20 each; interest in them seems to have been started by American soldiers in London during the war.

Since 1954 the firm had published an annual booklet, *The Trend of Prices*, which circulated in 7000 copies to the trade and interested customers, showing the levels averaged in the previous year. That for 1956 complained that 'it is almost impossible to value anything of real quality . . . it is the small, dainty piece which commands attention today and brings the high price'.

By 'dainty pieces' Guy Coleridge meant things like an Adam satinwood bureau which had realized £1300, or (in a sale at Burwarton Hall, Shropshire) a pair of Regency chiffoniers – only one had been catalogued, but a relative of the vendor suddenly remembered that she had the companion piece. The two were sold for £460. Separately they would have made only £150 each.

At Hanover Square Guy Coleridge was doing well with regular sales of carpets, furs, guns and fishing tackle. Too many people, he complained, stored carpets; the moths always got in; they should sell them and buy again if necessary. The 'credit squeeze' and international tension affected the demand for expensive furs. Mink and ermine were doing well but there was 'no demand at all for skunk and marmot'.

The sale at Burwarton, in July 1956, a four-day affair, had been helped by television publicity. The vendor was Lord Boyne, later an equerry to the Queen, and then aged twenty-five. The family were then living in the converted stables. Peter Harrison, as auctioneer and senior valuer, was asked by the BBC to take part in a TV programme to be made about a stately home auction. Sir John Betjeman was also in it. Three days before transmission, Peter Harrison went to Burwarton with Geoffrey Johnson-Smith, then a BBC anchor-man, not yet a politician, to set things up.

The opening shot, to establish the vendor's ancestry, was of a large picture of the Battle of the Boyne. Then Peter Harrison, sitting at a vast French desk which was one of the lots offered, forecast what prices various articles would fetch. The resulting sale made a grand total of £21,911. The family portraits by Kneller and Lawrence brought modest prices, but the sensation was Hogarth's 'Charity in the Cellar', showing four members of the Hellfire Club drinking a hogshead of claret at one sitting – it fetched £1000.

The most memorable shot of the film, Peter Harrison remembers, was Sir John Betjeman's first appearance, seemingly from a cellar, like the entrance of Mole in *Toad of Toad Hall.*

As 1956 drew to a close, Will Gibson announced his retirement. He was seventy; he had served the firm for thirty-eight years, combining the virtues of Scotland, the merchant navy, the army and his own upright, if occasionally austere, character.

He was succeeded, as Senior Partner – perhaps reluctantly – by Ted Fisher, a man universally liked and trusted, of whom his former colleague Geoffrey Gay says: 'A very quiet and modest man . . . I do not think I ever heard anyone make a nasty remark about him. He had a reputation for absolute honesty and forthrightness and he never, ever, went back on his word. His handshake was his complete bargain with anybody.' A man, too, of impish humour, conspiring with Willie Cunningham in harmless practical jokes, especially to while away a long railway journey (such as telling other passengers that Willie was his son). A man whose modesty was such that he refused to occupy the traditional and august Senior Partner's Room on the ground floor, preferring to remain in his first-floor room with its enchanting view of the square; and here he stayed until his retirement.

XV
Into the Sixties

The firm's work in West Africa was growing; Nigeria in particular was within three years of gaining independence, and its potential wealth suggested a big field for development. The new Nigerian Government would need a London headquarters, and Geoffrey Gay found one: Lincoln House, Northumberland Avenue, which had once belonged to the Society for Promoting Christian Knowledge and was now let to the Crown Agents for the Colonies for occupation, after substantial reconstruction, by the Federal Government of Nigeria. The refitting, carried out by Knight Frank & Rutley, included furnishing and equipment 'down to the knives and forks on the dining-table'.

Geoffrey Gay had been surveyor to Grosvenor House, Park Lane, for many years. This modern complex of an hotel and a block of flats had been built in 1930, with façades by Sir Edwin Lutyens, on the site of Lord Grosvenor's early nineteenth-century mansion. It was planned to add ninety-two new bedrooms (which were built in 1957), a new restaurant and a grill room which would be added in 1959 and 1961 respectively. The bedrooms were extended at record speed, because Geoffrey Gay had spotted a legal point: that the extension was part of the architect's original intention, and it therefore did not need a fresh planning permission. It was built by Taylor Woodrow, whom the firm had already met in West Africa, and with whom they were to enjoy increasingly close business relations, resulting eventually in enormous valuation tasks for the whole group worldwide.

One of Taylor Woodrow's subsidiaries was Myton Ltd, who were building the new BP House, an impressive office block in the City on a 1½-acre island site bounded by Chiswell Street, which was scheduled for completion by the end of 1958. Containing about 200,000 square feet, it had been let in its entirety to the British Petroleum Company Ltd, the lease having been negotiated by Knight Frank & Rutley. BP House, in which Geoffrey Gay and Laurence Knight played key parts, was one of several headquarters buildings occupied by BP over the years, and marked a stage in the growth of the Finsbury Square district as a centre for offices. BP had begun in 1909 as the Anglo-Iranian Oil Co. in Winchester House, Old Broad Street, moving in 1912 to Gresham House and in 1918 to the first Britannic House, Great Winchester Street. A second Britannic House, designed by Lutyens, was completed in 1920. Other buildings followed, until, in its Golden Jubilee year, 1959, BP finally took possession of a new Britannic House.

Negotiations had been complicated. BP's decision to consolidate their headquarters buildings had been strongly influenced by Geoffrey Gay. 'I realized that we had the opportunity of dealing with a much larger site,' he recalls. 'So I had some discussions with the City Corporation, who owned the freehold of all this land, and with the adjoining owners, and it seemed to me that we had the possibility of making a really fantastic site in the right position for BP. There would be no difficulty in sub-letting any space that might be surplus to their requirements . . . I met the Chairman and some members of the Board on the roof of BP House and we looked down over Moorfields and they were able to see for themselves the golden opportunity. I was then given the go-ahead.'

In 1955 Peter Masefield, chief executive of British European Airways, had announced details of a new London air passenger terminal to replace the one in Kensington High Street and Knight Frank & Rutley then found, as a temporary measure, the familiarly known Rocket Restaurant at Waterloo which had formed part of the 1951 Festival. It was to be an engineering feat – a huge triangular concrete raft to be built over the railway tracks at Gloucester Road underground station, involving the purchase of land around what was called the 'Cromwell Curve'. The land had been bought under the direction of Geoffrey Gay, who had acquired many other sites for BEA. The new terminal was opened on 6 October 1957 by the Minister of Transport and Civil Aviation, Mr Harold (afterwards Viscount) Watkinson. The structure was regarded as 'temporary', but it lasted until 1981 when it was acquired by Sainsburys for their new supermarket.

In the firm's traditional country estate market, two Scottish properties (Cambusmore and Flichity) and a Welsh castle (Glandyfi) were sold. For the Hon. David Astor, the firm bought a large part of the Countess of Craven's estate in Berkshire – 4800 acres of very productive land with eight attested hill and vale farms, in Ashbury, Compton Beauchamp, Woolstone and Uffington in the fertile Vale of the White Horse. There were sporting facilities, but that was not the new trend. The trend of the 1960s was buying farmland for investment, especially by the 'Institutions', a movement encouraged by Peter Oldfield, who was responsible for many land improvement schemes. Thus, in March 1957, Knight Frank & Rutley negotiated the purchase of the Tredegar estate for the Eagle Star Insurance Co. The executors of the late Lord Tredegar were disposing of over 50,000 acres of good agricultural land, since death duties were payable at 75 per cent. The mansion had passed to the National Trust. The Eagle Star's acquisition of the remainder (less the town sections in Monmouthshire) was one of the largest single land purchases in living memory, comprising over 700 properties – 122 farms, 5 public houses, over 100 cottages and 700 acres of woodlands. The whole came under the management of the new Hereford branch, which, with increased staff, had moved to its present office in Broad Street.

In November 1957 Alfred Burrows died at his home near Ashford at the age of ninety-three. It was typical of him that, in his will, he left some cottages in his village, Kennington, 'for the use of poor persons . . . agricultural labourers, if possible, having a preference.'

A new partner, Linton Roberts, arrived in 1958, a specialist in shop property, for which there was now a separate department. One of the biggest deals in commercial property this year was the sale of shops and offices in two large blocks on the south

Compton Beauchamp House. The 4800-acre Compton Beauchamp estate, comprising eight farms in the Vale of the White Horse, was purchased for the Hon. David Astor.

side of Piccadilly, Nos. 166–169, almost opposite the Burlington Arcade, and 174–176, which included the Piccadilly Arcade, with its twenty-five shops, extending through to Jermyn Street.

The architectural sensation of the year was Eero Saarinen's new eagle-topped American Embassy, believed to be 'the only American embassy in the world whose freehold is not owned by the US Government' (it is in fact owned by the Duke of Westminster). The buying up of all the west side of Grosvenor Square, acquiring the leasehold interests and negotiating with Grosvenor estates, had been going on since 1947 and had been achieved largely by Malcolm Mackenzie and Geoffrey Gay.

Knight Frank & Rutley's connection with the Foundling estate in Bloomsbury went back to the 1920s – they had been managing it since 1926.

In 1930, as we saw in the last chapter, the Mecklenburgh Square site was sold to the Dominion Students' Hall Trust, which bought the remainder of the property in 1948; they sold off parts of it to the University of London. What came up for sale in the autumn of 1958 was the remaining eleven acres, comprising some 250 freehold properties in Brunswick Square, Marchmont Street, Grays Inn Road, Guilford Street, Tavistock Place and Coram Street – shops, offices, private hotels, flats,

The sale of the Piccadilly Arcade, with its twenty-five shops, extending through to Jermyn Street, was one of the major deals of 1958.

houses, ground rents and vacant sites, producing a gross income of £113,500 a year and valued at nearly £2,000,000. The estate was sold before auction by Ted Fisher to the E. Alec Colman Group of Companies, centred in Birmingham, for a sum 'in excess of £1,750,000'. Mr Colman intended to develop much of the area by building flats.

Seven hotels and inns in the New Forest, near Brocenhurst, up for sale as part of the reorganization of the Morant Settled Estate, for which the firm had acted before; the Channel Island of Jethou, changing hands yet again as it was acquired by Group-Captain Cliff; and a new home for Sir Anthony Eden (afterwards Lord Avon), now in delicate health and retired after the débâcle of Suez two years before. Peter Oldfield acted for Sir Anthony, and found for him Fyfield Manor, near Pewsey, Wiltshire, formerly the home of Lord Hudson, with 50 acres and five cottages. The firm were to find him two more homes in the next few years – Rose Bower at Broad Chalke and Alvediston Manor near Shaftesbury. Rose Bower was a difficult negotiation. It was surveyed for him by Willie Cunningham, and the survey was not good. There was dry rot and some re-roofing to be done.

'If you decide to take the house, Sir,' Willie said, 'you ought to re-roof before next winter.'

But Eden spent the winter in the West Indies and no decision was taken. When he came back in the spring he was irritable: 'Why didn't you *tell* me it was so bad?'

'I did, Sir!'

'Then you should have told me more emphatically!'

Nevertheless he bought the house.

Great interest had been aroused in 1941 when Knight Frank & Rutley had negotiated the purchase by Oxford University Chest of about 3300 acres of the agricultural part of Earl Poulett's Hinton St George estate, near Crewkerne, Somerset. It had been renamed the University Estate, to avoid confusion with the Earl's own Hinton St George estate. Now, eighteen years later, the University's investment had matured, and the firm, in association with Jackson-Stops' Yeovil office, after giving sitting tenants the opportunity of buying their own farms, resold the estate for Talbot Estates (Nottingham) Ltd, for whom they had purchased it from the University earlier in the year. The sale realized £212,865.

Gerard (Pat) Heller was made a partner in January 1959. After experience in the Foundling estate office, he had worked in the Investment Department and eventually in the Valuation Department as surveyor and valuer of shops, offices and factories for company purposes, for purchase by clients as investments and for settlement of probate and on compulsory purchase. In 1957 he had become Investment Manager. With him, valuation was a science alerted by instinct. He could value *anything*. His wife Jean would greet him wearing a new dress when he came home in the evening: a mere man, he could not be expected to know that it was off the peg at Marks & Spencer.

'How much do you think this cost?'

'Oh, about seventeen shillings.'

'Sixteen and eleven actually!'

1959, the year of the 'you've never had it so good' election, certainly bore signs of prosperity. One sympton, perhaps, was the trend towards 'decentralized offices', modern ones, which were being built in the suburbs of cities, in particular along the North and South Circular Roads around London. The new Location of Offices Bureau helped the movement.

Sometimes an auctioneer or a property man, his eye straying momentarily from the main chance, will talk about 'a nice little auction' or a 'nice little sale'. It means that he has enjoyed the atmosphere. Country hotel sales are sometimes like this. Hotels like the George at Norton St Philip, six miles from Bath. This historic thirteenth- and fifteenth-century inn boasted a 'Monmouth Room . . . which was used by the Duke of Monmouth as his headquarters on 26 June 1685, and from which he is reputed to have escaped the King's forces moving from Bath'. The second floor consisted solely of the 80-foot-long Wool Store, used by local wool merchants in the fourteenth century. In the Monmouth Room were 'recently revealed Wall Paintings'. They dated from about 1500 and were the result of Bob Rutty's curiosity when surveying the building the year before – he had scraped away some plaster and there they were.

Lord Warwick sold 5100 acres of his estates (but not Warwick Castle and its parkland), including twenty-two dairy and stock farms and seventy houses in Warwick (among them the well-known 'black-and-white' Tudor houses in Mill Street) and other properties; they were mostly bought by a syndicate of sitting tenants. The estate trustees of Lord Darnley, whom the firm had advised for many years, finally disposed of Cobham Hall, near Rochester, to the Ministry of Works.

In the 'Swinging Sixties', a lot of people from nowhere became rich and famous very fast, bought property and often sold it again just as quickly. The typical figure of the decade was the pop star, who, if his agent or manager was wise, sought advice on how best to spend his unaccustomed wealth. It was thus that all the Beatles, Adam Faith and many more came to Knight Frank & Rutley to find homes. There were, too, the new small millionaires: a man who has just made his first million (often by building up a company and then allowing himself to be bought out by a big group) and wants a Rolls-Royce and a country house, in that order. He may get rid of both within two years, but at least he has had them. Thus a carpet magnate paid £75,000 for a modernized country rectory, saying: 'I want it in a month, please – furnished to the last ash tray!' He sold it again quickly because it was too far from his factory.

The 'institutions' – life assurance offices, pension funds, unit trusts – were now investing in property and even financing property companies; or buying whole buildings and 'leasing back' to the developer. Modern factories and warehouses were favoured, and offices and shops in 'prime' positions; but not residential properties. For property consultants, valuation work increased, as companies 'went public' and presented their prospectuses, in which the valuing firm's name was mentioned.

Prices were rising in the Galleries. For some years good antiques had been scarce: a few auctioneering firms had closed and others had amalgamated. Yet the London market had now overtaken New York: London commission rates were about half those in New York and Paris, so important collections were being sent to London. Auctions were becoming news, and this too pushed prices up. There was a shortage of Persian carpets and period silver.

Domestically, one of the memories of the 1960s for veterans of Knight Frank & Rutley is of the end of Saturday morning work. One was allowed to come to the office in a tweed jacket. Gradually it meant coming in on a duty roster every second or third Saturday. The building had to be open anyway on Saturdays to receive deliveries of chattels for the next week's sales. Not a great deal of work was done by the property staff; yet Alan Daniels remembers selling the Old Mint Inn at Southam, Warwickshire, for £6500 before going home for the weekend. There was one partner who came in on Saturday mornings theoretically to 'set an example', but actually to avoid being sent by his wife to do the shopping.

The sale of 1960 was the 5000-acre Red Rice estate at Andover (which the firm had last handled in 1912) – large Georgian house, sporting facilities ('one of the finest shoots in the country'), a good rent-roll and a lake garden. The firm, in conjunction with Strutt & Parker, sold it for Major P. Miller-Munday to Sir Richard Boughey, Bt, who then sold off about 1800 acres, including mansion, park, home farm and cottages for a price 'in the region of £300,000'.

1960 also saw the opening, in the City, of Barclays Bank International's new building in Old Broad Street. Knight Frank & Rutley had been acting for Barclays for many years, and the new building, known as Goodenough House, had been planned as long ago as 1947 when Barclays began looking for a separate international headquarters not too far away from their head office at 54 Lombard Street. Geoffrey Gay, and before him William Gibson, were chiefly concerned in the search. They found what Geoffrey Gay calls 'a smallish bombsite' at 34 Old Broad Street which also owned a nearby property in Union Court. A slow 'amassing' operation began, to buy adjoining properties. One legal oddity of the post-war years which delayed negotiations was that the site was subject to a war damage claim, and the authorities would not allow a value payment. In order to get what was known as the war damage claim 21B the original building had first to be re-built. It could then be demolished and replaced by a new modern building. After town-planning inquiries and tribunals and appeals, all the obstacles were skilfully removed, and Goodenough House at last arose.

Two new young partners were announced at the beginning of 1961: Geoffrey (Gerry) Akroyd and S. K. H. (Sam) Goodenough. Gerry Akroyd had arrived at Knight Frank & Rutley in 1955, having tried the Stock Exchange in his father's stockbroking firm Cazenove Akroyd (now Cazenoves), Shell and Lloyd's in rapid succession. His first inclinations had been towards the chattels side, perhaps Sotheby's or Christie's; but property soon claimed him and he joined the Country Department of Knight Frank & Rutley, soon laying the foundations of his career as the most skilful negotiator of his generation. We have already seen the early aspirations of Sam Goodenough, and how fate was to decree that he should be neither a bishop or a banker. As a principal in the firm he continued to specialize in Estate Management, and to be in charge of the Scottish Department. Being himself a farmer, he was well equipped to run the Farm Management team which prepared development plans, farming programmes and estimated capital requirements, engaging and supervising farm staff, buying equipment and supplies. His work was to take him abroad as the firm became more international – to Australia, the Caribbean and Nigeria in particular.

The firm was still not ready to 'go international' but a few exploratory tentacles seemed in order. Accordingly, Gerry Akroyd, accompanied by George Baker, was sent to the Bahamas to explore a threefold market: commercial property, residential 'homes' and tourism. Public figures like Noël Coward and Ian Fleming had started a trend among tax-exiles for having a second home in the West Indies. Gerry Akroyd went to work with Sir Harold Christie, doyen of real estate in Nassau. There were no death duties in the Bahamas then, and there was a lively market in 'death-bed purchases' of real estate owned by people who were domiciled elsewhere. It seemed as if half Bay Street (Nassau's commercial centre) was changing hands: for the latest news on who owned what, you had only to ask a taxi driver. The 'Bay Street boys' really ran the Bahamas then; and it was fascinating to study the name-plaques on office buildings and see how many foreign companies were registered in Nassau, sometimes several in one room.

There was a good deal of 'lease-back' of shop property and a residential market in houses on the seafront at Lyford Cay, in which E. P. (Eddie) Taylor the Canadian brewer was interested. Above all, where else could you meet people whom you would not so easily run across in London? Where else could you play golf with millionaires like Henry Ford II (now a client)? Gerry Akroyd's trip was rounded off by an island hopping flight all round the West Indies in a private plane to gather material for a survey of tourism in the Caribbean.

One of the British post-war developers – a man who acted on hunch and had a great talent for charming money out of bankers – was Jack Cotton, who had started as an estate agent's clerk in Birmingham. He had burst upon New York in 1959 to take part in the building of 'the world's largest office block', the $96 million Pan Am Building being constructed over Grand Central Station. In America, banks did not like lending money for such a project unless most of the space was sold in advance to a major tenant. The building (fifty-nine storeys giving 3 million sq. ft) was scheduled for completion by December 1962. By October 1961 it was known that Pan-American Airways had leased 613,000 sq. ft – and another superlative enhanced the publicity: 'The largest single rental transaction in the real estate world.' A group of New York banks provided a constructional loan of $65 million: Cotton's City Centre Properties held a 50 per cent interest. Permanent mortgages were arranged with 'New York's largest pension fund' up to $70 million, which thus became 'the largest mortgage financing transaction ever completed in the USA or the UK on a single commercial property'. Cotton had invested £2 million of his own money in it.

After all that, there were no superlatives left for the New York managing agents

The $96-million Pan Am Building over Grand Central Station, New York, built by Jack Cotton. As 'the world's largest office building', the fifty-nine storeys comprise over 3 million square feet.

The Covent Garden Market was moved to a site outside central London. The move was to take eleven years involving the acquisition of 80 acres of property at Nine Elms and the negotiation for the re-housing of over 100 families.

Cushman & Wakefield and the joint letting agents in Britain, Knight Frank & Rutley and Healey & Baker.

In London a vast plan was being prepared to transfer Covent Garden Market to a still undecided site outside Central London. This was to take eleven years of patient negotiation and political difficulty. Sites had to be examined, one had to be selected, and the likely cost of acquisition had to be assessed. Frank Hollins, CB, the then managing-director of the Covent Garden Market Authority, consulted architects Gollins, Melvin & Ward, and Geoffrey Gay of Knight Frank & Rutley. In due course Geoffrey Gay introduced David Gardner, then a senior member of staff and now a partner, to the Authority to undertake valuations and other property considerations in what was to become a major undertaking. It was decided to appoint Knight Frank & Rutley to act for the Authority on the economic and financial aspects of any schemes for redevelopment of either the new or the old site.

Knight Frank & Rutley's first task was to estimate the cost of acquiring 80 acres of property at Nine Elms near Vauxhall. So complex were the negotiations, and so good an example do they give of the professionalism of Knight Frank & Rutley, that we shall return to them in subsequent chapters.

The old Covent Garden market.

LOWER LYDE COURT FARM (*LOT 1*)

CHURCH FARM, MADLEY (*LOT*

THE RIVER WYE—HOM AND WEIREND BEATS (*LOT 108*)
(Reproduced by permission of the GLOSTER AIRCRAFT Co., Ltd.)

THE HOLSTY FARM (*LOT 29*)

WHITE HOUSE FARM, SELLACK (*LOT*

BY DIRECTION OF THE BOARD OF GOVERNORS.

GUY'S HOSPITAL
HEREFORDSHIRE ESTATE
16,000 ACRES

Divided into 15 *Blocks:*

Pipe and Lyde Section	1 Block	**970 acres**
Credenhill Section	1 Block	**1,340 acres**
Tyberton Section	4 Blocks (1,761, 850, 881 and 527 acres)	**4,019 acres**
Arkstone Section	1 Block	**522 acres**
Home Section	3 Blocks (1,982, 1,757 and 615 acres)	**4,354 acres**
Harewood End Section	1 Block	**849 acres**
Ross Section	2 Blocks (Salmon Fishing is second Block)	**1,698 acres**
Tretire Section	1 Block	**1,016 acres**
Llangarren Section	1 Block	**1,277 acres**

including

68 FARMS AND HOLDINGS

chiefly Stock and Arable Farms and with some Dairy units

VALUABLE STANDING TIMBER

included in over 1,300 acres of Woodlands

HOUSES, COTTAGES AND ACCOMMODATION LOTS

for investment or Early Possession

EXTENSIVE SHOOTING AND OTHER SPORTING RIGHTS

including

4 MILES OF FISHING IN THE RIVER WYE

Total Rental £53,400 per annum

To be offered for Sale by Auction, as a Whole, in 15 Blocks or in numerous Lots by Messrs.

KNIGHT, FRANK & RUTLEY

AT THE SHIRE HALL, HEREFORD

On Wednesday and Thursday the 20th and 21st days of September 1961, at 11.0 a.m. and 2.30 p.m. each day.

The actual division of the Sessions will be announced later.

(unless previously sold)

Solicitors: Messrs. PARKER, GARRETT & CO., St. Michael's Rectory, Cornhill, London, E.C.3. (*Tel.:* MANsion House 5071.)

Resident Land Agent: W. S. HOOD, Esq., F.L.A.S., Guy's Estate Office, Kingsthorne, Hereford. (*Tel.:* Wormelow 261.)

Auctioneers: Messrs. KNIGHT, FRANK & RUTLEY, 20, Hanover Square, London, W.1. (*Tel.:* MAYfair 3771.) and 14, Broad Street, Hereford. (*Tel.:* 3087.)

(Price : 30/- per copy).

A

The Guy's Hospital Estate in Herefordshire. Originally part of the investment made by Thomas Guy, founder of the hospital in 1731, it comprised almost sixty farms spread over 16,000 acres and was sold in 1961 to Mr Charles Clore. In 1978 Clore was to sell the estate to the Prudential Assurance Company for over £20 million.

The Earls of Dunmore have had two main links with Knight Frank & Rutley: one of them had once lived at 20 Hanover Square; and their descendant, Lady Elisabeth Murray, is married to Peter Oldfield. It was decided therefore, that when one of their former ancestral houses, Amhuinnsuidh Castle, came up for sale in June 1961, it should be sold by Peter Oldfield. The property with 35,000 acres, in North Harris, Outer Hebrides, now belonged to Sir Thomas Sopwith, one of the pioneers of British aviation and a famous yachtsman and sportsman. The Castle (barely 100 years old) had been on the firm's books before, and would be so again. It stood on the shores of West Loch Tarbert with views across the sea to the Isle of Taransay. The estate included six rivers, five major lochs full of fish, forty crofts, cottages and 'accommodation for nine ghillies'. It was sold as a whole to Captain Geoffrey Lowndes of Perthshire for a sum not far off the asking price of £65,000.

But the really news-making sale of the year was of Guy's Hospital Estate in Herefordshire. It was a subject of controversy during the spring and summer of 1961 and it took seven months to bring vendor and purchaser together.

Charles Clore has been described as 'a general entrepreneur with a leaning towards property'. He was seldom out of the news in the 1950s and 1960s. In 1959 he had acquired parts of the Stype estate, near Hungerford, from Lord Rootes, together with a famous flock of Hampshire Down sheep; he seemed to have an urge to go back to the land and farming. In 1961 the governors of Guy's Hospital in London, wishing for quicker capital appreciation by switching from property to equities, decided to sell their Herefordshire estate, spread out over about 16,000 acres – 'one of the biggest single land disposals for many years'.

Offers around £2 million were expected. The fact that the firm now had a branch in Hereford could promise continuity of management to any purchaser who did not wish to manage it himself. Peter Oldfield was in charge of the sale. The estate lay mainly between Hereford and Ross-on-Wye, but also to the north and west of Hereford. The land was originally part of the investment made by Thomas Guy, founder of the hospital, in 1731. Between fifty and sixty farms were involved, with a total annual rental of about £53,000. There were also extensive woodlands, shooting rights and four miles of fishing in the Wye.

In August it was announced that Guy's Hospital Estate would be put up for auction at the Shire Hall, Hereford, on 20 and 21 September. A week before this it was learned that the estate had been sold as a whole privately to Mr Clore. The price was not disclosed, but it was a good deal less than the £2 million asked for. It was understood that Mr Clore had bought Guy's estate as a personal investment.

Meanwhile several syndicates or tenants' associations had been formed to negotiate the purchase of individual blocks, and there was inevitably some criticism of the Governors of Guy's Hospital that tenants had not been given enough opportunity to buy at least their own holdings. The Governors therefore issued a statement, through Knight Frank & Rutley, saying that they had given tenants every possible chance, within a reasonable time limit: '. . . the Board regret that the tenants were unable to reach sufficient agreement among themselves to make a written offer for the estate as a whole . . . The Board of Governors feel that it is very satisfactory that it has not proved necessary to split up the estate and sincerely hope that the tenants will be happy with their new landlord.'

To which the honorary secretary of the tenants' association replied, 'While we are not entirely happy about the way Guy's Hospital governors handled these negotiations, I am quite sure that all the tenants will be very happy under their new landlord.'

XVI
Home and Away

In 1961 the firm had taken additional space in the house next door, No. 19 Hanover Square: the property side of the business was now so much greater than the Galleries that something had to give. So the weekly furniture sales were abandoned in 1962, and this coincided with the retirement of the two partners most concerned, Guy Coleridge and Rupert Richardson-Gardner. The main Auction Gallery was turned into offices for the expanding Town and Country Departments, and other sales continued in the Estate and North Galleries.

The Hotels Department was busy. Three typical smaller hotels on the market were the Fairmile Hotel, on the A3 at Cobham, Surrey, a former manor house with a Georgian frontage; the fifteenth-century Crown Hotel at Faringdon, Berkshire; and the Lord Leycester at Warwick, dating from the seventeenth century. The Fairmile went for £50,000, the Crown for £13,600, and the Lord Leycester was withdrawn.

For Grosvenor House, the firm obtained, from Town & City Properties, the lease of a fourteen-storey, 118-room hotel in Sheffield whose foundations had not yet been laid and which would not be complete for three years. It was part of a one-acre development with shops. Grosvenor had recently acquired the Dudley Hotel, Hove, and the Polygon, Southampton. This was before the Trust House Forte merger, and in the early 1960s Knight Frank & Rutley were busy selling off small Trust Houses which did not fit into the coming Forte pattern.

Three new partners were announced in January 1963. Richard Davis, who had been with the firm for fourteen years, beginning as assistant to Charles Stenholm, had carried out much of the famous 'PZ' valuation in West Africa, and was a valuation expert. Brian Hatcher had joined the firm from Hamptons in 1955 when he was only twenty-four. At Hamptons he had had the unforgettable experience of sharing an office with Harry Hyams, future developer of the long-empty thirty-two-storey Centre Point at St Giles's Circus. Brian Hatcher had been responsible for some big property deals, and would go on to still bigger ones, specializing in City and West End developments. The third new partner, George Baker had been with the firm since leaving school in 1934; he had experience of almost every department.

In Nigeria, the firm was steadily collecting clients: since the 'PZ' valuation they had done an increasing amount of work for Taylor Woodrow, the United Africa Company and John Holt & Co. (Liverpool) Ltd. Holts had began romantically as 'merchant venturers' when the original John Holt went to sea in 1856 at the age of fifteen in his grandfather's schooner *Thomas Holt*. He had traded, with his two brothers, up and down the West African coast, got to know H. M. Stanley and Mary Kingsley, and David Livingstone's brother who was British Consul at Fernando Po;

and nearly died of fever and lung disease, against which Primitive Methodist missionaries were fighting.

From these tough beginnings Holts had become general traders, buying and shipping Nigerian produce, arranging for its sale in Europe and importing consumer goods from Europe into West Africa – salt, bicycles, beer, wine and Ford motors, for which they were main agents. If you said 'Jonnolt' anybody in West Africa would know whom you meant. Still a family firm, they were now quoted on the Stock Exchange. Their depots in Nigeria, many of them up-country in the bush, often little more than corrugated iron sheds, were still called 'ventures'.

After Nigerian independence in October 1960, with the advice of Knight Frank & Rutley, Holts had set up a property department with Alan Shelley as manager with responsibility for the whole of Nigeria and also Ghana, Sierra Leone, Dahomey, Togo and Cameroons. Their headquarters was Ebani House, a valuable modern building in Lagos. Holts wanted to offer the services of their property department to third parties; and also to develop their principal site in Lagos. They felt they needed top-level advice on property, and appointed Knight Frank & Rutley to represent them.

To appreciate the opportunities in the Federal Republic of Nigeria, as they appeared in the 1960s, one has to remember that it was the largest of the West Coastal states with a population of 55 millions (more than any other African state), 650 miles north to south and 700 miles east to west. Only South Africa and Egypt, in that continent, had a larger gross domestic product. It produced oil (not yet fully exploited), ground-nuts, palm oil, cocoa, coal, tin and columbite (a salt of iron and manganese).

Alan Shelley had arrived in Lagos in 1955 at the age of twenty-four. After a few years as office boy in a small firm of estate agents in Nottingham, and an extremely short time as a surveyor to the Crawley New Town Development Corporation, he had answered an advertisement for a Lands Officer for the Nigerian Railways Corporation. Six years later he joined Holts.

When Geoffrey Gay came out from London in 1963 to advise Holts, an historic meeting took place with Alan Shelley. They were joined shortly afterwards by Paul Mitchell, a young surveyor of twenty-three who had just spent six years in a very different department, London Residential: he had come theoretically for one year, and stayed for eleven.

Shelley and Gay began to consider whether the 'third party' activity could be expanded into a partnership between the two concerns (with Holts as principal client). However, in those days the Royal Institution of Chartered Surveyors would not agree to partnerships with limited companies, and so Holts and Knight Frank & Rutley appealed to them for a dispensation. Meanwhile the Holts property department operated under the name of 'Shelley & Co.' from two rooms on the third floor of the Elder Dempster Building, a new office block at 47 Marina, Lagos, the chief commercial street along the harbour side of Lagos Island.

Social life in Lagos was hectic and enjoyable, especially for a fit young man with

Alan Shelley and Paul Mitchell in Lagos, Nigeria, 1963.

Calabar in the nineteenth century. Knight Frank & Rutley (Nigeria) opened an office in Calabar in 1978.

no attachments, but the work was in many ways harder than in the UK. Paul Mitchell remembers in particular two valuation safaris, one for Holts (4500 miles in Alan Shelley's ancient Borgward saloon in one month), the other for Leventis (a Cypriot trading firm) by Land-Rover to the edge of the Sahara, often through sheer bush with never a sign of a road. He was glad of two months leave a year, part of it spent working at Hanover Square.

There was slow progress at Covent Garden, where the Knight Frank & Rutley team found themselves in a tangled web of town planning, housing and road traffic problems at the Nine Elms site, involving much consultation and cooperation with the then London County Council and local authorities. It was at last decided to go ahead with legislation to acquire the Nine Elms properties, by agreement, but if necessary by compulsion.

The Market Authority and traders were anxious about the disposal of their properties, and Knight Frank & Rutley were concerned about the basis of valuation. Meanwhile the Greater London Council came into being, and the whole of the Covent Garden area was under scrutiny from the planning viewpoint. Pressure groups were agitating for more public consultation.

By comparison, the firm's ancient skills in handling country properties were easy to exercise. The sporting estate and agricultural investment, 2800 acres of their Hursley estate, between Romsey and Winchester, withdrawn from auction at £230,000 and sold privately for considerably more, to pay death duties following the death of Sir George Cooper; and in Sussex, a sign of the times: the executors of Mrs Nellie Ionides, daughter of Lord Bearsted, sold Buxted Park estate, near Lewes, to Mr Kenneth Shipman, of Bryanston Films, who proposed to convert the 100-acre property into a health hydro.

1964 was a year of uncertainty for the property market. Thirteen years of Tory rule were ended by the October general election which brought Harold Wilson to power with proposals for Corporation and Capital Gains Taxes and a Land Commission which would impose a levy of at least 40 per cent on the proceeds of land sold for development. In towns, this could mean a curb on new office blocks.

In the City, Brian Hatcher had met his second new young property tycoon, the then almost unknown Jim Slater. In about 1959 Knight Frank & Rutley had the task of finding tenants for a massive ex-garment factory called Beaufort House, in Gravel Lane, Houndsditch, which had been occupied by BP as a temporary accommodation for their shipping department. 'During the course of two years,' Brian Hatcher recalls, 'I showed many companies over the building, in particular insurance brokers. The insurance brokers, although interested in the space, as rent was only 12*s* (60p) per square foot per annum, could not accept the E1 address. It was on the wrong side of Houndsditch. Had it been on the other side, the postal address would have been EC3 and quite acceptable.

Brian Hatcher arranged two or three half-floor lettings, one of them to the Midland Bank, and then P & O expressed an interest in half the basement. 'Our client Harold Lotery was reluctant to let half the basement on its own, but I

Beaufort House, E1. Brian Hatcher's sale of this massive ex-garment factory provided Jim Slater with the base from which he built his financial empire.

persuaded him to do the deal, as it occurred to me that once P & O were in the building they might take more space. In the event, they subsequently took an overriding lease of the entire building.' While on holiday, Brian Hatcher heard that Harold Lotery had sold his company, H. Lotery & Co. Ltd, to two men called Jim Slater and Peter Walker. 'I knew that the main asset of this company was Beaufort House, and on my return to the office I contacted Jim Slater and suggested a meeting. I told him I had the impression that P & O might well be interested in buying the leasehold interest in Beaufort House – was he interested in selling?'

Jim Slater said he did not understand property, but was interested in cash for his other financial activities. Brian Hatcher arranged a meeting with P & O at Beaufort House at 9.30 one morning. By 9.55 Slater had not appeared, and eventually telephoned to say he could not find the building. When at last he appeared negotiations began, and 'we sold the leasehold to P & O on Mr Slater's behalf at a price in the region of £1¾ million. Mr Slater, being an accountant, had been content with the knowledge that the building was let to a first-rate Covenant and was producing an acceptable rent, and therefore he had not thought it necessary to

The Crown Inn, Chiddingfold. Well known to Canadian servicemen during the war, the Crown and the village green made an unforgettable picture of England as she was meant to be. In 1965 the hotel was bought by two former members of the Royal Canadian Air Force.

inspect the property. The proceeds of this sale provided Jim Slater with the base from which he built his financial empire.

Knight Frank & Rutley's advertising had always stood out from the rest, ever since the first full-page in *Country Life* in 1898 – at first by boldness, latterly by style. In 1964 Col Michael Barton joined the firm to take charge of both advertising and public relations. From 1965 onwards, the firm's direct advertising used innovations of style ahead of its competitors – colour, reversed blocks, bordered pages; property supplements in glossy magazines; and brochures and particulars which (as had been said of Sir Howard Frank's particulars forty years before) were 'works of art'.

Activity continued in the hotel market as big groups bought hotels. Examples were Ye Olde Bell, at Hurley-on-the-Thames, and the Crown Inn at Chiddingfold, Surrey, well-known to Canadian soldiers during the war. To many Canadians the Crown, and the village green, made an unforgettable picture of England as she was meant to be. The half-timbered, mainly fifteenth-century inn, which sometimes claims to be the oldest pub in the country, did not sell at auction. However, the circulation of *Country Life* is worldwide, and the advertisement for the Crown was seen by two Canadians in a Toronto club. They had been in the Canadian Air Force, which had also been stationed in Surrey. Said one: 'Hey, that's our pub!' Replied the other: 'What are we waiting for? Let's go over and buy it!'

Meanwhile, the RICS had given its dispensation for the partnership of Knight Frank & Rutley (Nigeria) to be formed, and it opened in Lagos on 1 February 1965, with a staff of four: Alan Shelley, Paul Mitchell, a secretary and a Nigerian clerk, Christopher Nwaokolo who is today office manager. Over the years this nucleus would grow to a partnership of eleven Nigerians and 200 staff, with branch offices at Kano, Port Harcourt, Calabar, Kaduna, Enugu, Benin and Jos.

To describe Ramsbury Manor, Wiltshire, as 'the perfect Charles II house' was not just estate agent's euphoria. Offers of around £300,000 were sought for the 460-acre property in the heart of the Kennet Valley, five miles from Marlborough – the river flows through the estate for more than a mile. It had belonged to Lord Rootes, the motor-car king. Caroline panelling, two dining rooms each with its Adam mantel-shelf, a drawing room with a chimneypiece carved by Grinling Gibbons, a tennis court, perpetual shooting rights – it could hardly have been more different from Centre Point. Yes, it was to Harry Hyams that Peter Oldfield sold Ramsbury.

On 24 January, Sir Winston Churchill died; and after the State funeral service at St Paul's Cathedral there was much speculation about what would happen to his London home in Hyde Park Gate, Nos. 28 and 27, the intercommunicating houses which the firm had found for him in 1945. Undoubtedly the sale of the year, it was one of the last auctions conducted by Alan Mann, manager of the Town Residential department for the last twenty years, who was due to retire at Christmas. He was assisted by Peter Kearon, who became his successor. Prospective buyers were expected from all over the world, and the sale took place in the glare of television lights. There were, indeed, more photographers than bidders. Just before the bidding started, an eccentric figure in a tail coat stood up and began making a long speech in praise of Churchill and had to be eased out of the room and into Hanover Square.

Bidding at the Churchill auction was short and sharp; there were, after all, few overseas buyers, and the second bidder, Dr Samuel Simpson, chairman of Simpsons of Piccadilly, eventually got the two houses for £102,500. A syndicate of businessmen from Baton Rouge, Louisiana, wanted to turn them into a museum, but did not bid enough. It was all over in four minutes. Dr Simpson was not certain whether he wanted to turn the houses into a Churchills shrine or just live there.

Up in Yorkshire, they were worrying about the future of Fountains Abbey, dating from 1132, one of the best preserved abbey ruins of Europe. It was part of the 19,000-acre Studley Royal estate, near Ripon, which had once belonged to John Aislabie, imprisoned in the Tower for making nearly £800,000 out of the South Sea Bubble. It was now being offered by Mr Henry Vyner for a price in the region of £1 million. The sale was conducted by George Baker, and the new owners were Broadlands Properties Ltd of Scarborough in association with Effold Properties Ltd, of London, who gave assurances that the Abbey would 'continue to be maintained as before and be accessible to the public' even if the estate were split up and re-offered in lots.

During the1960s, when so many people seemed to be making money, 'Overseas Residential' flourished, until much of its business was snuffed out by the oil crisis and foreign exchange restrictions of the early 1970s. Knight Frank & Rutley never regarded it as a natural market for them, but around 1965 they had arrangements with local offices in France, Switzerland, Italy, Spain, Portugal, the Mediterranean islands, and the West Indies. Gerry Akroyd, after his debut in the Bahamas, was spending much time abroad and so was Jeremy Haworth. The firm's advertising

Fountains Abbey, dating from 1132, one of the best preserved abbey ruins in Europe and part of the 19,000-acre Studley Royal Estate near Ripon. Once owned by John Aislabie, who had been imprisoned in the Tower for his dealings with the South Sea Bubble, the estate was sold in 1974 to Broadlands Properties Ltd, of Scarborough.

stressed, not only villas but 'land and sites for investment and development', commercial and industrial as well as tourist. Rich men were buying property in Bermuda and the West Indies, 'holiday playgrounds' were planned in faraway places like the Seychelles, even Fiji; and with the leisure-pleasure market came opportunities for commercial work – big valuations in the Bahamas, and a major task in the British Virgin Islands in which Knight Frank & Rutley, acting for the British Government, advised on a new development in Road Town, Tortola. Majorca was another development area; so was Sardinia, where the Aga Khan was creating the Costa Smeralda.

Nine new partners were announced in January 1966 – Jeremy Haworth, David Gardner, Peter Kearon, William Anderson, Arnold James, Jack Guy, Robert Rutty, Rowland Entwistle, and Gordon Wordsworth, direct descendant of the poet, who was based at Hereford. These were joined, in April, by Stanley Glynn, who had been a partner in Styles & Whitlock of St James's Place, having been originally trained before the War at Knight Frank & Rutley. He was now in charge of Business Premises, with plans to enlarge the Investment Department.

Peter Kearon, who had joined the firm in 1948, had specialized entirely in

'London Residential', formerly part of the Town Department. Much of his work, until the mid-1960s, had been letting large West End furnished and unfurnished flats to celebrities, especially visiting American film-stars. William Anderson had joined the old Structural Department after experience in three other property firms, and would take over that department when Willie Cunningham retired. Jack Guy, one of the first people ever to qualify as a 'chattels' auctioneer, had been running the Galleries ever since Guy Coleridge's retirement. Gordon Wordsworth had been a National Trust agent in Northern Ireland and had a sound knowledge of running estates as well as selling them.

On paper, it looked like a palace revolution as six partners retired. Edward Fisher, Alec Siese, Willie Cunningham, Edward Osborne, Charles Stenholm and Linton Roberts; but it was simply that they had all reached retiring age in the same year. Peter Oldfield was the natural successor to Ted Fisher as Senior Partner.

January 1966 brought the first rumbles of civil war in Nigeria. It began with the attempt by the Ibos of the former Eastern Region to set up a separate state. The Eastern Region, which included Port Harcourt, was under a military governor, Lt-Col O. Ojukwu. The Ojukwu family ran a major commercial transport firm in Nigeria: they were among the firm's clients.

There were riots in the West, and Chiefs Awolowo and Enahoro, both imprisoned, were charged with plotting to overthrow the Federal Government. On 15 January there was a military coup: the Sardauna of Sokoto and other leaders were assassinated by Ibo-led soldiers. In all regional capitals Parliament and Broadcasting Houses were seized. The country was ruled from Lagos by General Ironsi, and a Military Governor was appointed for each region. A decree of 24 May abolished the Regions and announced unification. There was a second coup when General Ironsi was shot and General Gowon (a Christian) came to power, in due course releasing Awolowo and Enahoro. In the east Ojukwu, bent on secession, sent to Europe for arms. It was still not clear how far conflict was likely to spread. Knight Frank & Rutley carried on in Lagos throughout the war and, amid considerable staff difficulties, made a profit each year.

At home, property was stagnant until the general election in April, when uncertainty ceased and more estates came on the market. In Wiltshire South Wraxall Manor came up for sale – it was by no means the first time the firm had handled it, for it had once belonged to Sir Howard Frank's old friend Walter Long. Mereworth Castle, in Kent, an eighteenth-century copy of Palladio's Villa Rotunda, near Vicenza, with 400 acres, had also been on the firm's books before, and would be so again. Little Durnford Manor, three miles north of Salisbury, with 890 acres, was sold before auction to the Earl of Chichester for a little under £400,000.

For Scotland, the most emotional transaction of the year was the offer, by Maj.-Gen. Sir John Laurie, former commander of the 52nd Lowland Division, of his ancestral home, Maxwelton House, Dumfriesshire. It was the birthplace, in 1682, of Annie Laurie, and the scene of the famous love-song by her first suitor, Captain

Douglas of Fingland. Annie Laurie is buried in Glencairn churchyard.

The *Sunday Times* was conducting a campaign of scrutiny of art dealers. In 1964 the paper had exposed 'dealers' rings', which are objected to in Bond Street but not in Madison Avenue. In August 1966 the paper planned to expose art forgeries and the degree to which even 'experts' could be hoodwinked. An Italian framer and a carver, Pirotta, were disturbed to find that their reproduction carved furniture was being sold in Europe as antiques. They made a pair of painted blackamoor torchères which could, they thought, be passed off as eighteenth-century Venetian work, especially with legs in the style of Viana. (They were in fact carved out of an old telegraph pole.) The *Sunday Times* Insight Team showed them to various West End dealers, none of whom seemed to think they might be modern. One of the figurines, for realism, had a broken arm. Jack Guy handled them warily: he at first thought they might be Regency, then catalogued them as 'in the style of Viana'. The *Sunday Times* representative, after making a great fuss about the reserve price, withdrew them at £650. To have let the sale go through would have caused legal risks.

Jack Guy, realizing the fickleness of fashion, had many ideas for sales of objects which could become collectors' manias – old coins and medals, railway relics, model soldiers. He had had some success with netsukes, Japanese carved ivory button ornaments much loved by Americans; now he discovered Stevengraphs, woven silk 'primitive' pictures first made in Coventry in 1879 by Thomas Stevens. His firm went on manufacturing them almost until the 'Baedeker' air-raid on Coventry in 1940. Portraits of politicians, views of the Crystal Palace, famous railway engines, scenes from American history, Lady Godiva trying to reduce taxation by riding naked – these became collectors' items, and there is a society for their study in the United States. In 1969 he was able to hold an exhibition of the Austin Sprake collection, with a sale in September at which one lot broke through the £500 barrier: most fetched £10–£25 each.

One of the immediate effects of Peter Oldfield's leadership, in which he was backed by Geoffrey Gay, Sam Goodenough, Bill Yates and all who thought of themselves as progressive, was the thrust overseas. Oldfield's own sphere was the Country Department, which he had helped to restore to its pre-war glory; but he had a quick intuitive grasp of the need to expand abroad, and also the need for a profession to adapt itself to the administrative techniques of modern business and industry.

It made sense, therefore, that in 1967 he should pick Richard Edwards, a chartered accountant, to be groomed as head of financial administration. Richard Edwards, who became a partner in 1969, had spent five years with Peat Marwick Mitchell & Co. and another five with Holland & Holland, the Bruton Street gunsmiths. He would eventually find himself in charge of all business management, accounting, financial planning and administration, answering the question, 'Is this new development viable?' with the counter-question, 'Can we afford it?' And in the fullness of time this would involve computers and word-processors, and something called Management-by-Objectives.

Seventeen years before, Malcolm Mackenzie had urged the case for development in Australia. Taylor Woodrow and other big firms were exploring it. On Peter Oldfield's first trip there, Frank Taylor generously lent him his private aircraft. Next year it was Sam Goodenough's turn, and he was able to conclude an 'association' with Baillieu Allard of Melbourne, who deal in both insurance and real estate. This involved Baillieu Allard Real Estate Pty Ltd of Melbourne and their own associates in Sydney (Hardie & Gorman) and in Perth (Milner & Co.); and led, in October 1969, to an Australian Land and Property Fund (registered in the Bahamas) formed between Knight Frank & Rutley and a unit trust group, First Investors & Savers. The recession of the early 1970s would hinder progress. But the firm persevered, and Sam Goodenough flew to Australia every spring for the next seven years.

In Scotland, Jessica (Mitford) Treuhaft, to whom Sam Goodenough had sold Inch Kenneth, the Mitford family island off Mull, in 1959, succeeded, with the firm's help, in selling it to Dr A. Barlow, of Norland Square, London W11, for something under the asking price of £30,000. And what is probably the remotest Scottish property ever handled by the firm, islands excepted, the 8500-acre Durness estate near Cape Wrath, came on the market in May 1967. Noted for its wild coastal scenery, bird-life, twelve trout lochs and off-shore islands (one of which, Eilean Hoan, is the haunt of the barnacle goose in winter), the estate contains some of the oldest rock formations in the world, and Smoo Cave, with its 90-ft waterfall. This chunk of leather-covered granite was sold by Sam Goodenough to a philanthrophic Mr Robinson, whose chief anxiety was to preserve the coast and the house, Smoo Lodge. He had also bought and restored Kilcoy Castle, ancient seat of the Mackenzies in Ross and Cromarty.

And by way of contrast, among many country properties handled this year, the firm sold the Wavendon Tower estate, land and cottages, near Bletchley, Bucks., to Johnny Dankworth the saxophonist and composer.

For years the firm had been recommending investment in property for long-term capital appreciation. That appreciation was getting shorter and quicker, and it was now possible to recommend property as a hedge against inflation, which, in the next few years, would accelerate alarmingly. The time was ripe for a scheme which had been maturing in the minds of Peter Oldfield and Sam Goodenough for some time, which was launched in the summer of 1967. It was not only a chance to invest in property – it was, from the firm's viewpoint, a useful means of attracting new clients.

The Hanover Property Unit Trust, formed in association with Samuel Montagu & Co., as bankers and financial advisors, Nabarro Nathanson, as solicitors, Duncan C. Fraser & Co. as consulting actuaries and Peat Marwick Mitchell & Co. as auditors, was advertised in a hardselling style: it had 'appointed Knight Frank & Rutley as property consultants and managing agents . . . The fund is actively investing in Shops, Offices, Industrial and Commercial Properties, including leasebacks. Progressive policy – quick decisions – introducing agents retained – no limit on size.'

Its assets now exceed £90 million, which Knight Frank & Rutley manage on behalf of the 150 pension funds who invested in Hanover.

XVII
Into Europe

In January 1968, Knight Frank & Rutley announced that they had acquired Wheatley, Kirk, Price & Co., a firm with specialized skills and experience which were particularly useful at the time. Knight Frank & Rutley's own industrial department would join with Wheatley, Kirk & Price in a combined operation specializing in the valuation and sale of industrial properties, plant and machinery. The acquired firm's senior partner, E. L. Judson, continued as a consultant, while another partner, George E. Gibbs, joined the Knight Frank & Rutley partnership.

In the spring, a famous conference hotel, the Norebreck Hydro, came on the market as a going concern. It is probably the largest British hotel the firm has ever handled, with over 20,000 square feet of conference and exhibition space, indoor swimming pool, sauna, nursery, five bars, lounges, ballrooms, 400 rooms and a restaurant for 600 people. It occupied 11 acres and had parking space for 300 cars.

Once again the firm found itself acting for an old client, Earl Poulett, authority on steam locomotives, who had been Director of Small Arms Ordnance Factories during the war. He wished, at last, to sell the Hinton St George estate in Somerset, where his ancestors had lived for 500 years (he had another house in Nassau, Bahamas). The property, extending to 1300 acres, realized £225,000. The buyers (as with Studley Royal three years before) were Effold Properties, in association with the agricultural tenants.

In Scotland, the 12,500-acre Lanfine and Auchmannoch estate, 25 miles south of Glasgow, was sold privately as a whole. But the sale of the year was that of the 'splendid' (*The Times* reporter's word, not the auctioneer's) Warter Priory estate near York – 'probably the most important sale of agricultural land ever to have taken place in England'. The 14,500-acre estate had been bought for his son by the late Lord Vestey, one of the founders of Union Cold Storage. The Hon. George Vestey, recently deceased, who had concentrated on the food retailing side of the family business, had had no son; and when the estate was placed on the market, his eldest daughter told the press: 'We would like to sell it in one lot to someone who will run it in the same way that Daddy did.' Knight Frank & Rutley, in conjunction with Henry Spencer & Sons of Retford, Notts., sold it to a trust formed under the will of the first Earl of Iveagh for 'a figure in the region of £4 million'.

In July came one of the first signs of the Arab invasion of the 1970s, when Sayed Mohamed Mahdi Al-Tajir (who would become Ambassador in London for the United Arab Emirates, still, however, known as the Trucial States) bought Sir Billy Butlin's house at Windlesham – not, apparently, for himself, but on behalf of Sheikh Rashid ben Said al Maktoum, Ruler of Dubai. Mr Al-Tajir eventually bought some half a dozen stately homes in London and the Home Counties, including Dropmore,

The Warter Priory estate near York. The 14,500-acre estate, property of the Vestey family, was sold to a trust formed under the will of the first Earl of Iveagh for 'a figure in the region of £4 million'.

not far from Cliveden, and the spectacular Mereworth Castle in Kent.

1969 began badly for the firm's communications. The new London telephone directory, completely reset as a result of the changeover to all-figure numbers, had omitted Knight Frank & Rutley and their new number, 01-629 8171. 'Many clients have complained that they cannot find our number,' the firm told the Post Office. 'The mistake could lose us quite a lot of business.' On 23 January Sir William Teeling, MP for Brighton Pavilion, asked a question in Parliament about it, and the Postmaster-General (who happened to be John Stonehouse) was able to assure him that the Post Office was taking the unprecedented step of paying for a series of national newspaper advertisements to publicize the number they had left out. They would be repeated throughout the year until the new edition of the directory appeared in 1970. It was all rather good publicity.

For the Galleries it was a middling year. There was a boom in silver, about which Jack Guy was extremely knowledgeable; but it quickly declined, and some speculators burnt their fingers. Prices of chattels and bric-à-brac receded. 'Many collectors who bought for pleasure and as a hedge against inflation have been forced to pay off overdrafts,' Jack Guy reported, 'and are temporily lost to the market. Such people rarely attend auctions, usually preferring to put their trust in a favourite dealer.'

The overseas thrust was further implemented by the first tentacle into Europe – the opening of an office in Geneva, headed by Bill Yates. Yates, who had joined

Knight Frank & Rutley in 1964 by way of Lancing, Sandhurst, the Royal Dragoons and a firm of estate agents in Cirencester, had been picked in 1967 as the future founder of the firm's European expansion – but it had taken two years to get a Swiss work-permit. The Geneva office was to be not so much a branch as a listening-post, in the days when the EEC was still in the contemplation stage. Why Geneva? It had a good international airport for travel to other parts of Europe, and it was a good centre for dealing with the international business community. 'Sitting in Geneva,' Bill Yates recalls, 'enabled me to have a very clear view of continental Europe and where I felt Knight Frank & Rutley should get established, and how.' He was well-placed to deal with valuation work connected with real estate financing on a worldwide scale for the massive quantity of institutional funds moving through Swiss banks. Certainly there would have been little point in setting up merely as estate agents – 'Geneva has, if possible, even more estate agents than it has banks.'

Nevertheless, there was a certain amount of business domestically within Geneva, in pure agency letting operations of office and shop space. 'However, the bulk of our work there was valuation and I must have valued 25 per cent of the buildings housing the Geneva branches of international banks, mostly on the Rue du Rhône.'

One thing Yates noticed was that 'many of our competitors were setting up in European cities by staffing their offices with British chartered surveyors rather than local real estate people'. So he got the London partnership to agree that the firm's policy should be different – 'in each place we should recruit a local and put alongside him one of our home-trained British chartered surveyors.'

By the end of the first year, the Geneva office had collected a number of interesting clients, among them the Credit Lyonnais Bank, Shell, the Agnelli family from Italy, two subsidiaries of the Onassis empire, and the principal property subsidiary of the D. K. Ludwig organization, Princess Property, much concerned with hotels and leisure in glamorous places like Acapulco. Mr Ludwig, one of the contenders for the title 'richest man in the world', had interests in oil tankers, chocolate, citrus fruit and salt as well as real estate. His shipping empire was said to be bigger than those of Onassis and Niarchos combined.

The Ludwig business had arrived in a curious way. One morning Bill Yates received a call from the London office of White Weld, the American merchant bank, saying that their New York office was about to do a major underwriting for 'a well-known client' and that they required a huge valuation of property assets in the USA, Mexico, Bermuda, the Bahamas and Australia. Could he attend an interview in London that evening or the following morning at latest? Bill Yates cancelled all other appointments and flew to London that evening. He learned that four competitors had also attended interviews. Having been told the size of the Ludwig job, he was asked whether Knight Frank & Rutley could do it, and if so, what fees they would quote.

'I haven't the slightest idea,' Bill replied. 'But if you'll buy me a round-trip air ticket I will look at all the properties and come back to you in ten days to tell you what we would charge.' This pleased White Weld; all the competitors had quoted a

The Acapulco Princess Hotel in Mexico owned by the D. K. Ludwig Group of Companies.

percentage of value. Bill Yates returned to London ten days later, looking (according to someone who had seen him at Heathrow) 'like a boiled cabbage'. A fee was agreed and the firm got the job. 'I had to obtain some very substantial support from Hanover Square,' Bill Yates says. 'We set up our headquarters in the King's Inn Hotel in Grand Bahama, the centre point of most of the work, and from there various teams went out to Mexico, North America and Bermuda.' And so the task was completed.

About this time, Credit Lyonnais set up a Swiss-based international property advisory company which they could consult on all real estate matters over a large number of countries in Europe and North America, and which could seek out suitable investments for Credit Lyonnais clients, both corporate and individual. In fact what they did was to create a separate unit trust for every single purchase selected by INCAS, the company so formed. 'It was an amazingly far-sighted scheme,' Bill Yates remembers, 'since it wasn't until the late 1970s that most of the other large international banks and many London merchant banks decided to set up their own property advisory services.' INCAS got Knight Frank & Rutley involved in a number of investment transactions in several countries, and also won them important friends in Paris and Geneva.

One partner in INCAS was Cushman & Wakefield, the American real estate firm, which had recently become a subsidiary of RCA, the international communication company. Cushman & Wakefield were represented on the board by Earl Reiss. The first meeting of Reiss and Yates was historic: in nine years' time it would lead to the foundation of Douglas Elliman Knight Frank.

Switzerland was also part of the leisure market, which Knight Frank & Rutley were now exploring. On the southern slopes of the 3247-metre Wildhorn, overlooking the Rhône valley, Anzère a new summer and winter resort was being built. Summer ski-ing would be possible on the glacier near the summit. The village consisted of chalet-style blocks of flats with all facilities. In spite of the property dollar premium, Knight Frank & Rutley were able to report outstanding sales in England.

The Algarve, in Portugal, was also much in demand, and the firm had just formed an association there with Miss L. de Sousa, who had been their consultant there for some years. Here, as in several countries, the developers slogan was 'a second home in the sun'.

We move suddenly to Regency London, or rather a remaining piece of it – Albany, between Piccadilly and Vigo Street, once the town house of the Duke of York and Albany (the one who 'had ten thousand men'). It is now residential chambers (you are not allowed to say 'flats'), and one of the few residential properties managed by Knight Frank & Rutley. Mainly for single gentlemen, Albany is guarded by porters in livery and top-hats, and no one enters casually. The famous Ropewalk created by Henry Holland when he converted the original building, remains largely unchanged today, paved and roofed and with the original oil lamps converted to electricity.

Albany's historian is Jean Love, Knight Frank & Rutley's first woman partner, who manages Albany and other London property. 'The Trustees of Albany,' she says, 'laid down rules at a meeting in 1804 and these remain substantially unchanged. Residents have always been carefully selected and it was not until 1889 that a woman was allowed to take rooms. In the early part of the nineteenth century a woman's reputation would be lost if she was seen entering chambers.'

One of the earliest tenants was Jane Austen's brother, Henry. Lord Byron lived there in 1814, Macaulay in 1841, Gladstone in 1842, and Compton Mackenzie in 1912. (Albany is one of the settings of *Sinister Street.*) The most famous fictional resident was A. J. Raffles, the burglar who played cricket for the Gentlemen. In recent years J. B. Priestley, Sir Terence Rattigan, Margaret Lane the author, Fleur Cowles, Graham Greene, Sir Isaiah Berlin the philosopher, Edward Heath and Terence Stamp have lived there – also Knight Frank & Rutley's own senior parter, Geoffrey Gay.

Until 1958, thirty-four of the sixty-nine sets of chambers belonged to William Stone, known as the Squire of Piccadilly, the delight of gossip columnists because he belonged to more clubs than any other man in London. When he died at the age of 101, he left his property to Peterhouse, Cambridge, and in 1967 Peterhouse appointed Knight Frank & Rutley managing agents. No longer bachelor chambers, they may

Dylan Thomas. Sixteen years after the poet's death, Knight Frank & Rutley was instructed to sell the Boathouse at Laugharne. The auction was broken up by Welsh Nationalists – there was no sale.

now be let to 'suitable single women' but 'no children under fourteen'.

A property that made international news was at Laugharne, at the mouth of the river Taf in Carmarthenshire. It is not often that an auction breaks up in disorder with hostile elements shouting slogans, but this is what happened on 24 September 1969 at Brown's Hotel, when Gerry Akroyd made a valiant attempt to sell Dylan Thomas's Boathouse sixteen years after the poet's death, since when it had been empty.

Trouble had been brewing for some weeks. Laugharne, a curiously un-Welsh town full of medieval traditions (such as a Portreeve who controlled a Court Leet and Court Baron) seemed apathetic; it did not want to buy the house, but neither did it want any foreigner to buy it, especially an American who might bodily remove it from the town. The Portreeve-Elect found that Laugharne was in dispute with Knight Frank & Rutley who had been instructed by the poet's widow, Mrs Caitlin Thomas. Dylan's 'small sea-shaken house on a breakneck of rocks . . . lost in a sad Kangaroo-pocket of the sad salt west' was expected to fetch £10,000. There had, it is true, been many American visitors, and a Dutchman had already offered £7000. A British trust was striving to raise £15,000 through an appeal fund.

At the auction Gerry Akroyd had barely secured an opening bid when there was a commotion at the back of the hall and menacing figures advanced on the rostrum. The Welsh Nationalists wished the Boathouse to remain Welsh, even if empty and derelict, even if no Welshman was willing to come forward and save it. There was no sale.

In January 1970 the Nigerian War came to an end just thirty months after the 1966 assassinations. About 200,000 people were under arms by this time. In Lagos British staff had few serious problems: they were occasionally raided by the security authorities, and their passports were temporarily confiscated, but the firm continued to make a profit, as it had done every year since 1965.

Business, for British firms, was almost 'as usual' in Lagos but by no means so in Port Harcourt, which was badly damaged. Shell-BP had resumed oil export from their Bonny terminal, about 30 miles south-east of Port Harcourt, as early as September 1968; but after the war they wanted to transfer their headquarters offices from Port Harcourt to Lagos.

In Lagos, where office space was in short supply, Shell took the unusual course of approaching half a dozen site owners or developers and asked them to tender for building an office block to their specification. 'At the time,' Alan Shelley recalls, 'we were acting for three of the developers approached by Shell, and we had to decide which client to act for. We decided that the best site was one on the Marina owned by the Methodist Church. The development was undertaken by Western Holdings Ltd, a company jointly owned by the Methodist Church and John Holt Investment Co. Ltd.' (Holts, today part of the Lonrho Group, had by 1970 left Knight Frank & Rutley [Nigeria]: the dissolution of the partnership had been friendly but delicate – too many of Knight Frank & Rutley's clients were Holt's competitors. But the two firms continued to help each other, and today Alan Shelley is a director of Holt's investment subsidiary.)

Part of the deal between Holts and the Methodist Church required Holts to pay for rehousing the President of the Church (his home was on the site to be developed) and also to build a new library for the Methodist Boys' High School. 'Construction of the 100,000 sq. ft office block began early in 1970,' Alan Shelley says, 'although during the piling stage we were held up for a few days because the wife of the President of the Church, who was still living on the site, complained that the piling affected the laying habits of her chickens.' This block became Freeman House, 21 Marina.

In London, the Oldfield policy of adapting professional practice to the sophisticated efficiency of modern business was about to be seen in several aspects. Urwick Orr & Partners, the management consultants, were asked to advise. Bearing in mind that Richard Edwards was the first chartered accountant the firm had ever had, there was quite a lot to learn. For instance, the departments tended to be cut off from each other with a lack of a central mechanism for decision-making. The answer to this was a Policy Committee and the introduction of Management-by-Objectives. Another important recommendation was that the firm had now reached a size when it could not be run by one Senior Partner. The consultants suggested that there should be a Managing Partner as well. (This was not implemented until 1978.)

With this modernization of structure went an overhaul of what commercial advertising men call the firm's 'corporate identity' or 'brand image' – a forthright visual quality in all its publicity. It began with a symbol or 'logo', either in red and dark green or in black and white, instantly recognizable, carried on all advertisements, brochures, particulars and leaflets. It was awarded a Certificate of Excellence in Milan in March 1974.

The 'logo' was later followed by another new look in property advertising: a system of Michelin Guide symbols (bathrooms, bedrooms, garage, tennis court, fishing, etc.) for shortening the amount of copy normally used by estate agents. Other property firms have imitated Knight Frank & Rutley's advertising style to a point, but they cannot use the symbol system – it is now copyright.

In February 1970 the firm launched a controversial publicity campaign to advertise its services. They explained it in a press statement: 'the traditional small illustrations and bald lists of details have been replaced by dramatic photographs, attention-getting headlines and copy which conveys the necessary information fully and compellingly . . .'

A very large insertion in *The Times*, under the headline *Knight Frank & Rutley Comes in All Shapes and Sizes*, showed and named a stately home, an Edgware factory, New Zealand House, a farm, a supermarket, an office block. The copy was businesslike: even a little brash. Publicizing services, if done with restraint, was professionally tolerable: but drawing attention to actual achievements was against the rules of the Royal Institution of Chartered Surveyors. A gauntlet had been thrown down.

The Institution received complaints from some of its members, and all those Knight Frank & Rutley partners who were Chartered Surveyors were called before a disciplinary committee. They were 'admonished' – the smallest reproof which could be given. Soon afterwards the Institution's rules for advertising were revised, allowing more commercial techniques to be used.

Two new partners were appointed in 1970 – Brian Shorter, an expert on rating, and John Inge, a specialist in country houses; and in Lagos, Paul Mitchell became a partner in Knight Frank & Rutley (Nigeria). From the staff's viewpoint, the innovation of the year was the new profit-sharing scheme which replaced the old bonus system.

There was a certain sadness, and a major break with the past, in the approaching closure of the Galleries. There were sound commercial reasons for it: they were less reliably profitable than the property side; they needed an army of porters to handle the chattels; they took up an enormous amount of space, and attracted throngs of bidders and dealers who made for a certain untidiness and excess of human traffic about the place. The clerical and detail work was excessive.

Among the famous names to be seen at 'chattels' sales (remembered by Doris White, who had been secretary to both Guy Coleridge and Jack Guy), either as sellers or bidders, were the Churchill family (certificates of authenticity were given to purchasers of their property), Noël Coward (who was not pleased when some of his furniture from his Gerald Road Studio was relegated to 'secondary goods'), Marius Goring, Sir George Robey (with his wife who had a fine taste in antiques), Dame Marie Tempest, Donald Sinden and Rosa Lewis of the Cavendish Hotel.

The timing of the closure was partly dictated by the expiry of the lease at No. 19

KF
+R

CERTIFICATE OF EXCELLENCE

This is to certify
that the trademark
owned by

KNIGHT FRANK & RUTLEY

has been selected
for its superior standard of design
amongst the most impressive
contemporary trademarks
to be included in
Top Symbols and Trademarks of the World
published by Deco Press

Milano, March 1974

The Chairman of the Committee — *The Editor*

The KFR logo. The Knight Frank & Rutley corporate identity, personified in its logo, which was awarded a Certificate of Excellence in Milan in March 1974.

Knight Frank & Rutley symbols, first used in 1970, were another step to enhancing the firm's individuality. But they made as many enemies as they made friends. The object was to reduce the amount of copy required for advertisements.

Hanover Square. On 1 October *The Times* announced 'a marriage of interests between Knight Frank & Rutley, the estate agents and auctioneers, and Christie, Manson & Woods, the fine art auctioneers' – not a take-over, but the two firms would operate 'in close liaison' in future. As the end of the year drew nearer, there was a little rush of sales at Hanover Square – sporting guns, vintage firearms, Stevengraphs, horse brasses, drawings and prints, rugs and 'illustrations of cats' – and the two final advertisements ended, inexorably, 'We cannot accept any more goods for sale . . . All goods sold and unsold must be removed by 31 December.'

The final sale, on 23 December, had a kind of sad Christmas feeling as Jack Guy sold, not only everything in the catalogue, but his microphone, the saleroom show-cases, his clerk's desk and stool, and last of all his own oak rostrum knocked down to Sotheby's for £230.

By the beginning of 1971 it was clear that Britain was to join the EEC, and that the Geneva office would soon be moving back to London before the firm began a truly international policy by opening offices, at carefully planned intervals, in European, and eventually world, capitals. Scotland is not precisely continental Europe, but it was in this year that an Edinburgh branch was opened, or perhaps reopened. The firm had always dealt in rural property in Scotland, especially sporting estates, but to build up a new commercial property side it was necessary to be on the spot. The nucleus of the Edinburgh office, which began in one room in the Forres Street office of Schomberg Scott, the well-known architect and expert on the work of the Adam brothers, was Geoffrey Forrest, for many years senior land acquisition officer in the Forestry Commission.

In June the office moved to its first official address, 8 Charlotte Square. It had struck a boom time in Scottish properties: 1971 saw Robert Louis Stevenson's home on the Isle of Erraid (an estate handled several times by the firm), the Earl of Seafield's Lochindorb and Carrbridge estates (22,400 acres), Culloden House, an estate on Islay, and others come on the market. In the next few years the firm sold Lord Seafield's 21,000-acre Tulchan estate (to Jim Slater), the 17,000-acre Suisgill estate on the river Helmsdale, the Gelston estate in Kirkcudbrightshire, and Hunthill in Angus which in 1973 was sold for over £2¼ million. In April 1972 Colin Strang Steel joined the Edinburgh office to help with the greatly increased workload – the demand for Scottish sporting properties was exceptionally strong – and eventually became partner in charge of Scotland on Geoffrey Forrest's retirement.

Internationally, the emphasis was on leisure, pleasure and overseas residential, often with a golf-course handy. On the Costa del Sol, at Sotogrande, half-acre plots were £9000 and upwards, with completed houses from £21,000 and apartment blocks under construction. At Vale de Lobo, Portugal, in a development by Costain and Trust Houses, 'complete homes in the Moorish-style village' cost from £9500, and the golf-course, designed by Henry Cotton, was a savage affair in which 'at one point two yawning chasms separate player from green'. Another 'instant village', also on the Costa del Sol, in the mountains above Marbella, was El Madronal, developed by Robertson 'Happy' Ward the architect who had successfully pioneered this sort of thing in the West Indies. El Madronal was 'within easy reach of some half-dozen golf courses, with the ski-lifts of the Sierra Nevada less than a morning away'.

The word 'village' is very persuasive. There were houses for sale in Ambelia Village, near Kyrenia, Cyprus. A strangely English-looking park, the Cap estate on St Lucia, Windward Islands, offered one-acre 'home sites' for £3000. And in the lazy Seychelles, a new development, Casuarina Hills, 'amid lush tropical vegetation', had split-level houses designed by British architects for £9000–£10,000 (including land).

'London Residential' was also approaching a boom, swollen by Middle East buyers. One of them would eventually buy 'the most expensive house in London', 26 Rutland Gate. It had belonged to Richard Gangel, of Bernie Cornfield's notorious Investors Overseas Services (IOS), and, in six storeys, it had an air-conditioned 'Moroccan style' swimming pool, a sauna, a lift, a ballroom, a cinema, a roof garden, gold taps in all four bathrooms, and 'twin Gothic loos for the children'. Although bankrupt, Mr Gangel was asking £400,000 – the sum he was said to have spent on 'improvements'. He had to be content with £250,000.

1972 saw a short land boom. Fringe banks were lending money to finance speculative purchases. In 1973 £2000 an acre was not unknown. This was the age of 'gazumping' – 'we'd never heard the word before,' say Knight Frank & Rutley people, wrinkling their noses distastefully. Valuation became farcical. It couldn't last, and didn't: the looming oil crisis, and Mr (now Lord) Barber's 1973 Budget, directed against the hoarding of land for building by speculators, put an end to it.

Bill Yates had closed the Geneva office and was now back in London, setting up an international commercial department, to provide a desk in London to service British property companies and institutions who would at the same time be dealing with the offices in Amsterdam, Paris and Brussels which the firm had now definitely decided to open. (This became something of an act of faith after the 1973–74 property crash!)

In 1972 Knight Frank & Rutley opened in Amsterdam under the name KFR Vastgoedadviseurs.

Just occasionally an auction is rendered invalid by the problem of the Bogus Bidder. This happened in the summer of 1972 when Newsells Park Estate, Royston, Herts., was sold under the hammer to a purchaser who failed to complete. It was eventually sold privately for a sum in excess of £2 million; but the vendors, Mr and Mrs Dermot Humphrey de Trafford, sued the original purchaser through his solicitors for their loss which they estimated at £300,000. At the auction Peter Oldfield, as auctioneer, suspected that something was wrong when he heard that someone in a Rolls-Royce had been visiting tenants and asking unprofessional questions. It was probably an attempt at a 'trading option' – to buy without capital and re-sell for a quick profit.

The Bogus Bidder did not come up for trial until 1975. When he did he turned out to be a solicitor bidding for a client who seemingly had vanished. Having bid £2,400,000 for the estate, he had got his uncle to pay the £240,000 deposit with the promise of a banker's draft the next day – which never arrived. He had, he said, 'left his cheque book at home'. Peter Oldfield and several other people at once offered him theirs, but the solicitor still insisted on a banker's draft. It turned out that, although he owned both a Rolls and a Jaguar, he had only £82 in the bank. Charged with perjury and fabricating evidence, he went down for four years.

Peter Oldfield had taken the unusual step of announcing his retirement a year before he actually went on 1 January 1973. While remaining a consultant, he would now have time to enjoy his island retreat on Corfu, whose people like the British and even know how to play cricket. His villa was surrounded by a beautiful garden designed by his wife; and he has one great gift that particularly endears itself to the Greeks for whom fresh water is as vintage wine: he is a dowser, and has found an underground river 33 metres deep. Whimsically, the staff's farewell gift to him was a portrait of 'Rutley', one of his horses, painted by the sporting artist, Peter Biegal.

He was succeeded, as Senior Partner, by Geoffrey Gay, a man of many parts who, in addition to being a General Commissioner for Inland Revenue, sometime member of Westminster City Council, and a Governor of Benenden School, had just been elected World President of the International Real Estate Federation (FIABCI). In January 1973 seven new partners were announced: Geoffrey Fisher, Colin Elliot, David McIntosh-Whyte, Alan Daniels, Martin Holgate, John Chambers and

The Case of the Bogus Bidder. Newsells Park was sold at auction for £2,400,000. It was later discovered that the purchaser, having persuaded his uncle to pay the 10 per cent deposit with the promise of a banker's draft the next day (which never arrived) owned both a Rolls and a Jaguar – but only had £82 in the bank.

Geoffrey Forrest. In Hereford, Hugh Preston had been made a partner in 1972.

The Paris office opened in one month, splendidly situated in the Place Vendôme and with François Boutet as Managing Partner. The London taxi owned by Knight Frank & Rutley, with the registration plate KFR 1, toured Paris and was parked outside the Ritz Hotel for the reception to welcome the new office. Established now in both Holland and France, with plans for further expansion, the firm was ready to launch a project which was very much linked to the EEC. EUPIC (European Property Investment Company NV), largely the creation of Bill Yates, had begun as the germ of an idea in Geneva three years before. Bill Yates discussed the idea with a friend, Sir John Montgomery Cuninghame, then running a finance company in Geneva. After preliminary research they needed the support of a bank of some standing to get the project moving.

1972 had found both Yates and Cuninghame back in London, the latter then with Morgan Grenfell, the merchant bankers. On Morgan Grenfell's advice and with their help, banks in Holland, France, Germany and Belgium were persuaded to join in, together with the Murray Johnstone Group of trusts in Glasgow and MEPC, the British property company. Morgan Grenfell then set about a Euro equity issue, the first-ever of its type. Stockbrokers Rowe & Pitman raised about 40 per cent of the issue in Britain.

'Alongside EUPIC, we formed a management company called EUPIC Services,' Bill Yates says. For fiscal reasons, Knight Frank & Rutley did not have a share, but had a contract to provide certain services, including that of Bill Yates who became one of the managing-directors, the Senior Partner of the day being a member of the Supervisory Board. The issue was completed by 30 June – 'We raised approximately £22 million from the public on a promise, having purchased absolutely no property.' Property was the 'in' investment in 1973; not so in 1974: 'By then, the hike in oil prices had occurred, the world economy had spiralled downwards and the property crash had resulted . . . but, by mid-summer, we were bold enough to start buying properties again, and during '74, '75 and '76 the company's portfolio began to take shape.' The firm had created an international investment client – something none of its competitors had done, or have since done.

More new partners were announced at the beginning of 1974: Ray Taylor (London Residential), John Grimshaw (plant and machinery specialist), and, in Edinburgh, Colin Strang Steel; and Stanley Glynn retired.

In March, Paul Mitchell, formerly a partner in Nigeria, joined the London partnership, being destined for the International Department and eventually for the new City of London office at 7 Birchin Lane with Martin Holgate as resident partner, and John Crickmay, formerly chief estates surveyor to the Legal & General Assurance Society, as consultant.

This move into the City was perhaps overdue, although the firm had handled many major properties in the Square Mile and in particular Peter Oldfield, Sam Goodenough and Gerry Akroyd had contacts there. It is generally agreed that, for the property business at least, the City is 'a different ball-game'. Who you know can be as important as what you know, and a huge chunk of business can sometimes result from a chance meeting in the street. The institutions are all within a stone's throw of each other; ears are to the ground; local intelligence in pubs and clubs is important. We shall see that the City office did not take long to bear fruit.

Two symptoms of slump (both temporary) were the markets in farms and hotels. The 1969 Development of Tourism Act, giving new hotel developers a grant of £1000 per bedroom or 20 per cent of the total cost, had been an artificial boost. Result: too many London hotels and too many inexperienced hoteliers. Yet three years later confidence returned, peaking at the Jubilee.

The 'second home in the sun' aspirations declined as foreign exchange grew difficult and the dollar premium level increased. But there were bigger projects abroad than the whims of 'overseas residential'. Jeremy Haworth and Michael Nicholson were in the team selected by the firm for a large international task in the West Indies – relocating the new town centre (with a Marina) at Road Town, Tortola, British Virgin Islands. This was a total project management job – advising

Wickhams Cay, British Virgin Islands. A 70-acre development in which the whole of the town centre of Tortola was re-built on a new site which included a marina.

on site acquisition, preparing a feasibility study and seeing the whole thing through to the last detail. The new development, in which the firm acted for the British Virgin Islands, covers about 30 hectares (70 acres), and is called Wickhams Cay. Among many responsibilities, the team were involved in coordinating the preparation of contracts for the development infrastructure, advising on town-planning aspects, raising finance and attracting participants to the scheme, together with the control of 'commercialization' and cash-flow of the project (in conjunction with the Financial Secretary of the Territory).

The Amsterdam office, in a difficult first year, proceeded cautiously, concentrating on commercial property, and among several minor instructions two deals stood out: the acquisition, for Barclays Bank International, of a freehold office building for their own use at Herengracht 504, Amsterdam; and the letting, for Amalgamated Investment Europe BV, of their 18,000 sq. ft office project at Noordhollandstraat 61 to Oxyde BV, a metals group who took a ten-year lease.

In November 1974 the new Covent Garden Market at Nine Elms was opened by the Queen, and Geoffrey Gay and David Gardner, who had done so much to bring about an orderly transfer, were invited to the ceremony. It had been a long haul since 1963. After the initial task of estimating the cost of acquiring 80 acres of property at Nine Elms came the second task – the promotion of the necessary legislation.

The third task had been to acquire the land at Nine Elms and effect clearance and demolition before redevelopment. Unforeseen problems had arisen: the scheme and extent of land interests was changed. Over one hundred families were rehoused by Knight Frank & Rutley by negotiation with Housing Trusts and Associations and local authorities.

The fourth task was to help prepare legislation for the discontinuance of the old Market and to advise on the basis of compensation, recognizing that certain hardships could arise.

Fifth and sixth tasks were to dispose of the Market Authority's interest in the Covent Garden area, and to purchase such traders' interests as might be necessary to ensure the move of the Market. For some time Knight Frank & Rutley opened a special office in Bedford Chambers, Covent Garden, to deal with the many technical problems that arose. David Gardner negotiated the disposal of the Market Authority's own interests, selling part to the Greater London Council and the remainder to the Arts Council. This was done against a background of pressure groups and a press campaign to 'save Covent Garden', where many buildings, including the Market itself, were 'listed' as being of historical and architectural importance. 'Wilderness Threat to Garden of Inigo Jones' was a typical headline.

For David Gardner, solving the human problem of rehousing the hundred families displaced at Nine Elms without litigation remains the most satisfactory achievement of the whole operation. 'I succeeded in this,' he says, 'by becoming involved in relocation of businesses – in mortgage arrangements and even transfers of certain people; for example a Post Office worker who wanted to move to Southampton, but the post office would not pay his removal costs although they were quite happy for him to work at Southampton. We arranged the move and the costs of the move, and so saved the Market Authority very considerable amounts of money.'

XVIII

'Probably the Most Diversified . . .'

In Belgium there had been a remarkable growth in property values during the early 1970s, due partly to the expansion of the Common Market administration and also to an influx of foreign manufacturers attracted by the high productivity of the Belgian workforce and excellent communications.

Knight Frank & Rutley had been involved in Belgium for about twenty-five years, especially during the boom decade after 1965, and had achieved some very large property deals, such as the sale of Manhattan Centre, at 30,000 sq. metres one of the biggest office buildings ever sold in Belgium. The firm had also acted for EUPIC in acquiring an industrial investment of 7000 sq. metres at Zaventem, near the international airport.

In spite of the recession, at a time when other foreign estate agents seemed to be pulling out of Belgium, and Brussels seemed threatened with an over-supply of new offices, Knight Frank & Rutley flew in the face of fortune and opened a Brussels office. Baron Paul Rolin, seven times Belgian golf champion, with long experience of the property market, agreed to become chief executive. By September 1975 Michael Nicholson, from Knight Frank & Rutley, London, and Jean-Pierre Washer from Richard Ellis, had joined the team to make a total office complement of five. By the end of 1980 the Brussels office had almost one million sq. ft of commercial property under management and an enviable client list.

Iran seemed an exciting prospect in 1975 – a rapidly expanding economy requiring buildings of all kinds. Several major British construction firms had established themselves in Teheran. Knight Frank & Rutley opened a Teheran office, in association with Morgan Grenfell Property Services, at 135 Kheradmand Shomali, and sat there for a year. Against a corrupt bureaucracy and the difficulty of getting paid for anything, little could be done: 'We didn't talk the same language at all,' say the survivors.

At home, there was a new Senior Partner – Pat Heller – succeeding Geoffrey Gay, who was retiring for health reasons. Apart from his obvious qualifications for the task, it was perhaps significant that Pat Heller was the only property management specialist ever to hold the top job, a recognition of the improved status of his department.

When the firm's lease in No. 19 Hanover Square had ended, and the house next door had been demolished and replaced by a new office building acquired by Lord Samuel's Land Securities group, the refurbishment of No. 20, the firm's traditional home, became necessary. Bill Anderson, head of the Building Surveyors' department, was in charge of this delicate task. There were difficulties of all kinds. Most of the work was carried out in 1972–73, a winter of discontent with power-cuts and a three-day week. There were problems with 'authorities': the District Surveyor insisted on top-lighting and better ventilation in the old sale-room (a slatted ceiling was one of the solutions). The work was phased so that staff could (uncomfortably) go on working. Perhaps the greatest technical difficulty, in preserving this eighteenth-century house, was the staircase, a stone cantilever type anchored into the wall between No. 19 and No. 20: it needed scaffolding for a year until it could be reinforced with steel.

1975 was 'European Architectural Heritage Year', and Knight Frank & Rutley were awarded a Commendation in recognition of 'structural repair and restoration, both inside and out, of an eighteenth-century five-storey town house for continued use as offices'.

As for No. 19, it was redeveloped and bought (at the depth of the property recession) by the BBC Pension Fund, for whom it has performed well: it is now let to Dalgety, the food conglomerate.

The Clore interests in Berkshire (Sir Charles lived at Stype Grange) now made it advisable to have someone on the spot. There were other clients in the area, or within a 20-mile radius, such as the Hon. David Astor at Compton Beauchamp, an estate with nine farms which the firm, led by Peter Oldfield and Sam Goodenough, had modernized.

An office was therefore opened in Hungerford – first as a sub-branch of Hereford, then as an independent office in its own right. The Berkshire-Wiltshire heartland of Southern England is full of wealthy men and big landowners, some of whom were already clients and others might become so. There was plenty of estate management, for both private or 'squire' landowners with two or three thousand acres and institutional or investment clients.

The Hungerford office started a building surveying department, and then went into farm management with Gordon Lugg as chief executive in charge. The next stage was to be country residential property . . .

In Nigeria, it was a seller's market: 'We do not sell, we allocate!' was one way of putting it. After Paul Mitchell's move to London, Peter Nwankwo, Joe Idudu and Jock Morris had joined the Partnership. Knight Frank & Rutley (Nigeria) had just valued all the properties of the largest Nigerian bank and succeeded in getting a 90 per cent reduction in a rating assessment on the second largest office building in Lagos; valued three breweries in Nigeria and one (for Guinness) in the Cameroons; and had been appointed letting and managing agents for a £6 million flat development.

In January 1976, three new partners were appointed to the London partnership – Peter Steward and Richard Edgell, both experts on property investment; and Jean Love, specialist in urban property management.

In London and the Home Counties, overseas buyers, more specially Arabs, were becoming a force in the market. This boom went on until 1980, when, partly through 'silly prices' and partly through the very real damage done by the TV film *Death of a Princess*, it subsided. The Arab influx came with the oil crisis, and with the fact that in London business, good medical attention and pleasure could all be combined.

There are, today, one or two Arab 'Lords of the Manor' in Britain, presiding benignly at village fêtes; but most of those who buy this privilege are solid British, and occasionally American. In the mid 1970s there was quite a brisk trade in 'lordships', many of which date from Norman, and a few from Saxon times, but since an act of Parliament in 1926 there have been no rights of 'escheat' or *droit de seigneur*. There are about 65,000 'lordships' in Britain. In 1976 and 1977 they were being offered at around £1000 a time; and most leading estate agents tell the anecdote of the German who paid £28,000, fully expecting to take his seat in the House of Lords.

1977 was Jubilee Year, and the influx of overseas visitors to London had a healthy effect on business confidence, and in particular on the hotel market, which was the special concern of Alan Daniels. No new foreign branches were opened in this year, but the *Country Life* image was consolidated by the acquisition of a branch at Ascot by arrangement with a very well-known local estate agent, Timothy Tufnell, who joined the partnership: this gave Knight Frank & Rutley an office at Sunninghill managed by Timothy Tufnell.

There were seven other new partners this year: Jonathan (Jon) Homan, specialist in industrial property, Peter Caröe (farms), Walter Conway (Building Surveyors), Christopher Kilduff (Professional Division), John Martin (shops), Peter Noest (Decentralized Offices) and Philip Fenwick Elliott (West End Offices).

At the Continental branches, nearly all the deals concerned offices. In Amsterdam clients were foreign banks requiring office space in Holland. In Brussels, the firm had recently completed, for Artagen Properties SA, one of the biggest sales of the year, getting over £3,500,000 for their vacant building at 63 Rue Montoyer. And in Paris the firm had achieved a number of major letting deals.

In April 1978 Pat Heller died at the early age of 61 – the first Senior Partner to die in office since Sir Howard Frank in 1932. He had modelled himself on his father-in-law, Will Gibson, to whom he had been articled when he had joined the firm in 1947, but had too much humour to be a martinet. He had originally wanted to be a farmer, but, like Peter Oldfield, he lacked the necessary capital. Just after the war he had narrowly escaped being sent to Hong Kong for ten years in the Hong Kong & Shanghai Bank; but they insisted that he should remain a bachelor, and he was already married. With his flair for valuation, his death was a great loss to the firm.

There now occurred a major constitutional change, one that had been recommended several years before by management consultants. The functions of Senior Partner and Managing Partner were separated: Sam Goodenough became Senior Partner and Bill Yates Managing Partner.

There was no overseas expansion this year, but a new office was opened in Boroughbridge, North Yorkshire, in May, and a local estate agent, John H. Jackson, joined the partnership, his office changing its name to Knight Frank & Rutley.

Sir Charles Clore, preparing to retire to Jersey, now wanted to sell his Stype Grange estate, on the Wiltshire-Berkshire border (but actually in Wiltshire). It had been managed for some time by the Hungerford office which was three miles away. Its 2060 acres, described as 'an important residential, sporting and agricultural estate', had been bought from Lord Rootes, and comprised the main house, annexe, a secondary house and forty-one other houses and cottages, a stud farm with twenty-two boxes, a dairy and arable farm and 645 acres of woodland. It was expected to realize 'more than £4 million' at auction in July. In the event, bidding stopped at £3,600,000, and Gerry Akroyd, who was the auctioneer, withdrew it. It looked as if it might have to be sold privately, in lots. And so, two years later, it proved. Part of the estate was retained by Clore's daughter Vivien after her father's death, the main house was sold to an Italian and the remaining properties were sold by auction on 10 July 1980 for £556,000.

Another interesting sale in the Hungerford area in 1978 was that of the 2700-acre Faccombe Manor estate (for about £2 million) to Brigadier Tim Landon, military adviser to the Sultan of Oman. Knight Frank & Rutley have provided consultancy management services ever since.

The firm's corporate advertising had increasingly concentrated on the international and agricultural services. The two themes would soon be combined to extend the firm's international agricultural services, but first there was a change of technique. A series of advertisements, both in the press and on television, featured a cartoon character called Mr Square Footage. The long-term aim of Mr Square Footage was to rectify the firm's excessive *Country Life* image by explaining that it also undertook a lot of commercial work, both at home and abroad – mundane things like shops, offices, factories and warehouses. To use television for this purpose, at peak viewing times when the public is generally being sold convenience foods and soap, was almost impudent. But it worked. The morning after the first showing of the commercial brought a telephone call from the managing-director of Thomas Tilling, an international 'conglomerate' group of companies: 'Congratulations! At last a property consultant has come out into the market place to talk about the services he offers! We have an idea that might interest you . . .' The result was an enormous valuation job involving properties right across North America . . .

Preparing for further expansion of agricultural services, especially in Africa, the firm engaged Dr John Stevens, a specialist in soil science who had lectured at Durham University and then worked for commercial concerns in the Sudan, Egypt, various deserts, and East Africa. He had then become Technical Manager, Dunlop Irrigation Services. Dunlop's saw irrigation as a big market for diversification of their own manufactures. John Stevens was to become one of Knight Frank & Rutley's most constantly travelling experts, as senior member of the International Agricultural Consultancy Team. Meanwhile, he was very fully occupied touring Nigeria and completing feasibility studies for a horticultural unit, a piggery and a poultry unit, with others in the offing.

In Edinburgh, the sale of the year was that of the Grantully estate in Perthshire, just before Christmas, for £2,700,000; and a number of islands, including Staffa (bought, unseen, by a retired chartered accountant from Inverness for £100,000).

Mr Square Footage featured in four television commercials and was designed to promote the firm's services to commercial property. The morning after the first showing a telephone call from an international group of companies offered a vast valuation task involving properties right across North America.

Perhaps the most travelled department this year was the Valuation Department, whose people visited the United States, four states of Australia, Singapore, Kuala Lumpur, Penang, Jakarta and Italy. Amid acquisitions such as a 15-acre plot of land at Reading, for development by Gillette Industries, and one of the largest industrial-commercial redevelopment schemes North London had seen since the war, the Industrial Department pulled off the ecumenical deal of the year – buying the Manchester Central Synagogue for an Arab client who wished to convert it into a mosque.

The end of 1978 saw two retirements – George Baker, who had been with the firm for forty-five years, and Gordon Wordsworth, who had been in charge of the Hereford office, where he was succeeded by Christopher Cornell. Both George Baker and Gordon Wordsworth continued as consultants.

Since the 1930s when Ted Fisher had pioneered the new shopping developments in the spreading suburbs of London, Knight Frank & Rutley had always been aware of new trends and patterns of shopping. In the mid-1970s there had been two such schemes in negotiation, in Aberdeen and Epsom: in each case a large site would be redeveloped with due regard for the local style of building and the preservation of listed buildings. In each case, too, the successful developer was Bredero, a Dutch firm whose Aberdeen tender was made through Knight Frank & Rutley in Edinburgh.

The Aberdeen development of nearly ten acres, announced in April 1979, would provide some 340,000 sq. ft of shops and and supermarkets, 90,000 sq. ft of offices, a leisure centre and two car parks, at an estimated cost of £30 million – 'the biggest thing' the Lord Provost was quoted as saying 'that has ever happened in Aberdeen.' As letting agents, Knight Frank & Rutley's first task was to ensure that a sizeable part of the shopping area was taken by big multiples, whereupon other shops would follow.

In Paris, 'small was beautiful', especially for suites of offices in the fashionable central business areas. 'Knight Frank & Rutley appears to have established a lead in this type of lettings,' said *The Times* property correspondent.

'Probably the biggest agricultural investment ever to change hands in this country.' The firm had no hesitation in so describing the sale of Sir Charles Clore's 16,627-acre Guy's estate in Herefordshire for over £20 million. It was bought by the Prudential Assurance Co. It was Sir Charles's wish that a buyer should be found who would retain the property as a whole. As we saw in an earlier chapter, he had bought it in 1961 (for a reputed £1,250,000) and, advised by Knight Frank & Rutley's Hereford office, had done a great deal to improve it. Farmland in Herefordshire at this time sold for about £1000 an acre (tenanted) and more than £2000 an acre for vacant possession. The estate contains 1475 acres of woodlands and a heavy-tree nursery; 'excellent pheasant shooting' and salmon fishing along four miles of the Wye. The Hereford office continues to manage this wonderful estate for the Prudential.

The management portfolio at Hungerford had just been increased by instructions from Lord Weinstock to manage his Bowden Park estate near Chippenham, Wiltshire; and at David Astor's Compton Beauchamp estate, a car park and landscaping scheme, conceived and coordinated by Knight Frank & Rutley on White Horse Hill, Uffington, Berkshire, was awarded a diploma in the Europa Nostra awards 'for the creation of a well-designed visitors' car park directly sited with due regard to the famous view'. It was the result of seven years' negotiation and planning.

In May 1979 it was announced that Knight Frank & Rutley were about to open a New York office. It was to be a joint venture between themselves and Douglas Elliman, a firm with whom they had co-operated in 1925, when they had been joint letting agents for New Devonshire House, Piccadilly. Bill Yates, now Managing Partner, had been responsible for most of the firm's overseas operations for the past ten years; and ever since his time in Geneva he had had his eye on one man to run the New York office, whatever form it took. This was Earl Reiss, then executive vice-president of Cushman & Wakefield, one of the biggest real estate firms in the world. 'We put a number of one-off deals together,' Bill Yates recalls, 'the most important of which was the sale of the Warner Building in Rockefeller Center in New

York to some investors in Abu Dhabi, who were clients of Morgan Grenfell.' Earl Reiss at first refused Knight Frank & Rutley's overtures on the grounds that Knight Frank & Rutley was not a sufficiently well-known name in the United States, however famous they might be throughout the rest of the world. Would it not be better to buy a small but well-known real estate firm in New York? But this would have meant risking too much capital.

'One day, just before Christmas 1978,' Bill Yates says, 'Earl called me to say he had found the answer: a joint venture with Douglas Elliman, whose name was "gold". Would I please jump on an aeroplane straight away?' However, not even partners of Knight Frank & Rutley transact business on Christmas Day, and Bill Yates flew to New York in the first week of the New Year. After two days of meetings, 'we had a meeting of minds. By April we had set up a joint-venture company called Douglas Elliman Knight Frank, and Earl Reiss left Cushman & Wakefield to become its President.' It quickly became established, with its offices in the same building (575 Madison Avenue) as Douglas Elliman Gibbons & Ives Inc., a full-service real estate organization which covers everything from 'fine urban and suburban homes' to insurance, international counselling and appraisals; and manages more than 240 buildings in New York City alone, among them such landmarks as Olympic Tower, Dakota, the United Nations Plaza and 10 Columbus Circle.

Lawrence P. McGauley, President of Douglas Elliman, was named as Chairman of Douglas Elliman Knight Frank. Within a year, the joint venture had a staff of twenty-five, and soon had a subsidiary operating on the other side of the Hudson river in New Jersey.

EUPIC, the firm's pan-European property investment scheme, now six years old, had been having a financially sound but adventurous life. For a concept that had been greeted with so much suspicion at first, it had had a remarkable number of suitors trying to bid for it. The first was the best: Wereldhave, a Dutch property company which built up a holding of somewhere between 22 and 27 per cent. 'Wereldhave at the time was 25 per cent owned by the Robeco group,' Bill Yates explains, 'who were themselves intending to launch a property fund, which they eventually did, called Rodamco. In a complex series of deals, Rodamco also built up a substantial position in EUPIC, and then acquired Wereldhave's interest to give them some 55 per cent of the company.' By 1980, Rodamco owned or controlled 85 per cent of the company, but still retained the services of the management company – and also of Knight Frank & Rutley.

During 1979, Nick Sheehan, of the Industrial Department, had been appointed a partner; and in the new year there were seven new partners, five in January (John Edge, John Rich, Tim St J. Russ, Michael Soames and Lindsay Wallace) and two in June (Paul Jarvis and Gus Stafford Allen). Martin Holgate, the partner in charge of the City office, left to devote himself to his dairy farm in Wales and was succeeded by Paul Mitchell.

* * *

Furzey Island, Poole Harbour in Dorset, which was sold to Algy Cluff, then the owner of the Spectator.

The time had come to hand over much of the control of Knight Frank & Rutley (Nigeria) to Nigerian partners, and the firm is proud of the success with which this was achieved. Alan Shelley, who had done so much in the last twenty-five years to build up the West African operation, which now had about 200 staff in eight offices, returned to London and was immediately given the task of exploring opportunities for expansion in the Third World. This was to have important results later in the year.

He had left Knight Frank & Rutley (Nigeria) in a prosperous and expanding condition. For a property consultancy to take on the job of project-managing a new town needs all the skills a 'probably-most-diversified' organization can muster. This is what happened at Agbara, 30 kilometres west of Lagos. In the early 1970s, the firm was approached by Chief A. O. Lawson, to advise on the economics involved in establishing a residential and industrial estate of 2000 acres on land he had amassed over a number of years.

'The land had been opened up by the construction of a highway between Lagos and the old slaving port at Badagry,' Alan Shelley says. 'Eventually a master plan was prepared for the development, and we began to let industrial sites and sell residential plots, the proceeds from which were used to provide infrastructure (roads, estate water and main drainage – virtually the first in Nigeria).'

Except for Lagos, there had been very little attempt to provide local authority revenue by the rating of property in urban centres of Nigeria. Since about 1970 this had (encouraged by Knight Frank & Rutley) been changing. 'It began in Aba

Reddish House, Broad Chalke, Wiltshire, for thirty years the home of Sir Cecil Beaton.

(about 50 miles north-east of Port Harcourt) where we were commissioned, with other surveyors, to value all properties within the township,' Alan Shelley recalls. 'After this, we were solely commissioned to value properties comprising the historic township of Calabar (about 30 miles from the Cameroon border), and we also did the rating valuation of part of Port Harcourt, Makurdi and part of Kano.'

There is very little investment property in Nigeria, but a great deal of valuation work, generally of owner-occupied premises; and since the mid-sixties the firm has valued breweries, cement works, soap factories, a tannery, tyre-making plants, hotels, and the largest flour-mill in the world.

At home, how different; or rather, how much the same. A 13,000-acre sporting estate, Simonstone, Wensleydale, Yorkshire; Culverthorpe Hall estate, Lincolnshire, with a beautiful manor, soon to realize £2 million (its farm management was done by Knight Frank & Rutley); Fairlawne estate, Kent, sold to a Saudi Arabian prince for more than £3 million; and Furzey Island, Poole Harbour, also in Dorset, a seven-bedroom house in 31 acres, sold eventually to Algy Cluff, the oil man who owned the *Spectator*.

The property which really hit the headlines, in June, was the late Sir Cecil Beaton's Reddish House at Broad Chalke, Wiltshire. This Queen Anne house in magnificent gardens, on which Beaton had lavished care for thirty years, was obviously not expected to take long to sell, since the auction of house and grounds was timed to start at 11 a.m. and the auction of the contents (by Christie's) for 11.30 a.m. The house was bought by Lady Chichester of Lymington, Hants. The sale was covered by almost every national and leading foreign newspaper; the house appeared three times on television, and the auctioneer, Gerry Akroyd, was interviewed by BBC News. The house alone realized £225,000 in spite of the fact that it needed about £60,000 worth of structural repairs.

In Scotland, the Edinburgh office sold Kellie Castle to an American lawyer from Germany, a deer forest on the island of Mull to the pop group Genesis, and the second section of the Delnadamph estate, near Tomintoul, to the Trustees of Her Majesty the Queen (the first section had been sold to them in 1977).

For some time the firm had been feeling the lack of representation between Boroughbridge, North Yorkshire, and London. They had had an 'evacuated' office during the war at Shrewsbury which had been closed down in 1946. Salop is full of Knight Frank & Rutley-type properties; and it is a fruitful area for introducing institutional investors. However, the firm did not open a new branch, but formed an 'association' with a well-established local firm, Balfour & Cooke, who have long experience of land management.

In the City of London, an ultra-modern office block known as Britannic House West, built on land belonging to Whitbread's Brewery, was the scene of Brian Hatcher's most spectacular deal. He bought it for BP in July 1980, for £93 million. Had it been rented, the rent would have been about £15 per square foot per annum. This is believed to be the biggest single property transaction ever seen in this country.

International Agricultural Consultancy this year found itself in Uganda, with a team drawn also from Country Surveyors and Plant and Machinery, plus a Kenya tea expert. The assignment was to value and assess the rehabilitation of almost derelict tea estates for the Mitchell Cotts Group. Years of neglect and destruction by civil war during the Idi Amin regime had left the tea bushes looking like overgrown tropical forest: some had reached a height of nine metres. The team roughed it in camp beds and shattered houses which had been used as billets by Amin's troops. Three tea factories were included in the valuation exercise – one of them had been the largest in the world when completed in 1957. Plant and machinery were in an extremely run-down state; one factory had also been looted. In all, over 900 buildings were valued, ranging from fertilizer stores to executive houses, and including hospitals, dispensaries and schools.

Wishing to decentralize their London Residential department, Knight Frank & Rutley began looking around the Knightsbridge area and what they found was a converted bank at 152 Sloane Street. The move was advertised with typical Knight Frank & Rutley pleasure-loving *panache*, impudently suggesting that Buckingham Palace, the Chelsea Flower Show, Harrods and Belgravia had all moved nearer to Knight Frank & Rutley, and showing a row of champagne bottles each representing one of the firm's branch offices. This was the year in which there seemed to be almost more Nigerian purchasers than Arabs; and a new record was set for 'the most expensive house in London' by the sale of 28 Wilton Crescent for 'well in excess of £1½ million'.

Britannic House West, adjacent to Whitbread's Brewery, which was bought for BP in July 1980 by Brian Hatcher for £93 million – the biggest single property deal ever seen in this country.

The Japanese language and modes of thought are very different from English. One-third of all Japanese companies operating in Europe have offices in the City of London, and another third are located in Greater London. There is plenty of Japanese business to be picked up, given the ability to communicate – and remembering that Japanese executives abroad seldom or never make off-the-cuff decisions. Decisions take a long time because they are always by consensus, and the consensus happens in Tokyo, not here.

It thus made sense to start a Japanese department within Knight Frank & Rutley's City office in Birchin Lane, and this opened in October 1980. Among the very long list of work undertaken for Japanese companies and institutions in various parts of the world, Knight Frank & Rutley were involved in both of the first two major commercial property investments in London, one by Mitsui, the other by Mitsubishi.

And what of Alan Shelley, whom we left in London, about to start a tour of African countries with stable political regimes? By March, he was in Nairobi (where the firm may eventually open an office); a few days later, in Lusaka; and by the end of the month he arrived in Salisbury (Harare) just as Robert Mugabe was elected. The regime was acceptable to other African countries, and this was important: Knight Frank & Rutley could not have opened up in a country that did not get on with Nigeria. In Harare, Alan Shelley met all the local estate agents (mostly white) who were glad to see him, having been cut off from Britain for more than a decade by UDI. He chose the biggest firm, Sagit Real Estate, which was owned by RAL, a firm of merchant bankers. Its main business comprised a large management portfolio (about 3000 residential properties and well over half a million square feet of commercial property with many shops, industrial properties and farms) and was being run by Jim Gibbons, FRICS, who had twenty years' experience of the country. A new partnership was formed, Knight Frank & Rutley (Zimbabwe), to take over the Sagit business. Christopher James, a product of the firm's highly successful Graduate Training Scheme, who had just completed a business training course at INSEAD, Fontainebleau, became Managing Partner. Jim Gibbons was also made a partner, and Alan Shelley became Chairman (resident in London).

XIX
And Now, the World . . .

The firm and its clients were shocked by the deaths of Gerry Akroyd in November 1982 and of Sam Goodenough in July 1983. Both men were in their early fifties, and apparently in robust health. Both, in different ways, were extrovert life-loving personalities, Sam with numerous professional qualifications, Gerry with none but a genius for negotiation. Sam Goodenough, following Pat Heller, was thus the third Senior Partner to die in office (Sir Howard Frank had been the first). The death of John Morgan in 1985 at the age of fifty-six was another untimely loss. He had taken over the old Professional Division from Richard Davis when the latter had retired at the end of 1981.

The ensuing reorganization left the firm divided into three main divisions, not counting Overseas. Because Gerry Akroyd had headed the largest division, Residential, Bill Yates gave up his responsibilities as Managing Partner and took it over. Alan Shelley became Managing Partner until Sam Goodenough's death, whereupon the two jobs were merged once again and Alan Shelley became Senior/Managing Partner.

None of these changes interrupted the firm's steady development and expansion at home and abroad. It is convenient at this point to take a cross-section of the firm as it is today. A group's corporate structure, shown diagrammatically as a family tree, can never express the mutual help, exchange of personnel and cross-fertilization of ideas that take place in an organization where a carefully-picked team works *as* a team.

There are now fifty-three partners and five associates. Due to expansion, the firm in 1984 took larger premises at 5 Hanover Square, giving up the office at 6 Princes Street; so that they now occupy space at 3, 5 and all of the original 20 Hanover Square.

The Investment and Professional Division, headed by Godfrey Richardson, comprises the investment, valuation, management, portfolio management, building surveyors', rating and planning departments.

Godfrey Richardson, 'second to none in the investment business' (the encomium comes from a rival firm), had set up an Investment department with Stanley Glynn in 1966. Over the years he has secured as 'in-house' clients a number of institutions, including the BBC Pension Fund, Hanover Property Unit Trust, Grand Metropolitan Pension Fund, Lancashire County Council Pension Fund, Reckitt & Colman Pension Fund, Croydon Pension Fund, and South Glamorgan County Council Pension Fund. Supported by David McIntosh-Whyte the Investment Department buys and sells property for these and other 'institutions', always with an eye to long-term rental and capital growth. All this is part of the growth, during the past eighteen years or so, of the commercial side of the Knight Frank & Rutley practice, now about two-thirds of the whole.

Six years ago Richardson created the Portfolio Management Department. Portfolio management involves scrutinizing every property for opportunities to improve its financial performance. The investor in property does not necessarily know how to run it, and so he often needs expert guidance. John Chambers, in charge of the Management Department, acknowledges his debt to Pat Heller, who taught him, among other things, how to collect rents without pain. The department can point proudly to a twenty-year period of growth and efficient service. The secret appears to be: choose only quality properties with quality tenants.

Building surveyors, in addition to carrying out structural surveys, often find themselves project-managing major development and refurbishment schemes. Some years ago the firm bought and fitted out the famous West Ilsley stables near Newbury for the Hon. J. J. Astor, who eventually sold them to Lord Weinstock. This involved new boxes, a covered ride, a hostel, building fourteen new cottages and refurbishing about twenty old ones in the village.

As surveyors to Wimbledon, Knight Frank & Rutley invented and managed an ingenious scheme for increasing the seating capacity of the Centre Court, by raising the height of the steel columns, winching up the whole roof to do so.

Not long ago the firm adapted two listed buildings in London to specific uses. The old Pharmaceutical Society building at the north-east corner of Bloomsbury Square (late seventeenth century with a façade added by John Nash) was converted by the Volkswagen Foundation who were seeking a new home for the German Historical Institute. And for Campbell Connelly, the music publishers, 37 Soho Square, dating back to about 1760 and almost derelict, was adapted, furnished and decorated with restored Adam ceilings.

Valuations, something of a mystery to the layman, grow more frequent in a period of inflation, and their size can be bewildering. For example, Knight Frank & Rutley value Taylor Woodrow's assets all over the world, and carry out investment valuations for property companies including Land Securities. John Edge and John Rich, protèges of the late John Morgan, now run this important part of the firm.

Brian Hatcher's Commercial Agency division has five main departments, City Office, West End Offices, Suburban and Provincial Offices, Shops and Industrial; and oversees the new Leeds office, set up in 1983 in partnership with Peter Munro and Keith Thompson, who had been practising in Leeds for more than twenty years. The Leeds office deals with commercial property in the North of England.

Brian Hatcher's own deals are often spectacular. We have already seen several of them (such as the £93 million acquisition for BP). He has always specialized in commercial property since he joined the firm in 1955. For BP too he found a brand-new 250,000-sq. ft office block in Buckingham Palace Road. He negotiated the site assembly and acquisition for the new headquarters in the City of Barclays Bank International: being a listed building, it was a costly development job behind an old façade.

The Qantas Centre, Sydney, sold in 1986 for A$200 million, the biggest single property sale in Australia. For many years Knight Frank & Rutley had an informal relationship with the major Australia firm Baillieu Real Estate. In the Far East the Knight Frank & Rutley group now comprises Baillieu Knight Frank in Australia, Knight Frank Kan & Baillieu in Hong Kong and Knight Frank Cheong Hock Chye & Baillieu in Singapore.

KFR Research, headed by Dr Fer Dijkstra, produces periodic reports on subjects like planning aspects of office development (within such constraints as the Green Belt policy) in likely areas such as the 'Western Corridor' along the M4 motorway and the M25 Corridor in the South. The firm is also financing research by the Centre for Agricultural Strategy at Reading University, whose first report in 1985 dealt with milk quotas.

As for shops, the word is now taken to mean any point where retailer meets consumer, including restaurants and bars as well as supermarkets and department stores. The firm has produced for their clients a special survey, *Shopping in the 1980s*, to show the changing pattern of retailing.

We have seen what is happening in Aberdeen. On a smaller scale the same thing has already happened at the Ashley Centre in Epsom, Surrey. Again, Knight Frank & Rutley were working with Bredero, the Dutch development and construction company. The letting has been shared with Hillier Parker, May & Rowden. Many features of the old market place, including the Clock Tower, have been preserved, as have the older shop fronts. The development is expected to establish the town as a shopping focus to rival Kingston, Croydon and Guildford. Like those towns, it has traffic and parking problems, and the scheme provides for a new link road round the back of the 6½-acre site.

The City office is run by Michael Soames. The City market place, like everything else in the City, has changed dramatically in the last few years. The trend is towards large lettings on the fringe of the Square Mile, where tenants are seeking quality accommodation – new air-conditioned buildings suitable for a 'high-tech' environment with computers and sophisticated communications.

Bill Yates now heads the Residential division, administratively the biggest 'home' division, since it embraces country houses, farms, Land Management (formerly led by Jeremy Haworth who retired in 1985), Country Surveyors, hotels, London Residential and the provincial offices, including the Scottish office in Edinburgh.

During the 1980s Knight Frank & Rutley have opened offices at Sherborne, Chipping Norton, Stratford-upon-Avon, Guildford and Cirencester. 'In 1983,' Alan Shelley explains, 'an informal association had been formed with the young firm of Lambert Way & Co. which had offices dealing with residential property and land management at Chipping Norton, Stratford and Kineton. This filled a geographical gap in our countryside representation, so in 1984 we took them over and the three founding partners of the firm, Stephen Lambert, James Way and Sam Butler, became partners of Knight Frank & Rutley. We later closed Kineton.'

Each department of Residential can bear witness to change in the last twenty years or so. Peter Caröe of the Farms department notes how the demand for farms is affected by the new motorways: a man makes money in the City, seeks country pleasures (and profits too) but wants to be able to get there quickly at weekends. Another trend seems to be the Common Market (usually German) buyer, who fears the ultimate Russian invasion of his own country and still has faith in 22 miles of Channel . . .

Peter Kearon, of London Residential, can recall a time in the 1960s when hardly anyone owned a *lease* of a flat. Now the rented flat has almost disappeared. In 1960, a three-bedroom small house in 'Kensington Village' (say, Victoria Grove or Canning Place) would have cost about £10,000 freehold. Now it would be upwards of £250,000 . . .

'They order things differently north of the border,' Colin Strang Steel, in charge of the Edinburgh office, explains. Although estate agents are plentiful in Scotland, solicitors often buy and sell houses and flats for their clients, especially in towns. It is wiser not to invade their territory, since they can bring in new business from other directions. The Scots do not much like auctions except for selling farms. One rather valuable difference in Scottish practice is the 'closing date' system. An offer has to be in by midday on a certain date. If you make it only at the last moment and arrive after midday because you have been held up in a traffic jam, you are out of the running. Your offer is legally binding and has to be put in by your solicitor. You cannot make an offer 'subject to survey' or 'subject to contract'. You are expected to have done your own survey, and your offer letter states at the bottom 'adopted as holograph' which gives it the legal force of a contract. So 'gazumping' cannot happen in Scotland.

The Knight Frank & Rutley companies abroad, autonomous in principle, are overseen from Hanover Square. The firm's agricultural expertise, which has been responsible for much of their growth, often goes hand-in-hand with property. Dr Steven's International Agricultural Consultancy has produced a number of reports (they cost anything from £25,000 to £100,000 each) on enormous schemes in under-developed countries, often funded by governments or the World Bank. In recent years there have been projects for Jordan, Egypt, Zambia and Saudi Arabia, often dependent on irrigation; for agro-forestry in Zimbabwe; for feedmill requirements in Nigeria . . .

Very different was a big international deal in September 1981, negotiated by Douglas Elliman Knight Frank in New York – the sale of Pan-American World Airways Intercontinental Hotels Corporation to Grand Metropolitan for $500 million – hailed by the press as 'one of the largest single real estate transactions ever recorded'. The deal, although finally negotiated between principals, was put together by a then twenty-seven-year-old Londoner, Rory Tagert, in about two months. He had been with Douglas Elliman Knight Frank since January 1981, and this was his first major deal. Before going into real estate he had worked for Grand Metropolitan, and he knew two things, that Grand Met wanted to buy an American hotel chain, and that Pan-Am were making heavy losses. Twice he was told by Pan-Am that their eighty-three luxury hotels (including the Barclay, New York and the Intercontinental in the Place Vendôme, Paris) were not for sale. Third time lucky; and the commission he collected made Rory Tagert a dollar millionaire overnight. It justifies Peter Oldfield's belief that, while qualifications are important, it is salesmanship that clinches the deal.

The 1980s have seen further overseas expansion, with new partnerships in Hong

The Mark Hopkins Intercontinental Hotel, San Francisco. One of the Intercontinental Hotels which were acquired by Grand Metropolitan for $500 million in 1981 and hailed by the press as 'one of the largest single real estate transactions ever recorded'.

Kong and Singapore, a stake in the Baillieu group in Australia, a new USA office in new Jersey, and (in 1982) another in Botswana – 'A logical step after Zimbabwe,' says Alan Shelley.

Why Botswana? This landlocked independent state in Southern Africa is about the size of France with a population of only 800,000 of whom 60,000 live in the capital, Gaborone. It is probably the most stable country in Africa, one of the few multi-party states of the continent, and its economy has been so well managed that it had resources of over £100 million (about five months' imports) as at 1982 and virtually no exchange control. The economy had been depressed because of the fall in demand for diamonds, Botswana's chief export, and other minerals. Cattle is the other major industry. Shell, BP and Anglo-American have identified enormous coal stocks (17 billion tonnes) and a rail link to the west coast is under consideration.

The other major gap in world coverage was that Knight Frank & Rutley were not represented in the Far East. 'For many years,' Alan Shelley says, 'we had had an informal relationship with a major Australian firm, Baillieu Real Estate, and when we decided to open in Hong Kong and Singapore we did so in partnership with Baillieu's.' In early 1983 Knight Frank & Rutley joined up with a prominent surveyor in Hong Kong, Mr F. Y. Kan, and formed Knight Frank Kan & Baillieu. Since then, the firm has grown to fifty staff with some prestigious instructions, including acting for the Bank of China on what will be the most important office development in the Colony.

In Singapore, at the same time, Knight Frank & Rutley set up Knight Frank Cheong Hock Chye & Baillieu – a partnership with a Singaporean firm headed by a very respected local surveyor (and eminent amateur golfer) Cheong Thiam Siew.

A still stronger link was forged in 1985 by the purchase of a significant shareholding in the Baillieu group, whose name was changed to Baillieu Knight Frank. 'Some of the firms in the group are of more ancient lineage than Knight Frank & Rutley themselves,' Alan Shelley observes. The Adelaide office dates back nearly 140 years. Sam Goodenough, whose pioneer visits to Australia in the late 1960s laid the foundations, would be gratified.

On the other side of the world, in Belgium, there had been another change with Jean Claude Vandecauter taking over the office in Brussels; despite a difficult market, the change at the helm soon began to take effect.

Sir Howard Frank would certainly have approved: he had initiated overseas expansion before 1914. He would be impressed by the quality of young executives throughout the organization today, some of them products of the firm's Graduate Training Scheme; and pleased that there are still partners who have an eye for a good horse. He might find it a little strange that few personnel retain their military ranks in civilian life: Peter Oldfield was the last veteran to be known as The Major, and only in the Farms department.

Sir Howard never saw television, but if he lived today it would please him, watching a revival of a series called *To the Manor Born*, to note that the period country

The Holme, Regent's Park, the famous Palladian villa designed by Decimus Burton, which was sold in 1985 on behalf of the Crown Estate Commissioners.

house in the opening shot is in fact Cricket Court in Somerset, which has been on Knight Frank & Rutley's books more than once.

Two recent spectacular deals would strike him as traditional to the firm – the sale, on behalf of the Crown Estates Commissioners, of The Holme, in Regent's Park, the famous Palladian villa (designed by Decimus Burton in 1818 when he was only eighteen) for which more than £5 million was expected for a new sixty-year lease; and the Adelphi complex near Charing Cross station, found after a difficult search for Phillips Petroleum, with a thirty-five-year lease at an annual rental in the region of £4 million.

Sir Howard would approve of the firm's bold advertising, developed over sixteen years by Michael Barton, who retired in 1981, and continued by his successor Shaun Longsdon, as head of advertising and public relations. He would enjoy the many sponsorships, all over the country, of sporting events and local good causes, from the International Driving Grand Prix at the Royal Windsor Horse Show, to the Newbury Music Festival, from the Pitlochry Festival Theatre to a clay pigeon shoot at

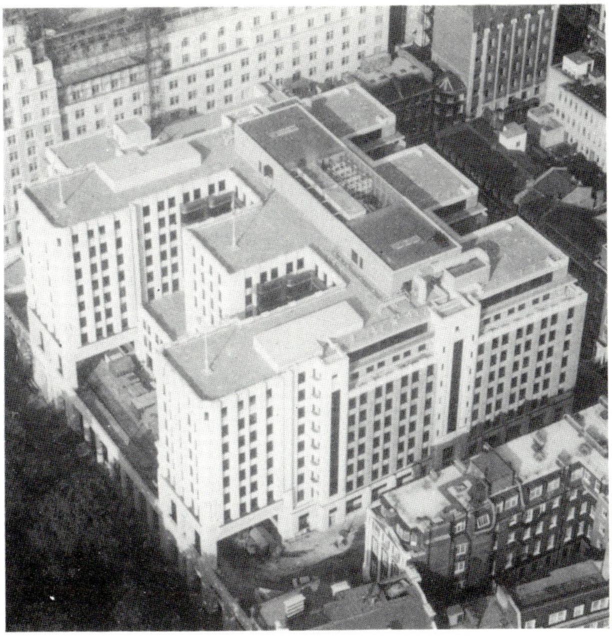

The Adelphi Complex near Charing Cross, acquired for Phillips Petroleum at an annual rental in the region of £4 million.

Teesdale County Fair. He would be particularly gratified that the Driving Grand Prix was won in 1982 by the Duke of Edinburgh, who wrote to the Senior Partner: 'I am more than delighted to accept your very generous offer of this splendid Knight Frank & Rutley Driving Grand Prix Trophy. As you can imagine, it was the one event I really wanted to win . . .'

Sir Howard might perhaps be a little perturbed by the informality and democratic atmosphere at Hanover Square, where Christian names are universal and nobody is afraid of anybody. What, no Galleries, no grandfather clocks, no Ming vases and fishing tackle and Holland & Holland guns lining the corridors? For these he would not have grieved: he was first and last a property man.

As for the future of the profession, and of Knight Frank & Rutley in particular, only a severe assault from the Left, and the old threat of nationalizing land which we have lived with since Lloyd George, could seriously damage the firm's hopes for the future, about which it is possible to be optimistic as long as we remain a property-owning democracy; for land, and what stands upon it, is the true wealth of men and nations.

The Overseas United Bank Centre, 1 Raffles Place, Singapore, which, when completed, was the tallest office building in Asia – but only until the 72-storey, 1033-foot Bank of China Building in Hong Kong was topped out. Letting agents Knight Frank Cheong Hock Chye & Baillieu.

The Bank of China Building, Hong Kong. Knight Frank Kan & Baillieu were letting agents.

In 1981, the twenty-fifth anniversary as Surveyors to Wimbledon, Knight Frank & Rutley were appointed Surveyors to the MCC.

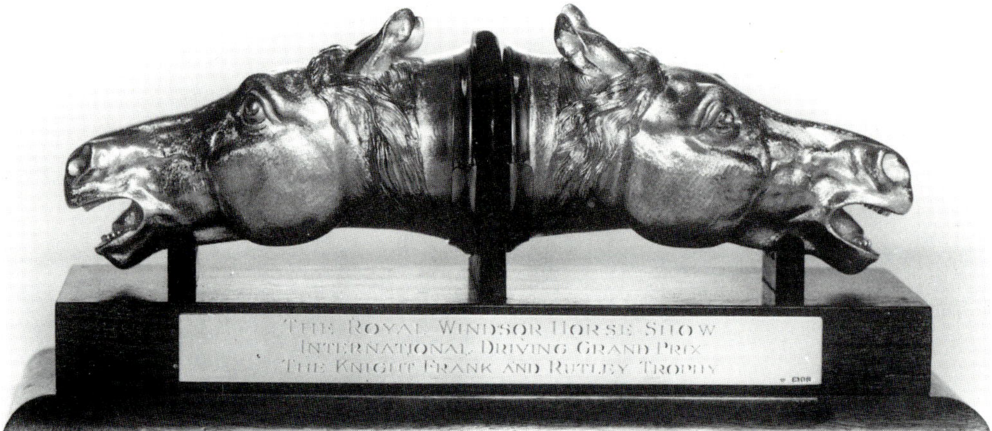

The silver trophy for the Knight Frank & Rutley International Driving Grand Prix at the Royal Windsor Horse Show. The trophy was won in 1982, the final year of the sponsorship, by the Duke of Edinburgh who now retains the trophy.

Appendix

United Kingdom

Knight Frank & Rutley

Partners

A J Shelley FRICS FNIVS
B W Hatcher FRICS
G E Richardson FRICS
W H Yates FRICS
R A Edwards FCA
P Mitchell FRICS
P R Caroe FRICS
P M Steward BSc FRICS
J E M Inge FRICS
D McIntosh-Whyte FRICS
J H S Martin FRICS
J A Edge FRICS
J S Rich MA FRICS
D W Gardner FRICS
W F Anderson FRICS
B E Shorter FRICS
G S Fisher FRICS
A C Elliott FRICS
A F Daniels FRICS
J T Chambers FRICS
J M Grimshaw FSVA
Jean D Love BSc FRICS
J P Homan FRICS
W Conway FRICS
C J Kilduff FRICS
P M Fenwick Elliott FRICS
P A Jarvis BSc FRICS
N G Stafford Allen FCA
P A B Prag MA FRICS
G R McLeod FRICS
P W M Ramsay ARICS
H R Woolaston BSc FRICS
R H Haynes BSc ARICS
N R Clough MA ARICS
R J Hannington BSc ARICS
R R Tee FRICS

Associates

C E Evans-Tipping
K W Stubbs FSVA
D J Large BSc ARICS
N B Asbury ARICS
G J Hayman
P P S Barnard BSc ARICS
J W Snow
A J R Macpherson ARICS
G N G Smith BSc ARICS
J F Woolsey ARICS

City Office

M S Soames BSc FRICS
N H Thomlinson MA ARICS
P J Willis BA ARICS
S H P Edge-Partington BSc ARICS

London Residential

P H A Kearon FRICS
R T Taylor FSVA
R G Ford MA FRICS
R D Crosthwaite

Ascot

H Eastwood

Chipping Norton

S U Lambert MA FRICS

Cirencester

C R Cornell FRICS
S M G Butler ARICS

Edinburgh
Knight Frank & Rutley Scotland

C B Strang Steel FRICS

Glasgow
Knight Frank & Rutley Scotland

A R M Stewart FRICS FRVA ACI Arb
David Harvey FRICS FRVA
J Iain Hay FRICS FRVA
Iain Wiseman FRICS ACI Arb

Guildford

R E G Gayner BSc

Hereford

K G Mason FRICS
A D G Douglas FRICS

Hungerford

N H van Zeller ARICS

Leeds

P C Munro FRICS ACI Arb
K C Thompson FRICS

Sherborne

M R A de Pelet ARICS

Shrewsbury

L A Wallace TD FRICS
T M Evans BSc FRICS
J R B Lovegrove-Fielden FRICS

Stratford-upon-Avon

J V E Way FRICS

Australia

Baillieu Knight Frank Australia Pty Ltd

E R Salisbury FAIV FREI FSLE
Chief Executive & Managing Director-Australia

New South Wales **Sydney**

Directors
D H Archbold B Comm AASA AREI ASLE
R M Wappet FREI FSLE AAIV
C R Weir FAIV FSLE AAIA
B C Challen AREI
C L Cotman ASLE
C S Dalrymple-Hay AAIV
N P Lucas AREI AAIV

Associate Directors
K L Goddard FAIV
R A Young AAIV
S E Matthews
B J Rath FSLE
D M Coupland
T J G Donlea
D W Morton BSc ARICS
D L Brown AREI

Also offices at:
Parramatta, North Sydney

Australian Capital Territory **Canberra**

Directors
R L Davis FSLE AAIV
P W L Marshall AREI

Victoria **Melbourne**

Directors
R E Woodhouse FREI FSLE AAIV
B J Baker FRICS FSLE
M R Burrows
B H Capp AASA AREI
G J Hay AREI
J H Hull AREI
I H Lyall FAIV FREI

Associate Directors
R L Allison AD Vals CREM BEc Dag Sci
R G Altson AAIV
J C Love AAIV
P R Randell AREI AAIV
E E Wood AREI

Also offices at:
South Yarra

Queensland **Brisbane**

Directors
R Sung Cert RE Val FSLE AREI
R J S Bean AREINZ FSLE
J Ferguson Cert RE Val ASLE
M O'Reilly ASLE
P Rushworth

Associate Directors
H T Ward
R M Tovey AAIV
P L Manthey

Also offices at:
Gold Coast

South Australia **Adelaide**

Directors
G W Dee FAIV FSLE AREI AAIA
Chief Executive SA
T S Andrew AAIV
C E Ingham B App Sc (PRM) AAIB (Snr)

Associate Director
J L Kenny AAIV

Tasmania Hobart

Directors
D M Pitt FAIV
D R Creese AAIV
I G Wells AAIV

Associate Director
C Brothers AAIV

Also Eastern Shore Branch at Bellerive

Western Australia Perth

Directors
G I Gauntlett BA FAIV
R W Glendinning
S J Seward
L M Seward B Comm AASA
I R Watson Dip CE

Associate Directors
D J Hunt AAIV
G B Davies Dip Val
J D McIntosh

Also offices at:
Claremont, Wembley, Canning Bridge

Belgium

Knight Frank & Rutley s.a.

J C Vandecauter

Botswana

Knight Frank & Rutley Botswana

M A Simpkin ARICS

France

KFR France

F R Boutet ESSEC

Hong Kong

Knight Frank Kan & Baillieu

F Y Kan FRICS FCI Arb FIAS FFB
Pat J Kelly AAIV AREI
R A Fry OBE FRICS

Nigeria

Knight Frank & Rutley (Nigeria)

J I Ojo-Osagie BSc FNIVS FRICS
S N Okeke BSc FNIVS FRICS
S Udo-Akagha FNIVS FRICS
P C Nwankwo FNIVS FRICS
O J A Idudu BSc FNIVS FRICS
S A Otegbola FNIVS FRICS ACII
M A Ogunbodede ANIVS ARICS
S A Ojo MSE PEng ASVA
O E Bassey MSc ARICS
P J Welborn BSc ARICS

Kano

M O Jawando FNIVS FRICS

Kaduna

S C Chineke BSc ANIVS

Also offices at:
Port Harcourt, Calabar, Jos

Singapore

Knight Frank Cheong Hock Chye & Baillieu

Cheong Thiam Siew FSVA FSISV
Tan Tiong Cheng Dip Urb Val (Auk NZ) ANZIV MSISV
Roger Parsons BSc ARICS
David Ong Liang Bong MSISV
Lydia Wong Loo Kuan BSc (Est Man) MSISV

United States of America

Douglas Elliman Knight Frank Inc

Earl Reiss, President
Nicholas Dana
Raymond A Koski
E Rodney Smyrk
Jeffrey Urstadt

John K Glaister Bsc ARICS
Rory A Tagert

New Jersey

Robert Rudin

Zimbabwe

Knight Frank & Rutley Zimbabwe

J K Gibbons FRICS FEI
P D A MacColl BSc FRICS

Index